Have Your Cake
and Eat It, Too

ALSO BY SUSAN G. PURDY

A Piece of Cake (1989)

As Easy as Pie (1984)

Christmas Cooking Around the World (1983)

Christmas Gifts Good Enough to Eat! (1981)

Jewish Holiday Cookbook (1979)

Halloween Cookbook (1977)

Christmas Cookbook (1976)

Let's Give a Party (1976)

Christmas Gifts for You to Make (1976)

Books for You to Make (1973)

Costumes for You to Make (1971)

Jewish Holidays (1969)

Holiday Cards for You to Make (1967)

If You Have a Yellow Lion (1966)

Be My Valentine (1966)

Christmas Decorations for You to Make (1965)

My Little Cabbage (1965)

Have Your Cake

and

Eat It, Too

200 Luscious
Low-Fat Cakes, Pies,
Cookies, Puddings, and
Other Desserts You Thought
You Could Never Eat Again

Susan G. Purdy

WILLIAM MORROW AND COMPANY, INC.

New York

The following recipes were previously published in *Eating Well, The Magazine of Food & Health*:

Chocolate-Peppermint Angel Pie, Raspberry Mousse Angel Pie, Apricot-Orange Soufflé Pie, No-Bake Berry Pie, Strawberry-Rhubarb Streusel Pie, Individual Meringue Pie Shells with Berries, Cappuccino Mousse Pie, Burgundy Cherry Mousse Cake with Cassis Glaze, Cocoa Roulade with Raspberry Cream, Cranberry-Raisin Tart, Panetela Borracha, Pineapple Chiffon Cake, Frozen Framboise Chiffon Cake, Spiced Apple Chiffon Cake, Orange Chiffon Cake, Cocoa Chiffon Cake, Chocolate Soufflé, Apricot Soufflé, Lemon Soufflé, Orange Soufflé, Raspberry Soufflé, Plum Soufflé, Pineapple-Banana Cake, Orange Yogurt Crumb Cake, Prune Cake, Chopped Apple Cake, Nectarine Raspberry Coffee Cake, Raspberry Marble Cheesecake, Lemon Ricotta Cheesecake, Pumpkin Cheesecake Pie, No-Bake Pineapple Cheesecake, Café au Lait Cheesecake, Brown Sugar Cheesecake with Spiced Blueberry Sauce

The following recipes were adapted from recipes that appeared in *Eating Well*:
Brandy Snap Tulips ("The New Christmas Goose"; copyright © Susan Stuck, November/December 1992), Caramel Sauce ("Fall Temptations"; copyright © Susan Herrmann Loomis, September/October 1991), Lemon Madeleines ("Fresh Market Menu"; copyright © Nina Simonds, July/August 1992)

Library of Congress Cataloging-in-Publication Data

Purdy, Susan Gold
   Have your cake and eat it, too : 200 luscious low-fat cakes, pies, cookies, puddings, and other desserts you thought you could never eat again / Susan G. Purdy.
      p. cm.
   Includes bibliographical references and index.
   ISBN 0-688-11110-6
   1. Desserts. 2. Low-fat diet—Recipes. I. Title.
TX773.P984   1993
641.8'6—dc20   93-1507
                                                                        CIP

Printed in the United States of America

First Edition

1 2 3 4 5 6 7 8 9 0

BOOK DESIGN BY RICHARD ORIOLO
ILLUSTRATIONS BY SUSAN G. PURDY

Acknowledgments

◆ ◆ ◆

The preparation of this book has taken me on a long and surprisingly difficult journey through uncharted culinary terrain. Not for one moment was it simply a matter of going into the kitchen to develop a delicious cake recipe. Each recipe, by definition, had to be not only delicious but also seriously reduced in total fat, saturated fat, and cholesterol. The process involved the study of food chemistry and nutrition and myriad consultations with nutritionists, doctors, food scientists, and other food professionals. Since my approach to this material was often based on a comparison of classic recipes and lightened versions, I also had to master new computer skills that often seemed more frustrating than mastering the art of low-fat baking. I could never have made this journey alone. That I made it at all is a tribute to those who helped me. To all, I say a heartfelt thank you.

To begin, I am grateful to my mother, Frances Joslin Gold, both for giving me the idea for the book and for convincing me years ago that nothing is impossible. As always, I relied upon the moral support and critical palates of my skeptical, butter-loving husband, Geoffrey, and our daughter, Cassandra, who shared her creative baking skills and helped develop and test some of the recipes.

Recipe development and testing is a long and unpredictable process that necessarily involves family, friends, neighbors, and professional colleagues. I want to thank everyone who crossed our threshold during the past several years as well as all who crossed my path, whether they tasted, tested, or listened; all had to endure my fascination with low-fat baking. For carefully testing and annotating recipes, I thank Tracy Glaves Spaulding, Mary Pat Glaves, Arietta Slade, Claire Rosenberg, Susan Rush, Lee Rush, Janie Peterson, Judy Perkins, Jolene Mullen, and Stephanie Lyon.

I am especially indebted to Judy Fersch, baker/owner of Concord Teacakes, Concord, Massachusetts, who urged me to write this book because she needed the recipes, encouraged me along the way, and proved her support by extensively testing my cakes in her shop and reporting her customers' comments.

For teaching me how to approach the subject of reduced-fat cooking and baking in the first place, I owe a great debt to the editorial staff of *Eating Well, the Magazine of Food and Health.* Most particularly, I thank Rux Martin (now editor of *Chapters*) for bringing me into the magazine; Patricia Jamieson, Test Kitchen Director, for generously sharing ideas and suggesting solutions to fat-reduction problems; Elizabeth Normand Hiser, Nutrition Editor, for answering endless questions and for introducing me to two key elements for this book—my nutritional analysis computer software, and registered dietician Marsha Hudnall, R.D., M.S., who reviewed and revised the technical material and Light Touch notes with skill, patience, and good humor.

Atlanta-based food scientist, writer, and friend Shirley Corriher and her husband, Arch Corriher, generously shared their time, expertise, and collective wisdom. Not only did they both review my technical chapters, but also tasted some of the cakes and offered solutions for problem recipes. Dr. Paul D. Doolan, Clinical Professor of Medicine at Yale University, tutored me in the theory and chemistry of lipids and thoughtfully reviewed the technical chapters. Paul maintained his sense of humor in spite of the fact that I insisted on concessions for nonmedical readers. Needless to say, I accept all technical errors as my own.

A good part of my work on this book involved learning to use specialized computer software to calculate and compare the nutritional analyses of recipes. I could neither have mastered nor applied this skill without the help of my friend and patient computer consultant, Jan Pieter Hoekstra. Jan cheerfully answered desperate midnight calls and kept me laughing as he solved every problem and saw me through a maze of computer-generated frustrations.

I want to thank my literary agent, Susan Lescher, for her support throughout the project and for placing this book in the capable hands of Harriet Bell, my editor at William Morrow. I am grateful to Harriet for her skillful editing of the manuscript, thoughtful tasting of cakes, and empathetic mothering. For their help in producing this book, I thank editorial assistant Valerie Cimino, copy editor Judith Sutton, designer Richard Oriolo, and remarkable food photographers Alan Richardson, Jerry Simpson, Ellen Silverman, Randy O'Rourke, and Tom Eckerle. For their enthusiastic skill in making connections for me in so many areas, I am indebted to Lisa and Lou Ekus, public relations impresarios extraordinaire.

For sharing their spiritual insights as well as their wonderful pie crust recipe, I thank two very special ladies, Elmira Ingersoll and Mary Muhlhausen. For suggesting that I include steamed pudding recipes, I thank my delightful, supportive colleague Ann Amendolara Nurse, cooking teacher and founding member of the New York Association of Cooking Teachers (NYACT). For suggesting muffin recipes and taste-testing the results, I thank my sweet-butter friend and real estate colleague, Lauren Lieberman. Rebecca Tatel, Vermont friend and UVM nursing student, shared her enthusiasm and loaned me her nutrition course notes and textbooks. For contributing good humor and armloads of apples, I thank Vermont friend and neighbor Sonny Sweatt. For their interest in my books and my work with low-fat baking, I appreciate the support of Pamela Knights, Public Relations Director, and the students and staff of the New England Culinary Institute in Montpelier and in Essex, Vermont. For sharing their prize-winning recipes from the Vermont Apple Bake-Off sponsored by the New England Culinary Institute and the Vermont Apple Board, I thank Karen Lanzer and Connie Waller. For contributing her expertise with gluten-free recipes, as well as sharing delectable home-baked samples, I thank Beth Hillson, friend and Hartford food writer. For sharing his Exotic Fruit Soufflé recipe, I thank Chef Jean-Pierre Vuillermet and restaurateur Jo MacKenzie of Robert Henry's Restaurant in New Haven, Connecticut.

For taste-testing the good, the bad, and the indifferent, I thank my sister, Nancy Gold Lieberman; her family, Steve, David, and Scott Lieberman; and our friends: Charley Kanas; Elizabeth and Pirie MacDonald; Scott Hanna; Hila Colman; Woody Dugan; Seymour Surnow; Paul, Nellie, and Amy Doolan; Judith Navia Auchincloss, The Two Strother Purdys; and Alexander and John Williams.

For general encouragement, support, creative inspiration, and baking ideas, I thank cookbook author Paula Wolfert, baking associate Barbara Went Cover, baker Linnea Milliun, food writer Bonnie Tandy Leblang, cookbook author Lora Brody, Thérèse Davies, and Halle and Bob Brooks. For giving me the opportunity to experiment with recipes using corn syrup to replace oil, I thank Sue B. Huffman and Jane Uetz of Best Foods Corporation. For technical information and for recipe suggestions utilizing prune purée, I thank food writer Marialisa Calta as well as the California Prune Board. For technical information about egg safety and cooking temperatures, I thank Kate Englehardt of the American Egg Board in Chicago. For chocolate and cocoa information, I thank Dr. Applebaum of the American Cocoa and Chocolate Manufacturers Association, and Rena Cutrufelli of the USDA Human Nutrition Information Service. For information about edible flowers, I appreciate the help of ethnobotanist and food writer E. Barrie Kavasch and botanist/landscape designers Moira and Paul Sakren. For their interest in and support of my book, I thank Knox gelatine, and particularly Pam Stetson and the staff at the Knox kitchens.

Contents

•◆· ·◆· ·◆·

Recipes for Special Diets

◆ ◆ ◆

Egg-Free Recipes

Lactose-Free Recipes
(eggs but no milk products)

Especially for Children

Holiday Gifts from Your Kitchen

Gluten-Free Recipes

(*From bottom*) Cape Cod Upside-down Muffin Cranberry Muffins,
Carrot-Currant Muffins, Yogurt Scones

Frozen Framboise Chiffon Cake

(*From top*) Poppy Seed Lemon
Cake, Strawberry- Rhubarb
Streusel Pie, and Blitz Torte
with Strawberries and Cream

Orange Chiffon Cake

Chocolate Soufflé

Whole Wheat Blueberry Kuchen

Raspberry Mousse
Angel Pie

Cranberry-Raisin Tart

Top: Chocolate-Peppermint Angel Pie
Bottom: Individual Meringue Shells with Berries and Cassis

(*From left to right*) Oatmeal Raisin Cookies, Cut-Out Cookies, and Pfeffernusse

Introduction

◆ ◆ ◆

Having spent a good part of my professional career dipping my fingers into batters made of sweet butter, heavy cream, and melted chocolate while writing my dessert cookbooks, the subject of reduced-fat baking was not necessarily next on my list. As often happens, however, real life intervened and sent me in a new direction.

Several years ago, my mother was advised to go on a low-fat diet. The prospect of ending our delicious afternoons together in her kitchen covered from our aprons to our noses with flour and chocolate as we tested new recipes and discussed the new portraits she was painting was unthinkable. But she could no longer even taste the newest version of buttery puff pastry or creamy yolk-rich custard. No longer could I, the designated baker, bring a traditional heart-shaped butter cake filled with buttercream to family birthday parties. Neither could I, after the first unconsciously rude attempt, bring two cakes, a plain, low-fat angel food cake for my mother and a rich chocolate cream cake for the rest of us. Angel food cake, no matter how we tried to disguise it, became old very quickly. Devil's food cake beckoned seductively. I began to hear a voice in my head asking, "Can you have your cake and eat it, too?" Now, after years of testing and developing, retesting and redeveloping, the answer is a resounding yes.

My philosophy has always been that one should bake the richest dessert possible and, if watching dietary fat or calories, eat only a small piece. A little slice of heaven: Who says you have to eat the whole cake? On a recent radio call-in show I listened to an obsessed young woman explain to a psychologist that her diet forbade any desserts. She longed for, and dreamed of, a piece of rich chocolate cake; every waking hour was spent planning ways to avoid giving in to her craving. The psychologist's advice, of course, was to rush out, eat some chocolate cake, and get on with her life. The lesson here is to remember that it is all right, even essential, to indulge sometimes, to give in to luxuriously sensual pleasures. Eat dessert first now and then, and if it happens to contain excessive grams of fat, then eat a penitential salad for dessert.

This "odd indulgence" theory is fine unless there are medical problems that preclude eating even a small slice of cake, as in my mother's case. When I began to immerse myself in reduced-fat thinking, baking, and eating, however, I became convinced that cutting back on saturated fat is a healthier way of eating. And, best of all, low-fat food can taste good too. I learned that we can combine the notions of pleasure and reduced fat and eat sensational food that inspires the spirit, food we would go out of our way to find, not food that is prescribed.

My goal was to develop a collection of delicious, inviting dessert recipes that were not only appealing to the palate and to the eye, but also were so good you couldn't wait to make them. If they also happened to be low in fat and more healthful, that was a secondary bonus. This is neither a deprivation diet book nor was it written with the intention of being what I call "CC" (Culinarily Correct).

When testing and developing recipes, I aimed to cut out excessive fat but save taste. First, it's a given that by reducing fat to any degree you will never achieve the identical rich mouthfeel of a full-fat dessert. However, if a recipe did not taste good, and I mean really good, not "okay, but a little weird," or "passable for a low-fat thing," it did not make the cut. My tasters, particularly my husband and our daughter (who, at age nineteen, is also a baker), were very severe critics. Some notable failures (like a rubbery chocolate zucchini cake) even bypassed my testing crew and went straight to the raccoons.

While it is easy to reduce the quantity of fat in a stew and slightly trickier to devise a rich, butterless sauce, it can be a nearly impossible chemistry problem to bake a totally fat-free but flavorful cake with a light, tender crumb. As anyone who has tried will tell you, reducing or removing fat from baked goods is, at best, frustrating, and, at worst, makes you long for an overdose of sweet butter. But when it works, and you create a dish everyone raves about, sweet victory is yours.

I began my work on each recipe by analyzing the ingredients to understand the function of each; then I made appropriate changes and significant reductions in fat, especially saturated fat and cholesterol. I reduced sugar and salt where possible. I devised, developed, and dropped many recipes that seemed logical on paper, but were disasters in practice. As with any recipe, only much more so because I was in uncharted territory, I baked, tasted, made notes, added this, dropped that, fine-tuned, then baked again. Once the taste was right, I analyzed, with the help of a software program, the nutritional components of each recipe; if the fat reduction was significant and the taste good, the recipe was a go. If the numbers were good but taste or texture was not, the recipe was discarded. If the numbers were grossly off, but I felt the recipe still had possibilities, I made adjustments and retested it. If it still didn't work, I finally conceded that some baked goods cannot and should not be made without lots of butter, egg yolks, and cream. Finally,

I passed the recipes on to others to test in their own kitchens. Every recipe in this book has been tested at least five times, some a dozen or more.

The American Heart Association recommends limiting dietary fat intake to no more than 30 percent of total daily calories. As I worked, I did not adhere strictly to the famous 30 percent quota or any other preconceived formula for two reasons. First, this percentage refers to daily fat intake for total foods consumed by people over the age of two years, not the fat content of one single food or dish. Second, it is impossible to calculate the formula in advance when trying to reduce fat in baking. One recipe can turn out wonderfully with 11 percent of its calories from fat, while another may need 22 percent calories from fat to have the right taste and texture. A few of these recipes, for correct taste and texture, are slightly above 30 percent calories from fat although saturated fat and cholesterol are reduced. In most cases, I succeeded in lowering the total fat content well below the 30 percent mark, and, with few exceptions, have kept the grams of fat per serving between 5 and 10. This is good news when you compare these recipes to conventional fat-laden ones that often weigh in at about three times that number.

Some of the recipes in this book are new and original, some are reduced-fat variations of classic favorites. Many first appeared in my articles in *Eating Well* magazine, while others come from my family and friends, and from professional colleagues, many of whom now are working on, and are fascinated by, the same subject. Whether you want to change your eating patterns as a preventive measure or a member of your family has been advised to follow a reduced-fat diet, there is no question that a reduced-fat diet is important. Even if you just want some great new dessert recipes, the good news is you can have your cake and eat it, too.

Have Your Cake and Eat It, Too

If Fats Are Good for Us, Why Are They Bad for Us?

⬦ ⬦ ⬦

What Is Fat?

For good health, the human body needs more than forty different nutrients. These are divided into five major classes: fats, proteins, carbohydrates, minerals, and vitamins. Of these, fats seem to have suffered the worst press. In a culture that believes you are what you eat, fats are perceived as sinful, and fat people are no longer "jolly" or even "voluptuous." *Fats* has become a four-letter word. Clearly, we need some perspective on this complex subject.

First, it is essential to remember that fats are a vital nutrient. The body needs some fats for good health, even for life itself. Second, food would simply not taste good without any fat. The goal is to balance the amount and type of fat needed with the amount of fat desired.

Chemically speaking, fats belong to a group of organic compounds called *lipids* (from the Greek word *lipos,* meaning fat). In the simplest sense, lipids are compounds that will not easily dissolve in water, but will dissolve in special solvents such as benzene and ether. Lipids can be either solid or liquid.

Fat's essential characteristic is that its chemical structure is made up of fatty-acid chains (see page 455) composed of carbon, hydrogen, and oxygen, the same three elements found in carbohydrates, though in differing proportions. For the purposes of this book, we are concerned with two types of lipids: triglycerides (and the fatty acids they contain) and cholesterol.

Why Do We Need Dietary Fat?

Fats play many roles in the body: They supply a fuel source for many tissues, they aid in the synthesis of cell membranes, they participate in the synthesis of cholesterol and sterol hormones. Fats provide the most concentrated source of energy in our diet, actually $2\frac{1}{4}$ times more than an equal weight of proteins or carbohydrates. When fat is ingested, the body utilizes some of the fat it needs for energy, then stores the rest in various tissue, increasing the concentration of fat in blood plasma and other body cells. The majority of the excess is stored in fat cells. Body fat also serves as insulation against climatic temperature changes, prevents bodily heat loss, and protects vital organs.

A totally fat-free diet is not healthy under normal circumstances. Fat serves as a carrier for four essential fat-soluble vitamins: A, D, E, and K. Without fat, these vitamins could not be absorbed by the body. Fat also helps the body use carbohydrates and proteins more efficiently.

There are many different types of fats contained in food; all but three of these types can be made in the body. The three that cannot, yet are essential for good health and necessary in the structural integrity of some cellular membranes, are called essential fatty acids: linoleic, linolenic, and arachidonic acids.

Linoleic acid, found in vegetable and seed oils, is essential for proper growth as well as the prevention of skin disorders. The other essential fatty acids are required for maintenance of healthy skin and regulation of cholesterol metabolism; they also act as precursors of prostaglandins, hormone-like substances that regulate certain body processes.

Fat helps to make our food taste good. Fats hold and carry flavors and aromas, contributing to taste appeal. Oil-soluble flavors coat the taste buds, so they remain on the tongue, lingering to create a complex taste quality scientists call "mouthfeel." Foods lacking fat lack mouthfeel; they neither taste as good nor subliminally urge us to take another bite. Oil-soluble aromas also linger, remaining to give pleasure even after food is swallowed. After dietary fats are eaten and digested, they tend to leave the stomach slowly, thereby contributing to a feeling of satiety, or fullness.

If you consume more calories, especially calories from fat, than are necessary for maintaining good health and optimum weight, you will gain weight. All calories are *not* created equal—50 calories of butter are not the same as 50 calories of sugar or starch. The body converts fat calories to bodily fat more easily than it converts carbohydrate calories; in other words, fats are metabolized more efficiently. The body uses less energy for this process and has more energy left over to use for other activities, or to store as fat. Thus, excess fat calories make you fat faster than excess carbohydrate calories, although an excess of these will also, eventually, end up as fat cells.

While it is important to watch total caloric intake, the easiest way to reduce your total calories from fat is to reduce your total fat intake. If you reduce the intake of fatty foods, you almost always cut calories. People who are put on low-fat diets for cardiovascular problems often simultaneously lose weight. Just because fat can be delectable to taste, however, it should not necessarily be condemned as sinful; it is just something to be reckoned with ... mathematically speaking.

According to the American Heart Association, the average American diet presently derives as much as 40 percent of its total calories from fat. Most health authorities agree this is excessively high. AHA authorities recommend a daily fat intake of no more than 30 percent for individuals over two years of age; conservative voices prefer 25 to 20 percent or less.

Research indicates that diets excessively high in fat, particularly saturated fat and cholesterol, may be bad for our health. Diets high in saturated fats are the worst culprits, with high-cholesterol diets running a close second. They are known to raise blood cholesterol levels, a major risk factor for coronary artery disease: arteriosclerosis (clogging of the arteries) can lead to heart attacks, inadequate circulation to the extremities, and blockage of blood vessels, thereby preventing blood supply to the brain and causing strokes. It is also possible that a high-saturated-fat, high-cholesterol diet may be a contributing factor in late-onset diabetes and certain cancers.

For many people, reducing excessive dietary intake of saturated fat and cholesterol results in a reduced risk of many of these diseases. Other individuals, however, suffer high blood cholesterol levels even when their diets are low in fat and cholesterol; these cases are generally related to genetic factors.

Cholesterol and Other Fats

Cholesterol has become one of our buzz words, yet few of us really understand what it is. First isolated from gallstones in 1784, this compound has become so important that, to date, thirteen Nobel prizes have been awarded to scientists devoting the major parts of their careers to its study.

Cholesterol is a type of lipid found in foods from animal sources; cholesterol is also synthesized in the body. Cholesterol is never present in vegetable or plant fats.

Our bodies need cholesterol for the creation of cell walls and the formation of many bodily substances, including sex hormones, bile salts, and the organic membranes covering nerve fibers. Most of the cholesterol found in the blood is synthesized in the liver, although it is also made in the adrenal cortex, testes, aorta, skin, and small intestine. The amount and type of fat in the diet also affects the cholesterol level in the blood. Since the body naturally supplies a sufficient amount of cholesterol, humans do not *need* to eat more; dietary cholesterol may be strictly limited without ill effect. It should be noted that not everyone needs to limit cholesterol intake; some people can eat all they want without problems. Within limits, cholesterol is beneficial to the body. The total amount of cholesterol in the blood depends on the body's natural production, dietary intake, and bodily absorption. This interaction is complex and affected by many factors, including genetics. High blood cholesterol levels do not necessarily mean high risk of coronary disease; the most important factor is the relative level of certain lipoproteins that circulate in the blood, carrying both cholesterol and fat.

To supply what is needed, bodily production of cholesterol changes in relation to diet. In other words, when we eat a lot of foods high in dietary cholesterol (such as organ meats or red meat) or foods high in saturated fats (butter and animal fats), natural production of cholesterol by the body slows down. If the intake of dietary cholesterol is reduced, then production by the body revs up.

In order for dietary fat to be used by the body, it must first be broken down chemically in order to pass through cell walls. This process begins in the mouth, when food is chewed, and continues as a series of special enzymes (lipases) break down the fat molecules. Then the fat is digested in the small intestine, where it is broken down and absorbed into the bloodstream as chylomicrons (complex compounds containing triglycerides and other components) or carried directly to the liver for transformation into lipoproteins.

Lipoproteins are lipids (including triglycerides and cholesterol) combined with protein. Visualize them as little transportation balloons or particles enveloped by the protein, designed to carry fats, proteins, and cholesterol through the blood to the body's cells, where they can be broken down by enzymes and used for various purposes. Without this protective protein wrapper, the fat, which floats in water (the main ingredient in blood), would separate out.

There are three major types of lipoproteins: very-low-density lipoproteins (VLDLs), low-density lipoproteins (LDLs), and high-density lipoproteins (HDLs).

Fat floats because it is less dense than water or blood. A lipoprotein that contains a very high proportion of fat is thus very light. In addition to the fat molecules (primarily triglycerides) in the lipoprotein particle, or balloon, there are also proteins, cholesterol, and other types of fat. This very light (low-density) particle is called a very-low-density lipoprotein (VLDL). Its job is to whiz around the circulatory system dropping off bits of its cargo to the cells to be transformed into bodily energy. Once most of the fat is dropped off, the particle is a little less light and then is called a low-density lipoprotein (LDL); it continues the delivery circuit begun by the VLDLs.

When supply exactly meets demand in the delivery process, all is well. Trouble arises when there is anything left over...excess cholesterol in particular: LDLs simply dump the leftovers, leaving fatty deposits called *plaque,* which can build up in the blood vessels and cause blockages that reduce blood flow and contribute to heart disease. The length of time LDLs remain in circulation and the rate of plaque buildup varies among individuals and is influenced by many factors, including smoking and high blood pressure. The longer the LDLs stay in the body, the more leftovers they can dump and the more damage they can do. LDLs are "lousy," the bad guys.

HDLs, in contrast, are the "helpful" good guys. Smaller in size than LDLs, HDLs are simply lipoprotein particles that contain fewer lightweight fat molecules than the LDLs. With less fat, they are heavier (more dense) and thus are called the high-density lipoproteins (HDLs). In a process known as reverse cholesterol transport, these heavy little particles act like vacuum cleaners zipping through the circulatory system, scooping up the leftover fat or cholesterol and returning it to the liver for reprocessing or excretion.

Interpreting Blood Cholesterol Tests

When your doctor tests your blood to measure the total blood (serum) cholesterol levels, he is looking at the number of milligrams of cholesterol per 100 milliliters, or 1 deciliter (dl) of blood. A level of 200 means you have 200 milligrams of cholesterol per 100 milliliters of blood. (Over 50 percent of American adult males have levels above 200.) According to the recommendations for adults by the National Institutes of Health, total serum cholesterol ideally should be under 200; the HDLs should be over 35, and the LDLs at or below 130. According to the National Institutes of Health, healthy individuals as well as anyone whose cholesterol count varies seriously from these parameters should be on a low-fat, low-cholesterol diet.

More important than the total overall cholesterol level, however, is the relationship between the levels of LDLs and HDLs in the blood. The higher the number of HDLs, the *lower* the risk. As a general rule, physicians measure the amount of HDLs and LDLs in the blood only when total cholesterol levels exceed 240 (or 200 in those with coronary heart disease or with two risk factors for the disease). If the total is at a desirable level, it indicates that neither type of lipoprotein is too high.

There are a variety of ways to improve HDL–LDL ratios and lower total blood cholesterol levels. For example, the American Heart Association recommends limiting dietary intake of saturated fat, total fat, and cholesterol. In addition, doctors can prescribe various appropriate drugs, including one that blocks cholesterol synthesis and others, generally less effective, that reduce serum levels by trapping fats in the intestine and increasing excretion.

Personal Fat Math

To determine your own personal health requirements and desired weight and/or desired weight loss, you must evaluate such factors as how much you exercise, the state of your present health and/or risk of illness, and your family hereditary patterns. You should consult with your doctor and/or nutritionist to prepare a suitable dietary program. The information following is intended to be a general guideline, not an individualized program.

According to the American Heart Association, the average American adult derives about 40 percent of his or her daily total of calories from fat. As mentioned above, most authorities agree this is too high and recommend that the daily fat intake not exceed 30 percent, while more conservative voices look for 25 to 20 percent or even less.

Calories are a measure of food energy. A woman weighing 125 pounds and leading an active life requires approximately 1800 calories per day. If 40 percent of these calories came from fat, she would consume 720 calories (40 percent × 1800) from fat per day. If the same individual is to cut fat intake down to 30 percent, she should derive no more than 540 calories from fat (30 percent × 1800).

Pure fats all weigh the same amount and contain the same number of calories from fat. For example, all oils—including canola oil and peanut oil—are 100 percent fat. One tablespoon of any one of these weighs 13.6 grams, usually rounded to 14 grams, and therefore contains 14 grams of fat. (These fats do, however, differ in their degree of saturation: Canola oil is approximately 6 percent saturated, while peanut oil is 17 percent.)

Every gram of every fat (solid or liquid) provides 9 calories (more exactly, kilocalories, kcals), a measure of energy. Thus, one tablespoon (13.6 grams weight) of any type of oil equals 13.6 × 9/kcal, or 122 calories (usually rounded to 120). One tablespoon of butter weighs 14.2 grams. Butter is 80 percent fat. Thus, 80 percent × 14 = 11.2, and 11 × 9/kcal = 99 calories per tablespoon of butter.

How to Calculate Fat Grams

There are three easy ways to calculate the total number of grams of fat (fat grams) allowed per day.

1. Simply divide the number of calories required to maintain your ideal weight (or your goal for percent of calories from fat per day) by 30 percent. (Check your doctor's weight charts. For example, say 1800 calories: 1800 ÷ 30 percent = 60 grams of fat per day.)

2. Another method is to calculate the number of calories per day derived from fat—in our example, 30 percent of 1800 = 540—and divide this figure by 9, which is the number of calories in each gram of fat. Thus, 540 ÷ 9 = 60 grams of fat per day.

3. The third method is to divide your ideal weight in half. If, for example, you weigh, or wish to weigh, 125 pounds, you should consume no more than 62.5 grams of fat per day (125 ÷ 2 = 62.5). If you weigh 180 pounds, you can consume 90 grams of fat per day and still meet the 30 percent goal.

How to Allocate Your Daily Fat Grams

Pay attention to three factors: the total quantity of fat, the type of fat, and the amount of cholesterol you consume. The American Heart Association *Dietary Guidelines For Healthy American Adults* recommends that total daily intake of fat grams (60 in the example above) be divided roughly in thirds by type of fat, to provide a ratio of one third mono-unsaturated fat, one third polyunsaturated, and one third saturated. Each third should be no more than 10 percent of the total daily caloric intake, for a total of 30 percent calories from fat.

How can I do this, you ask? Too many calculations, too much trouble. My advice: Simplify the numbers game and watch only one ball—*the total number of fat grams you eat in a day.* Forget counting calories. Forget counting milligrams of cholesterol. Remember that saturated fats are worse for your health than dietary cholesterol anyway. Just try to cut down on eating high-fat foods, which are often also high in calories, saturated fats, and cholesterol. Beyond counting fat grams, of course, one has to be conscious of total weight management, behavior, and lifestyle: in other words, how you think and live as well as how you eat.

Nutritional Analyses in This Book

The nutritional analyses of recipes in this book should be viewed as guides rather than gospel, even though every attempt has been made to ensure accuracy. The analyses were calculated using the Nutritionist III computer software program and are based upon the entry of nutritional data for all ingredients in each recipe. The data are supplied by various sources, from the USDA to manufacturers. Occasionally, data is incomplete or unavailable; in those cases, substitutions of similar ingredients are made.

Each recipe analysis is per serving and lists total calories, proteins, total fat, saturated fat (satfat), carbohydrates, sodium, and cholesterol. When yield varies (12 to 14 crêpes), analysis is calculated on the first, smaller figure. Fractions are rounded off to the nearest whole number, except for saturated fats, which frequently appear in trace amounts and are so noted. When total fat is less than 0.5 g, it is considered a trace amount. Note: If you try to calculate the percentage of calories from fat in these recipes using the printed rounded-off figures, your results will not always agree with mine. This is because my calculations were done by computer using figures carried to three decimal places instead of being rounded off.

Portions are based on average-size servings and have not been shaved to "cook" the numbers. In the Light Touch notes following each recipe, I give the percentage of calories from fat to show the difference between a traditional full-fat version and my lighter, fat-reduced recipe. Bear in mind that in a few cases, in order to have proper taste and texture, a particular recipe will derive more than 30 percent calories from fat even in its reduced-fat version. The great majority of recipes in this book are well below this percentage and all are significantly below the fat content of conventional recipes. In some recipes, even a small amount of fat will register as disproportionately high, while the actual per serving figures are low in grams of fat. This is because there are relatively few ingredients in the recipe and/or those that are there contribute few calories. For example, the Almond Tile Cookies (page 322) are models of dietary restraint compared to their traditional counterparts (with 45 percent calories from fat). The lightened version is cholesterol-free and each cookie contains only 1 gram of fat. The total recipe, however, gets 34 percent of its calories from fat, the minimum needed to achieve proper taste and texture; there are very few ingredients and few of these contribute any calories, so the proportion of fat appears to be relatively high.

In a few cases, the total fat will be above 30 percent simply because the recipe requires more fat to achieve the proper taste and texture. These recipes are still below the fat content of the conventional versions of the same recipe. While accommodating as healthy a regime as possible, it is my priority to offer baked goods that give pleasure rather than simply adhere to strict numerical rules.

The American Heart Association's recommended health guideline of no more than 30 percent calories from fat refers to *total daily caloric intake,* meaning that not every recipe or single food must be below 30 percent fat. Thus, a low-fat meal might be capped off with a dessert that is relatively higher in fat. The total dietary intake should be considered (fats plus other calories) to determine the percentage.

It is important to remember that low-fat foods, especially baked goods and desserts, are not necessarily low in calories. In fact, sometimes sugar or starch must be increased to maintain flavor when fat is reduced; when that happens, the total calories may not drop, or may even increase slightly. What changes is the proportion of calories from fat, which drops considerably. Do not be put off when you see a nutritional analysis of a low-fat recipe with total calories per serving reading nearly as high as for a traditional recipe; look again at the amounts of fat, saturated fat, and cholesterol. And enjoy yourself.

Understanding Ingredients

❖ ·❖· ❖·

I am often asked to judge baking contests where the competition is based upon a single recipe distributed to all contestants. I am always astonished at the variety of results. The cakes, pies, or breads never have the same texture or appearance—although there is a similarity in the taste because the ingredients are the same.

Different bakers achieve different results for many reasons. There is, fortunately, the element of human creativity, and the fact that some cooks have a natural instinct for baking while others simply do not. More than that, understanding the nature and function of each ingredient helps greatly in determing the results.

Good dessert recipes are careful formulas that balance a variety of elements to produce specific chemical reactions. It is true that if you can read you can follow a recipe, but if you do so with intelligence and understanding, it will be reflected in the results.

In baking, and especially in cake baking, each ingredient has a particular function. In the professional baking guide *Practical Baking,* author William J. Sultan devised a convenient system for characterizing baking ingredients. I have modified it slightly, but find it a useful guide, particularly when working to remove fat from baked products:

Binders and Tougheners (provide structure and bind ingredients): flour, milk solids, egg whites.

Tenderizers (soften the crumb by cutting the development of gluten in wheat flour, prevent toughness): sugar; fat; egg yolks; chocolate; acidic foods such as yogurt, sour cream, buttermilk, and vinegar; honey; molasses.

Moisteners (moisten the crumb, lengthen storage time): milk, water, and some other liquids, such as eggs; sugar syrups; honey; brown sugar.

Driers (absorb and retain moisture, provide body): flour, milk solids, starches, egg whites.

Flavorers (enhance or provide flavor): chocolate/cocoa; butter; eggs; fats; specific flavoring agents, including extracts, citrus zests, coffee, and nuts.

The following section explores in depth the basic baking ingredients and their relation to low-fat desserts.

Flour

For bakers, one of the most important elements in wheat flour is gluten, the stretchy, elastic substance that develops when two of wheat's proteins mix with liquid and blend together. There are actually several proteins present, but the main ones are glutenin (located in the outer layer of the kernel) and gliadin (found in the endosperm, the core of the wheat kernel). Glutenin provides strength and gliadin provides elasticity; both are needed to give flour the characteristics required for successful baking. The flour with the highest protein content (the most glutenin and gliadin) will also absorb the most water, which can be useful in bread doughs but leads to toughness in delicate baked products such as cookies and fine cakes.

Different types of wheat and different milling methods produce flours with more or less of these proteins. The type of flour used should be specific to the needs of the product baked. Be sure to note the protein content of the wheat flour you use; it is indicated on the bag label under the nutrition information, in grams per cup measurements.

Bread flour is milled from hard wheat and has a high gluten content, 12 to 15 percent. This means that it is strong and stretchy, good qualities to contain the gases given off by expanding yeast when bread rises. Bleached and unbleached all-purpose flour is milled from a blend of hard and soft wheats and contains roughly 10 to 13 percent gluten. It is good for most baking, especially when there is enough fat in the recipe to tenderize the protein. Pastry flour is milled from soft wheat only and has a gluten content of 8 to 12 percent. Cake flour, also milled from soft wheat, has even less gluten, about 6.5 to 10 percent, with 8 percent the average. Cake flour is specifically formulated to produce a tender grain in delicate cakes. In low-fat baking, cake flour is preferred over all-purpose because less fat is needed to tenderize it. Self-rising cake flour is altogether different, containing added calcium acid phosphate or monocalcium phosphate, bicarbonate of soda, and salt. Do not substitute self-rising for other types of flour. I do not use it at all, first, because I prefer to control the amount of salt and leavening in my recipes, and second, because baking powder loses strength after long storage so old packages can cause baking failures.

You can make your own cake flour by replacing 2 tablespoons of the all-purpose flour with 2 tablespoons cornstarch in every cup. To substitute cake flour for all-purpose flour, use 1 cup plus 2 tablespoons cake flour for each cup of all-purpose.

Fats inhibit the creation of gluten in wheat flour by coating the glutenin and gliadin so that they cannot bond together to form their elastic strands. Rule: The more fat, the more tender the product. Problem: Reduce fat, but obtain a tender product. One solution: Reduce the fat and use cake flour.

To add nutritional value to baked goods, you can substitute whole wheat pastry flour for one quarter to one third of the all-purpose flour or cake flour called for in the recipe. Note that moisture absorption differs with each type of flour and you will have to adjust or add more liquid to compensate if the batter looks too dry. Whole grain flours are also heavier than white, and they are not recommended for sponge or fine-grained layer cakes. One or two tablespoons sifted soy flour or sifted non-instant powdered milk can be substituted for an equal amount of flour in most cookie or muffin recipes (cakes are more temperamental). Soy flour causes quicker browning, so when baking with it, lower the oven temperature by 25°F.

Many individuals have gluten intolerance: They are allergic to wheat products. Flour milled from a variety of other grains (such as rice or quinoa) or starch made from potatoes or corn can be substituted in carefully formulated recipes. As a general rule, these nongluten flours work best when blended together. See page xiii for a list of gluten-free recipes in this book.

Sifting and Measuring Dry Ingredients

Flour is often sold with a label that reads "presifted"; ignore it. The bags have been stacked and stored so many times that the contents will have settled. When you open a bag of flour, pour it into a wide-mouth canister with an airtight lid. The pouring will aerate the flour slightly.

An important fact to remember about flour is that too much can toughen baked goods; use only as much as a recipe requires. This is not as easy as it sounds, because if you measure by volume, as most Americans do, you can pack as much as two extra tablespoons of flour into a cup by tapping it on the counter as you handle it. A scale is the most accurate tool for measuring, because 100 grams cannot vary no matter how you tap it, but many find the technique cumbersome.

When a recipe in this book calls for "½ cup unsifted flour," it is measured by the scoop-and-sweep method: Dip a dry measuring cup (page 55) into the canister of flour, or spoon it from the canister into the cup. Then take the back of a knife or icing spatula and sweep off the excess, leveling the top. Do not tap the cup, or the flour will compact.

When the recipe calls for "½ cup sifted flour," scoop the flour from the canister and pass it through a fine or medium-fine mesh strainer set over a piece of wax paper or a bowl. With a large spoon, scoop this sifted flour into the dry measuring cup, heaping it up slightly. Then take the back of a knife or icing spatula and sweep off the excess, leveling the top. Do not tap the cup, or the flour will compact.

Liquids

For the baker, liquids include eggs, water, milk, cream, sour cream and yogurt, fruit juices, alcohol, honey, molasses, oil, melted butter, and coffee. Liquids have many functions in a batter: They dissolve salt and sugar, create steam to push apart cells and aerate the structure of the final product, and moisten the leavening agent to begin production of carbon dioxide gas, causing rising.

Liquids should be used with caution because too much can activate the gluten in wheat flour and cause extra elasticity, resulting in toughness in cakes and pastries. Acidic liquids such as citrus juices, vinegar, sour milk, and buttermilk inhibit production of gluten and thus tenderize baked goods. Honey, molasses, sour cream, and yogurt are all acidic and will alter the pH balance of a batter; when these are present, baking soda (an alkali) is added to neutralize some of the acidity. Liquid quantities must be adjusted when baking at high altitudes (ask your County Agricultural Extension Service for recipe adjustments).

Dairy Products

Milk

Milk products contribute moisture, color, and richness to baked goods and also prolong their freshness. Milk products derive from an animal source, so they contain cholesterol and about 64 percent of their fat is saturated. However, they also contain protein, calcium, and a variety of vitamins and minerals. Note that as you remove fat from milk products, you reduce the amount of saturated fat and cholesterol but increase the proportion of calcium.

Milk is generally identified by its fat content. Whole milk contains 3.3 to 3.5 percent butterfat, by weight. This is a significant amount when you realize that one cup of whole milk receives 49 percent of its total calories from fat. To reduce fat in baking, use skim milk (whole milk minus the cream), low-fat milk (1 percent or 2 percent fat), or nonfat instant dry milk reconstituted with water (see manufacturer's directions for quantities).

Buttermilk is the liquid by-product of churned milk or cream. Because the solids and most fats are removed, "regular" buttermilk is low-fat; you can also purchase nonfat buttermilk. Cultured buttermilk is pasteurized skim milk mixed with a lactic-acid bacteria culture. Whether the label on the container says cultured or not, either one can be used. Cultured buttermilk powder, available in cans in the baking section of supermarkets, is a convenient dry mix that must be reconstituted with water. I use it frequently and always try to keep a container in the pantry. It saves buying a quart of buttermilk, using just a little bit, and then waiting for the rest to turn sour so you can throw it out.

If substituting buttermilk for whole or skim milk in a cake or other baking recipe, remember to add a little baking soda to balance the acidity (approximately ⅛ teaspoon baking soda for up to 2 cups buttermilk; ¼ teaspoon if over 2 cups buttermilk). Buttermilk is a welcome ingredient for the low-fat baker because it is both naturally low in fat and its acidity slows the development of gluten in wheat flour, tenderizing baked products.

As a substitute for buttermilk (though lacking its rich flavor), you can make your own soured milk by adding 1 tablespoon white vinegar or lemon juice to 1 cup 1% or 2% milk; let it sit for about 3 minutes before using it. Or, blend 1 cup of skim milk with 2 or 3 tablespoons nonfat yogurt.

Canned evaporated skim milk is skim milk minus about half its water content; it is processed by cooking and heat-sterilizing so it has a long shelf life. Once opened, it must be refrigerated, covered, and used within a week.

Symptoms of lactose intolerance, a physiological inability to digest and absorb lactose (a disaccharide) or so-called "milk sugar," present in many dairy products, can usually be alleviated by using lactose-free milk. Whole, skim, or low-fat milk with the lactose removed, it is sold alongside regular milk in the supermarket. Lactose-free milk is available as nonfat and 1% and 2% milk and can be used as a substitute for regular milk in all baking.

Comparative Table of Whole and Low-Fat Milk, Buttermilk, Evaporated Skim Milk, and Lactaid

1 cup	Calories	Percentage of calories from fat	Total grams of fat	Grams of saturated fat	Cholesterol (mg)	Calcium (mg)
Whole (3.3%) milk	150	49	8	5	33	291
2% milk	125	37	5	3	18	313
1% milk	119	23	3	2	10	349
Skim milk	86	4	0.4	0.3	4	302
Buttermilk (low fat)	99	18	2	1	9	285
Buttermilk (3 T powder + 1 cup water)	79	0.3	1	1	5	176
Evaporated (skim/canned)	199	2	1	0.3	10	740
Lactaid (lactose-reduced low-fat milk)	102	unknown	3	unknown	10	300

SOURCE: Anna dePlanter Bowes and Charles F. Church, *Food Values of Portions Commonly Used*, rev. by Jean A. T. Pennington, 15th ed. (New York: Harper & Row, 1989); *USDA Agricultural Handbook 8-1*, 1976.

Cream

Obviously, in low-fat baking, heavy cream is a no-no. One cup of heavy (whipping) cream, which contains 36 to 40 percent butterfat, obtains 95 percent of its calories from fat, contains 821 calories, 88 grams of fat (of which a whopping 55 are saturated), and 326 milligrams of cholesterol (more than a day's allowance, according to the American Heart Association).

That said, there are going to be a few times when nothing else can be substituted. Go ahead! Use the minimum possible to add the effect or the flavor desired. For whipping, use a minute amount of heavy (whipping) cream (no other type of cream holds a whip very long) and whip it extra-stiff. You may want to fold the whipped cream into a meringue or yogurt for a thick, rich but reduced-fat sauce.

As a substitute for heavy cream as a sauce, not for whipping, you can use "light" ricotta cheese (which has a faintly nutty flavor) or low-fat cottage cheese, whipped in a blender, then stirred into a little low-fat vanilla or plain yogurt.

Sour Cream

Sour cream is basically fermented heavy cream. Commercially marketed sour cream is cultured sour cream, a rich, tangy product made from 18 percent butterfat cream injected with a bacterium, *Streptococcus lactis,* and allowed to thicken. For the low-fat baker, there are now several fine brands of low-fat and fat-free sour cream that can be used as alternatives to the fat-rich original (see accompanying table). Choose brands made from cultured skim milk (read the label); do not use imitation or nondairy sour creams, because they frequently contain highly saturated tropical oils or are made with hydrogenated fat. If you cannot find one of these substitutes, use low-fat or nonfat yogurt or homemade Yogurt Cheese (page 405).

Yogurt

One of the oldest known foods, yogurt has been made for thousands of years. It may have originated as a deliberate method for preserving milk, or been a happy accident resulting when a desert nomad left milk in the hot sun and it combined with airborne cultures and turned into custard. Yogurt can be made from the milk of cows, horses, sheep, goats, camels, and buffalo; most yogurt sold in America today is made from cow's milk, although some small producers use sheep's and goat's milk.

While yogurt is neither a cure-all nor a perfect food, as sometimes claimed, it is a nutritious, low-fat, low-cholesterol product containing, among other virtues, high levels of calcium, protein, and B-vitamins.

Yogurt's annual sales in the United States exceed 1.2 billion pounds. This includes over thirteen different categories and a variety of flavors, from plain custard, nonfat, and Swiss-style to whipped low-fat with fruit on the bottom or blended in and frozen yogurt. Yogurts play the numbers game, ranging from a relatively spartan cup of "light" yogurt with 90 calories or plain nonfat yogurt with 127 calories and trace amounts of fat and saturated fat to heavily sweetened creamy fruit yogurt offering up to 250 calories and 9 to 12 grams of fat. The question is, when exactly is it really yogurt, and when is it a high-calorie, high-fat pudding?

Yogurt is made from skim milk, sometimes enriched with extra nonfat milk solids, that is homogenized, pasteurized, and injected with live bacteria: *Lactobacillus bulgaricus* and *Lactobacillus thermophilus,* plus, in some but not all cases, the most highly valued *Lactobacillus acidophilus.* These bacteria feed on the milk sugar to produce lactic

Comparative Table of Heavy Cream, Sour Cream, Yogurt, Frozen Yogurt, and Ice Cream

8 ounces/1 cup	Calories	Total grams of fat	Grams of saturated fat	Cholesterol (mg)	Calcium (mg)
Heavy cream (36%)	821	88	55	326	154
Cultured dairy sour cream	493	48	30	5	268
Lite sour cream (Land O Lakes)	293	15	ND*	ND*	ND*
Nonfat "Free" sour cream (Light n' Lively)	151	0	0	0	ND*
Low-fat yogurt with fruit	225	3	2	10	314
Low-fat (1.5%) vanilla yogurt	194	3	2	11	389
Plain whole yogurt	139	7	5	29	274
Plain low-fat yogurt	144	4	2	14	415
Plain nonfat yogurt	127	0.4	0.3	4	452
Frozen yogurt (Colombo low-fat chocolate)	240	3.7	ND*	13	26.6
Ice cream (rich vanilla; 16% fat)	349	23.7	14.7	88	151

*ND—no data available.
SOURCE: Anna dePlanter Bowes and Charles F. Church, *Food Values of Portions Commonly Used*, rev. by Jean A. T. Pennington, 15th ed. (New York: Harper & Row, 1989); *USDA Agricultural Handbook 8-1*.

acid. At this point, the milk is incubated, or allowed to ferment, in order to let it coagulate into yogurt and develop its characteristic tangy flavor. To keep the cultures alive and active, yogurt should be chilled and shipped at this stage. Live cultures are required in the yogurt sold in Europe, but not in the United States. Here, some companies pasteurize the product once more, killing the bacteria. Read the label to tell the difference. The most desirable yogurts contain "live, active cultures"; better yet, look for those containing "live, active Lactobacillus acidophilus cultures."

Yogurt that has been injected with bacteria in its individual tub or retail container is considered superior to that injected in batches in huge vats, then transferred to smaller containers. Transferring breaks the coagulation, or set; for this reason, some brands include added vegetable gum, modified food starch, or gelatine to hold or "reset" the yogurt.

Yogurt offers many health advantages. Yogurt containing live Lactobacillus acidophilus culture has the ability to replace beneficial bacteria wiped out by illness or antibiotics and may help prevent yeast infections. The lactic acid that transforms milk into yogurt also turns lactose into lactase, a form of the milk sugar that can generally be tolerated by individuals suffering from lactose intolerance. Thus, they can eat most brands of yogurt and frozen yogurt, while they cannot eat other milk products.

Low-fat or nonfat yogurt is a good substitute for sour cream or heavy cream. Low-fat homemade Yogurt Cheese (page 405) may be used in place of cream cheese, though the flavor is less sweet.

Frozen Yogurt

Frozen low-fat yogurt contains roughly half the calories and fat of butterfat-rich ice cream. Like other forms of yogurt, the frozen varieties supply calcium, minerals, vitamins, and amino acids. The frozen version also includes emulsifiers and stabilizers added to create a creamy consistency, and some brands contain active cultures. However, the fat content can vary considerably. While low-fat frozen yogurts may have less fat than ice cream, some are high in added sugars and are actually quite fattening; read labels carefully.

Eggs

Eggs are vitally important to successful baking: They aid in leavening, add richness, proteins, vitamins, and minerals, and contribute to the structure, texture, color, and flavor of baked goods. Eggs are a liquid that helps bind a batter together. When a cake rises during baking, the proteins in the egg combine with the proteins in the flour to support the structure. When whole eggs and/or egg whites are whipped, they incorporate air, which expands in the heat of the oven, leavening the product.

One large whole egg weighs 50 grams and contains 75 calories (of which 62 percent come from fat). The yolk, which weighs 17 grams, contains all the egg's fat (5.5 grams, of which 1.6 grams are saturated) and 59 calories (of which 79 percent come from fat). The yolk also contains all the egg's cholesterol (213 milligrams). Because of the yolk's saturated fat and cholesterol content, the American Heart Association currently recommends that the adult diet include only four whole eggs or four yolks per week—or any number of whites.

The egg white is more friendly to low-fat bakers. One large white weighs 33 grams and has 17 calories, 3.5 grams protein, and zero fat. Obviously, in low-fat baking, one uses more whites and fewer yolks; for cholesterol-free baking, one must eliminate the yolks entirely. In general, as a substitute for one whole egg, use two whites; for two whole eggs, use one egg plus one extra white, or three whites. Be aware that too many egg whites in a batter can have a drying effect; use them judiciously.

If you are trying to reduce fat in a conventional recipe and can tolerate cholesterol, often you can improve the taste and texture by using some yolk; for example, one yolk, one whole egg, or one egg plus one or two whites. Think of it this way: The yolk does contribute fat, but only 5.5 grams of it. If you divide this among eight servings, each one contains only about 0.7 gram of fat.

Whole eggs and egg yolks tenderize baked goods because their fat content helps to inhibit the development of potentially toughening gluten in wheat flour. In addition to fat, yolks also contain natural lecithin, an emulsifying agent that helps yolks whip into a stabilized foam.

To the cook, there is no difference between brown and white eggs, but eggs do vary in freshness, size, and whipping qualities. For use in cake batters, eggs should be at room temperature. If they are very cold, set them, in the shell, in a bowl of warm water for about ten minutes.

Storing and Freezing Eggs

Egg whites can be stored, refrigerated for up to a month. Egg yolks can be refrigerated in a covered jar for two or three days. (I like to put a drop or two of water on the yolks to keep a skin from forming.) But the best way to store eggs is in the freezer. Whites and yolks can be frozen separately; add a pinch of sugar to yolks to prevent stickiness when thawed. Lightly beaten whole eggs can be blended with a few grains of salt or sugar and then frozen in ice cube trays (one cube equals one whole egg). Frozen eggs, whole or separated, should be thawed overnight in the refrigerator before use. Never refreeze thawed frozen eggs.

What to Do with Leftover Egg Yolks

Since low-fat bakers use whites with impunity, the question always arises of what to do with all the leftover yolks. Here are a few ideas to get you started: Blend them with pure pigment to make egg tempera paint like the fourteenth- and fifteenth-century Old Masters did; cook the yolks and feed them to your dog or cat—the lecithin in the yolks is believed to make animal coats glossy; or mix an egg yolk into your shampoo—the lecithin makes human hair shine, too. Or, toss out the yolks; save them for a few days because you feel guilty about wasting them and then toss them out; or save them up until you cannot stand another low-fat dessert and make yourself a yolk-rich crème caramel! Remember, I do not suggest a total deprivation diet.

Egg Glazes

Whole-egg or egg-yolk glazes are often used in classic baking to give a sheen or gilded appearance to breads and pastries. For low-fat baking, substitute a lightly beaten egg white, or brush the top of a pie with skim milk and sprinkle with some granulated sugar.

Measuring Eggs

Egg size is very important in baking. In the recipes in this book, all eggs are U.S. Grade A "large," weighing two ounces in the shell. By U.S. law, one dozen large eggs must weigh twenty-four ounces, although the eggs will vary individually within that dozen. In low-fat baking, this is a critical point. When you are already cutting down on eggs, you need to have full value when you do use one. Keep a sharp eye out; if an egg looks especially small, select a larger one or weigh it or measure its volume.

1 large egg yolk	= 1 tablespoon
1 large egg white	= 2 tablespoons = 1/8 cup
4 large egg whites	= 8 tablespoons = 1/2 cup
4 large egg whites beaten with sugar until stiff	= approximately 4 cups meringue

Whipping Egg Whites

Beaten egg whites foam because of the combined actions of several proteins. Albumen is thick and viscous, made up of large molecules that resemble loosely coiled strands of twine. When beaten or heated, these strands unwrap and stretch out. When stretched around whipped-in air bubbles, they make a strong self-bonding skin. Ovomucin and globulins increase the viscosity of the albumen, helping it make a fine foam with many cells. Together with conalbumin, these proteins help stabilize the foam at room temperature and prevent it from draining liquid.

When meringue is exposed to the heat of the oven, the molecules of air in the foam cells get warm, expand, and enlarge the cells; they might actually grow so large they would burst if not for the ability of another protein, ovalbumin, to coagulate around and strengthen each cell wall. This prevents the collapse of the cell walls, even when the meringue is baked and the water in it evaporates.

Stabilizers are often added to egg whites. Acidity (in the form of cream of tartar, vinegar, or lemon juice) lowers the pH of the albumen slightly and slows down the unfolding of the protein strands, helping them to resist overbeating and leaking of liquid. When whites are whipped in a copper bowl, the copper ions interact molecularly with the albumen, just as an acid would.

There are several important things to remember when whipping whites into meringue. First, keep all utensils scrupulously clean; the smallest speck of fat prevents the whites from beating to full volume because the fat becomes suspended in the natural moisture of the whites and softens the protein, weighing them down. Avoid whipping whites in plastic bowls, which can never be washed completely grease-free. To rid any bowl of a hint of grease, wipe the bowl and your beaters with a paper towel dampened with white vinegar.

Eggs separate most easily when cold, but they whip to greatest volume when at room temperature (about 68°F). The paradox can be solved if you separate the eggs as soon as they come from the refrigerator, placing yolks and whites in separate bowls. Place the bowl of whites in a pan of warm water for about 10 minutes, stirring occasionally until the whites feel lukewarm to the touch.

To hold its shape, meringue must be properly whipped. For best results with least effort, use an electric mixer with a balloon-type wire whip and a closely fitting bowl. The point is to keep the entire mass of whites in constant movement. To begin, add a pinch of cream of tartar (or other acid if called for) and salt to the whites and whip on low speed, gradually working up to medium. When the whites are foamy, but not before, begin to add sugar (if used) gradually, while continuing to whip. Whipping on low to medium speed gives smaller bubbles, which are more stable than the large bubbles produced if whipped only on high speed. If the sugar is added too soon, it will dissolve into the whites and hinder the development of the meringue.

Continue to whip until the meringue looks glossy and smooth and forms slightly droopy peaks. To test this, turn off the machine and scoop out some whites on a spoon, or turn the beater upside down. Then beat a few seconds longer (some bakers prefer to do this final stage by hand with a whisk) until almost-stiff peaks form and you can see beater or whisk tracks on the surface of the meringue. This is the moment just before the maximum volume is reached. At this stage, you should be able to turn the bowl of whipped whites completely upside down (over a sink if you are nervous) without the whites budging. This is the point referred to in the recipes as "stiff but not dry."

Avoid overbeating egg whites. Overbeating occurs when the albumen strands are bonded and stretched so tightly that they squeeze the water molecules right out of the foam. Overbeaten, meringue looks lumpy and dry, and a film of water forms in the bottom of the bowl. If turned upside down (this time you would need a sink), the mass of whites would slide around precariously. You can try to salvage and revive overwhipped whites by gently whipping in one extra egg white for every four in the meringue.

Egg and Meringue Safety

Recently, egg safety and the possible health hazards of eating uncooked eggs and meringues has become a hot topic for cooks and food writers. Some incidents of bacterial contamination, or salmonella, have been attributed to raw, improperly cooked, or undercooked eggs. The cause and its cure are not fully understood. Until the hazard is eliminated, be prudent when using eggs and follow these simple guidelines.

When shopping, open the cartons and look at the eggs; reject any cartons that have cracked or unclean eggs. Be sure the store has properly refrigerated egg cases. At home, refrigerate eggs promptly, storing them inside the refrigerator itself, where it is colder than the shelves on the door.

Wash any container or food preparation surface that has come in contact with raw eggs before reusing it. Avoid eating raw eggs or raw egg whites. Refrigerate cheesecakes and all baked goods containing custards or meringues.

While the bacteria causing the common food poisoning *salmonellosis* is sometimes present in egg whites, it has also been found on the skins of fruits grown in contaminated soil; its origin is the subject of some debate. Washing produce carefully helps; there is no question, however, that the bacteria cannot survive high temperatures. Commercial food handlers and many restaurants avoid the possibility of the problem by routinely cooking with pasteurized liquid eggs instead of fresh eggs.

Cooking Meringues and Egg White Icings

For the baker, egg white caution means following instructions carefully when preparing meringues, boiled or seven-minute icing, or other preparations such as mousse. While it is highly unlikely that eating a small amount of icing will make you sick, at least you should be informed. Most of the meringue recipes in this book call for cooked syrup or cooked meringue; the few that give you a choice are so noted. You be the judge.

According to the American Egg Board, to destroy the bacteria, egg whites must be brought to a temperature of 140°F for 3½ minutes, or 150°F for 2 minutes, or at some point reach 160°F. I have done some testing on temperatures of cooked meringues. When I started each test, the whites were at room temperature (68°F). I began with Seven-Minute Icing (page 439), the bottom line: This is an easy and safe solution to the safety problem. My first trials were over direct heat rather than in a double boiler. After I whipped the meringue with a hand-held beater on medium speed for 3½ minutes, the temperature of the meringue reached 140°F. In the following 30 seconds, the temperature increased to 145°F and remained there for the next 4 full minutes while I increased the beater speed to high. This was well within the acceptable range. (My only problem with this method was that if I did not constantly manipulate the beater over the entire bottom surface of the pan, the meringue began to scorch and brown.)

Making Seven-Minute Icing (I now prefer to call it Five-Minute Icing) in a double boiler is much easier. First I whipped the meringue with a hand-held beater on medium speed for 4 minutes (1 minute longer than over direct heat), and the temperature reached 140°F; then it rapidly climbed to 150°F and stayed there for the next 3 minutes. I had no scorching problems with the double boiler. I believe that this is the most reliable method available at this time, and it produces the most silken icing texture. Unfortunately, Seven-Minute Icing cannot be used for all desserts requiring meringue because the ratio of sugar to egg whites must be high enough for the cooking meringue to foam properly before it poaches; in my tests, it poached too soon if the sugar dropped below ¾ to 1 cup per 2 whites. Atlanta food scientist Shirley Corriher explains that sugar prevents coagulation of the egg white proteins; when you cut down on sugar, the whites coagulate (in this case, poach) faster.

To test Boiled Icing (page 441), I prepared a sugar syrup and heated it to 242°F, the temperature recommended by the American Egg Board. I whipped the egg whites to soft peaks in the electric mixer, then poured the 242°F syrup in a steady stream into the continually whipping meringue. Once the hot syrup was incorporated, the meringue reached 145°F, and it held this temperature for 45 seconds. Then, as the whipping continued (per the recipe), the temperature started to descend; after 60 seconds, it plummeted to 125°F. After 2 minutes, it was at 100° and falling. Seven-Minute Icing is easier to make and stays hot longer than Boiled Icing, but Boiled Icing is the only possibility in certain recipes.

I have not used commercial egg replacements in any of the recipes in this book because I prefer fresh, natural products. The replacements (such as Eggbeaters) are safe and work well if you wish to use them; follow the manufacturer's instructions for quantities to use. The one product I have used with success is Simply Eggs, processed by Michael Foods and found in the refrigerator cases of supermarkets. Simply Eggs are natural whole eggs with 80 percent of the cholesterol removed; they are also pasteurized to eliminate bacteria like salmonella. The yolk and white are blended; they can replace whole eggs in baked goods without detection.

Cheese

Cream Cheese

Cream cheese is a soft, rich, fresh unripened cheese made from milk and cream, with a mild but slightly acidic flavor. The whey is first separated and drained from milk curds, then milk and cream are added to the curds.

The fat content of regular cream cheeses ranges from 35 to 40 percent. Kraft's Philadelphia Regular Cream Cheese, a widely available brand, is sold in 3- and 8-ounce foil-wrapped blocks that are freshness-dated (see table on page 26 for nutritive values).

"Light" or low-fat cream cheese is regular cream cheese minus part of the fat. One widely available brand, Philadelphia Light Cream Cheese, sold in an 8-ounce tub, is similar to the regular style in texture and taste but contains just half the fat. Buyer beware: Kraft also packages "Soft" regular cream cheese in an identical tub; it does not have the same properties for baking and should never be substituted. Philadelphia also sells "Fat-free" cream cheese in a tub; it looks like the Light version but is greasier, does not taste as good, and should never be cooked. Avoid it. My choice is the Light, or low-fat, Philadelphia version, even though it has some fat.

As a substitute for cream cheese, you can use homemade Yogurt Cheese (page 405), although it is less sweet. Or you can substitute nonfat or low-fat cottage cheese that is drained and pressed dry in a strainer, then whipped absolutely smooth in a blender.

Neufchâtel cheese is creamy, made from milk, and similar to regular cream cheese in texture. It originated in Normandy, France, and is cured for a period of several weeks, which gives a particular flavor some perceive as slightly tangy or leaving a faint bitter aftertaste. It is usually softer in texture and not quite as mild as cream cheese. There are several low-fat Neufchâtel cheeses on the market. The most widely available brand in my area is marketed by Kraft/Philadelphia, wrapped in a foil brick looking remarkably like the Original Philadelphia cream cheese; whichever one you want, be sure you select the correct package. Philadelphia brand Neufchâtel has one third less fat than regular cream cheese, but is not quite as calorie- and fat-reduced as Philadelphia Light Cream Cheese (see table on page 26). You can use Neufchâtel or light (low-fat) cream cheese interchangeably unless the recipe is specific about the type.

Ricotta Cheese

Fresh, unripened, and similar to cottage cheese, ricotta has fine moist clumps and a bland, faintly bitter or nutty taste. Italian ricotta is often made from sheep's milk drained from the curds when provolone cheese is made. In the United States, ricotta is usually made from cow's milk whey, which contains a protein called lactalbumin that, when heated, causes the whey to coagulate, or set. At this point, acids are added, and sometimes extra milk as well. Because ricotta is a fresh cheese, it does not have a long shelf life and should be used soon after purchase; watch the date on the package. Ricotta can also be frozen, but its texture changes slightly; this does not harm it for baking use. Regular ricotta has between 4 and 10 percent fat and about half the calories of cream cheese per ounce (see table on page 26).

Low-fat ricotta is made from skim milk. There are several brands, of ricotta "Lite" available, with about half the calories, fat, and saturated fat of the regular type.

Part-skim ricotta is made from partially skimmed milk, and while it is lower in calories and fats than the original, it has slightly more of both than the "light" type.

The low-fat ricottas are slightly blander than the regular in taste, but there is not enough difference to affect use in baking. When drained well and blended smooth, ricotta can be substituted for cream cheese although you should compensate for the difference in sweetness.

Type	Amount	Calories	Total grams of fat	Grams of saturated fat	Cholesterol (mg)	Calcium (mg)	Protein (g)
Philadelphia Regular Cream Cheese	8 ounces	784	76	43	224	160	18
Philadelphia Light Cream Cheese	8 ounces	496	38	22	128	304	23
Neufchâtel	8 ounces	592	53	34	176	168	23
Ricotta (whole milk)	8 ounces	432	32	21	126	514	28
Ricotta (part skim)	8 ounces	340	20	12	76	669	28
Ricotta (Lite)	8 ounces	280	16	8	40	ND*	32
Cottage cheese (creamstyle whole milk)	8 ounces	217	10	6	31	126	26
Cottage cheese (1% low-fat)	8 ounces	164	2	2	10	138	28
Cheddar (medium sharp)	1 ounce	114	9	5	28	208	7
Cheddar (low-fat)	1 ounce	72	4	3	12	192	6

*ND—no data available.
SOURCE: Anna dePlanter Bowes and Charles F. Church, *Food Values of Portions Commonly Used*, rev. by Jean A. T. Pennington, 15th ed. (New York: Harper & Row, 1989); *USDA Agricultural Handbook 8–1*.

Cottage Cheese

A fresh, unripened cheese, one of the oldest types known to man, cottage cheese was originally made from naturally soured milk, probably left in the sun until it curdled. Today, the milk is set with a lactic starter, then cut, drained of whey, and packaged. Cottage cheese is a lumpy white cheese with either small or large curds and a mildly acidic flavor. Because of the rounded curds, this cheese is also known as popcorn cheese. Cream is often added to give more moisture and flavor; this type is called creamed cottage cheese. The fat content of cottage cheeses varies. The richest can have up to 15 percent fat, while the average has

4 percent, and low-fat only 1 or 2 percent; dry-curd varieties contain only 0.5 percent fat.

Low-fat (1%) cottage cheese is similar to regular cottage cheese in taste and texture, but has about one quarter fewer calories, one fifth the fat, and one third the saturated fat. It also has more calcium and more protein than the regular version. Use the low-fat type for baking. If the curds are pressed relatively dry in a strainer and then puréed in a processor or blender until completely smooth, it can be substituted for cream cheese. Some brands contain gums that inhibit release of the whey; if you are trying to drain this type, just press out as much liquid as possible.

Farmer's or Pot Cheese

This cheese is similar in taste to cottage cheese, but has a much drier texture. As a substitute, use cottage cheese drained in a sieve to remove most of the excess liquid (whey). Farmer's or pot cheese is often bulk-packed. It is not as widely available as cottage cheese. Look for it in specialty delicatessens and supermarkets with large cheese departments. Farmer's or pot cheese can contain as much as 8 percent fat, according to the National Dairy Board.

Cheddar Cheese

Cheddar cheese is named for a village in Somerset, England, where it originated. The word *cheddar* also refers to a step in the manufacturing process (cheddaring), during which blocks of cut cheese are continually turned and stacked for a period of about one and a half hours. A firm aged cheese that varies in color from white to orange, Cheddar is made all over the world. The taste varies depending on aging and manufacturing technique. American Cheddars range from mild to strong. Regular Cheddars contain about 45 percent fat.

Reduced-fat Cheddar has about half the calories and fat of regular, and the taste is almost the same. Use it in low-fat baking, especially for muffins and quick breads.

Fats

Baking fats include butter, margarine, vegetable shortening, lard, and oil. Used in baked goods, fats tenderize, moisturize, add flakiness, and carry flavors, aromas, and nutrients. Fats also add smoothness to the texture. Different fats have different melting points and contain different percentages of water. For these reasons, the type of fat used affects the tenderness, texture, taste, and shape of baked products.

Understanding Ingredients

Fats are either saturated or unsaturated; unsaturated fats tend to be liquid at room temperature (e.g., oils) and saturated fats tend to be solid. In addition to differences in saturation levels, solid and liquid fats differ in moisture content, melting point, and additives. These qualities affect their uses in baking and should be considered when choosing fat substitutes. Remember that the preferred choice for fat in low-fat baking is always the one lowest in saturation, or the one with the highest P/S ratio, which indicates the relative balance between polyunsaturates and saturates (see page 458).

The fat used in baking affects tenderness. Soft or liquid fats (including oils) coat the proteins in wheat flour more completely than solid fat; coating prevents development of the gluten and contributes to tenderness. Since solid fats are more highly saturated than soft or liquid fats, it is important for the low-fat baker to know that a light flavorless vegetable oil (such as canola) can often be substituted for (or combined with) solid fat in a recipe that calls for "creaming butter (or shortening) and sugar." The grain of the cake will be more dense, but acceptable. When a recipe calls for melted butter or melted shortening, oil can be substituted. The results will be similar to the original, except in flavor— unless the recipe requires the eventual hardening of the melted butter for texture, as is the case with certain icings.

For aeration of cake batters, solid fat at room temperature (68°F) or semisolid shortening gives best results. When these types of fat are beaten, creamed, or whipped with sugar, the rough-edged sugar crystals cut air bubbles into the flexible fat, which then stretches and expands, enveloping the bubbles. If the fat is too cold, the walls around the air bubbles will be brittle, cracking and releasing air and thereby causing the cake to fall. Shortening contains no water and thus has the capacity to absorb air to its full volume. It can whip in more air than either butter or margarine, which contain milk solids, salt, and water and can only absorb beaten-in air in their fat portions. In low-fat baking, aeration is accomplished by using the reduced quantity of fat plus the addition of stiffly whipped egg whites or a viscous substance like fruit purée, applesauce, or certain syrups that hold the air bubbles.

For flaky pastry, a cold solid fat is desirable. The colder it is, the less it soaks into the starch in the flour and the more separate it stays, creating little flakes or layers as it is pinched into the flour. In the heat of the oven, the liquid in the pastry dough makes steam that pushes up the layers while the heat sets them firmly; this action creates the quality of flakiness in a pie crust. In contrast, oil blends right into flour, tenderizing the crust but never making it flaky. Solid fat does not have to mean highly saturated butterfat. You can combine low-fat milk and oil with a little flour and freeze it (see page 278), then work this into the flour for a low-fat flaky pastry.

The amount of water released by the fat used contributes to the total liquid in a recipe. In baking, a fat that contains a lot of water can require more flour and thus result in a tough product. Some margarine spreads (as opposed to solid margarine) contain well over 50 percent water. Light or diet margarines contain so much water (and occasionally additives or air) that they are not reliable for use in baking unless specifically called for in the recipe.

Butter and stick margarine contain roughly 20 percent water. The presence of so much liquid means an all-butter cookie will require more flour, and will usually be less tender than one made with 100 percent fat such as oil or shortening.

Butter and margarine are food spreads that melt in the mouth; they have melting points near body temperature (approximately 92°F). Some brands of margarine stay solid a little longer, melting near 100°F. Hydrogenized vegetable shortening has the highest melting point, from 110 to 120°F.

If you baked the same cookie recipe using each of these fats, you would see that butter and margarine doughs soften in the oven and spread relatively quickly, before their starches are set; the cookies are usually thin and crisp. Shortening cookies are puffed up and thick because they set up before the fat melts. For low-fat baking, oil can be used successfully in soft, moist, or bar cookies, particularly those made with fruits. I find it difficult to make crisp buttery cookies without some solid fat. Let's face it, sometimes you just need some butter, in combination with oil or shortening or margarine. (Use it, just don't eat the whole batch.)

Butter

Butter has the best flavor of all baking fats. Besides its taste, unsalted butter is preferred because it is (or should be) either dated or sold frozen, and should be fresher than salted butter. Salt is added to butter for flavor, but also to prolong shelf life; it often masks off flavors in older butter. Made from pasteurized sweet cream, butter is an animal fat and thus contains cholesterol (33 milligrams per tablespoon), and it is a solid fat and thus contains saturated fat (7.1 grams per tablespoon). Its fat content ranges from 80 to 86 percent. Water content varies from 18 to 20 percent plus 2 percent milk solids. For cake baking, select butter with the least water; melt a variety of brands and compare the liquid that settles out upon cooling. The low-fat baker must consider butter a luxury: always tempting, often to be lived without, but sometimes absolutely essential to spiritual and gustatory life.

Margarine

Margarine was invented by a French chemist during the late nineteenth century, to provide an inexpensive fat for the army of Napoleon III. It is made from a variety of oils and solid fats that are blended, heated, and combined with water, milk, or milk solids; emulsifying agents; flavorings; preservatives; coloring; and vitamins. Margarine is partially hydrogenated (see below) to make it solid. Soft margarine spreads usually list water as the first ingredient; they contain unspecified quantities of water and air and about 60 percent fat. Diet imitation margarine and reduced-fat spreads can contain about 40 percent fat and at least 50 percent water; they, as well as soft tub margarines, are absolutely unreliable for baking.

While it lacks the good taste of butter, solid margarine has roughly the same fat content—around 80 percent—but it is much lower in cholesterol. Many brands in fact contain no cholesterol, a big plus. To satisfy kosher dietary laws, one can select a brand made without milk solids or animal fats; read the labels. Select a margarine in which the first ingredient on the label is a liquid oil high in polyunsaturates (such as liquid safflower oil); avoid products in which the first ingredient listed is a hydrogenated or partially hydrogenated oil.

From the point of view of dietary health, margarine—once considered the perfect alternative to the cholesterol and saturated fat of butter—is now being scrutinized along with other hydrogenated shortenings.

Solid Shortening

To transform liquid vegetable oil into solid or spreadable form (margarine or solid shortening), the oil must be hydrogenated. This involves a commercial process by which hydrogen molecules under pressure are forced through the oil. In addition to hardening the fat, hydrogenation increases its stability and prolongs its shelf life.

During the process, the molecular structure of the oil is changed. The more an oil is hydrogenated, the greater the change and the more solid the final product. Squeeze-bottle or soft tub margarines are less hydrogenated than hard stick margarines. Many margarines and shortenings contain a high percentage of unsaturated fatty acids (oils). For example, Crisco contains 80 percent liquid soybean oil suspended in a honeycomb matrix of 20 percent hardened (hydrogenated) oil. It is 100 percent fat, contains no water, and has high levels of emulsifiers (mono- and di-glycerides) added to stabilize the structure of baked goods and increase their absorption of moisture. Crisco, like most shortening, is made of highly polyunsaturated vegetable oil; it contains about half the saturated fat of butter.

Solid shortening is designed to go in, not on, food. As it does not have to taste good or feel good in the mouth, it can contain a generous quantity of emulsifiers to preserve the suspension of the fat in liquid, to hold more air, and to stabilize the moisture content of batter.

Lard

Lard is rendered pork fat, plus a very small amount of water. It is 100 percent animal fat and has 14 milligrams cholesterol per tablespoon. It is 39.2 percent saturated fat—less than one might think. Lard seems to be less harmful to the diet than previously believed, but, nevertheless, is not really an option in low-fat baking.

Cocoa Butter

Cocoa butter, once prized for cosmetic use, is a highly saturated fat created as a by-product of processing cocoa beans to make chocolate. As a vegetable fat, it contains no cholesterol. Most of the cocoa butter is removed during the processing of cocoa powder (which is thus extremely low in fat and saturated fat).

Vegetable Oils

All liquid oils (see table on page 33) have almost the same caloric content. Oils contain primarily unsaturated fats and are liquid at room temperature. They are predominantly of vegetable origin (although fish oil is also unsaturated). Vegetable oils contain different amounts of mono- and polyunsaturated fatty acids. Oils high in polyunsaturates include safflower, sunflower, corn, soybean, and cottonseed. Research has shown that polyunsaturated fat can lower harmful serum cholesterol LDLs, but large amounts in the diet can also lower the desirable HDLs.

Mono-unsaturated oils may be the most desirable of all oils. Recent research has shown that these oils can lower the levels of LDLs without affecting the levels of HDLs. Oils high in mono-unsaturates include canola oil, peanut oil and other nut oils, and olive oil. The most highly praised member of this family is olive oil, which is 77 percent mono-unsaturated fat.

Vegetable Oil Spray

To grease pans in low-fat baking, use the minimum amount of fat possible. I use no-stick vegetable oil cooking spray. My personal preference is for butter-flavored PAM, recommended for use with the recipes in this book. This brand leaves no unpleasant aftertaste on delicate cakes and other baked goods. PAM and other no stick spray oils contain lecithin, which is an excellent release agent; with this product, cakes and muffins are easily removed from their pans. When I use this spray, I do not need paper or foil muffin cup liners. Often, to facilitate removal of certain types of cakes, I recommend that the pan be coated with cooking spray or brushed with oil and then dusted with flour. Another pan-greasing alternative is a light vegetable oil (canola, safflower, and corn are my choices) brushed onto the pan with a pastry brush or put into a new pump-type spray bottle (available in hardware stores). You can select PAM or any one of a number of other commercial oil sprays in a pump.

To be an ecologically responsible baker, one must question the use of aerosol sprays. I, for one, am perfectly willing to pump or brush on my oil if that will protect the endangered ozone layer. Nevertheless, I was happy to take the suggestion of my eco-cop daughter and contact a variety of manufacturers of spray oils. They confirmed my information from the Aerosol Education Bureau: Since 1978, nearly all United States aerosol manufacturers have stopped using chloroflurocarbon propellants (CFCs), which are thought to injure the ozone layer, in compliance with bans by the Environmental Protection Agency, Food and Drug Administration, and Consumer Product Safety Commission. PAM, for example, uses a hydrocarbon propellant blending propane, isobutane, and n-butane, gases that I am assured are "environmentally safe." The small percentage of CFC users exempted from the ban are in the medical and pharmaceutical industries. If you are unsure about a particular product, contact the manufacturer.

Should I Bake with Margarine or Vegetable Shortening or Oil Instead of Butter?

Butter has all the taste, but also all the cholesterol and most of the saturated fat. The bottom line, however, is that solid margarine is not a perfect butter substitute. It lacks butter's flavor and contains some saturated fat—slightly less than one third that of butter. Its advantage is that it does not (usually) contain cholesterol. You certainly can bake with margarine. Solid shortening has a neutral (or an artificial butter) taste, is reliable for achieving certain qualities in baked goods, has about half the saturated fat of butter, and has no cholesterol. But because both margarine and shortening are hydrogenated, vegetable oil plus a small amount of butter is often the best alternative.

Storing Fats

Fats have a tendency to absorb strong odors, so all fats should be stored covered, away from strong-scented ingredients. To prevent rancidity,

Liquid and Solid Fats Listed from Best-for-Health (Lowest Amount of Saturated Fat) to Worst

Fat	Amount	Percentage of fat	Calories	Total grams of fat	Grams of saturated fat	Grams of monounsaturated fat	Grams of polyunsaturated fat	Cholesterol (mg)
Vegetable oil spray	2.5-second spray	—	6	0.7	0.1	—	0.4	0
Canola oil	1 T	100	120	13.6	0.9	7.6	4.5	0
Safflower oil	1 T	100	120	13.6	1.2	1.6	10.1	0
Walnut oil	1 T	100	120	13.6	1.2	3.1	8.6	0
Hazelnut oil	1 T	100	120	13.6	1.0	10.6	1.4	0
Sunflower oil	1 T	100	120	13.6	1.4	2.7	8.9	0
Corn oil	1 T	100	120	13.6	1.7	3.3	8.0	0
Olive oil	1 T	100	119.3	13.5	1.8	9.9	1.1	0
Sesame oil	1 T	100	120	13.6	1.9	5.4	5.7	0
Soybean oil	1 T	100	120	13.6	2.0	3.2	7.9	0
Peanut oil	1 T	100	119.3	13.5	2.3	6.2	4.3	0
Margarine (corn/stick)	1 T	80	101.4	11.4	1.8	6.6	2.4	0
Margarine (corn/tub)	1 T	80	101	11.4	2.1	4.5	4.5	0
Crisco	1 T	100	106	12.0	3.2	5.7	3.3	0
Lard	1 T	100	116	12.8	5.0	5.8	1.4	14
Palm oil	1 T	100	120	13.6	6.7	5.0	1.2	0
Butter, salted	1 T	80	102	12.2	7.15	3.3	0.4	33
Cocoa butter	1 T	100	120	13.6	8.1	4.5	0.4	0
Palm kernel oil	1 T	100	120	13.6	11.1	1.5	0.2	0
Coconut oil	1 T	100	120	13.6	11.8	0.8	0.2	0

SOURCE: Anna dePlanter Bowes and Charles F. Church, *Food Values of Portions Commonly Used*, rev. by Jean A. T. Pennington, 15th ed. (New York: Harper & Row, 1989); *USDA Agricultural Handbook Series 8–4.*

special care must be taken. Rancidity not only alters taste but is potentially toxic; it can result when fats are exposed to air and combine with oxygen and water. Research shows that by-products of rancid fats can cause damage to the lining of blood vessels, which may later lead to cardiovascular disease.

In general, unsaturated fats (oils) have a less stable molecular structure than saturated (solid) fats. They are more vulnerable to changes from exposure to heat and light and moisture. Oils should be stored in opaque containers in a cool, dark location or refrigerated. Cold temperatures sometimes turn oil cloudy; this is not harmful and clarity returns as the oil returns to room temperature. Dark-colored specialty oils, such as walnut and hazelnut, are the least stable. Their shelf life is from four to six months. Refined vegetable oils (such as canola, safflower, and corn) should be stored away from air, heat, and light in a cool, dry location. They generally stay fresh for six to ten months. Many vegetable oils naturally contain vitamin E or similar antioxidants; safflower oil, an exception, does not, and must always be refrigerated.

Some home cooking oils (and all commercial cooking oils) contain silicones, added to inhibit foaming during frying. These should be avoided and silicone-free oils used for baking, because some cake batters, for example, require foaming.

Saturated fats such as butter and cream contain enzymes that can affect and accelerate rancidity. Thus it is best to use unsalted butter because the salt in salted butter may mask the smell of rancidity. Butter and margarine should be refrigerated and/or frozen for short-term use; for long-term storage they should be frozen.

Fats that are rancid or are being reused present a safety hazard. Vegetable oil used for frying should never be reused. The high temperatures required for frying cause chemical changes in the molecular structure of the oil, releasing free fatty acids and lowering the flashpoint, or burning temperature, of the oil. Reused cooking oils may burst into flame when reheated to normal temperatures.

Measuring Fats

Oil is a liquid fat: It is measured in a liquid measuring cup. Solid fats such as butter and margarine usually are conveniently sold in quarter-pound sticks, marked on the wrapper to indicate tablespoon and cup divisions. (One stick = 8 tablespoons = ½ cup; ⅓ cup = 5 ⅓ tablespoons; ¼ cup = 4 tablespoons.) To measure solid fat using measuring spoons or cups, pack it into dry (not liquid) measuring cups or measuring spoons, taking care not to trap air pockets in the bottom. Level off the top with a straight edge before use. I prefer not to use the water displacement method—in which solid fat is added in increments to a specific amount of water in a measuring cup until the water reaches the desired level—because water left clinging to the fat may disrupt the balance of liquid in the recipe.

Reducing the Fat in Your Favorite Recipes

The special qualities of fat are hard to replicate and successful substitutions, especially in baked goods, are tricky. Generally, when you cut back or cut out fat, you need to readjust a whole range of elements in a carefully balanced formula. You must enhance flavors by increasing or adding flavoring agents, such as citrus zests, various extracts, and sometimes sugar. To maintain the desired texture in baked goods, a suitably viscous aerating and moisture-holding fat substitute is needed: fruit purées (prune, apple, banana), corn syrup, various vegetable oils, whole eggs or stiffly whipped egg whites. Sometimes, for successful baking, a little butter must be used to achieve the proper taste. To restore the tenderness contributed by the fat in the original recipe, cake flour often is used instead of higher protein all-purpose flour. But cake flour absorbs a different quantity of moisture than all-purpose flour, so then the liquids must be adjusted; acidic dairy products such as yogurt or buttermilk may be added, as they inhibit gluten development. Sometimes when acids are added, they must be balanced by the addition of neutralizing baking soda.

Remember that this book focuses on low-fat, not totally fat-free, baking. With very few exceptions (meringues and a few unusual cakes, for example) totally fat-free baked goods taste unspeakably rubbery and pasty and are boring beyond endurance. You can, however, reduce the fat with success in many cases. Beware of tinkering too much when reducing fat in your own baking recipes. Baking recipes are carefully balanced formulas; eliminating fat drastically upsets the balance. The recipes in this book have all been carefully tested and are reliable. Study their proportions if you want to alter another recipe. As a general rule, it is possible to cut fat from a "traditional" recipe by about one quarter to one third; the resulting texture may be more dense because solid fat creamed with sugar will incorporate more air than oil.

Many companies are trying to develop acceptable fat substitutes. While the research is intense and looks promising, the results to date are inconclusive.

Sugar and Other Sweeteners

Sugar in baking provides sweetness, aids the creaming and whipping of air into batters, and contributes grain, tenderness, and texture. In addition, sugar's ability to caramelize adds flavor to baked goods. Sugars, particularly sugar syrups, and honey have the ability to attract and absorb moisture, which helps keep baked goods moist and fresh. In fat-reduced baking, since flavor is often reduced, sugar is needed to retain or enhance flavor and can't be drastically reduced. As a general rule, I cut about one quarter to one third of the sugar from traditional recipes, more if fresh or dried fruit or a fruit purée or sauce can be added.

Sugar plays many roles in baking. In the creaming process, the sharp edges of the sugar crystals bite into solid fat and open up pores that grow into air cells and ultimately expand during baking to leaven and lighten the product. Sugar thus contributes to structure and volume.

In cakes leavened with eggs or egg foams, sugar interacts with egg proteins to stabilize the whipped egg foam structure. This makes the foam more elastic so air cells can expand more. In fat-free or low-fat cakes, particularly angel food and chiffon cakes with their large proportion of egg whites, the leavening agent is the air whipped into the whites. Sugar helps to stabilize the whipped foam. In addition, the presence of sugar molecules among egg proteins tends to raise the temperature at which egg proteins set, thus slowing the coagulation, or set, of the egg proteins until cells have expanded in the oven to encompass the maximum amount of air to leaven the product. This delaying action ensures good texture and volume.

Sugar also slows the development of gluten in wheat flour, causing the cell walls to stretch slowly so a cake, for example, can rise to the maximum before it is set by oven heat. High-ratio cakes are those with more than one cup of sugar per cup of flour; these cakes have an especially fine texture because of the slowness with which their cell walls have stretched.

During baking, oven heat causes starch to absorb liquid and swell, an action called *gelatinization.* The quicker the process, the faster the cake becomes set, or solid. Sugar slows this process by competing with the starch to absorb the liquid. As sugar liquefies, the batter remains viscous longer than it would without the sugar, allowing time for the maximim amount of leavening gases to develop before the batter sets. This results in a fine-grained product with a smooth crumb and good volume.

Sugar

Sugars are the simplest carbohydrates. Many different types of sugar exist in nature, but only three are primarily used in cooking: glucose, fructose, and sucrose.

The sugar most commonly used in baking is sucrose, a natural sugar found in plants. It is a complex sugar, or disaccharide, composed of one fructose and one glucose molecule joined to form a simple carbohydrate; it can be rapidly absorbed by the body to provide quick energy.

For the baker, sucrose is available as white sugar, brown sugar, or molasses. Each type comes from a different stage of the refining process. Granulated sugar is available in a variety of different crystal sizes, providing unique characteristics that suit the baker's special needs.

White sugar comes in a variety of crystal sizes, from regular granulated to superfine or bar sugar, plus confectioners' sugar. The amount of air each type of sugar can incorporate into a batter when creamed or beaten with fat is related to the size of the crystal. Obviously, granulated sugar will cut open larger holes in the fat than powdered sugar. The size of the crystals also determines how quickly the sugar will dissolve in a batter. Superfine (also called ultrafine or bar sugar) crystals dissolve much more quickly than regular granulated, so they are best for drinks or meringues. Make your own superfine sugar by grinding granulated sugar in the food processor. Extrafine sugar is slightly finer than regular granulated and is used primarily by professional bakers. Baker's Special sugar is slightly finer than extrafine and is also used by commercial bakeries. British castor sugar is similar to Baker's Special; superfine sugar can be substituted. Granulated sugar should be sifted if it has been stored for a long time and is caked or lumpy.

Confectioners' sugar is granulated sugar that has been ground to a specified degree of fineness. For home use, powdered 10X is generally used but 4X and 6X are also available. A box of confectioners' sugar usually contains about 3 percent cornstarch to prevent caking and crystallization. This gives the sugar a raw taste that is masked by adding flavorings if the sugar is not to be cooked. Confectioners' sugar dissolves almost instantly, so it is good for meringues, icings, and confections. It is sometimes used for tenderness in cookies and may even be added to cake batters to produce a denser and more silken texture than that created by granulated sugar. Confectioners' sugar should always be sifted before using.

Brown sugars, whether turbinado, dark brown, or light brown, are all less refined than white sugar. The darker the sugar, the more molasses and moisture it contains. Turbinado, usually sold in natural food shops, has a coarser grain than granulated white. It also has a variable moisture content, which makes it unpredictable in baking, although it can be sprinkled on top of cobblers or cookies. Brown sugars, both light and dark, add color, flavor, and moisture as well as sweetness to baked goods. Brown sugars tend to make baked goods heavy and should be avoided in light, fragile cakes. In general, the darker the color, the more intense the flavor. Both dark and light brown sugar have the same sweetening power as an equal weight of white sugar; however, white sugar is more dense. To achieve an equivalent degree of sweetness, brown sugar must be firmly packed before measuring.

To avoid lumping, store brown sugar in a covered glass jar or heavy plastic bag in the refrigerator or a cool dry cupboard. To make your own brown sugar, add 2 tablespoons unsulfured molasses to 1 cup granulated sugar for 1 cup brown sugar.

Molasses is the liquid separated from sugar crystals during the first stages of refining. The color and strength of the molasses depends on which stage it comes from in the separation process during a series of spinnings in a centrifuge. The first liquid molasses drawn off is the finest quality; the second and later drawings contain more impurities. The third, called blackstrap (from the Dutch word *stroop,* or syrup), is the darkest and has the strongest flavor. The most common types available for cooking blend the first, finest molasses with some cane syrup to standardize quality.

Some processors treat their sugarcane with sulfur dioxide to clarify and lighten the color of its juice. This produces a sulfur taste in molasses that many find distasteful, so it's best to use only "unsulfured" molasses, which has not been treated.

Honey

Honey is not a sugar, but it is one of the sweeteners used in baking. It contributes softness and chewiness to baked goods. Because of its chemical structure, it is particularly hygroscopic (moisture-retaining), so it helps keep baked goods moist and increases their shelf life. Honey has the same sweetening power as sugar, but does not have the same properties in baking. Honey caramelizes quickly at low temperatures, causing baked goods to brown more quickly. Its natural acidity varies and thus it should be used in conjunction with baking soda as a neutralizer. To substitute honey for sugar, use about seven eighths the quantity of sugar called for and decrease the liquid in the recipe by about 3 tablespoons. (One cup granulated sugar = 7/8 cup honey.)

Maple Syrup

Pure maple syrup comes from the boiled-down sap of the sugar maple tree. Avoid imitation maple syrups, which are basically corn syrups with artificial flavoring and coloring added. Use maple syrup as a sweetener in baked goods as you would honey (being conscious of the fact that syrup is sometimes more liquid and the proportions may need adjustment). Also use it as a low-fat sauce on cobblers, pancakes and waffles, of course, and yogurt or homemade yogurt cheese.

Corn Syrup

Corn syrup has been produced in the United States since the mid-nineteenth century. Starch granules are extracted from corn kernels, and then treated with acid or various enzymes to break them down into a sweet syrup. Corn syrup, made up of glucose from the corn sugar plus some added fructose and about 24 percent water, is valued because of its sweetness and various physical properties. By controlling the thoroughness of the enzymatic action on the starch, the chemical structure can be altered, affecting the sweetness and viscosity of the syrup. Because of its viscosity, corn syrup imparts a chewy texture to baked goods. Because it is hygroscopic (moisture-retaining), it helps baked products retain moisture and increases their shelf life. In certain carefully reformulated cake batters, corn syrup can be used in place of a portion of the vegetable oil.

Leavening Agents

Leavening agents added to batters make baked goods rise and produce a light, porous structure. Air, steam, and carbon dioxide gas (produced by baking powder and baking soda) are the principal leaveners.

In reduced-fat baking, egg whites are sometimes used as a substitute for all or part of the whole-egg content of the original recipe; often the egg whites are stiffly whipped, both to contribute to the leavening effect and to lighten the texture that, without much fat, might be too dense.

Baking Powder

Baking powder is a chemical leavening agent. It is made up of acid-reacting materials (tartaric acid or its salts, acid salts of phosphoric acid, compounds of aluminum) and alkali bicarbonate of soda. Most brands of baking powder have a starch filler (cornstarch or potato starch) added as a stabilizer to keep the acid salts from reacting with the bicarbonate of soda and to act as a buffer in case any moisture gets into the mixture.

There are three main types of baking powders: single, fast-acting, tartrate baking powder, which releases gas quickly, as soon as it is mixed with a liquid; slow-acting or phosphate baking powder, usually used in commercial bakeries; and double-acting baking powder, sometimes referred to as SAS. The last is the one I recommend and the one most widely used in home kitchens. It is composed of cream of tartar, tartaric acid, sodium aluminum sulfate (or sodium acid pyrophosphate), and the monocalcium phosphates. It produces two separate reactions.

When double-acting baking powder is mixed with the liquid in a batter, it forms a solution, causing a reaction between the acid and the alkali, which begins to let off carbon dioxide gas. When the batter is placed in a hot oven, a second reaction occurs, releasing about 12 to 14 percent carbon dioxide.

Some bakers detect an aftertaste from baking powder containing sodium aluminum sulfate and prefer Rumsford, an all-phosphate double-acting brand sold in natural food stores.

Baking powder absorbs moisture from the air, causing it to begin to deteriorate and lose its power after three months. The average shelf life of an opened can is about 1 year. (Yes, that's why your cakes are falling.) You can erase this item from your list of bargains at the buy-by-the-case warehouse market. Unless you do high-volume baking, purchase small containers of baking powder. Write the date of purchase on the next can you buy. Store baking powder in a cool, dark place.

If you suspect you are dealing with an antique product, perform this simple experiment: Combine 1 teaspoon baking powder with ½ cup hot water; if it bubbles vigorously, it is still usable. If it sits in stern silence, toss it out.

If you run out of baking powder, you can make this single-acting substitution in an emergency (but do not try to store this mixture): For every 1 cup flour in the recipe, combine 2 teaspoons cream of tartar, 1 teaspoon baking soda, and a few grains of salt. Noted chef and food writer Edna Lewis recommends a blend of 2 tablespoons cream of tartar, 1 tablespoon baking soda, and 1½ tablespoons cornstarch; use 1 to 1¼ teaspoons of the mixture per 1 cup flour.

For high-altitude baking where the air pressure is lower and gas expansion in the batter is increased, the amount of baking powder must be adjusted.

Baking Soda

Baking soda, also known as bicarbonate of soda, is another common leavening agent. Unlike baking powder, it lasts indefinitely. An alkaline product, it is used in baking when there is an acid agent present (such as buttermilk, sour milk or yogurt, molasses, honey, chocolate or cocoa) to neutralize some of the acidity as well as to provide leavening. The alkaline soda needs an acid in order to react and release carbon dioxide gas. This reaction is similar to that of fast-acting baking powder, for it reacts just once, as soon as it blends with liquid when the batter is mixed. For this reason, baked goods that use baking soda alone must be placed in the oven as soon as they are prepared, before the rising action begins to dissipate.

Bicarbonate of soda has other properties in baking as well. Because it is an alkali, it darkens the color of chocolate or cocoa in a cake. It also causes reddening of cocoa, giving devil's food cake its name.

Be judicious when using baking soda. An excess in baking results in off odors, a soapy taste, and darkened or yellowed white cakes.

Old cookbooks often instruct the cook to mix the baking soda with boiling water before adding to the batter. This is because baking soda originally was very coarsely ground. Today, however, it is very fine and may simply be sifted into the other dry ingredients.

Salt

"Sodium," often confused with salt by the layperson, actually means sodium chloride, a chemical that accounts for about 40 percent of a salt molecule. In other words, salt is just a little less than half sodium. Nevertheless, too much is not good. The National Academy of Sciences recommends a daily sodium limit of 2400 milligrams, the equivalent of about 6 grams of salt, or roughly 1 teaspoon.

In low-fat baking, removing fat results in removing some flavor. To make the recipe taste good, it is nearly impossible to cut the salt drastically as well, although it is always possible to cut back. Sometimes flavor can be sparked by adding extra grated citrus zest or more flavoring extract. Nevertheless, an absence of salt leaves baked products flat; salt also has the ability to combine with sugar to bring out and balance its sweetness. In this book, every attempt has been made to reduce salt and sodium while maintaining flavor.

Cream of Tartar

An acidic by-product of winemaking, cream of tartar is a white powder used in baking to help prevent overbeating of whipped egg whites and to stabilize egg white foam during baking. In addition, it is used when making sugar syrups to inhibit crystallization of the sugar.

Gelatine

Gelatine is a natural product derived from collagen, the protein found in bones and connective tissue. In the United States, unflavored gelatine is most commonly sold in dry granulated form; in Europe, it is often sold in leaves or sheets that are reconstituted by soaking in water. Knox granulated gelatine is available in bulk or packed in small envelopes. Bulk packages are usually freshness-dated (very old gelatine often does not work), but the envelopes are not dated. Each envelope contains 1 very scant tablespoon (actually a generous 2 teaspoons), or ¼ ounce (7 grams). This is enough to set 2 cups of liquid.

To dissolve granulated gelatine, sprinkle it on top of a small amount of cold liquid in a small saucepan, and let it sit for a few minutes so the granules swell. Then, set it over moderately low heat and stir just until the granules dissolve completely. Do not let the gelatine boil, or it will lose some of its setting strength. Another method is to stir the swollen granules into boiling water until dissolved.

For the low-fat baker, gelatine is a user-friendly product. One envelope has 25 calories, 6 grams of protein, 8 milligrams of sodium, and not a bit of fat, carbohydrates, or cholesterol.

Chocolate

Chocolate is an important ingredient in any cookbook with an emphasis upon desserts, even one on reduced-fat baking. A glimpse at the index will show that chocolate recipes are presented here in number and in depth. Certainly chocolate is used in low-fat baking, but it is used with caution—and with cocoa.

Chocolate is processed from the pods of the *Theobroma cacao* tree, which is native to South and Central America and cultivated in Africa and Southeast Asia. The pods are cut from the tree and the inner beans and pulp are scooped out, dried, fermented, and cured. Different beans from different geographical areas have particular characteristics; many manufacturers blend them to combine the best taste, texture, and aroma. At the factory, the beans are roasted, their hulls are removed, and the inner nibs, containing up to 54 percent cocoa butter, a saturated fat, are crushed and ground, or rolled between steel disks. The heat from this process liquefies the cocoa butter, most of which is removed. The dark brown paste remaining, called chocolate liquor, is further refined by a churning procedure known as conching, to enhance its quality.

Unadulterated chocolate liquor is molded, solidified, and sold as unsweetened or bitter chocolate. Varying amounts of sugar and cocoa butter are combined with this liquor to create the blends known as bittersweet, semisweet, and sweet; each type has a different percent of calories from fat, and a large portion of the fat is highly saturated cocoa butter.

To reduce fat, and particularly saturated fat, in your baking, use as little solid chocolate as possible. One ounce of solid unsweetened chocolate has 15 grams of fat, 8.7 of them saturated. To give the illusion and some of the complex taste of solid chocolate, you can grate a small amount of it into a cocoa-based dessert; however, as a general rule, substitute cocoa (see below) for solid chocolate.

Store chocolate in a cool, dry location, preferably about 60°F. At warmer temperatures, a gray or white bloom may develop on the surface; this does not affect flavor, however, and will disappear when the chocolate is warmed or melted.

Cocoa

To make cocoa, chocolate liquor is pressed to remove more than half of its remaining cocoa butter. The dry cake of residue is pulverized and sifted into a fine powder containing very little fat. One ounce of alkalized cocoa has 63 calories and 4 grams of fat.

In reduced-fat baking, cocoa is a very handy product; it imparts the intense taste of chocolate with only a trace of its saturated fat. Since you are counting on it for flavor, use the best brand of cocoa you can afford.

There are different types of cocoa, each treating the natural acidity of the cocoa in a specific way. To neutralize some of the acidity and darken the color, some cocoas are Dutch-processed, or factory-treated with alkali (for example, Fedora, Droste, and Van Houten). "Natural" cocoas, such as Hershey's and Baker's, are not Dutch-processed. These have higher acidity and are used in recipes in conjunction with baking soda, to neutralize some of the acidity. The soda darkens and reddens the color of the cocoa. Do not mistake instant cocoa mixes for pure cocoa; the mixes are produced specifically for blending into drinks and have dry milk solids and sugars added.

To substitute cocoa powder for solid unsweetened chocolate, use 3 level tablespoons cocoa plus 1 tablespoon of vegetable oil per each ounce of chocolate. For mail order suppliers of chocolate and cocoa, see page 460.

Finally, it appears that there may be good news for those chocoholics (I count myself among them) who dream about mountains of creamy bittersweet chocolate oozing cocoa butter from every pore. It turns out that stearic acid, one of butter's primary saturated fatty acids, makes up about half the saturated fat in cocoa butter. Research has shown that stearic acid does not raise the levels of blood cholesterol.

Comparative Table of Calories and Fat in Chocolate and Cocoa

Ingredient	Amount	Calories/ ounce	Total grams of fat	Grams of saturated fat	Percent of calories from fat
Unsweetened baking chocolate (square)	1 ounce	148	15.7	9.2	89
German Sweet	1 ounce	143	9.6	5.6	58
Semisweet or bittersweet	1 ounce	135	8.4	4.9	53
Milk chocolate	1 ounce	145	8.7	5.2	52
Cocoa, unsweetened	1 ounce	64.9	3.8	2.2	50
Cocoa, unsweetened nonalkalized (Dutch-processed)	1 ounce	62.9	3.7	2.1	49

SOURCE: *USDA Agricultural Handbook 8–19.*

The bad news is that it is still fat that makes you fat; in other words, a 4-ounce bar of milk chocolate contains about 588 calories and 36 grams of fat.

Flavorings

Flavoring agents are especially important in reduced-fat baking because flavor is lost when fat is cut. Use fresh aromatic spices, pure extracts, and full-flavored zests and fruits to enhance the taste and bring baked goods to life.

Spices

The aroma of any spice is volatile and fades once the spice is ground. It also fades if the spice container is exposed to air, heat, or sunlight for a period of time. Ground spices should be stored in airtight containers in a cool, dark location. Whole seeds and spices keep better, but should be stored the same way as ground. If you have the choice, always use freshly ground spices—they give greater flavor.

Check the strength of spices by smelling them before tossing them into your perfect batter: A dash of old, pallid nutmeg is useless; a grating of fresh nutmeg is pungent.

Extracts

Extracts are the concentrated natural essential oils of a flavoring agent, commonly dissolved in alcohol. Some extracts are made from the oils found in the rind of citrus fruits, others are made from the pulp of the fruit.

Most essential oils are volatile and thus dissipate when exposed to the heat of baking. To have good flavor in your finished product, you must start with the best flavoring agent. Pure extracts cost a little more than imitation flavorings but really are worth it. The difference is critically important in reduced-fat baking, where flavor is lost when fat (especially butter) is cut. You need a strong replacement. For this reason, in many of the recipes in this book, you will see that the amount of vanilla extract is double that of the original recipe, and other extracts may be added along with it. Some essences and extracts (maple, for example) are generally unavailable in pure form; if you cannot find a pure extract, use the imitation or artificial if you must. The artificial flavorings, which are synthetic, are weaker in flavor and sometimes impart a chemical taste.

There are several suppliers of fine pure extracts in this country, such as the Cook Flavoring Company in Washington State, for example, or Nielsen-Massey. Their products, and others, are available by mail order from Williams-Sonoma and the King Arthur Flour Baker's catalogue (see page 460); they are also sold in gourmet shops.

Vanilla extract varies greatly in quality and strength. Some bakers believe the finest is made with the vanilla beans from Tahiti; others prefer beans from Madagascar or Mexico.

For the purest vanilla, make it yourself. It is easy. Buy four fresh, pliable aromatic vanilla pods (in a gourmet shop) and slit them lengthwise. Soak the pods in 2 cups vodka in a covered glass jar for at least two weeks. After this time, you can remove the pods and strain the liquid if you prefer, or just leave them in; the extract is ready to use. Store all liquid extracts in dark-colored glass containers, tightly closed, in a cool, dark space.

I also keep a canister of vanilla sugar on hand for baking. Simply stick a vanilla bean into a jar of granulated sugar and use as needed. The vanilla enhances the sugar and can be used in any baked product complemented by vanilla.

Zest

Zest is the brightly colored part of the peel of citrus fruit. The white pith beneath the zest is bitter and shouldn't be used. Zest contains all the essential oils or flavors of the peel. Usually the fruit is grated on the small holes of a grater to remove the zest. Alternatively, a zester—a small tool with a sharp scooped "eye"—is used to remove shallow strips of peel. The strips can be finely minced and used instead of grated peel.

Dried Fruits

Dried fruits add flavor and their natural sugars provide sweetness. Chopped dried fruit can be a useful textural substitute for nuts, which are much higher in fat. Most fresh and dried fruits are not only low in fat, they are also a valuable source of vitamins, minerals, and fiber. There are a few exceptions to the rule that fruits are low-fat, notably avocados (16 percent fat) and ripe olives (30 percent fat).

When purchasing dried fruits, look for those with good color and plump, full shape; avoid those that are hard as rocks. The chances are that in a natural foods store the product will be good, but it is best to taste one piece (ask first, please) before buying. Dates and prunes are sold pitted or with pits. Pitted are easier to work with and can easily be chopped. I prefer whole pitted dates to the packaged chopped dates, which often seem to be either covered with crystallized sugar or dried out. In any case, dates are easy to chop by hand.

Dried prunes are also available slightly moist (for snacking); some brands are good, others too gooey. Test these before adding to a cake.

Prune Purée and Lekvar

Prune purée is sometimes used in low-fat baking as a partial substitute for fat. The purée has many desirable characteristics: viscosity, an ability to attract and retain moisture in baked goods, a tendency to extend shelf-life, and an unobtrusive flavor when combined with chocolate or certain spices. On the negative side, baked goods with a high proportion of prune purée develop a sticky or soft exterior and occasionally have a peculiar—if undefinable—aftertaste. That said, a few recipes are really successful when made with this product; several are included in this book.

The low-fat baker has two choices when using prune purée. The first, which I generally prefer, is made by combining 1 cup dried pitted prunes (about 18) with 1 cup of water in a heavy-bottomed saucepan. Cover, bring to a boil, then reduce heat and simmer about 5 minutes or until prunes are soft. Add ½ cup more water and purée the mixture in a food processor; this makes about 1½ cups. The second choice is a commercially prepared prune butter called lekvar, sold in 1-pound or 17-ounce jars, manufactured by several companies and available in many supermarkets and Eastern European specialty food shops. Lekvar usually contains corn syrup, water, sugar, pectin, and citric acid. Because of the additives, it is both sweeter and more viscous than homemade prune purée. In the recipes in this book, use whichever type is specifically called for.

Nuts

The good news is that nuts impart unique flavor and texture to baked goods. The bad news is that they are high in fat; walnuts contain 64 percent fat, pecans 65 percent.

In baking, one of the easiest ways to cut fat is to cut out or cut back on the nuts. You can safely reduce the nuts in most recipes by as much as three quarters without fear of failure. Replace nuts with a crunchy low-fat cereal such as Grape-Nuts or with chopped dried low-fat fruit such as apricots or raisins. In some recipes, I use nut oils, especially hazelnut and walnut, to impart the flavor of a particular nut, but without the high fat. The oil must be absolutely fresh. Walnut oil, especially, has a tendency to become rancid quickly; smell the oil before using it. Always store nut oils in the refrigerator.

If you use nuts, see how little you can use and still retain some nut flavor and texture. Put the nuts on top of a cake or muffin, rather than in the batter. The exposed nuts will toast during baking, so their flavor will be enhanced. Also, they are visible and so more noticeable.

If you are going to use nuts, be sure they are fresh. The oils in nuts are volatile and lose their flavors and/or go rancid when exposed too long to heat, moisture, or light. Nuts keep longest when stored in their shells; next best are whole nuts rather than chopped. Store nuts in sealed bags in a cool, dry place, the refrigerator, or the freezer, although I have found that nuts stored in the freezer lose some of their flavor after about a month). Purchase your nuts from a reliable source to be sure they are flavorful and fresh.

Because nuts, particularly walnuts, contain a lot of oil, they often become pasty when ground. To prevent this problem, dry out the nuts before grinding. Bake the nuts in a shallow pan in a preheated 300°F oven for about 6 to 10 minutes, tossing occasionally. To toast nuts, instead of simply drying them out, increase the oven heat to about 325°F. Toast the nuts for 12 to 15 minutes, tossing or stirring several times, until the nuts are aromatic and beginning to turn golden. Nuts can also be toasted in a heavy-bottomed frying pan over medium heat

Nuts and Seeds, Listed from Lowest in Saturated Fat to Highest

Type	Amount	Calories	Total grams of fat	Total grams of saturated fat
Chestnuts, roasted	1 ounce	70	0.6	0.1
Poppy seeds	1 ounce	90	8	1
Black walnuts	1 ounce	172	16	1
Sesame seeds	1 ounce	165	14	1
Almonds, blanched	1 ounce	166	15	1
Hazelnuts, unblanched (filberts)	1 ounce	179	18	1
Sunflower seeds, dry	1 ounce	165	14	2
Pistachio nuts	1 ounce	164	14	2
Peanuts, dry roasted	1 ounce	161	14	2
English walnuts	1 ounce	182	18	2
Pecans	1 ounce	190	19	2
Cashews, dry roasted	1 ounce	163	13	3
Peanut butter (Skippy chunk)	1 ounce	190	17	3
Macadamia nuts	1 ounce	199	21	3
Brazil nuts, unblanched	1 ounce	186	19	5
Coconut (dry, sweet, flaked, canned)	1 ounce	126	9	8

SOURCE: Anna dePlanter Bowes and Charles F. Church, *Food Values of Portions Commonly Used*, rev. by Jean A. T. Pennington, 15th ed., (New York: Harper & Row, 1989); *USDA Agricultural Handbook 8–12*, 1984.

for 3 to 5 minutes; stir or toss continually to avoid burning.

To remove the skin from hazelnuts after toasting, wrap the hot nuts in a coarsely textured towel and allow to sit for a few minutes. Then rub the skins off with the towel. To remove the skins from almonds or pistachios, blanch the shelled nuts (skins still on) in boiling water for about 2 minutes, then drain and drop them into cold water. Pinch off the skins with your fingers; they should pop right off.

All nuts are high in total fat and saturated fat. If you use nuts at all, stick to walnuts, almonds, peanuts, hazelnuts, and pecans; absolutely avoid the fat-rich Brazil nut, cashew, macadamia, and coconut. (See the accompanying table.)

Equipment

⬧ ⬧ ⬧

The recipes in this book are written with the assumption that your baking pantry includes the basics described below. While creative substitution is a virtue to be admired, there are times when the correct tool is essential. Read through the notes describing equipment before beginning to bake.

The Special Equipment note in each recipe lists the specific baking pan recommended and any out-of-the-ordinary items, such as parchment paper.

Baking Pans

Baking pans are available in an amazing array of materials, sizes, and shapes. For the basic pantry, a few sizes and shapes will suffice. To substitute pans, see the chart on page 52. Select the best quality you can afford. Look for sturdy, durable pans with smooth seams. For low-fat baking, Teflon, Silverstone, or other nonstick pans are a great help but not essential. Avoid the cheapest nonstick products because the coating will be thin and wear off quickly.

An important factor in pan selection is the pan size. Maddeningly, every manufacturer seems to use a different system. Some measure a pan from rim to rim, others across the lip to the outer edges, others across the bottom. I measure across the top inner edge. I also measure the volume of a pan by noting the cups of water needed to fill the pan to the brim (see chart on page 52). Many cakes can be baked in pans of a variety of shapes and sizes; recipes that are flexible in this regard have the volume of batter noted in cups in the Yield section of the recipe. Select alternate pan sizes from the chart by comparing volumes. Note that pans should be filled about two thirds full so there is room for the batter to rise.

Something as simple as using the wrong pan size may result in baking failure. Batter that is too thin when poured into a large pan bakes into a cake that is too flat; if the pan is too small, the batter may overflow when it rises.

Buy layer cake pans in pairs or threes in 8- or 9-inch rounds. Also select one or two 8- or 9-inch square pans at least 1½ to 2 inches deep. Look for sturdy aluminum or heavy-gauge tinned steel. Avoid using dark or black pans, which give a dark crust undesirable in delicate cakes. Springform pans are two-piece pans with a flat or tubed bottom surrounded by a hoop fastened with a spring latch. These are used for delicate tortes, cheesecakes, and constructed layer cakes that are built up, chilled, and then unmolded.

Tube pans vary in manufacture, size, shape, and name. Whether they are called plain tubes, rings, Bundts, or kugelhopf molds, all have a central tube designed to conduct heat to the center of the batter, allowing the dough to rise and bake evenly. When selecting a tube pan, remember that the heavier the metal, the more evenly the cake will bake. Select the sturdiest pans, such as tinned steel (I like the Kaiser pans imported from Germany). Teflon-lined Bundt pans are made of aluminum and of heavy cast aluminum; both give good results.

Angel food cake pans are tube pans, but most have removable bottoms, as well as small feet sticking up around the rim so the baked cake can be inverted and suspended as it cools. Some pans lack the feet but have a long tube for the pan to sit on when inverted. If your pan lacks both, simply invert the pan over the neck of a tall bottle and let it hang upside down until the cake is thoroughly cooled.

A jelly-roll pan commonly measures 10 × 15 inches by 1 inch deep. It should be of sturdy construction with a good lip all around. Use it for thin sheet cakes and petits fours. In a pinch, turn the pan upside down and use it as an extra cookie sheet. It also makes a fine tray for catching drips when icing a cake or cookies placed on a wire rack.

Sheet cakes can be baked in oblong or rectangular pans 1½ to 2½ inches deep. I often use a lasagne pan for a sheet cake, and I prefer a pan with a nonstick lining.

Pie plates can be made of metal or Pyrex heatproof glass or pottery. If you prefer metal, select pans with sloping sides in 9- and 10-inch diameters in aluminum with a dull or dark finish, which absorbs heat quickly. Avoid highly polished metal pans, because the shine tends to deflect heat, causing the crust to bake more slowly. I prefer Pyrex pie pans because they conduct heat quickly and brown crusts nicely, and I can see the color of the bottom crust as it bakes. I could not do without my 10-inch Pyrex pans in regular depth and deep-dish, both purchased in the hardware store. (These are not always available in cookware shops; I don't know why.)

Tarts are generally baked in fluted-edge metal or ceramic pans. The ones I prefer are imported from France and have a removable flat bottom. They are available in a range of sizes, but for home baking try the 7- to 11-inch rounds, as well as a variety of rectangular sizes. To unmold a tart, set the center of the baked tart on a widemouthed canister and press lightly on the edge of the pan. The edging ring will drop away, leaving the tart to be carried and served on its metal bottom. Individual tartlet pans made of the same materials as the full-size pans are also available.

Use cookie sheets made of heavy metal with a shiny surface. The best designs have only one narrow lip, for a handle, so the hot air can easily circulate around the cookies. Avoid cookie sheets with full edges that block the heat. If you notice cookies browning too fast on the bottom, slide a second flat sheet beneath the first to insulate it slightly from the heat.

Muffin pans come in a variety of sizes, from mini-muffin tins, with $1\frac{3}{4}$-inch-wide cups, to giant, with $3\frac{1}{3}$- to 4-inch diameters. The average size, used in this book, is a $2\frac{1}{2}$-inch diameter. Select a pan with a dark, dull finish that absorbs heat rather than a shiny surface that deflects it. Muffins bake well in either heavy or thin pans; weight does not seem critical. Teflon or nonstick coatings are a great help in baking low-fat muffins.

Charlottes are made in tapered molds. Nearly any widemouthed mold will do. The classic charlotte mold, imported from France, is a slightly tapered cylindrical form made of tinned steel. It is available in graduated sizes from 6 ounces to 2 quarts. Avoid molds made of aluminum, because the metal can interact with certain fillings and/or acidic fruits, causing them to darken. If you do have an aluminum mold, line it with plastic wrap before filling it. For nonbaked charlottes, simply use a round plastic freezer container (1- or 2-quart capacity).

To allow for even circulation of oven heat, be sure all baking sheets or pans allow 2 inches of clear air space between them and the oven walls.

Electric Mixers

While most batters can be beaten by hand with a wooden spoon, and some are best done that way, electric mixers save time and whip in more air than one can incorporate by hand. There are a wide variety of mixers on the market: hand-held electric (cord) and battery-operated (cordless) mixers; stand-type homestyle mixers of moderate price having two or more bowls; and heavy-duty professional mixers with stainless steel bowls of various sizes and several beaters (balloon whip, flat paddle, dough hook), such as the English Kenwood Stand Mixer and the American KitchenAid.

Pan Volume and Serving Chart

Pan shape and size	Maximum cups fluid to fill to capacity	Maximum cups batter (allowing for rise)	Approximate number of servings
Round Layers			
6 × 2 inches	4	2 to 2½	6
8 × 1½ or 8 × 2	4½ to 5	2	8 to 10
9 × 1½ or 9 × 2	6 to 6½	3 to 3½	8 to 10
10 × 2	10	4½ to 6	14
12 × 2	14	7½ to 9	22
14 × 2	19½	10 to 12	36 to 40
Square Layers			
8 × 2	8	3½ to 5	9 to 12
9 × 1½	8 to 9	4½ to 5	9 to 12
9 × 2	10	5½	9 to 12
10 × 2	12⅓	6	20
12 × 2	16	10 to 12	36
14 × 2	24	12 to 14	42
Rectangular (Sheet Cakes)			
8 × 12 (7½ × 11¾ × 1¾)	8	4 to 5	12
9 × 13 (8¾ × 13½ × 1¾)	16	8 to 9	20 to 24
11 × 17 (11⅜ × 17¼ × 2¼)	25	14 to 15	24 to 30
10½ × 15½ × 1 (jelly-roll pan)	10	4 to 5 for butter cake or 8 for génoise	24 to 35
Heart			
9 × 1½	5	3 to 3½	16
Tube, Ring, Bundt, and Kugelhopf			
9 × 2¾ plain tube	6 to 7	4 to 4½	8 to 10
9 × 2 springform tube	9 to 10	6 to 7	10 to 12

$9\frac{1}{4} \times 3\frac{1}{4}$ fluted tube or Bundt	9 to 10	5 to 6	10 to 12
$9\frac{1}{2} \times 3\frac{3}{4}$ or 10-inch plain tube or springform	12	6 to 7	12 to 14
9×4 kugelhopf	10	5 to 6	10 to 12
$9\frac{3}{4} \times 4\frac{1}{4}$ kugelhopf	12	6 to 7	12 to 14
$10 \times 3\frac{1}{2}$ Bundt	12	6 to 7	14
10×4 angel cake tube	16	8 to $8\frac{1}{2}$	12 to 14

Loaves

$5\frac{1}{2} \times 3 \times 2\frac{1}{8}$	$2\frac{1}{4}$	$1\frac{1}{2}$ to $1\frac{3}{4}$	6 to 8
$6 \times 3\frac{1}{2} \times 2$ (baby)	2	$1\frac{1}{4}$ to $1\frac{1}{2}$	6 to 8
$7\frac{1}{2} \times 3\frac{1}{2} \times 2$	5 to 6	3	7 to 8
$8\frac{1}{2} \times 4\frac{1}{2} \times 2\frac{3}{4}$ (average)	$5\frac{1}{4}$	$3\frac{1}{2}$ to $3\frac{3}{4}$	7 to 8
$9 \times 5 \times 3$ (large)	8 to 9	4 to 5	9 to 10

Charlotte Molds

$5\frac{1}{2}$-inch base, $3\frac{1}{2}$-inch height	6	—	8
6-inch base, 4-inch height	8	—	10

Soufflé Molds

$6\frac{1}{2}$-inch base, $3\frac{1}{4}$-inch height	6	4 to 5	8
7-inch diameter, $3\frac{3}{4}$-inch height	8	6 to 7	10

Muffin Pans/Cupcakes

$1\frac{3}{4} \times \frac{3}{4}$ (baby)	4 teaspoons	3 teaspoons	1
2×1	3 tablespoons	2 to $2\frac{1}{2}$ tablespoons	1
$2\frac{1}{2}$-inch diameter	$\frac{1}{3}$ cup	$\frac{1}{4}$ cup	1
$2\frac{3}{4}$-inch diameter	$\frac{1}{2}$ cup	$\frac{1}{3}$ cup	1
$3 \times 1\frac{1}{4}$	$\frac{1}{2}$ cup	$\frac{1}{3}$ cup	1
$3\frac{1}{2}$-inch diameter	1 cup	generous $\frac{3}{4}$ cup	1

Remember that homestyle mixers do not have the power of the professionals, so take longer to achieve the same result; adjust your technique and recipe times to your appliance. I use the heavy-duty KitchenAid Model K45SS, with a head that tips back to raise the beater, making it easy to scrape the bowl and beater or add ingredients. For whipping cream, I often use the half-size KitchenAid bowl, or simply a small deep bowl and a hand-held mixer.

Food Processors, Blenders, and Mincers

A blender does a good job of chopping and mixing and puréeing, but overall it is not as versatile as the food processor. The now-ubiquitous food processor is a great time-saver for making bread crumbs, shredding carrots, apples, or potatoes, and chopping nuts or dried fruits. The processor also does a fine job of mixing creamed icings and glazes that do not need air incorporated. In general, I do not recommend the processor for cake batters, although a few recipes in this book are specifically designed for its use; the speed and power of the processor blade can quickly overwork the mixture and overdevelop the gluten in the flour, producing a tough product. In my home kitchen, I use a Cuisinart DLC 7 Superpro.

To grind herbs and poppy seeds, I recommend an electric herb mincer such as the one made by Varco. It consists of a small cup with a set of thin sharp blades that sits on a base containing the motor. One adds the herbs or seeds to the cup, places the cover on top, and pushes down to engage the motor on contact. The electric blender will grind poppy seeds, but you can add only ½ cup of seeds at a time and must stir them down once or twice. The food processor, on the other hand, will not grind poppy seeds because they are too small and just fly about the blade.

Nut Grinders

For European nut tortes and some other pastries, nuts must be ground into a fine, dry powder rather than finely chopped. The easiest method is to use a hand-held food or nut mill in which a presser bar pushes down on the nuts, forcing them onto a rotating cutting disk. A blender or food processor can also be used, if some of the sugar used in the recipe is added, but the nuts will never be as light or fine as when shaved with a nut mill. Before grinding walnuts (or other oily nuts) to a fine grade, dry them out in the oven first (see page 47).

Mixing Bowls

You can never have too many bowls in too many different sizes. However, you *need* only a few. I recommend heavy pottery for hand mixing and stainless steel bowls with flat bottoms (so they don't tip) for use with an electric mixer. Metal bowls are not subject to thermal shock; these are best for mixtures such as mousse that you sometimes whip over heat, then set into an ice bath to chill.

For general use, you need a set of bowls sized 1, 1½, 2, and 3 quarts. Life will go on without a copper bowl for whipping your egg whites, but it is a classy (and surprisingly efficient) addition to your pantry. Pyrex bowls are useful; one of my favorites is a 2-quart measuring cup/bowl marked in increments. Use it to measure the total volume of cake batters, a help when you're not sure which cake pan to use. Do not use plastic bowls for mixing batter or whipping egg whites; it is virtually impossible to remove all odors and grease from plastic, and the merest trace of fat will inhibit whipped meringue.

Sifters and Strainers

The distinction between a sifter and sieve is often as fine as the mesh that distinguishes them. In theory, a sifter has from one to three screens of medium-fine wire mesh. It is used for dry ingredients (flour, baking powder, confectioners' sugar). A sieve has a slightly coarser single-screen mesh and is used for draining fruits and straining sauces. I have several of these in my kitchen, each slightly different in mesh size. For most of the sifting operations in this book, I use a single-screen sifter with medium-fine mesh. None of the recipes in this book requires a triple-tier sifter. A handy addition to the pantry is a 3-inch-diameter, medium-fine sifter with a 3- or 4-inch handle. I use this for sifting (dusting) flour or cocoa onto greased pans; the sifter can reach into a tube pan to direct powder onto the sides of the greased tube, normally a difficult task.

Measuring Cups and Measuring Spoons

Dry measuring cups are designed specifically for measuring dry ingredients (e.g., flour, sugar). Fill the cup to the top, then level the ingredient off by passing a straight edge over it. Dry measuring cups are commonly available in nesting sets, in graduated sizes from ⅛ cup to 1 or 2 cups. They do vary in quality, and cheap plastic cups are not as accurate as sturdy metal. My favorites, available from specialty cookware shops such as Williams Sonoma (see page 460), are heavy-duty stainless steel and precisely calibrated in ¼-, ⅓-, ½-, and 1- and 2-cup sizes.

Liquid measuring cups are very different. They have pouring spouts and are commonly available in 1-, 2-, and 4-cup sizes. The best are made of Pyrex. To use, you simply fill the cup to the desired mark, set the cup flat on the counter, and bend down so you can check it at eye level.

Dry and liquid measuring cups should not be used interchangeably.

Measuring spoons come in graduated sizes from ⅛ teaspoon to 1 tablespoon; metal spoons are more accurate than those of flimsy plastic. My favorite type is similar to the heavy measuring cups; stainless steel, sturdy, and relatively expensive.

Wire Whisks

Wire whisks are used for whipping or folding certain ingredients together. The multiple wires have the effect of opening the batter and incorporating a lot of air when beating. Whisks come in a variety of sizes, from about 3 inches long for whipping melted butter in a measuring cup to enormous whisks for oversized commercial bowls. Select a whisk that is all metal, with the wires soldered into a metal handle. The whisks with wires poked into a wooden handle are impossible to clean, and eventually old unmentionable food particles collect in the tube and begin to discolor your meringue or your batter.

Rubber Spatulas

Rubber spatulas (often made of plastic) are invaluable for mixing, stirring, and folding ingredients together. The blade is a flexible tongue perfect for scraping down bowls and beaters or turning batters out of bowls into baking pans. Rubber spatulas come in all sizes, from 4 or 5 inches long to 18 or more for the professional kitchen. I prefer the type with a wooden handle affixed to a flexible blade that is acid- and heat-resistant and will not stain or deteriorate. This type, exclusively available from Williams-Sonoma, is made of silicone rubber developed for medical equipment. It is nonstick, stain- and extra-high-heat resistant, and holds its edge without chipping. For many scooping/stirring tasks, I use a spatula with a scooped head, a cross between a spatula and a spoon (Rubbermaid calls its version the Spoonula).

Graters

I recommend a stainless-steel box grater or a flat mandoline with a variety of hole sizes. For grating citrus zest or fresh ginger, I use the finest holes; for grating carrots, apples, and potatoes, I use the medium-sized holes.

Wax Paper and Baking Parchment

Wax paper is useful for collecting sifted dry ingredients or grated zests, or for lining baking pans for cookies and cakes. It will brown in the oven, but, in my experience, will not burn. When pans are lined with wax paper, the paper should be greased, and then dusted with flour if the recipe specifies. Baking parchment is a specially formulated paper designed for lining baking pans to prevent baked goods from sticking. The paper does not generally have to be greased; exceptions in this book are so noted. You can draw on baking parchment with a pencil, for guidelines to follow when making cookies or meringue shapes. Parchment is more durable than wax paper and thus ideal for making paper decorating cones (see page 62). It is available from supermarkets, restaurant supply houses, and baking specialty shops (see page 460) in dispenser rolls, in precut triangles (for decorating cones), and in rounds to fit various cake pans.

Pastry Brushes

A pastry brush is used for applying egg washes to doughs and jelly glazes to tarts. It is also useful for spreading syrups and preserves on cake layers. For the most delicate tasks, I prefer an imported European goose-feather brush with a handle of braided quills. This lovely tool, available from fine cookware shops, lasts a long time, is inexpensive, and can be washed in warm water and air-dried. For ordinary tasks such as brushing glazes and for brushing oil on baking pans, I use a natural or nylon bristle brush, available in sizes from 1 to 2½ inches wide. Keep a sharp eye out for fallen bristles in the glaze. No matter how thoroughly you wash them, brushes tend to hold a trace of past flavors. Since I also use pastry brushes for savory uses such as spreading garlic butter on bread, I have learned to use an indelible pen to mark the handles of my brushes "savory" and "pastry." This keeps my icing glaze from smelling like garlic.

Cardboard Cake Disks

Corrugated cardboard rounds are invaluable for supporting cakes and cake layers. They are sold in disks ranging from 6 to 14 inches in diameter. They are available in plain brown paper or with one side covered with white, or in gold or silver foil; some have fluted edges. Basic disks are sold in restaurant supply or party and paper goods shops. If you cannot find them, you may be able to buy them at a local pizzeria; they often use the same boards for pizza, and you can cut them down to any size you need and cover them with aluminum foil.

Cooling Racks

Cooling racks are essential for baking. When a baked cake or tart or sheet of cookies comes from the oven, it should be set on a raised rack so it can cool with air circulating all around it. The rack prevents condensation of moisture on the bottom of the baked goods and promotes even cooling. Most cakes have a fragile structure and need to cool in the baking pan for about 10 to 15 minutes before unmolding. After unmolding, cakes should continue cooling on a wire rack so air circulation will draw off the moisture or steam. If the steam remained inside the cake, it would become soggy. Other baked products benefit from cooling on a rack for the same reasons.

Racks range from flimsier ones of thin wire to heavy-gauge ones, and from 8-inch rounds perfect for a single cake layer to broad rectangular racks, holding a dozen layers, for the professional kitchen. The best racks are the most sturdy and have the mesh close enough together to prevent cookies from sliding between the wires.

Cake Testers

One of the tests for doneness for many baked products is to stick a cake tester into the cake: If it comes out clean, the cake is done; if covered with wet crumbs, the cake needs more baking time. Theoretically, this is a fine test, but you also need to watch for other signs noted in the recipes, such as color and springiness when touched, because an *overbaked* cake will also produce a clean testing pick.

In my grandmother's day, the preferred cake tester was a clean broom straw. My favorite is a thin bamboo saté skewer, inexpensive and readily available at Oriental food markets and gourmet shops, but a toothpick can also be used. Special metal cake testers that look like long hatpins with a big handle are sold in hardware and bakeware shops. In general, I prefer a wood pick to metal, because metal heats up quickly and batter may cling to it even when the cake is completely baked.

Thermometers

Specialized thermometers are important for accuracy at different stages of baking and in general food preparation. Take care of your thermometers. Do not put a cold one directly into boiling syrup, but rather warm it in hot water first; thermal shock can crack the glass tubes.

For making candy, sugar syrups, and pastry creams, I use a candy-jelly-deep-fry thermometer with a mercury-filled glass tube fastened to a stainless-steel casing.

For instant read-out temperatures for sauces, soufflés, meringues, melting chocolate, and so forth, I use a special thermometer with a stainless-steel stem and a large round dial mounted on top (with a narrower temperature range than regular thermometers). Instant-read thermometers are not meant to be left in food throughout the cooking time, but rather inserted from time to time to check the temperature; the thermometer reacts within seconds, then should be removed. Called Instant Bi-Therm thermometers, they are made by Tel-Tru and Taylor, among others, and are available in hardware stores and cookware shops.

Ovens and Oven Thermometers

Even heat is essential for accurate baking. Both electric and gas ovens produce good results, but you must know your oven well and watch it carefully, for even the best seem to lose accuracy easily and often. While it is a good idea to have the calibration checked occasionally (and certainly if you suspect it is off), it is also important to be sure the doors close tightly, their rubber gaskets are still flexible, the vent filters are clean, and hot spots (which most ovens have) are monitered. Hot spots mean that baked goods color more in one spot than another on the oven shelf. If this happens, turn the item, transfer it to another shelf, or move it front to back on the same shelf halfway through the baking time. My own ovens have distinct personalities and we have a decided love/hate relationship, though we tolerate each other and have learned how to work well together. The secret of our success, and it can be yours too, is that I rely on auxiliary thermometers placed inside my ovens; in some cases I use two, one in front, one in the rear. Small mercury-type thermometers, the best style, are available mounted on metal stands. They are sold in hardware and cookware shops. Set the thermometer in place on the oven rack or wire it in place, then adjust the outer oven thermostat if necessary to match the interior thermometer. If a recipe fails, don't blame the cookbook, or yourself, until you have your oven temperature checked.

For accuracy when baking, always preheat your oven for at least fifteen to twenty minutes. Ingredients will react in unexpected ways if set into the oven at the wrong temperature, and results can be disastrous. Check the interior auxiliary thermometer before putting in the baking pan.

Allow at least an inch and preferably two between baking pans to allow heat to circulate properly. If baking several cake layers at one time, stagger them on two shelves so they are not directly in line with each other.

Positioning Oven Shelves

The recipes in this book specify the position of the oven shelf upon which the item is to be baked. This is important because the heat circulation varies within the oven chamber. Different types of baked goods bake better in different temperatures. The topmost shelf is hotter than the middle, the oven floor the hottest spot of all. Single-layer cakes can be baked in the lower third of the oven or the middle, where the heat is moderately hot. Thicker cakes, with more than two inches of batter, or cakes with delicate structure should be baked in the center, where the heat is more even and moderate. If you have doubts, use the middle. If you are baking cookies or several layers at one time, position two racks to divide the oven evenly in thirds.

Convection and Microwave Ovens

Convection ovens contain an interior fan to blow the heat around. This constant circulation causes them to cook baked goods about 25 percent faster than regular ovens and produces a nicely browned crust on pies and breads and fine interior crumb in breads and cakes. However, the rush of air produced by the fan is too gusty for fragile meringue cookies and may blow them off the pan. Convection ovens are preferred by many professionals for specific uses and are used by many bakeries. When converting ordinary recipes for use in a convection oven, lower the baking temperature about 50°F.

I use my microwave for melting butter and chocolate and for defrosting and even warming baked goods. But I continue to feel that my conventional ovens give me more control, produce a better texture, and are generally better for baking.

Pastry Bags and Decorating Tips

Pastry bags are used for piping icing, meringue, and soft doughs like pâte à choux for eclairs. Bags are available in materials ranging from cotton canvas to nylon and sizes from 7 inches to nearly 24 inches long. Select the bag fitted to the task: small bags for delicate designs and melted chocolate, large ones for piping meringue and batter. For all-purpose use, I use a 16-inch nylon bag. I prefer the nylon for ease in cleaning. It is also flexible, feels comfortable in the hand, and will not leak fat from the fabric as cotton will. Wash the bags in hot water and air-dry them after use.

To fill a decorating bag, fold back a 4- or 5-inch cuff and set the tip down into a 2- or 4-cup measure for support. Fill the bag, then squeeze the icing down into the tip and twist the bag closed. To use the bag, hold the twist-closure between the thumb and fingers of one hand. This way, you hold the bag closed while applying pressure to squeeze out the icing. The other hand guides the bag and helps support its weight.

Decorating tips made of metal are the best; avoid flimsy plastic tips because they crack easily. Tips and bags, manufactured by such companies as Ateco and Wilton, are available from cookware shops. Be sure to select tips that fit the bags—small tips for small bags, extra-large tips

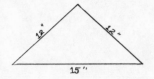

for the long bags. When you have a new bag, you must trim the tip so a decorating tip can fit inside. Then drop the decorating tip into the bag, allowing the nose to peek out, so the icing will be forced through it. Or use a plastic 2-piece coupler (sold with tips); this device allows you to fasten the tip on the outside of the bag so you can change it for another without changing the bag.

The simplest decorating bag of all is a heavy-duty plastic bag with a small hole cut in one corner. Spoon in the icing or melted chocolate, roll the top closed, and then squeeze it out through the hole. Discard the bag when done: no clean-up. To use a plastic bag for a finer design, drop a metal decorating tip into the bag and force the icing through the tip. The plastic bag method is ideal for children to use when decorating cookies.

Disposable paper decorating cones can be purchased precut or homemade of wax paper or baking parchment. To make a cone, cut a triangle about 12 × 12 × 15 inches (a). Pull one long side of the paper up around its midpoint, making a cone (b). Hold the cone tight while wrapping the second point around (c); tuck in all the ends (d) to hold the cone in place. Use a piece of tape to fasten the side, securing the shape. Cut a tiny piece off the cone tip, or cut a hole that permits the nose of a metal tip dropped into the cone to peek through. Fill the cone, fold down the top (e), and squeeze out the icing or melted chocolate.

About the Recipes in This Book

1. Before baking from this book, read the sections on ingredients and equipment. The information and the techniques described will help you achieve success.

2. Read each recipe from beginning to the end before starting. This will help you plan your time efficiently and enable you to discover whether or not you have all the ingredients and equipment on hand before beginning.

3. All dry measurements are level.

4. All eggs are U.S. Grade A large (2 ounces).

5. "Grated zest" of citrus fruits refers to the brightly colored outer layer of the peel, not the bitter white inner layer, or pith.

6. When a recipe says "½ cup chopped nuts," the nuts are chopped *before* measuring; "½ cup nuts, chopped" means they are chopped *after* being measured.

When a recipe says ½ cup *unsifted* flour, it means that the flour is simply scooped from the canister into a measuring cup and leveled off with a knife. When it says ½ cup *sifted* flour, it is sifted, then spooned into a measuring cup and leveled off with a knife.

7. For reliable baking results, use the type of flour (cake or all-purpose) specified in each recipe. Flours differ in protein (gluten) content and absorb moisture differently.

8. If you find you don't have the baking pan recommended, turn to the Pan Volume and Serving Chart (page 52) for substitutions. Most recipes include total batter volume in the Yield; use this figure to calculate pan size following the guide.

9. Room temperature means 60° to 70°F. It is important to have baking ingredients at room temperature so they will blend together properly.

10. Check your oven temperature. Inaccurate oven temperature is one of the most common causes of baking failure. Use a separate oven thermometer (see page 60) purchased in the hardware store. Set it on the oven rack; adjust your oven dial as necessary for the correct internal temperature. External oven calibrations are frequently incorrect.

11. When two times are given for doneness (e.g., 10 to 15 minutes), check the oven at the first time, then watch closely until the second. Your oven may vary from mine; the most important thing to watch is the baked product to observe signs of doneness (cake is springy to touch, tester comes out clean, etc.). Watch what's in the oven, not the clock.

12. Where alternative ingredients are listed (e.g., skim or 1% milk), the nutritional analysis has been calculated on the first-mentioned item.

13. When measuring yogurt, pour off the excess liquid before measuring. Drain yogurt through a sieve only if directed in the recipe.

14. Use pure extracts (vanilla, almond, orange) whenever possible; they do not leave any chemical aftertaste. "Imitation" flavors are most commonly available for maple, pineapple, coconut, and other unusual or exotic flavors; for mail order sources for pure extracts, see page 460.

15. In instructions for freezing baked goods, the terms "airtight" or "double-wrapped" mean cooling the product completely, setting it on a stiff foil-covered cardboard disk, then wrapping it first in an airtight layer of plastic wrap, then in a layer of aluminum foil (preferably heavy-duty with double-folded edges to keep out air) or in a heavy-duty plastic bag. Label carefully and include the date.

Breakfast
and
Brunch

I f you are paying attention to your total fat intake and going to the trouble of making reduced-fat desserts, it only makes sense to extend the process to the morning hours and include breakfast and brunch. After all, it is the total daily fat content of your diet that counts.

The following recipes are high in flavor and style, low in fat. Crunchy granola is a staple for me—enjoyed for breakfast, added to bread and muffin batter, sprinkled on yogurt and fruit for a snack, used to top frozen yogurt scooped into a molded cookie for dessert. Pancakes and waffles are synonymous with Sunday brunch in our house; Buttermilk Pancakes are favorites because they taste so good with any type of chopped fruit or berries added to the batter. Cornmeal Pancakes, Great-Grandmother's Potato Pancakes, and Whole Wheat Applesauce Waffles are crowd pleasers for brunch parties. Baked Blueberry Puff is my own personal vice—a dream to make and seductive to eat. Versatile crêpes should be in every cook's repertoire; the fillings are limited only by your imagination. Serve them for breakfast, brunch, lunch, or even for family desserts.

Basic Buttermilk Pancakes

◆ ◆ ◆

This light, delicious pancake owes its tenderness to the presence of buttermilk in the mix and yogurt, both of which inhibit the development of potentially toughening gluten in the flour. Nutritional value is enhanced by the addition of wheat germ. I have made this recipe in dozens of side-by-side tests comparing pancakes made from scratch to those made with packaged buttermilk baking mix; my preference is always for the mix. It just gives the best texture: tender, yet with body. Low-fat or nonfat scratch pancakes made with white flour are often too soft or insipid in texture. Let's face it, made-from-scratch isn't always best. Bisquick is the only mix I use, and I do so without shame. First, it is not laden with additives and preservatives, although its sodium content is relatively high. Second, it produces the right texture because it utilizes some partially hydrogenated shortening (yes, that is fat) blended into the dry ingredients; the in-factory, high-speed commercial mixing process blends in less fat for better results than we could at home. In fact, when I added enough fat to duplicate the Bisquick results, the calories-from-fat percentage went through the roof.

It is a Sunday morning tradition in our family to make this recipe with lots of sliced fruits or berries added to the batter. Our maple syrup comes from Tony Jones's family farm in Craftsbury, Vermont. It is hard to beat, especially the Grade B, which has a stronger maple flavor than the clear, fancy Grade A sold commercially. (Native Vermonters think we "downstaters" from Connecticut are crazy to like Grade B; they prefer the "fancy.") To avoid this controversy altogether, try the Orange Syrup (page 422) or Blueberry Syrup (page 423).

◆ ◆ ◆

Yield

About twelve 4-inch pancakes without fruit added, or 14 to 15 with fruit; 6 servings

Advance Preparation

Prepare the batter just before making the pancakes.

Special Equipment

12-inch nonstick skillet or electric frying pan

1 large egg plus 1 large egg white

3 tablespoons nonfat plain or vanilla yogurt

3 tablespoons toasted wheat germ

2 cups Bisquick

1 cup skim milk, or as needed

⅔ to 1 cup fresh berries, peeled and thinly sliced peaches or nectarines, or sliced bananas (optional)

Butter-flavor no stick cooking spray

1 cup pure maple syrup, warmed

Nutritional Analysis per 2 pancakes (with about 2½ tablespoons maple syrup but no fruit)

357 calories

8 g protein

7 g fat

2 g satfat

69 g carbohydrate

567 mg sodium

36 mg cholesterol

1. In a large bowl, whisk together the egg and egg white, yogurt, and wheat germ until well blended and creamy. Add the Bisquick and the milk alternately, whisking until smooth. (If the batter stands for a while and thickens, add 1 to 2 tablespoons more milk.) If using fruit, stir in just before you make the pancakes.

2. Lightly coat the griddle or skillet with cooking spray. Heat the skillet until a drop of water sizzles when dropped onto the surface. Use a large serving spoon to drop the batter onto the hot surface (2 tablespoons make a 4-inch pancake). Cook the pancakes for about 2 minutes on the first side, until bubbles appear on the surface. Turn and cook on the other side for 45 to 60 seconds, until golden brown. Watch the pancakes, not the clock. Repeat until all the batter is used. Serve the pancakes hot, with the warm syrup.

Light Touch: This recipe obtains only 17 percent of its calories from fat; when you add ⅔ cup fruit, the figure drops to 15 percent. The wheat germ contributes 3 grams of dietary fiber per serving. Compare this to my old recipe, also using Bisquick but combining it with 1 cup whole milk, 2 whole eggs, regular yogurt, and 2 tablespoons melted butter: 28 percent calories from fat (pretty good, really)—but per 2-pancake serving it packs nearly twice the fat (13 grams), three times the saturated fat (6 grams), and about two and a half times the cholesterol (88 milligrams). You can eliminate the cholesterol altogether by using 2 egg whites in place of the whole egg and white.

Cornmeal Pancakes

◆ ◆ ◆

ornmeal gives crunch to these light, flavorful pancakes. The batter is also fine for waffles. I like to serve these with hot maple syrup and a spoonful of vanilla or plain yogurt on the side.

◆ ◆ ◆

1 large egg

3 tablespoons canola or safflower oil

1 cup nonfat buttermilk

2 tablespoons toasted wheat germ

½ cup yellow cornmeal, preferably stone-ground

1⅓ cups plus 1 tablespoon unsifted cake flour

1 tablespoon granulated sugar

2 teaspoons baking powder

¼ teaspoon baking soda

⅛ teaspoon salt

Butter-flavor no stick cooking spray

½ to ¾ cup pure maple syrup, warmed

1. In a large bowl, whisk together the egg, oil, buttermilk, and wheat germ. Stir in the cornmeal.

2. Set a strainer over the bowl and add the flour, sugar, baking powder, baking soda, and salt. Stir and sift the dry ingredients onto the wet ingredients. Whisk until combined. Do not overmix.

3. Lightly coat the skillet with cooking spray. Heat the skillet until a drop of water sizzles when dropped onto the surface. Use a large serving spoon to drop the batter onto the hot surface (about 1½ tablespoons makes a 3-inch pancake). Cook the pancakes for a minute or 2, until bubbles appear on the surface and they just begin to look firm around the edges. Turn and cook on the other side until golden brown. Watch the pancakes, not the clock. Repeat until all the batter is used. Serve the pancakes hot, with the warm syrup.

Light Touch: The cornmeal contributes vitamins and minerals as well as flavor and texture. With the added wheat germ, 2 pancakes contribute 2 grams dietary fiber. Cake flour works better here than all-

(continued)

Yield

Twelve 3-inch pancakes; 6 servings

Advance Preparation

Prepare the batter just before using it.

Special Equipment

12-inch nonstick skillet or electric frying pan

Nutritional Analysis per 2 pancakes (with 2 tablespoons syrup)

316 calories

6 g protein

9 g fat

0.9 g satfat

54 g carbohydrate

270 mg sodium

36 mg cholesterol

purpose; it gives a lightness that balances the weight of the cornmeal granules. If you substitute all-purpose flour, which absorbs more water, you may need to add a few more tablespoons of liquid to keep the pancakes from being too dry and heavy. The recipe obtains 25 percent of its calories from fat. If you want to eliminate the cholesterol, use 2 egg whites instead of the whole egg.

Gluten-Free
Cornmeal-Buttermilk Pancakes

◆ · ◆ · ◆ ·

B eth Hillson, Hartford-based food writer and friend, gave me the recipe for these delicious pancakes that just happen to be gluten-free. Crisp and crunchy, they also just happen to be low in fat. For more information about gluten-free foods, see the recipe for Gluten-Free Apricot Lemon Scones (page 98). Gluten-free flours and cereals are available in natural food stores. (To purchase gluten-free vanilla, see page 461.) Serve these pancakes with warm maple syrup.

◆ · ◆ · ◆ ·

Yield

About twenty 3-inch pancakes; 4 to 6 servings

Advance Preparation

Prepare the batter just before using.

Special Equipment

12-inch nonstick skillet or electric frying pan

1 large egg

1½ cups nonfat buttermilk

2 tablespoons canola oil

½ teaspoon gluten-free vanilla

1 cup yellow cornmeal

½ cup brown rice flour

½ cup crunchy rice cereal (such as Perky's Nutty Rice Cereal)

1 teaspoon salt

1 tablespoon granulated sugar

½ teaspoon baking soda

Butter-flavor no stick cooking spray

1 cup pure maple syrup, warmed

1. In a large bowl, whisk together the egg, buttermilk, oil, and vanilla.

2. Add all the remaining ingredients except the cooking spray and the syrup. Whisk just to blend. Set the batter aside for 4 to 5 minutes.

3. Lightly coat the skillet with cooking spray. Heat the skillet until a drop of water sizzles. Drop the batter by large tablespoonfuls onto the hot griddle. Cook until the top looks dry and bubbly and the bottom is browned, 1 to 2 minutes. Turn and cook for 1 to 2 minutes on the other side. Use more cooking spray as needed. Serve the pancakes hot, with the warm syrup.

Light Touch: Beth's original recipe called for 3 tablespoons melted butter or margarine and obtained 30 percent of its calories from fat. Cutting the fat down to 2 tablespoons oil (which is 100 percent fat, unlike butter, which is 80 percent) lowers the fat content to 26 percent, but each pancake drops 0.4 gram fat, 1.1 gram saturated fat, and 5 milligrams cholesterol.

Nutritional Analysis per pancake (without syrup)

....

68 calories

2 g protein

2 g fat

0.2 g satfat

10 g carbohydrate

158 mg sodium

11 mg cholesterol

Crunchy Granola

· ◆ · ◆ · ◆ ·

Granola is a crunchy, healthy blend of whole grains, dried fruits, seeds, and nuts. It is a concept, rather than an exact recipe, a designer food that varies depending upon one's mood, larder, and low-fat requirements. Every chef has a favorite mixture. Fifteen years ago, I published my first, and favorite, granola recipe in a children's Halloween Cookbook. The only real change I have made since then is to add, when I have them, half a cup of dried blueberries, cherries, or cranberries for flavor. This recipe is similar, but with fewer nuts and less oil, and without high-fat coconut or sesame seeds. The inspired additions of cinnamon, orange zest, orange juice, and apple juice were suggested by Tamara Frey, breakfast chef at Rancho La Puerta in Baja California. Her recipe for Ranch Granola was shared with me by my editor, Harriet Bell, who adds her own touches: a generous teaspoon of ground ginger, some nutmeg, cranberry or apple-pear juice, and she uses Lactaid nonfat milk (for lactose intolerance). I serve my granola with either regular skim or 2% milk for breakfast, and also use it as a topping on fresh fruit and yogurt desserts or in Granola Bars (page 336) or muffins.

Since granola requires assembling quite a few ingredients, I like to make a big batch.

· ◆ · ◆ · ◆ ·

Yield

Approximately
10¼ cups granola;
21 servings (about
½ cup each)

Advance Preparation

Granola can be stored in an airtight container in a cool location for 2 to 3 weeks.

Special Equipment

Extra-large mixing bowl, roasting pan

Temperature and Time

300°F for 60 to 75 minutes

¾ cup apple cider or other fruit juice

¼ cup canola or safflower oil *or* walnut or hazelnut oil

⅓ cup honey

Grated zest and juice of 1 orange (about 2 tablespoons zest and 6 tablespoons juice)

1 tablespoon vanilla extract

1 cup All-Bran cereal

4 cups old-fashioned rolled oats

1 cup wheat or rye flakes

1 cup toasted wheat germ

¼ cup chopped blanched almonds

½ cup sunflower seeds

1 teaspoon salt

1½ teaspoons cinnamon

1 cup seedless raisins

½ cup dried apricots, chopped

½ pitted prunes, chopped

½ cup dried pitted whole dates, chopped

¼ cup dark brown sugar, packed (optional)

*Nutritional Analysis
per ½ cup serving
(without optional
sugar)*

261 calories

8 g protein

8 g fat

1 g satfat

43 g carbohydrate

126 mg sodium

0 mg cholesterol

1. Position a rack in the center of the oven and preheat it to 300°F.

2. In a saucepan, combine the cider or juice, oil, honey, and orange zest and orange juice. Heat until just about to boil. Stir, remove from the heat, and add the vanilla.

3. In a large bowl, combine the All-Bran, oats, wheat or rye flakes, wheat germ, nuts, sunflower seeds, salt, and cinnamon. Toss well. Pour on the hot liquid, and stir and toss with 2 wooden spoons to coat thoroughly.

4. Spread the mixture in a large roasting pan and bake for 1 hour, or until the cereal is dry and golden brown. Using a spatula, stir the mixture every 10 or 15 minutes. Do not overtoast, or the granola will become too hard to chew.

5. When thoroughly dry and crisp, remove the granola from the oven and mix in the raisins and chopped dried fruit. I like to add the optional brown sugar, but it depends upon your sweet tooth. Stir well, then allow to cool completely. Store in lidded jars or plastic bags.

Light Touch: While traditional granola mixtures provide dietary fiber, vitamins, and minerals, they usually contain a substantial amount of relatively high-fat coconut, nuts, sesame or other seeds, and oil; some also contain sweetened condensed milk. These blends get from 41 to 50 percent of calories from fat.

I have reduced calories from fat to 26 percent by increasing the proportion of fruits and grains, decreasing the quantity of nuts and oil, and dropping the sesame seeds and coconut. Each serving contains 6 grams of dietary fiber. If you omit the nuts entirely, you can cut an additional 1 gram of fat per serving. Wheat flakes and rye flakes (sold in natural food stores) are interchangeable; if you don't have them, use all rolled oats (fat increases 1 gram per serving). One-half cup dried sweetened coconut will add 11 calories and 0.8 gram of fat per serving. Walnut or hazelnut oil adds a nutty flavor that is welcome since the proportion of nuts has been cut; however, be sure the oil is fresh and not rancid.

Whole Wheat Applesauce Waffles

◆ ◆ ◆

This is a delicious cinnamon-scented batter that makes a crisp, tasty waffle. Don't try to use this for pancakes, however, because the batter is too moist. It needs to be baked in a waffle iron to set properly.

◆ ◆ ◆

Yield

Fifteen to sixteen 4-inch square waffles; 5 to 6 servings

Advance Preparation

Prepare the batter just before using it.

Special Equipment

Electric waffle iron, preferably with a nonstick surface

Butter-flavor no stick cooking spray

1 large egg

2 tablespoons canola or safflower oil

3 tablespoons nonfat vanilla or plain yogurt

½ cup unsweetened applesauce

1 tablespoon dark corn syrup or granulated sugar

¼ cup toasted wheat germ

¾ cup 1% milk, or as needed

½ cup unsifted all-purpose flour

½ cup whole wheat flour or buckwheat flour

2 teaspoons baking powder

¼ teaspoon baking soda

⅛ teaspoon salt

½ teaspoon cinnamon

1 cup pure maple syrup, warmed

1. Lightly coat the waffle iron with cooking spray. Preheat the waffle iron according to manufacturer's directions.

2. Meanwhile, in a large bowl, whisk together the egg, oil, and yogurt. Beat in the applesauce, corn syrup or sugar, wheat germ, and milk.

3. Set a strainer over the bowl and add both flours, the baking powder, baking soda, salt, and cinnamon. With a spoon, stir and sift the dry ingredients onto the wet ingredients. Mix well. (If the mixture must stand for any length of time, you may need to add a little more milk, a tablespoon at a time.)

4. Spoon the batter onto the bottom panel of the waffle iron, close it gently, and cook for 2 or 3 minutes (models vary in timing), until the jaws can be opened easily. If the iron sticks, the waffle is not yet baked through. When the waffle is done, use a fork to gently pry it up. Repeat until all the batter is used. You should have to regrease the surface only rarely, but if the waffles seem to stick, lightly spray the waffle iron again. Serve the waffles hot, with the warm maple syrup.

Light Touch: This recipe obtains only 17 percent of its calories from fat. The whole wheat flour and wheat germ contribute vitamins and minerals; with the applesauce, you have over 2 grams dietary fiber per (4-inch) waffle. To eliminate the cholesterol, use 2 egg whites in place of the whole egg.

Nutritional Analysis calculations based on 15. Per one 4-inch waffle (with about 1 tablespoon syrup)

133 calories

3 g protein

3 g fat

0.4 g satfat

26 g carbohydrate

111 mg sodium

15 mg cholesterol

Baked Blueberry Puff

◆ ◆ ◆

This recipe appears in many guises in numerous German and Eastern European cookbooks. I believe the origin is German, though it is not purebred, or even "purepancake." In any case, an egg batter is quickly tossed together, poured into a buttered skillet, and popped into a hot oven. In a few minutes, it magically puffs into a crisp golden cloud. (Chemically, if not genealogically, it is related to Yorkshire pudding and popovers.)

When it emerges from the oven in all its glory (gather the breakfast crowd around to admire it, because the show is short), top it with some lemon juice and sifted sugar. As it begins to cool, it deflates. By the time you cut and serve a slice, you have an almost flat pancake, but with a sublimely creamy texture and flavor. One recipe serves four if you have other accompanying treats, but two or three of us have been known to polish it off with pleasure and wish there were more.

Although this recipe contains blueberries, I often make it with other berries or sliced fruit. My favorite, actually, is plain, without any berries, just lemon juice and sugar on top. Or prepare the pancake plain and serve it with Dried Fruit Compote (page 397) and vanilla yogurt.

◆ ◆ ◆

Yield

One 10-inch pancake; 4 servings

Advance Preparation

Baking pan must be preheated in the oven for at least 15 minutes before adding the batter. The pancake must be served as soon as it is baked.

Special Equipment

10-inch ovenproof skillet or pie plate, small sifter

Temperature and Time

425°F for 20 minutes to preheat pan, plus 15 minutes to bake pancake

1 tablespoon unsalted butter

Butter-flavor no stick cooking spray

1 large egg plus 1 large egg white, lightly beaten

½ cup unsifted all-purpose flour

½ cup 1% milk

½ teaspoon vanilla extract

1 tablespoon granulated sugar

Pinch of nutmeg

Pinch of salt

1 cup fresh blueberries, picked over, rinsed, and patted dry on paper towels

½ lemon

¼ cup confectioners' sugar

1. Position a rack in the lower third of the oven and preheat to 425°F. After preheating for 10 minutes, add the butter and a 5-second spray of cooking spray to the pan (if you have only unflavored spray coating on hand, use it). Set the pan in the oven to preheat 10 minutes.

2. In a large bowl, whisk together the egg and egg white, then whisk in flour, milk, vanilla, sugar, nutmeg, and salt. Stir in the berries.

3. Set a small sifter in a dish and pour the confectioners' sugar into it. Set this and the lemon half (plus a reamer if you have one) near the stove.

4. Pour the batter into the preheated pan and return it to the oven to bake for 15 to 20 minutes, until the edges are puffed up high and are golden brown. Remove the pan from the oven. Squeeze the juice of the halved lemon over the whole surface of the pancake, and sift on the confectioners' sugar. Serve hot, directly from the baking pan, cut into wedges. Spoon a little of the pan sauce over each slice.

Light Touch: This recipe obtains just 26 percent of its calories from fat. This is a significant reduction in fat when compared to my original recipe, which contains 2 whole eggs, ⅓ cup whole milk, and ¼ cup butter: It gets 57 percent of its calories from fat, and each serving has 65 more calories, over twice the cholesterol, three times the fat (16 grams), and over three times the saturated fat (9 grams). To achieve the fat reductions, I have cut one yolk, replaced whole milk with low-fat, and reduced butter. I added vanilla and sugar to the light version to compensate for flavor lost from using less butter. If you cut the berries to ⅔ cup, the puff will rise a little higher.

*Nutritional Analysis
per serving*
....

184 calories

5 g protein

5 g fat

2.6 g satfat

29 g carbohydrate

117 mg sodium

63 mg cholesterol

Basic Crêpes

◆·◆·◆·

Yield

About twelve 6-inch crêpes

Advance Preparation

Batter can be made up to 1 hour in advance and refrigerated until ready to use. Cooked crêpes can be cooled completely, stacked with wax paper between the layers, wrapped in plastic wrap and placed in a heavy-duty plastic bag, and refrigerated a few days or frozen for up to 1 month. Thaw at room temperature before using.

Special Equipment

6-inch (bottom diameter) crêpe pan or skillet, preferably nonstick or Teflon-coated; clean tea towel or paper towels

*T*hese are all-purpose French crêpes, very close in formula to Jewish blintzes. Although water is used because it makes a very light, flexible crêpe, you can replace it with skim milk. When either beer or hard cider (which contain some yeast) is used to replace the water, the result is a light, airy crêpe with a tangy taste—good for savory fillings. There is a tiny bit of sugar in the batter for flavoring but it does not make the crêpes sweet; you can use this recipe for both sweet and savory fillings.

For brunch, or for dessert, spread the pale side of each warm-from-the-pan crêpe with your favorite fruit preserves, roll up, and top with a little sifted confectioners' sugar. To make crêpes au citron, squeeze a little fresh lemon juice over the pale side of each warm crêpe, sift on some confectioners' sugar, roll up, and then sift on a little more sugar. Keep the rolled crêpes warm on a hot plate until all are made. For other ideas, see the crêpe and blintz entries in the Index.

The crêpes can be baked in a small omelet pan or a crêpe pan (a pan with sloping sides that facilitate turning the crêpes), an ordinary small skillet, or an electric crêpe maker (follow the manufacturer's directions). Pan measurements vary with the manufacturer. Measure across the bottom, as this will be the crêpe size. Select a pan that measures about six inches across the bottom and about eight inches across the top, rim to rim.

When making crêpes the pan must be hot enough for the batter to stick lightly and spread into an even layer without splattering or burning. The batter must be like cream, thin enough to run smoothly over the bottom of the pan, not so thick that it will puddle like a pancake. Adjust the heat as needed and add a little more liquid to the batter if it seems too thick. You may need to make one or two test crêpes before you get them just right. Yield will vary slightly depending upon the size of the eggs, the length of standing time before the batter is used (the longer it stands, the thicker it becomes), and the amount of liquid added. If you are not getting as many crêpes as indicated, add another tablespoon of water to the batter, and be sure to pour any excess batter back into the bowl as you form each crêpe.

◆·◆·◆·

2 large eggs plus 2 large egg whites

¾ cup plus 2 tablespoons water, or as needed

½ teaspoon salt

¼ teaspoon granulated sugar

1 cup unsifted all-purpose flour

Butter-flavor no stick cooking spray or about 1 tablespoon
canola or safflower oil

*Nutritional Analysis
per crêpe*
....
54 calories

3 g protein

1 g fat

0.3 g satfat

8 g carbohydrate

109 mg sodium

36 mg cholesterol

1. In a bowl, or in a blender or food processor, combine the eggs and egg whites, water, salt, and sugar. Whisk or blend well, then beat in the flour. The batter should be the consistency of heavy cream. Allow to stand for at least 5 minutes, or refrigerate for up to 1 hour. (If the batter seems too thick or stands for more than 30 minutes, you may need to beat in 1 or more tablespoons of water.)

2. Set a tea towel or a paper towel alongside the stove to hold the cooked crêpes. Lightly coat the crêpe pan or skillet with cooking spray or lightly brush with the oil. Heat the pan over medium-high heat until a drop of water sizzles when sprinkled on the surface.

3. Pour a scant ¼ cup batter into the hot pan. *Immediately* lift the pan and tilt it until the batter coats the bottom of the pan in an even layer, then quickly (before the batter sets) pour any excess batter back into the bowl, leaving just a thin coating of batter in the pan. Return the pan to the heat and cook for 15 to 20 seconds, until the edges of the crêpe just start to curl away from the pan, the top of the crêpe looks dry, and the underside, when you pry up an edge with the tip of a knife to peek, is a pale golden color.

4. Run the tip of a paring knife or spatula around the edge of the crêpe to free it from the pan, then use the knife to help you flip the crêpe over, and cook it for 10 to 15 seconds on the other side. (For Cheese Blintzes [page 84], cook only on one side.)

5. Flip the crêpe out onto the tea towel. Inspect the crêpe: It should be thin, flexible, and delicate. If it seems rubbery, pasty, or thick, feed it to the dog, and whisk 1 tablespoon more water into the batter. Repeat the cooking procedure until all the batter is used, stacking the crêpes on the towel. If the crêpes begin to stick to the pan, lightly spray or oil the pan. Use the crêpes as directed in the following recipes.

Light Touch: This recipe obtains 16 percent of its calories from fat and it is the one I usually use. Occasionally I use 4 whole eggs instead of eliminating 2 yolks; that version has 26 percent calories from

(continued)

fat; per crêpe the whole eggs add only 0.6 gram fat and scarcely change the saturated fat, but they increase the cholesterol to 53 milligrams.

Traditional crêpe recipes vary considerably depending upon their country of origin. French crêpes often call for extra egg yolks and use cream for the liquid; they usually are cooked in clarified butter. My basic extra-rich French recipe (weighing in at 72 percent calories from fat) uses ½ cup flour, 4 whole eggs, and 1 cup heavy cream, plus a little brandy, sugar, and salt. This recipe produces sixteen 6-inch crepes. Compared to the recipe above, each rich crêpe contains more than one and a half times the calories (85), with 7 grams fat, 4 grams saturated fat, and twice the cholesterol (74 milligrams).

Crêpes with Fresh Berries and Vanilla Cream

◆ · ◆ · ◆ ·

 quick and easy brunch or dessert dish.

◆ · ◆ · ◆ ·

Yield
....
12 filled crêpes;
6 servings

Advance Preparation
....
Plain crêpes can be prepared ahead and refrigerated or frozen. They can be filled, rolled, and refrigerated about 2 hours before serving; if they stand longer, they may get soggy.

Special Equipment
....
Pastry brush

1 recipe Basic Crêpes (page 78)

⅔ cup apricot or other fruit preserves

2 tablespoons orange-flavored liqueur (such as Grand Marnier), peach liqueur, or kirsch

3 cups fresh berries (use any type or mixture of berries) or 3 cups total berries and thinly sliced peeled peaches or nectarines (out of season, use canned Elberta peaches and/or other fruits in light syrup, well drained, or unsweetened frozen fruit such as berries or peach slices, thawed)

2 tablespoons light brown or granulated sugar, or to taste

Confectioners' sugar

1 recipe Vanilla Custard Sauce (page 410)

1. In a small saucepan, stir the preserves with the liqueur over low heat until melted and of spreadable consistency. Set the glaze aside.

2. Place the berries or fruit mixture in a bowl, and toss with the sugar.

Nutritional Analysis per 2 filled crêpes with sauce

352 calories

10 g protein

5 g fat

1.4 g satfat

65 g carbohydrate

274 mg sodium

179 mg cholesterol

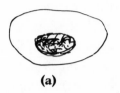
(a)
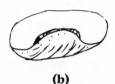
(b)

(c)

(d)

3. Place 1 crêpe pale side up on a work surface and brush on some preserves glaze. Using a slotted spoon to drain excess juices, place 1 to 2 tablespoons of the fruit on the crêpe (a) following the diagrams. Lift up the bottom edge of the crêpe over the fruit (b). Fold over the sides (c), then roll up from the bottom and set seam side down on a serving plate (d). Repeat until all the crêpes are filled.

4. Just before serving, sift a little confectioners' sugar over the crêpes. Spoon on some of the remaining berries or fruit mixture, and serve with the Vanilla Custard Sauce.

Light Touch: This recipe gets 12 percent of its calories from fat. The cholesterol count is relatively high because both the crêpes and the custard sauce contain egg yolks. To get only 8 percent calories from fat while dropping 108 milligrams cholesterol, substitute ¾ cup low-fat yogurt for the custard sauce. Top each filled crêpe with 1 tablespoon yogurt.

Crêpes with
Caramelized Pears

．◆．◆．◆．

Plain crêpes can be
prepared well ahead and
refrigerated or frozen.
The pears can be
caramelized a day in
advance and kept
covered in the
refrigerator. Fill the
crêpes up to 3 hours in
advance. Warm the filled
crêpes in the oven just
before serving.

12-inch skillet with
cover, 9 × 12-inch oven-
to-table baking dish

F*resh pears cooked in caramelized brown sugar scented with
lemon zest, pear brandy, and a touch of ginger make a
delectable crêpe filling. The pears are so tasty you may want to hold the
crêpes and serve them alone. You can also use the pears as a pie or tart
filling (double the recipe), or serve the fruit inside crisp cup-shaped tulip
cookies. Peach or apple slices can be substituted for the pears with equal
success.*

*My daughter, Cassandra, created this recipe. It was inspired by, and
is dedicated to, the memory of our friend, Sonja Plaut, a sculptor who
made her garden into a living work of art. Sonny preserved everything
she grew, including pears from her orchard, which she put up in Mason
jars with lemon zest, ginger, and brandy.*

．◆．◆．◆．

1 recipe Basic Crêpes (page 78)

Pear Filling

    4 ripe Bosc, Anjou, or Bartlett pears, peeled, cored, and
        coarsely chopped (pieces about ½ × ½ × ¼ inch; about
        4 cups fruit)

    2 tablespoons fresh lemon juice

    1 tablespoon butter

    ¼ cup dark brown sugar, packed

    3 tablespoons orange or apple juice *or* pear brandy

    ½ teaspoon grated lemon zest

    Scant ⅛ teaspoon each nutmeg and ground ginger

1 recipe Caramel Sauce (page 421), warmed (optional)

1. Put the chopped pears in a bowl and toss them with the lemon
juice to prevent discoloration.

2. Add the butter and pears to a large skillet. Crumble the brown
sugar over the pears. Heat over medium-high heat, stirring gently with
a wooden spoon, for about 2 minutes, until the sugar melts and coats
the fruit.

3. Add the fruit juice or brandy, lemon zest, and spices. Cover the skillet, and lower the heat. Simmer for about 3 minutes (depending on the type and ripeness of the pears), or until the pears begin to be tender but are not completely soft; to test, pierce with the tip of a paring knife. Remove the lid, raise the heat to high, and boil rapidly for about 3 minutes, until most of the liquid has evaporated and only about 3 tablespoons of syrup remain clinging to the pears. Watch the pears carefully to be sure they do not burn. Remove the skillet from the heat and let the filling cool to lukewarm.

4. To assemble, place 1 crêpe pale side up on a work surface. Following the diagrams (page 81), place 1½ to 2 tablespoons of the caramelized pears on the crêpe. Lift up the bottom edge of the crêpe over the filling, fold over the sides, and roll up from the bottom. Set the crêpe seam side down on an ovenproof serving platter. Repeat with the remaining crêpes. Spoon any remaining filling around the filled crêpes.

5. About 20 minutes before serving, preheat the oven to 350°F. Ten minutes before serving, place the crêpes in the oven to warm them through. Serve plain or with warm Caramel Sauce.

Light Touch: One tablespoon butter adds richness to the caramel flavor of the pears. There is little other fat, however; the recipe has only 17 percent calories from fat. If you omit the butter in the filling (use a little butter-flavor no stick cooking spray in the skillet), you drop 2 grams of fat and 1 gram of saturated fat per serving, lowering the calories from fat to 10 percent. The fruit adds 3 grams of dietary fiber per serving.

Nutritional Analysis per 2 filled crêpes (without optional sauce)

220 calories

6 g protein

4 g fat

1.8 g satfat

41 g carbohydrate

222 mg sodium

77 mg cholesterol

Cheese Blintzes

◆ · ◆ · ◆

Advance Preparation

Plain crêpes can be made in advance and refrigerated or frozen. Cheese filling can be made a day in advance and kept covered in the refrigerator. Before frying, the filled blintzes can be set on a plate, double-wrapped, and frozen for up to 1 month; defrost overnight in the refrigerator before frying. Filled blintzes can be fried, then cooled, covered, and refrigerated for up to 8 hours; serve the blintzes cold or for better flavor reheat in a 350°F oven for about 10 to 15 minutes.

Special Equipment

10-inch frying pan, preferably nonstick or Teflon-coated

Blintzes are one of my mother's many culinary triumphs. My sister and I still vie for leftovers to take home after we visit her. She prepares dozens of these delectable golden crêpes, bursting with creamy, cinnamon-sweet cheese, served barely warm with a little sour cream and a sprinkling of sugar. We each have our favorites; I like blueberries in the cheese filling and a little light brown sugar sprinkled on the sour cream topping; my sister, Nancy, prefers hers plain with Spiced Blueberry Sauce (page 415). Since blintzes can be prepared in advance and frozen, they are perfect for brunch or for supper on a hot summer day.

The classic crêpe used for blintzes is made with water because it produces a lighter texture than cream or milk. Generally, the filling contains cottage cheese and farmer's or pot cheese, and sometimes a little cream cheese, mixed together with an egg and some sugar. Pot cheese or farmer's cheese is favored over cottage cheese because the curds are drier. However, since pot and farmer's cheese can be difficult to find, I have used a combination of nonfat low-fat cottage cheese and cottage cheese that has had most of its liquid (whey) pressed out through a strainer. Note that some brands have more gums added than others and so some curds will scarcely drain at all, while others will drain easily and become nearly dry.

◆ · ◆ · ◆

1 recipe Basic Crêpes (page 78)

Cheese Filling

1 large egg

1 teaspoon vanilla extract

Pinch of salt

1½ tablespoons granulated sugar, or to taste

¼ teaspoon cinnamon, or to taste

1¾ cup (14 ounces) nonfat cottage cheese, preferably without added gums (see introduction)

¾ cup (6 ounces) 2% low-fat cottage cheese

1½ to 2½ tablespoons matzo meal or plain dry bread crumbs, as needed

Butter-flavor no stick cooking spray or about 1 teaspoon
   canola or safflower oil

⅛ teaspoon unsalted margarine or butter

Topping

¾ **cup light sour cream**

*Nutritional Analysis
per 2 filled blintzes
fried in cooking spray
and margarine and
each topped with
1 tablespoon light
sour cream*

160 calories

14 g protein

5 g fat

0.7 g satfat

17 g carbohydrate

429 mg sodium

44 mg cholesterol

1. In a large bowl, whisk together the egg, vanilla, salt, sugar, and cinnamon.

2. Set a strainer over another bowl and place the nonfat cottage cheese in it. Place a piece of plastic wrap over the cheese and press down on the curds to expel most of the excess whey.

3. Add the pressed nonfat cheese and low-fat cottage cheese to the egg mixture and beat well to blend. Add enough of the matzo meal or crumbs to make a mixture that is neither runny and wet nor stiff and dry, but will hold together. Taste and adjust the sugar and cinnamon.

4. To fill the crêpes, follow the diagrams (page 81). Place 1 crêpe pale side up on a work surface and place 1½ to 2 tablespoons of the filling about ½ inch above the bottom edge. Fold the bottom edge up over the filling. Fold over both sides, and roll up tightly from the bottom, making a puffy envelope. Place the filled blintz seam side down on a plate. Repeat with the remaining crêpes and filling. Cover and refrigerate up to 8 hours or fry blintzes now.

5. To fry the blintzes, coat a large frying pan with cooking spray or brush with the oil, and the margarine or butter. Heat the pan over medium heat until a drop of water sizzles when sprinkled on. Add 3 or 4 of the blintzes, seam side down, without crowding, and fry until the bottom surface is golden brown, about 35 seconds. Turn and brown on the other side. Remove to a serving platter. Repeat with the remaining blintzes, adding a little more spray or oil if necessary. Cover blintzes to keep warm if serving them soon.

Light Touch: This recipe, including the low-fat sour cream topping, obtains 25 percent of its calories from fat. If the sour cream is omitted, the count drops to 19 percent (but they're better with sour cream, believe me). This recipe received rave reviews from my family, the toughest critics of all, and I didn't even tell them that my mother's original version, with full-fat cottage cheese plus farmer's cheese, fried in margarine, and topped with dairy sour cream, contained more than twice the calories from fat (59 percent) plus significant amounts of saturated fat and cholesterol: per serving, 17 grams fat, 9 grams saturated fat, and 72 milligrams cholesterol.

Great-Grandmother's Potato Pancakes

◆ ◆ ◆

These are my maternal great-grandmother Sophia's Chanukah latkes. I always knew they were delicious, but until recently I never thought about the fact that they are also very low in fat.

Sophia was apparently a very savvy cook. I grew up on stories about how lovely, resourceful, and clever she was. Known for her wicked sense of humor, a helpful trait for a single parent who raised three daughters (including a pair of twins) by selling sewing notions door-to-door, she ultimately outlived three husbands.

I like to serve these potato pancakes for brunch with a side dish of chunky homemade applesauce (Golden Delicious apples peeled, cored, cut in large chunks, and simmered with a little cider and a cinnamon stick until tender-soft). A nonstick frying pan enables you to fry the pancakes with less fat; however, a regular pan is fine if you watch the quantity of fat carefully.

◆ ◆ ◆

Yield

About twenty 3-inch pancakes

Advance Preparation

The grated potatoes need to drain at least 15 minutes before being added to the batter, so plan ahead. The pancakes can be kept warm in a hot oven on a baking sheet in a single layer, but are best served soon after they are fried.

Special Equipment

Box or mandoline grater or food processor fitted with grating disk, 12-inch skillet or electric frying pan, preferably nonstick

---

6 medium white potatoes (1½ pounds), peeled

1 medium yellow onion

1 large egg plus 1 large egg white

¾ teaspoon salt

⅛ teaspoon freshly ground black pepper

2 tablespoons matzo meal or plain cracker crumbs

1 tablespoon margarine, or more as needed

1. Grate the potatoes on a box or mandoline grater, or use the food processor. If using the processor, remove the grated potatoes and replace the grating disk with the steel blade. Return the grated potatoes to the processor and pulse a few times to cut up the long shreds.

2. Place the potatoes in a strainer set over a bowl and cover the top of the potatoes with a piece of plastic wrap to retard their turning brown from oxidation. Allow to drain for at least 15 minutes to remove excess liquid. (Don't worry if the potatoes discolor anyway—this won't affect the flavor.)

3. Grate the onion on the box or mandoline grater, or coarsely chop it in the food processor. Place the onion in a large bowl. Add the egg and egg white, salt, pepper, and matzo meal or cracker crumbs. Add the drained grated potatoes and stir well to blend.

4. Melt the margarine in the frying pan and heat until a drop of water sizzles when sprinkled on. Add 1 heaping tablespoon of batter per pancake to the pan, spreading or pressing each one into a 3-inch round. Fry until golden brown on the bottom, about 4 minutes, then turn and fry until crisp and browned on both sides. Transfer to a platter and repeat with the remaining batter, adding more margarine to the pan if necessary. Serve immediately, or arrange in a single layer on a baking sheet, so they do not get soggy, and keep warm in a low oven.

Light Touch: This recipe gets 19 percent of its calories from fat. The only change I made from the original was to drop 1 egg yolk, a remarkably minor variation considering that the recipe goes back at least three generations.

*Nutritional Analysis
per pancake*
....

42 calories

1 g protein

1 g fat

0.2 g satfat

7 g carbohydrate

95 mg sodium

11 mg cholesterol

Biscuits, Scones, Muffins, *and* Popovers

S teaming hot, feather-light biscuits or luscious crisp popovers are just the thing when you want a bit of bread, but not necessarily a loaf of...with a luncheon salad or a dinner roast, for example. For mid-morning coffee or afternoon tea, scones or muffins are my choice: irresistibly homey, old-fashioned comfort foods. And since muffins and scones freeze successfully and travel with ease, they are also high on the list for lunch-box and picnic snacks.

Muffin Notes

• All the muffin recipes in this book were baked in 2½-inch muffin cups. They can, of course, be baked in any size pan; smaller or larger cups will produce different quantities and require different baking times. Check the volume amount of batter under the yield for each recipe, and then use the table on page 91 to estimate quantity and time. Watch carefully when muffins are in the oven, and test doneness with a cake tester as described in each recipe. Times and temperatures are for electric or gas ovens; if you use a convection oven, reduce the heat by about 50°F and adjust the baking time accordingly.

• In place of metal muffin tins, you can substitute Pyrex or ceramic custard cups or any similar-size ovenproof vessels. Muffin batter can also be baked in a square or oblong pan for a coffee cake; an 8-inch square pan of muffin batter bakes for 20 to 25 minutes.

• Traditionally, muffins are baked in paper- or foil-lined cups. But I prefer to coat the cups with butter-flavor no stick cooking spray. The lecithin in the spray prevents sticking and enables the muffins to be released easily, making extra liners unnecessary.

• When preparing muffins, use this simple mixing technique: Combine all the liquid ingredients in a bowl and blend together. Set a strainer over the bowl and add the dry ingredients, including spices. Stir the

Diameter of individual muffin cups	Maximum amount of fluid to fill to brim	Maximum amount of batter (allowing for rise)	Approximate baking time (in minutes)
1¾ × ¾ inches	4 teaspoons	3 teaspoons	12 to 15
2 inches	3 tablespoons	2 to 2½ tablespoons	18 to 20
2½ inches	⅓ cup	scant ¼ cup	20 to 22
2¾ inches	½ cup	⅓ cup	20 to 22
3 inches	½ cup	generous ⅓ to scant ½ cup	20 to 22
3½ inches	1 cup	generous ¾ cup	25 to 30

dry ingredients together, sifting them down onto the wet. Blend together with a wooden spoon. Finally, stir in any dried or fresh fruit or other remaining ingredients. Avoid overbeating; it makes muffins tough and dense.

• A perfect muffin has a domed or rounded top, usually with an irregularly bumpy surface (depending upon ingredients), golden brown color, no splits or chasms across the top, and a moist, slightly crumbly, tender texture. Some variations, of course, depend upon specific ingredients; heavy, dense batters with fruit will rise less than plain simple batters. Muffins should never be concave or utterly flat, leaden, or pudding-like.

• The old rule to fill muffin cups only two thirds full *can* be broken. I like my muffins oversize and prefer to fill the cups nearly to the top with batter; the muffins rise higher this way.

• If you have any empty cups in a muffin pan, add some water to them to prevent scorching during baking.

• To give muffins crunchy crisp tops, before baking, sprinkle with granulated or brown sugar, or cinnamon sugar, plain or with a few finely chopped nuts.

• Muffins are best served warm or split and toasted. They can be wrapped airtight and frozen, but should be warmed before serving.

Basic Biscuits

◆ · ◆ · ◆

Buttermilk makes these biscuits especially tender. They are light, "high-rise," and as delicious covered with gravy as they are in strawberry shortcake.

◆ · ◆ · ◆

Butter-flavor no stick cooking spray

2 cups sifted all-purpose flour

2 teaspoons baking powder

¾ teaspoon baking soda

½ teaspoon salt

Pinch of granulated sugar

¼ cup canola oil

¾ cup cultured regular or nonfat buttermilk

1. Position a rack in the center of the oven and preheat it to 425°F. Lightly coat the baking sheet with cooking spray or line with baking parchment.

2. In a large bowl, combine the flour, baking powder, baking soda, salt, and sugar. Whisk to blend well. Add the oil and buttermilk and whisk just until the mixture forms a ball. Transfer the dough to a lightly floured surface and knead four or five times.

3. Pat the dough into a rectangle about ½ inch thick and cut with 2- to 2½-inch round cutters; a 2-inch round cutter yields 12 to 14 biscuits, a 2½-inch cutter yields 10. Set the rounds on the prepared pan and bake for about 12 minutes, or until lightly golden and well risen. Serve warm.

Drop Biscuits

Increase the buttermilk to 1 cup. Do not form the dough into a ball or knead it; instead, mix it well. Drop by tablespoonfuls onto the prepared pan. Bake as directed. Drop biscuits will not rise quite as high as cut biscuits.

Light Touch: These biscuits are cholesterol-free and significantly lower in fat than those from a traditional recipe. Using ¼ cup canola

---

Yield

Twelve 2-inch biscuits

Advance Preparation

If serving as savory biscuits, do not bake in advance; they take little time and are best prepared just before serving. If using in shortcake, bake as near serving time as possible.

Special Equipment

Baking sheet, preferably nonstick, baking parchment (optional), 2- to 2½-inch round cookie cutter

Temperature and Time

425°F for 12 to 15 minutes

oil to replace ½ cup butter reduces calories from fat to 36 percent, a 27 percent reduction from the original 49 percent calories from fat. When I reduced the fat below 36 percent, the texture changed too much, and the biscuits became tough and rubbery. Although 36 percent total fat appears at first to be relatively high, it is because there are so few ingredients in the recipe and so few that contribute calories that the ¼ cup oil is disproportionately weighted. The per serving figures are well within acceptable limits and the recipe can easily fit into a low-fat plan for healthy eating.

Yogurt Scones

◆ · ◆ · ◆

Yield

Yield
8 wedge-shaped scones

Advance Preparation
Scones are best when freshly baked, but will keep well for several days if stored airtight. They can be wrapped airtight and frozen; serve warm or toasted.

Special Equipment
Baking sheet, baking parchment (optional)

Temperature and Time
425°F for 15 to 20 minutes

*T*hese are light, high-rising scones studded with raisins. The mixing technique is unusual: A small quantity of butter is melted and browned to enhance its flavor, combined with a little flour and frozen, then pinched into the dry ingredients in coarse flakes. This contributes to the flaky texture.

My daughter, Cassandra, often bakes scones (with lots of butter) that are sold at our local village store, and they have become one of her specialties. Since she has the knack, she perfected this recipe for me.

◆ · ◆ · ◆

Butter-flavor no stick cooking spray

2 tablespoons lightly salted butter

2½ cups sifted all-purpose flour

3 tablespoons cornstarch

1 tablespoon baking powder

1 teaspoon salt

¼ teaspoon nutmeg

1 large egg

½ cup nonfat plain or vanilla yogurt

2 tablespoons canola or safflower oil

½ cup water

⅓ cup granulated sugar

½ cup seedless raisins or dried currants

1. Position a rack in the center of the oven and preheat it to 425°F. Coat the baking sheet with cooking spray or line with baking parchment.

2. Melt the butter in a small saucepan over medium-low heat, and cook until the butter begins to turn golden brown and has a nutty aroma, about 4 minutes. Watch carefully so the butter does not burn. Transfer the browned butter to a small bowl and stir in 2 tablespoons of the flour. Place in the freezer for about 15 minutes, or until solid.

3. Sift together the remaining flour, the cornstarch, baking powder, salt, and nutmeg into a large bowl. Scrape in the frozen butter in pieces. With your fingertips, pinch the butter into the dry ingredients, as you would for a pie crust, creating coarse flakes.

4. In another large bowl, beat together the egg, yogurt, oil, water, and sugar. Add the dry ingredients and raisins or currants and blend just to combine; do not overbeat. Gather the dough into a ball.

5. On a very lightly floured surface, pat the dough into a 9-inch round about ½ inch thick. Cut into 8 wedges. With a floured spatula, set the wedges on the prepared baking sheet.

6. Bake for about 15 minutes, until the scones are lightly golden and a cake tester inserted in the center comes out dry. Transfer the scones to a wire rack to cool slightly. Serve warm, or reheat before serving.

Light Touch: Scones are notorious for containing a high proportion of fat, usually in the form of butter. My favorite classic recipe is similar to this one but uses ⅔ cup butter and weighs in at 49 percent calories from fat; each scone packs 377 calories and 21 grams of fat, half of which is saturated fat.

In my attempts to cut the fat drastically, I substituted oil, changed the type of flour, and altered proportions of skim milk or buttermilk. I succeeded only in producing enough dry, hard, and tasteless hockey pucks to fill a skating rink.

I concede that I needed, in addition to a little oil, at least some of the real thing—butter—to get a tender flaky texture and buttery flavor. I browned the butter to enhance the flavor, then froze it and worked it into the flour. Tenderness and moisture are provided by the yogurt, which works better than other liquids because it has a high proportion of milk solids and so can retain moisture during baking. These lightened scones have 25 percent calories from fat—half that of the original version. The variation that follows raises the count to 38 percent calories from fat because the pine nuts contain a relatively high proportion of fat.

Pine Nut and Golden Raisin Scones

Add ¼ teaspoon cinnamon and 2 teaspoons grated orange zest to the dry ingredients. Substitute golden raisins for the dark ones, and add to the dough ⅓ cup pine nuts, lightly toasted for 3 to 4 minutes in a frying pan.

Nutritional Analysis per scone

273 calories

6 g protein

8 g fat

2.4 g satfat

46 g carbohydrate

412 mg sodium

35 mg cholesterol

Nutritional Analysis per scone

277 calories

8 g protein

12 g fat

3 g satfat

48 g carbohydrate

412 mg sodium

35 mg cholesterol

Oat Scones

❖ ◆ ❖

Yield

8 wedge-shaped scones

Advance Preparation

Scones are best when freshly baked, but will keep well for several days stored airtight. They can be wrapped airtight and frozen; serve warm or toasted.

Special Equipment

Baking sheet, baking parchment (optional)

Temperature and Time

425°F for 15 to 20 minutes

*C*risp and golden on the outside, tender and buttery within, Scottish oat scones studded with currants or raisins are one of life's great treats. The nutty-tasting oats contribute texture as well as flavor. The mixing technique is similar to that for Yogurt Scones (page 94). To achieve a buttery taste and relatively light texture—even with oats—a small amount of butter is melted and browned, then mixed with flour and frozen. When it is worked into the dry ingredients, it results in a flaky texture. I prefer raisins, as they are usually plumper and sweeter than currants, but both are good, and as a matter of fact, so are dried sour cherries or dried cranberries or blueberries.

I prefer to use old-fashioned rolled oats for this recipe as they absorb less moisture from the batter than quick-style oats, but either will work.

❖ ◆ ❖

Butter-flavor no stick cooking spray

2 tablespoons lightly salted butter

1½ cups plus 2 tablespoons sifted all-purpose flour, divided

2 tablespoons cornstarch

1 tablespoon baking powder

¾ teaspoon baking soda

½ teaspoon salt

½ teaspoon cream of tartar

1 cup old-fashioned rolled oats

½ cup seedless raisins or currants

¼ cup plus 2 tablespoons granulated sugar

½ cup nonfat plain or vanilla yogurt

2 tablespoons canola or safflower oil

⅓ cup water

1 large egg

1. Position a rack in the center of the oven and preheat it to 425°F. Coat the baking sheet with cooking spray or line it with baking parchment.

2. Melt the butter in a small saucepan over medium-low heat, and cook until the butter begins to turn golden brown and has a nutty aroma, about 4 minutes. Watch carefully so the butter does not burn. Transfer the browned butter to a small bowl and stir in 2 tablespoons of the flour. Place in the freezer for about 15 minutes, or until solid.

3. Sift together the remaining flour, the cornstarch, baking powder, baking soda, salt, and cream of tartar into a large bowl. Scrape in the frozen butter in pieces. With your fingertips, pinch the butter into the dry ingredients, as you would for a pie crust, creating coarse flakes.

4. In a small bowl, toss together the oats and raisins or currants.

5. In a large bowl, whisk together the sugar, yogurt, oil, water, and egg. Add the flour mixture and the oats and raisins and beat just to blend; do not overbeat. Gather the dough into a ball.

6. On a very lightly floured surface, pat the dough into a 9-inch round about ½ inch thick. Cut into 8 wedges. With a floured spatula, set the wedges on the prepared baking sheet.

7. Bake for about 15 minutes, until the scones are golden and a cake tester inserted in the center comes out dry. Transfer the scones to a wire rack to cool slightly, and serve warm, or reheat before serving.

Light Touch: These scones obtain 27 percent of their calories from fat. The yogurt contributes to their moisture and tenderness.

Nutritional Analysis per scone
....
262 calories

6 g protein

8 g fat

2.5 g satfat

43 g carbohydrate

278 mg sodium

35 mg cholesterol

Gluten-Free
Apricot-Lemon Scones

◆ ◆ ◆

Yield

18 scones

Advance Preparation

Scones are best served the day they are baked, but they can be wrapped airtight and frozen. Warm before serving.

Special Equipment

2 baking sheets, pastry brush

Temperature and Time

400°F for 14 to 16 minutes

A delicious recipe full of fruit and flavor, with a hidden surprise: It is gluten-free as well as reduced in fat. The recipe originated as a classic scone formula created by Boston food writer Roberta Dehman Hershon. Beth Hillson, a friend and food professional, adapted Roberta's recipe to her own needs; she has celiac disease and has developed many recipes for gluten-free foods. According to Beth, over 120,000 people in the United States suffer from this disorder, which causes the body to attack gluten, resulting in severe digestive distress. Eating gluten causes flu-like symptoms in individuals with this condition. Another more common allergy is to wheat; reactions usually show up as respiratory or skin problems. Gluten-free recipes work for both categories.

Gluten-free flours have distinctive properties. Generally, they are a blend of several types of starch or flour, combined because of their individual qualities and flavors. Because the natural elasticity of gluten—the stretchy protein found in wheat flour and other wheat products—is missing in these products, other binders must be added to give "stretch." These include eggs, buttermilk, yogurt, fruit purées, and xanthan gum, termed the "wonder food" of gluten-free baking by Beth. Available by mail order, xanthan gum is a powder used sparingly to bind certain baked goods, particularly yeast products. Though xanthan gum is included in this recipe (it makes the scones slightly less dry and crumbly), I have made the scones without the gum and find the recipe works either way. To purchase gluten-free products, see page 461 or look in natural food stores.

Beth adds a strong ginger accent to the scones by grating in a chunk of fresh ginger. If you really like ginger, use the fresh instead of the 1/2 teaspoon powdered ginger, which gives them just a hint of ginger flavor.

◆ ◆ ◆

Butter-flavor no stick cooking spray

2 tablespoons pecans, halved or chopped

1 cup dried apricots

1/3 cup dried currants or seedless raisins

1/2 cup crunchy rice cereal (such as Perky's Nutty Rice Cereal)

1 tablespoon grated lemon zest

⅓ cup dark brown sugar, packed

1¾ cups brown rice flour

½ cup potato starch

½ cup cornstarch

1 tablespoon baking powder

¾ teaspoon baking soda

1 teaspoon salt

¼ teaspoon xanthan gum (optional)

½ teaspoon ground ginger or 1 tablespoon grated fresh ginger

3 tablespoons cold unsalted butter, cut up

2 large egg whites

1 tablespoon canola oil

3 tablespoons fresh lemon juice

1 cup low-fat vanilla yogurt

Glaze (optional)

2 tablespoons skim milk

1 tablespoon granulated or brown sugar

Nutritional Analysis
per scone
....

177 calories

3 g protein

4 g fat

1.4 g satfat

33 g carbohydrate

239 mg sodium

6 mg cholesterol

1. Position a rack in the center of the oven and preheat it to 400°F. Coat the baking sheets with cooking spray.

2. To toast the pecans, place them in a small frying pan over medium heat for a few minutes, tossing them until they start to smell aromatic and darken slightly in color. Transfer the toasted nuts to a food processor and add the apricots. Pulse until the apricots are coarsely chopped (¼-inch bits). Transfer to a medium bowl, and add the currants or raisins, rice cereal, and grated lemon zest.

3. In the bowl of the processor, combine the brown sugar, rice flour, potato starch, cornstarch, baking powder, baking soda, salt, xanthan gum, if using, and ginger, and pulse a few times to blend. Add the butter and process for a few seconds, until the mixture resembles coarse meal.

4. In a large bowl, whisk together the egg whites, oil, lemon juice, and yogurt. Add the dry ingredients, and stir just to blend. Stir in the apricot-nut mixture.

5. Using a ¼-cup measure, scoop the batter onto the baking sheets, setting the scones about 1 inch apart. If desired, brush them with the milk and sprinkle the tops with sugar for a glaze.
Bake for 14 to 16 minutes, until the scones are golden brown. Use a broad spatula to transfer them to a wire rack to cool slightly. Serve warm.

(continued)

Light Touch: These scones obtain 20 percent of their calories from fat. Margarine may be substituted for the butter to reduce the cholesterol, but the fat content will stay the same. I prefer the butter for its flavor. Furthermore, when it is replaced entirely by oil (which is 100 percent fat as opposed to about 80 percent fat for butter), the texture suffers and the total fat content actually increases, although the saturated fat level drops slightly.

Popovers

· ◆ · ◆ · ◆ ·

*P*opovers are so named because when the thin flour-egg batter is poured into a preheated pan and set in a very hot oven, the liquid in the butter forms steam that causes the batter to puff quickly into high, hollow shells that swell over the top of the baking pan. The trick to making successful popovers is not in the mixing technique, but in the pan preparation and baking. The pan must be preheated so the batter can immediately begin its climb up the sides; the oven must be hot enough to cause the rapid expansion of the steam. Once the hollow shell of the popover is set, the heat is lowered to bake the interior. Resist peeking in the oven for the first 25 minutes.

A perfect popover is high, golden brown, crusty outside, and slightly moist but not wet on the inside.

Cast-iron popover tins are best but not essential; muffin tins or earthenware custard cups (set on a cookie sheet) can also be used. Whatever type you use, preheat them for 3 to 4 minutes before spraying with no stick vegetable oil or greasing them with a paper towel dipped in vegetable oil.

· ◆ · ◆ · ◆ ·

Yield

12 popovers

Advance Preparation

Popovers are best served hot from the oven.

Special Equipment

12 cast-iron popover pans (approximately 1½ inches deep and 2¼ inches in diameter) or 2½-inch muffin cups

Temperature and Time

450°F for preheating pan and for 10 minutes baking; 350°F for 25 minutes. (If using muffin tins, which have cups that are wider than they are deep, bake for only about 15 minutes at 350°F.)

1 cup 1% milk

1 teaspoon canola or safflower oil

1 large egg plus 2 large egg whites

1⅓ cups unsifted all-purpose flour

1 teaspoon granulated sugar

¼ teaspoon salt

Butter-flavor no stick cooking spray

Have Your Cake and Eat It, Too

1. Position a rack in the center of the oven and preheat it to 450°F.

2. In a bowl, whisk together the milk, oil, and egg and whites until well blended. Add the flour, sugar, and salt and whisk until nearly smooth.

3. Place the baking pans in the oven for 3 to 4 minutes. Remove and quickly spray or wipe with vegetable oil. (Use potholders to handle the pans.)

4. Divide the batter among the hot oiled pans, filling the cups about half full. Bake for 10 minutes. Then reduce the heat to 350°F (do not open the oven door) and bake 25 minutes longer, or until the popovers are well risen, firm to the touch, and golden brown. If the inside of the popovers still seems wet, pierce each one with a fork and bake 5 minutes longer to dry them out. Remove the popovers from the pans and serve immediately.

Light Touch: Classic popovers call for 2 whole eggs, 1 cup whole milk, 2 tablespoons melted butter, 1 cup flour, and a little salt. The butter, milk, and eggs push the ante up to 40 percent calories from fat. I have slashed away nearly two thirds of the fat, cutting it down to 14 percent calories from fat, by substituting 2 egg whites for one of the eggs and using low-fat milk and only a touch of oil. The cheese in the following variation contributes a small amount of extra fat, raising the total calories from fat to 20—still only half of the classic recipe.

Cheese Popovers

Prepare the recipe as directed but add 2 ounces low-fat Cheddar cheese, grated (about ⅔ cup); 2½ tablespoons grated Parmesan cheese; and ¼ teaspoon each dry mustard powder and paprika after the salt in step 2.

Nutritional Analysis per popover

73 calories

3 g protein

1 g fat

0.3 g satfat

12 g carbohydrate

69 mg sodium

19 mg cholesterol

Nutritional Analysis per cheese popover

90 calories

5 g protein

2 g fat

0.5 g satfat

12 g carbohydrate

102 mg sodium

21 mg cholesterol

Boston Brown Bread

◆·◆·◆·

A New England specialty, steamed Boston brown bread is dark, moist, and studded with raisins or currants. It dates back at least three hundred years, and it was especially favored by the Puritans, who served it on the Sabbath with baked beans. Brown bread is still just as good with baked beans, or as an accompaniment to a turkey dinner. Or warm a slice, spread it with light cream cheese, and enjoy it with a cup of coffee.

Most recipes for brown bread use a blend of three grains; cornmeal (not corn flour) and rye flour are standard, and the third can be either whole wheat flour or graham flour. You can find all of these flours in natural food stores and some supermarkets, or purchase them— individually or blended in a brown bread flour mix—from special millers (see page 460).

The steaming procedure is a simple one. The batter is poured into a mold, set into a water bath in a large covered pot, and then steamed on the stove top.

◆·◆·◆·

Yield

8 servings

Advance Preparation

Bread can be steamed a day in advance; it is moist and keeps well. Note that it takes 2 hours to steam, so plan ahead.

Special Equipment

1-quart pudding mold with lid or 1-quart heatproof bowl or baking dish, with aluminum foil and string or a heavy-duty rubber band to fit the circumference of the container if it does not have its own lid; Dutch oven with lid or other deep lidded pot to hold the steaming mold; bain marie trivet or similar steamer rack to support the mold (I have even used several metal Mason jar lids wired together side by side into a ring.)

Temperature and Time

(stove top) 2 hours minimum

Butter-flavor no stick cooking spray
½ cup rye flour
½ cup whole wheat flour
½ cup yellow cornmeal
¾ teaspoon baking soda
½ teaspoon salt
⅓ cup unsulfured molasses
1 cup cultured buttermilk
½ cup seedless raisins

1. Coat the inside of the mold and its lid with cooking spray. Or spray the bowl and piece of foil that will be used as the top.

2. In a large bowl, whisk together all the dry ingredients. Make a well in the center of the dry ingredients and add the molasses, buttermilk, and raisins. Beat hard with a wooden spoon to blend everything together.

3. Spoon the batter into the greased mold. Add the lid, or top with the foil, greased side down, and fasten with string or a sturdy rubber band. Set the steamer rack or trivet in the bottom of the Dutch oven, place the mold on it, and add hot water to reach one half to two thirds of the way up the side of the mold. Cover the pot, set it over high heat, and bring to a boil. Reduce the heat to medium and boil very slowly for 2 hours. Add boiling water as needed to keep the water level constant.

4. Lift the mold from the pot and remove the lid or foil. The bread should be well risen and springy to the touch, and a thin wooden skewer or cake tester inserted into the center should come out dry. If necessary, cover the bread and steam for an additional 10 to 15 minutes.

5. Uncover the mold and place on a wire rack to cool for about 20 minutes. Then top with a plate and invert. Lift off the mold, then invert the bread onto the wire rack, so the rounded top is up, and let it cool completely.

6. To serve, turn the bread on its side on a board or a plate and slice into ½-inch rounds. Store any leftover bread in a plastic bag.

Light Touch: Boston brown bread has never had a fat problem, except in those versions that use whole milk in place of buttermilk. This recipe obtains a slim 3 percent of its calories from fat. All the grains provide a healthy amount of vitamins and minerals (including 96 milligrams calcium and 455 milligrams potassium) and 2 grams of dietary fiber per slice.

Nutritional Analysis per serving

194 calories

4 g protein

1 g fat

0.2 g satfat

45 g carbohydrate

382 mg sodium

1 mg cholesterol

Buttermilk
Wheat-Germ Muffins

❖ ◆ ❖

Yield

3 cups batter; twelve 2½-inch muffins

Advance Preparation

Muffins can be baked in advance, wrapped airtight, and frozen. Defrost and warm before serving.

Special Equipment

2½-inch muffin cups

Temperature and Time

400°F for 20 to 25 minutes

*T*his basic all-purpose muffin lends itself to endless variations. Toasted wheat germ provides a nutty flavor as well as a golden color, a slight crunch, and nutritional virtues galore, including dietary fiber, extra protein, and vitamins.

For even greater nutritional enhancement, you can substitute whole wheat pastry flour for half of the all-purpose flour and then replace one or two tablespoons of the all-purpose flour with an equal amount of nonfat dry milk powder. For variety, add ⅓ cup golden or dark raisins, chopped dried apricots, or any other fresh or dried fruit.

◆ ❖ ◆

Butter-flavor no stick cooking spray
1 large egg
¾ cup nonfat buttermilk
¼ cup canola or safflower oil
2 tablespoons honey
1¼ cups unsifted all-purpose flour
¼ cup granulated sugar
2½ teaspoons baking powder
½ teaspoon baking soda
½ teaspoon salt
¼ teaspoon cinnamon
⅓ cup toasted wheat germ
Granulated sugar

1. Position a rack in the center of the oven and preheat it to 400°F. Coat the muffin cups with cooking spray.

2. In a large bowl, whisk together the egg, buttermilk, oil, and honey. Set a strainer over the bowl and add the flour, sugar, baking powder, baking soda, salt, and cinnamon. Stir and sift the dry ingredients onto the egg mixture. Add the wheat germ and stir to blend well.

3. Divide the batter among the prepared muffin cups. Sprinkle a little granulated sugar on top. Bake for 20 to 25 minutes, or until the tops of the muffins are golden and a cake tester inserted in center of a muffin comes out clean. Cool the muffins in the pan on a wire rack for about 5 minutes, then use a fork to gently pry them from the pan. Serve warm.

Light Touch: Anything as virtuous as wheat germ has to have at least one minor drawback. Since the germ is the embryo portion of the wheat kernel, it carries most of its fat as well as the vitamins, minerals, and protein. Although this recipe gets 36 percent calories from fat, each muffin contains only 6 grams of fat, along with 2 grams dietary fiber. For cholesterol-free muffins, substitute 2 large egg whites for the whole egg. In both the cranberry and pineapple variations below, the preserves add calories in the form of carbohydrates but do not add fat. However, the extra ingredients cause calories from fat to fall to 24 percent.

Cape Cod Cranberry Upside-Down Muffins

These delicious and pretty-to-look-at muffins are bejeweled with a burgundy-colored cranberry-raisin glaze. Prepare the preserves first, then mix up the batter.

In a food processor, combine 1½ cups fresh or frozen (unthawed) cranberries and ¼ cup seedless raisins. Pulse to chop coarsely. Transfer to a heavy-bottomed nonreactive saucepan, and stir in ¾ cup dark brown sugar, packed, and ½ teaspoon cinnamon. Place over medium heat and stir until the sugar dissolves. Then cover the pan and cook for 5 minutes longer. Remove from the heat.

Spray the muffin cups well with cooking spray, then place about 1 tablespoon of the cranberry-raisin preserves in each cup. Prepare the muffin batter as directed. Divide the batter among the prepared cups, spooning it on top of the preserves. Bake as directed. Cool the muffins in the pan for 3 to 5 minutes, then cover the muffins with a large tray and invert. Lift off the pan, and serve the muffins warm, cranberry side up.

Pineapple Upside-Down Muffins

Sticky but heavenly, these are a favorite of my family. Put a tablespoon of pineapple preserves in the bottom of each well-oiled muffin cup before adding the batter. Bake as directed, then cover the baked muffins with a tray and invert. Serve the muffins warm, preserves side up.

Nutritional Analysis per blueberry muffin

137 calories

4 g protein

6 g fat

1 g satfat

19 g carbohydrate

213 mg sodium

18 mg cholesterol

Nutritional Analysis per cranberry or pineapple muffin

204 calories

4 g protein

6 g fat

1 g satfat

36 g carbohydrate

218 mg sodium

18 mg cholesterol

Old-Fashioned Blueberry Muffins

◆ ◆ ◆

Yield

3½ cups batter; twelve 2½-inch muffins

Advance Preparation

Muffins can be baked ahead, wrapped airtight, and frozen. Defrost and warm before serving.

Special Equipment

2½-inch muffin cups

Temperature and Time

400°F for 20 minutes; slightly longer with frozen berries

*L*ight-textured, fine-grained, and not too sweet, these fruit-filled muffins are picture perfect and taste as good as they look. This recipe works equally well as a coffee cake baked in an 8 × 8 × 1½-inch pan (25 to 30 minutes at 400°F).

For variety, use any type of fruit or berries. My favorite combinations are half blueberries and half raspberries or cut-up peeled peaches or nectarines. Or try the variations that follow. For extra nutritional value, you can substitute whole wheat pastry flour for half the all-purpose flour and add two tablespoons toasted wheat germ.

◆ ◆ ◆

Butter-flavor no stick cooking spray

1 large egg

½ cup skim or 1% milk

½ cup nonfat plain or vanilla yogurt

3 tablespoons canola or safflower oil

½ cup granulated sugar

2 cups unsifted all-purpose flour

1 tablespoon plus 1 teaspoon baking powder

⅛ teaspoon baking soda

½ teaspoon salt

1½ cups fresh blueberries, picked over, rinsed, and dried gently on paper towels, or frozen unsweetened berries (do not thaw)

Granulated sugar

1. Position a rack in the center of the oven and preheat it to 400°F. Coat the muffin cups with cooking spray.

2. In a large bowl, whisk together the egg, milk, yogurt, oil, and sugar. Set a strainer over the bowl and add the flour, baking powder, baking soda, and salt. Stir and sift the dry ingredients onto the egg mixture, then stir just to blend. Don't overbeat. Stir in the berries.

3. Divide the batter among the prepared muffin cups. Sprinkle a little granulated sugar on top. Bake for about 20 minutes, or until the tops of the muffins are well risen and golden brown, and a cake tester inserted in a muffin comes out clean. Cool the muffins in the pan on a wire rack for about 5 minutes, then use a fork to gently pry them from the pan. Serve warm.

Light Touch: Most blueberry muffins are made with 2 eggs, whole milk, and up to ½ cup melted butter, pushing the total calories from fat to about 41 percent, with about 214 calories, 10 grams fat, 6 grams saturated fat, and 60 milligrams cholesterol per muffin. By using skim milk and yogurt, cutting the amount of fat and replacing it with oil, and reducing the sugar and eggs, I have dropped calories from fat to 23 percent and lost 50 calories, 42 milligrams cholesterol, and 6 grams fat per muffin. To make these cholesterol-free, replace the whole egg with 2 large whites plus 1 tablespoon oil. The Orange-Blueberry variation following has 21 percent calories from fat, the Cranberry-Nut 25 percent calories from fat.

Nutritional Analysis per muffin

163 calories

4 g protein

4 g fat

0.4 g satfat

28 g carbohydrate

227 mg sodium

18 mg cholesterol

Orange-Blueberry Muffins

Prepare the recipe as directed, but add 1 teaspoon orange extract and 1 teaspoon grated orange zest to the liquid ingredients. Orange juice can replace the milk if desired. For the topping, blend 2 tablespoons granulated sugar with 1 teaspoon grated orange zest and sprinkle over the muffins before baking.

Nutritional Analysis per muffin

172 calories

3 g protein

4 g fat

0.4 g satfat

31 g carbohydrate

222 mg sodium

18 mg cholesterol

Cranberry-Nut Muffins

Prepare the recipe as directed, but replace the blueberries with whole or coarsely chopped fresh or frozen (unthawed) cranberries. For the topping, combine 2 tablespoons chopped walnuts, 2 tablespoons granulated sugar, and ¼ teaspoon cinnamon, and sprinkle over the muffins before baking. (The slight increase in fat comes from the addition of walnuts.)

Nutritional Analysis per muffin

175 calories

4 g protein

5 g fat

0.5 g satfat

30 g carbohydrate

226 mg sodium

18 mg cholesterol

Apple Oat Bran Muffins

◆ · ◆ · ◆ ·

G rated apples and cider give moisture and a delightfully sweet, nutty flavor to these super-healthy muffins. Made with whole wheat flour and oat bran, they are full of vitamins, minerals, and fiber, low in fat, and, as an added bonus, are cholesterol- and lactose-free.

· ◆ · ◆ · ◆ ·

Yield

3 cups batter; twelve 2½-inch muffins

Advance Preparation

Muffins can be baked in advance, wrapped airtight, and frozen. Defrost and warm before serving.

Special Equipment

2½-inch muffin cups

Temperature and Time

400°F for 25 to 30 minutes

Butter-flavor no stick cooking spray

1½ Golden Delicious or Granny Smith apples

2 large egg whites

½ cup plus 2 tablespoons apple cider or apple juice

3 tablespoons canola or safflower oil

⅓ cup dark brown sugar, packed

½ cup unsifted all-purpose flour

½ cup unsifted whole wheat pastry flour

2 teaspoons baking powder

½ teaspoon salt

1 teaspoon cinnamon

1 cup oat bran

½ cup seedless raisins

Granulated sugar

1. Position a rack in the center of the oven and preheat it to 400°F. Coat the muffin cups with cooking spray.

2. Peel apples and grate on medium-size holes of box or mandoline grater to make 1½ cups grated apple.

3. In a large bowl, whisk together the egg whites, cider or juice, oil, brown sugar, and apples. Set a strainer over the bowl and add both flours, the baking powder, salt, and cinnamon. Stir and sift the dry ingredients onto the egg mixture. Add the oat bran and raisins and stir well to blend.

4. Divide the batter among the prepared muffin cups. Sprinkle a little granulated sugar over the batter. Bake for about 25 to 30 minutes, or until a cake tester inserted in a muffin comes out clean. Cool the muffins in the pan on a wire rack for about 5 minutes, then gently pry them from the pan with a fork. Serve warm.

Light Touch: During the height of the oat bran craze, recipes for these muffins were as ubiquitous as their life-giving claims. Recipes varied as wildly as the hopes swallowed with each bite. Even if slightly overrated, however, they supplied vitamins, minerals, and fiber, if also, unfortunately, more fat and calories than necessary.

This enlightened version gets 23 percent of its calories from fat. Since I reduced the sugar, I replaced some of the sweetness with the natural sugar of apples and raisins. Because bran is so drying, I use a generous quantity of grated apples plus juice. The first version supplies over 2 grams of dietary fiber per muffin; the all-bran variation below has 27 percent calories from fat and 3 grams fiber per muffin.

All Oat Bran Muffins

Prepare the recipe as directed, with the following changes: Omit the flour and use a total of 2 cups oat bran. Increase the amount of cider or juice to ¾ cup and use only 1 cup grated apples. Combine the oat bran with the egg white mixture in step 2, then sift in the remaining dry ingredients.

Nutritional Analysis per muffin

145 calories

3 g protein

4 g fat

0.4 g satfat

27 g carbohydrate

156 mg sodium

0 mg cholesterol

Nutritional Analysis per muffin

126 calories

4 g protein

5 g fat

0.5 g satfat

25 g carbohydrate

156 mg sodium

0 mg cholesterol

Bran-Raisin-
Apricot Muffins

◆ ‧ ◆ ‧ ◆

*M*ade with whole wheat and all-bran cereal (not to be confused with wheat bran), these hearty muffins are surprisingly light-textured, sweetened moderately with honey and molasses, and brightened by the contrasting tastes of raisins and dried apricots.

◆ ‧ ◆ ‧ ◆

Yield

Scant 4 cups batter; fourteen 2½-inch muffins

Advance Preparation

Muffins can be baked in advance, wrapped airtight, and frozen. Defrost and warm before serving.

Special Equipment

2½-inch muffin cups

Temperature and Time

400°F for 20 to 25 minutes

Butter-flavor no stick cooking spray
1½ cups shredded 100% all-bran cereal
1¼ cups low-fat buttermilk
1 large egg
3 tablespoons canola or safflower oil
¼ cup honey
2 tablespoons unsulfured molasses
¾ cup unsifted all-purpose flour
½ cup unsifted whole wheat pastry flour
2 teaspoons baking powder
¾ teaspoon baking soda
⅛ teaspoon salt
½ cup seedless raisins
½ cup dried apricots, coarsely cut up into ¼-inch pieces
Granulated sugar

1. Position a rack in the center of the oven and preheat it to 400°F. Coat the muffin cups with cooking spray.

2. In a small bowl, combine the bran and buttermilk and set them aside to soak for about 5 minutes.

3. In a large bowl, whisk together the egg, oil, honey, and molasses. Set a strainer over the bowl and add both flours, the baking powder, baking soda, and salt. Stir and sift the dry ingredients onto the egg mixture. Stir just to blend, then stir in the raisins, apricots, and soaked bran.

Have Your Cake and Eat It, Too

4. Divide the batter among the prepared muffin cups. Sprinkle a little sugar on top of each muffin. Bake for about 20 minutes, or until the tops are well risen and a cake tester inserted in a muffin comes out clean. Cool the muffins in the pans on wire racks for about 5 minutes, then use a fork to gently pry them from the pans. Serve warm.

Light Touch: For years, I have been tinkering with Kellogg's back-of-the-box recipe for 100% All-Bran Muffins. This is my reduced-fat, energized version, substituting buttermilk for whole milk and adding whole wheat flour, molasses, and honey. Classic bran muffins contain about 35 percent calories from fat and 6 grams of fat each; my lightened recipe obtains only 22 percent of its total calories from fat, and each muffin contains just 4 grams of fat, yet offers 55 milligrams of calcium, 307 milligrams of potassium, and over 4 grams of dietary fiber. If you prefer to eliminate the cholesterol, substitute 2 large egg whites for the whole egg.

*Nutritional Analysis
per muffin*

154 calories

4 g protein

4 g fat

0.4 g satfat

30 g carbohydrate

243 mg sodium

16 mg cholesterol

Vermont Maple-Apple Muffins

◆ ‧ ◆ ‧ ◆ ‧

You can see the maple trees blazing burgundy and crimson against the cobalt sky of an autumn Vermont morning when you smell these muffins baking. Maple, apple, walnuts, cinnamon, oats, cider . . . all the perfume of fall in farm country, and the taste is as vivid as the image it conjures.

I devised this recipe at our summer home in Vermont's Northeast Kingdom one day late last August after our friend and neighbor Sonny Sweatt arrived at the door and literally handed me the shirt off his back. Smiling and tan, he laughed as he presented me with a work shirt cradling a huge mound of apples he had just picked for me. He knew I liked to bake, and thought these apples were the best. When I asked Sonny if he had used some of the apples himself, he shyly admitted that he had recently baked twenty-three apple pies, plus a few pumpkin and lemon, in one evening just to keep his building crew content during the starting week of construction on a new log cabin. My own baking marathon was not nearly as ambitious, but I had enough apples for a pie as well as applesauce, apple butter, and several batches of apple muffins.

Since I had so many apples, I began by creating a totally fat-free recipe substituting freshly made apple butter for vegetable oil. I thought this would be an improvement on a similar recipe in which I had replaced oil with prune purée. It was not. Both were a disappointment; without any fat you achieve a tough, chewy outer crust and a soggy, rubbery interior texture. After several trials, I conceded yet again that low-fat is better than no-fat.

This recipe works equally well as a coffee cake, baked in an 8 × 12-inch baking pan (25 minutes at 350°F).

◆ ‧ ◆ ‧ ◆ ‧

Yield

4 cups batter; twelve 2½-inch muffins

Advance Preparation

These muffins keep well for several days because the fruit keeps them moist. Wrapped airtight, they can be frozen. Serve warm.

Special Equipment

2½-inch muffin cups

Temperature and Time

350°F for 22 to 25 minutes

Butter-flavor no stick cooking spray

3 tablespoons canola or safflower oil

1 large egg plus 1 large egg white

¼ cup pure maple syrup

½ cup unsweetened applesauce

½ cup apple cider or apple juice *or skim milk*

½ cup dark brown sugar, packed

½ teaspoon maple or vanilla extract (optional)

1 medium tart apple, peeled, cored, and finely diced (about 1 cup)

½ cup seedless raisins

1 cup old-fashioned rolled oats

¾ cup plus 2 tablespoons unsifted all-purpose flour

½ cup unsifted whole wheat pastry flour

2 teaspoons baking powder

½ teaspoon baking soda

½ teaspoon salt

2 teaspoons cinnamon

Topping

2 tablespoons granulated sugar

2 tablespoons chopped walnuts

½ teaspoon cinnamon

*Nutritional Analysis
per muffin*

217 calories

4 g protein

5 g fat

0.5 g satfat

40 g carbohydrate

199 mg sodium

18 mg cholesterol

1. Position a rack in the center of the oven and preheat it to 350°F. Coat the muffin cups with cooking spray.

2. In a large bowl, combine the oil, egg and egg white, maple syrup, applesauce, cider or apple juice, brown sugar, extract, chopped apple, and raisins. Beat well with a wooden spoon, then stir in the oats.

3. Set a strainer over the bowl, and add both flours, baking powder, baking soda, the salt, and cinnamon. Using the back of a spoon, stir and sift the dry ingredients onto the egg mixture. Stir well to blend.

4. Divide the batter among the muffin cups. Combine the granulated sugar, walnuts, and cinnamon and sprinkle over the muffins. Bake for about 25 minutes, or until the tops of the muffins are well risen and crisp and a cake tester inserted in a muffin comes out clean. Cool in the pan on a rack for a few minutes, then use a fork to lift out the muffins and cool completely on the rack. Serve warm.

Light Touch: This recipe obtains only 21 percent of its calories from fat, and it packs a tremendous amount of flavor and nutrition. The whole wheat flour, apple, applesauce, raisins, and oats all contribute vitamins and minerals, as well as 2 grams of dietary fiber per serving. The applesauce replaces part of the fat in the traditional recipe, leaving only the few tablespoons of oil needed for flavor and texture. The cinnamon-nut mixture makes a crisp, crunchy topping, but the nuts add about 15 calories and 0.75 gram of fat per serving; omit them if you wish. To eliminate all cholesterol, substitute 2 egg whites for the egg plus white.

Biscuits, Scones, Muffins, and Popovers   **113**

Pumpkin Bran Muffins

◆ · ◆ · ◆ ·

I developed these muffins on assignment from Best Foods, the makers of Karo syrup. We were looking for good taste and texture while replacing all the fat with corn syrup. The muffins have a slightly chewy crust, a soft, moist crumb, and a lightly spiced flavor. Egg whites are stiffly whipped and folded into the batter to lighten it. Raisins add sweetness and textural contrast, as does the sugar-glazed crusty topping.

◆ · ◆ · ◆ ·

Yield

4 cups batter; fourteen 2½-inch muffins

Advance Preparation

Muffins can be baked in advance, wrapped airtight, and frozen. Defrost and warm before serving.

Special Equipment

2½-inch muffin cups

Temperature and Time

400°F for 20 to 25 minutes

Butter-flavor no stick cooking spray

1 cup unsweetened pumpkin purée (canned or fresh)

1 cup 100% Bran cereal

¾ cup nonfat buttermilk

⅓ cup dark or light corn syrup

⅓ cup dark brown sugar, packed

1¼ cups unsifted cake flour

2 teaspoons baking powder

½ teaspoon baking soda

½ teaspoon salt

1 teaspoon cinnamon

¼ teaspoon ground cloves

¼ teaspoon ground ginger

2 large egg whites, at room temperature

3 tablespoons granulated sugar

1 cup seedless raisins

Topping

2 tablespoons granulated sugar

¼ teaspoon cinnamon

1. Position a rack in the center of the oven and preheat it to 400°F. Coat the muffin pans with cooking spray.

2. In a large bowl, whisk together the pumpkin purée, bran, buttermilk, corn syrup, and brown sugar. Set a strainer over the bowl and add the flour, baking powder, baking soda, salt, and spices. Set aside while you beat the egg whites.

3. In a grease-free bowl, using an electric mixer, whip the egg whites until foamy. Slowly add the sugar and continue whipping until the whites are stiff but not dry.

4. Stir and sift the dry ingredients onto the pumpkin mixture, and stir just to blend. Add the raisins. Add about one quarter of the beaten whites to the batter to lighten it, and gently stir. Fold in the remaining whites.

5. Divide the batter among the prepared cups. Combine the sugar and cinnamon and sprinkle on top of the batter. Bake for 20 to 25 minutes, or until the muffins are well risen, the tops feel springy to the touch, and a cake tester inserted in the center of a muffin comes out clean. Cool the muffins in the pans on a wire rack for about 5 minutes, then use a fork to pry them gently from the pans. Serve warm.

Light Touch: Because these muffins lack added fat, the outside crust is chewier and slightly tougher and the inside a little less tender than muffins made with even a small amount of oil. Nevertheless, these won high praise from my testers, and their nutritional value is worth noting: They get less than 3 percent of their calories from fat, yet supply many vitamins and minerals, and each muffin contains 3 grams of dietary fiber.

Nutritional Analysis
per muffin
....

153 calories

3 g protein

0.5 g fat

0.1 g satfat

37 g carbohydrate

215 mg sodium

0 mg cholesterol

Carrot-Currant Muffins

· ◆ · ◆ · ◆ ·

I was in the process of adapting my favorite carrot cake to a recipe for reduced-fat muffins when I came upon a similar idea developed by Barbara Albright for Chocolatier magazine (December 1990). The recipe following is my own version, with a nod to Barbara. The results are neither too sweet nor overly dense in texture, and highly flavorful.

The muffins are made with egg whites and thus are cholesterol-free; moisture, sweetness, and texture are provided by the carrots, pineapple, and currants.

· ◆ · ◆ · ◆ ·

Yield

About 3 cups batter; twelve 2½-inch muffins

Advance Preparation

Muffins can be baked in advance, wrapped airtight, and frozen. Defrost and warm before serving.

Special Equipment

2½-inch muffin cups

Temperature and Time

400°F for 20 minutes

Butter-flavor no stick cooking spray

2 large egg whites, at room temperature

½ cup nonfat plain yogurt

3 tablespoons canola or safflower oil

½ cup dark brown sugar, packed

2 teaspoons vanilla extract

1 cup unsifted all-purpose flour

½ cup plus 2 tablespoons unsifted whole wheat pastry flour

1¼ teaspoons baking powder

½ teaspoon baking soda

Generous ¼ teaspoon salt

1 teaspoon cinnamon

½ teaspoon nutmeg

2 tablespoons toasted wheat germ

1 cup grated or shredded carrots, lightly packed (about 2 carrots, peeled and grated on medium-sized holes of a box or mandoline grater)

¾ cup drained sweetened crushed pineapple

½ cup dried currants

Granulated sugar

1. Position a rack in the center of the oven and preheat it to 400°F. Coat the muffin cups with cooking spray.

2. In a large bowl, whisk together the egg whites, yogurt, oil, brown sugar, and vanilla. Set a strainer over the bowl and add both flours, the baking powder, baking soda, salt, and spices. Stir and sift the dry ingredients onto the yogurt mixture. Blend lightly. Add the wheat germ, carrots, pineapple, and currants and stir to blend well.

3. Divide the batter among the prepared muffin cups. Sprinkle a little granulated sugar over the batter. Bake for about 20 minutes, or until a cake tester inserted in a muffin comes out clean. Cool the muffins in the pan on a wire rack for about 5 minutes, then use a fork to remove them from the pan. Serve warm.

Light Touch: My classic carrot cake recipe obtains 56 percent of its calories from fat. By contrast, this lightened version gets only 20 percent of its calories from fat. I cut out the egg yolks and replaced the granulated sugar with a smaller amount of moist brown sugar. For better nutritional value, I added wheat germ and replaced some of the all-purpose flour with whole wheat, to give over 2 grams of dietary fiber per muffin. If you prefer, the Carrot-Banana variation below gets 23 percent of its calories from fat.

Carrot-Banana Muffins

Prepare the recipe as directed but replace the 2 egg whites with 1 whole large egg, replace the pineapple with 1 cup mashed ripe bananas (2 medium bananas), and use light brown sugar instead of dark. For a crunchy topping, blend 2 tablespoons finely chopped walnuts with 1 tablespoon granulated sugar and sprinkle it over the muffins before baking.

Nutritional Analysis per muffin

172 calories

4 g protein

4 g fat

0.4 g satfat

31 g carbohydrate

136 mg sodium

0 mg cholesterol

Nutritional Analysis per muffin

195 calories

4 g protein

5 g fat

1 g satfat

35 mg carbohydrate

132 mg sodium

18 mg cholesterol

Fabulous Five-Week
Fiber Muffins

◆ ◆ ◆

*T*his is a streamlined version of a highly nutritious 1940s favorite, the Five-Week Refrigerator Bran Muffin. The idea is to whip up a big batch of raisin-bran muffin batter and refrigerate it, then simply scoop out some batter whenever you feel like baking a muffin or two. My original recipe came from friend and fellow baker Lauren Lieberman. I agree with her that it is a great concept, although I have tinkered with the formula. In addition to cutting back on fat, I have changed the original all-bran formula to a more interesting and even healthier combination of bran, oats, wheat germ, and whole wheat flour. These muffins are high in vitamins and minerals as well as fiber and flavor. They taste great and the batter really *does* keep for five weeks without waving at you from the refrigerator shelf. It is a luxury to be able to have a freshly baked muffin on a whim.

For added nutritional value, with a slight change in taste and texture, you can substitute soy flour or quinoa flour for ½ cup of the all-purpose flour. You can also add some chopped walnuts, sunflower seeds, or chopped dried apricots along with the raisins.

◆ ◆ ◆

Yield

6 cups batter; eighteen 2½-inch muffins

Advance Preparation

Batter can be prepared in advance and refrigerated, covered, for up to 5 weeks. Dip in and bake a fresh muffin whenever you wish. Baked muffins can be wrapped airtight and frozen. Defrost and warm before serving.

Special Equipment

2½-inch muffin cups

Temperature and Time

350°F for 20 to 25 minutes

Butter-flavor no stick cooking spray

1 cup boiling water

2 cups All-Bran Cereal or 100% Bran cereal

¾ cup granulated sugar

¼ cup canola or safflower oil

1 large egg plus 1 large egg white

¾ cup old-fashioned rolled oats

¼ cup toasted wheat germ

1½ cups unsifted all-purpose flour

1 cup unsifted whole wheat pastry flour

2½ teaspoons baking soda

½ teaspoon salt

¾ teaspoon cinnamon

2 cups low-fat buttermilk

¾ cup seedless raisins

Granulated sugar

1. Position a rack in the center of the oven and preheat it to 350°F. Coat the muffin cups with cooking spray.

2. In a small bowl, pour the boiling water over the bran cereal. Stir, and set aside until cool (about 10 minutes).

3. In a large bowl, whisk together the sugar, oil, and egg and egg white. Add all the dry ingredients and the buttermilk and stir well to blend. Beat in the soaked bran and the raisins.

4. Cover the bowl and refrigerate until ready to bake, up to 5 weeks.

5. To bake, scoop out the batter, without stirring, and pour it into the prepared muffin cups. Sprinkle a little sugar on top. Bake for 20 to 25 minutes, or until the muffins are springy to the touch and lightly browned, and a cake tester inserted in the center comes out clean.

Light Touch: Although low in cholesterol and calories, of which only 22 percent come from fat, each of these tasty muffins contains 51 milligrams calcium, 284 milligrams potassium, and a whopping 5 grams of dietary fiber—that's a good way to start a day.

The original recipe used about ½ cup solid shortening, between 1 and 1½ cups sugar, 2 whole eggs, and all white flour. To cut fat and cholesterol without losing flavor, I halved the solid fat and substituted canola oil, removed 1 egg yolk, reduced the sugar, and added whole wheat flour plus a variety of grains.

Nutritional Analysis
per muffin
....
168 calories

6 g protein

4 g fat

0.6 g satfat

30 g carbohydrate

317 mg sodium

13 mg cholesterol

Double Corn Muffins

◆ ◆ ◆

*I*f you like classic corn muffins, you will like these twice as much! The addition of canned cream-style corn adds extra corn flavor, moisture, and texture. For this secret, I am indebted to Lil Thompson, who bakes delectable giant muffins each morning to sell in the general store in the village of Bridgewater, Connecticut. For a sweeter breakfast muffin, you can increase the sugar to a quarter cup and omit the cayenne pepper.

A colorful and spicy variation, Santa Fe Green Chile and Cheese Muffins, follows.

To make corn bread instead of muffins, pour the batter into an oiled 8-inch square pan and bake for 20 to 25 minutes. Or, use a cast-iron corn stick mold, which shapes "ears," or corn sticks. My antique mold contains seven ears, each holding ¼ cup of batter, and the corn sticks bake in about 12 to 15 minutes. If you use a different size baking pan, adjust the baking time accordingly.

◆ ◆ ◆

Yield

3 cups batter; twelve 2½-inch muffins

Advance Preparation

Muffins can be baked in advance, wrapped airtight, and frozen. Defrost and warm, or split and toast, before serving.

Special Equipment

2½-inch muffin cups

Temperature and Time

400°F for 20 to 25 minutes

Butter-flavor no stick cooking spray
1 large egg
¾ cup skim milk
¼ cup canola oil
½ cup canned low-sodium cream-style corn
3 tablespoons granulated sugar
1 cup plus 3 tablespoons unsifted all-purpose flour
2 teaspoons baking powder
½ teaspoon salt
⅛ teaspoon cayenne pepper
1 cup yellow cornmeal

1. Position a rack in the center of the oven and preheat it to 400°F. Coat the muffin cups with cooking spray.

2. In a large bowl, whisk together the egg, milk, oil, canned corn, and sugar. Set a strainer over the mixing bowl and add the flour, baking powder, salt, and cayenne. Stir and sift the dry ingredients onto the egg mixture. Add the cornmeal and stir well to blend.

3. Divide the batter among the prepared muffin cups. Bake for about 20 to 25 minutes, or until the muffins are golden and well risen and a cake tester inserted in a muffin comes out clean. Cool the muffins in the pan on a wire rack for about 5 minutes, then use a fork to gently pry them from the pan. Serve warm.

Light Touch: Plain corn muffins have never ranked among the high-fat items, but once you enrich them with creamed corn to add moisture, the numbers begin to add up quickly. I began by transforming my original basic corn bread recipe, which includes wheat germ, into a moist double-corn version by adding ½ cup frozen corn kernels, chopped and blended with ¼ cup heavy cream. The result was a recipe with 38 percent of the total calories from fat, and 183 calories and 8 grams of fat per muffin. To lighten this to 30 percent calories from fat, cutting 24 calories and 3 grams of fat per muffin, I replaced heavy cream with canned cream-style corn and skim milk, cut back on oil, and dropped the wheat germ. In the following variation, the addition of cheese pushes the calories from fat to 31 percent, and the calories to 180 per muffin but only raises the fat in each by 1 gram.

Santa Fe Green Chile and Cheese Muffins

Prepare the recipe as directed but reduce the sugar to 1½ tablespoons and add 3 ounces grated sharp low-fat Cheddar cheese (about ¾ cup grated); ¼ cup chopped canned mild green chilies; 2 tablespoons minced red bell pepper; 3 tablespoons finely chopped pitted black olives; 3 tablespoons hot chunky salsa; and 2 tablespoons chopped fresh cilantro or 1 teaspoon dried. If you like them hot, add another ⅛ teaspoon cayenne pepper.

Nutritional Analysis per muffin

159 calories

3 g protein

5 g fat

0.5 g satfat

24 mg carbohydrate

158 mg sodium

18 mg cholesterol

Nutritional Analysis per muffin

180 calories

6 g protein

6 g fat

0.5 g satfat

25 g carbohydrate

223 mg sodium

20 mg cholesterol

Coffee Cakes
and
Quick Breads

Warm, welcoming, easy-to-make coffee cakes are just "muffins-in-a-pan," as my daughter once observed. She was about six at the time, helping me prepare Sunday breakfast. Is there anything more appealing on a lazy Sunday morning, to adult or child, than the fragrance of a hot, just-baked cake filled with fruit, topped with sugar-crackled glaze or a tumble of crisp crumbs?

While it requires only minutes to throw the ingredients together, coffee cakes and quick breads always look inviting. They are perfect for bringing people together, whether for a family breakfast, a coffee klatch, or an office meeting. They are simple and portable (take them to a bake sale or picnic), they freeze well, and all the ones in this book are both nutritious and low in fat.

Compared to those made from traditional recipes, the nutritional content of these coffee cakes and quick breads has been significantly enhanced. I have added lots of fruit, as well as whole wheat pastry flour and/or wheat germ. Vegetable oil stands in for butter, and flavors are accented with spices and citrus zest. When nuts are included in a recipe, they are used in small amounts in a topping, to give greatest "taste visibility" and texture. To save calories and fat, none of these cakes needs icing on top, although a dusting of sugar may be appropriate in some cases.

There is a wide variety of recipes here, but I think of four of them as basic, all-purpose coffee cakes, utterly reliable formulas you can personalize by varying the type of fruit: Orange Yogurt Crumb Cake, Whole Wheat Blueberry Kuchen, Everyone's Favorite Coffee Cake (my personal favorite), and Nectarine-Raspberry Coffee Cake. For a family dessert, a coffee klatch, or a picnic, serve Hungarian Plum Cake or its apple variation, or Chopped Apple Cake, or Cocoa-Prune Cake, cut into squares. For holiday gift-giving, or just to accompany a quiet afternoon pot of tea, try extra-moist, fruit-filled Applesauce Cake, Pineapple-Banana Cake, Florida Orange Kiss-Me Cake, or Cinnamon-Cider-Cranberry Cake. Poppy Seed Lemon Cake has a strong fruit flavor complemented by the sweetness of the poppy seeds; bake small loaves for gifts. And four quick breads are favorites for brunch or luncheon buffets and Thanksgiving groaning boards: Spicy Apple Corn Bread, Blueberry Gingerbread, Carrot-Rosemary Bread, and Irish Soda Bread (special for Saint Patrick's Day).

Orange Yogurt Crumb Cake

❖ · ❖ · ❖

This is my idea of a farmhouse coffee cake. It has a moist orange-flavored crumb with a nutty topping baked right in . . . just the thing to dunk into a steaming mug of coffee on a crisp fall morning. You can vary the flavor of the cake by changing the type of yogurt—try raspberry or apricot. The recipe calls for a blend of white and whole wheat pastry flour, but you can use all white flour.

❖ · ❖ · ❖

Butter-flavor no stick cooking spray

Crumb Topping

3 tablespoons unsifted all-purpose flour

3 tablespoons granulated sugar

2 tablespoons finely chopped walnuts

Pinch of salt

½ teaspoon cinnamon

¼ teaspoon nutmeg

2 teaspoons unsalted butter, at room temperature

1 teaspoon hazelnut or canola oil

1½ to 2 teaspoons orange juice or water, as needed

Cake

2 large egg whites

2 tablespoons canola or safflower oil

2 tablespoons honey

2 tablespoons orange juice

¾ cup granulated sugar

1 teaspoon vanilla extract

1 teaspoon orange extract

Grated zest of 1 orange

1 8-ounce container low-fat orange or lemon yogurt

1 cup plus 2 tablespoons unsifted all-purpose flour

½ cup unsifted whole wheat pastry flour

1¾ teaspoons baking powder

¼ teaspoon baking soda

½ teaspoon salt

(continued)

Yield

2⅔ cups batter; one 8-inch or 9-inch square cake; 12 servings

Advance Preparation

Cake can be kept covered at room temperature for several days or wrapped airtight and frozen.

Special Equipment

8 × 8 × 1½-inch or 9 × 1½-inch baking pan

Temperature and Time

350°F for 35 to 40 minutes

191 calories

4 g protein

5 g fat

0.8 g satfat

35 g carbohydrate

175 mg sodium

3 mg cholesterol

1. Position a rack in the center of the oven and preheat it to 350°F. Coat the baking pan with cooking spray.

2. Prepare the crumb topping: In a medium bowl, toss together the flour, sugar, nuts, salt, and spices. Add the butter and pinch the mixture together with your fingers until crumbly. Add the oil and toss with a fork. Add 1½ teaspoons of the juice or water and mix with the fork until small crumbs form, adding ½ teaspoon more liquid if necessary. Set aside.

3. In a large bowl, combine the egg whites, oil, honey, orange juice, sugar, both extracts, the zest, and yogurt, and whisk or beat to blend well. Set a strainer over the bowl and add both flours, the baking powder, baking soda, and salt. Stir and sift the dry ingredients onto the yogurt mixture. Beat just to blend well.

4. Turn the batter into the prepared pan. Sprinkle the crumbs evenly over the top. Bake for about 35 minutes, or until the cake is golden brown on top and a cake tester inserted in the center comes out clean. Cool for 5 minutes in the pan on a wire rack. Cut the cake into squares, and serve warm.

Light Touch: Because this cake has real substance, I find that it amply serves 12, but even if you cut it into only 9 pieces, you will have just 6 grams of fat per serving.

I modeled this cake on an old family favorite made with 1 whole egg, 6 tablespoons butter, some wheat germ, and 2 cups rich walnut-streusel crumbs, half of which went inside the batter and half on top. This cake obtained a relatively sober 31 percent of its calories from fat, but the butter, nuts, and egg contributed 10 grams of fat (4 of them saturated), plus 34 milligrams of cholesterol and 296 calories, to each serving. I shaved the total calories from fat to 21 percent, dropped 100 calories and half the fat from each serving, and eliminated nearly all the cholesterol by replacing the butter with a small amount of oil and cutting out the egg yolk and wheat germ. The trick for accenting the flavor and increasing the moisture is to use fruit-flavored yogurt (stir the container if fruit is on the bottom) with a little honey. To whittle down the fat contributed by the crumbs, I cut the amount in half and removed most of the nuts. Then, to bolster the nut flavor, I used hazelnut oil; ½ teaspoon almond extract can be substituted.

Whole Wheat
Blueberry Kuchen

❖ ❖ ❖

This simple kuchen will remind you of blueberry muffins, and it is even easier to prepare. Made with whole wheat pastry flour and wheat germ, it is light-textured, fine-grained, and not too sweet. You can use whatever berries are available—blackberries or raspberries, for example. For the best texture, beat the batter as little as possible, and do not use a mixer.

❖ ❖ ❖

Butter-flavor no stick cooking spray

1 large egg

½ cup skim milk

3 tablespoons canola or safflower oil

½ cup nonfat plain or vanilla yogurt

1 cup unsifted all-purpose flour

1 cup unsifted whole wheat pastry flour

3 tablespoons toasted wheat germ

1 tablespoon plus 1 teaspoon baking powder

⅛ teaspoon baking soda

½ teaspoon salt

½ cup granulated sugar

1½ cups fresh blueberries, picked over, rinsed, and gently dried on paper towels, or frozen (unthawed) whole unsweetened berries

Topping

3 tablespoons granulated sugar

¼ teaspoon cinnamon

2 tablespoons finely chopped walnuts (optional)

1. Position a rack in the center of the oven, and preheat it to 400°F. Coat the baking pan with cooking spray.

2. In a large bowl, combine the egg, milk, oil, and yogurt. Whisk to blend. Set a strainer on top of the bowl and add all the dry ingredients. With a spoon, stir and sift them onto the liquid mixture. Stir just

(continued)

Yield

3½ cups batter; one 8-inch or 9-inch square cake; 9 servings

Advance Preparation

Cake is best fresh from the oven, but can be prepared a day or two in advance and kept covered at room temperature. It can be wrapped airtight and frozen. Warm before serving.

Special Equipment

8 × 8 × 2-inch or 9 × 9 × 2-inch baking pan

Temperature and Time

400°F for 20 to 25 minutes with fresh fruit, 40 to 45 minutes with frozen fruit

to blend; do not overbeat. Stir in the berries. Turn the batter into the prepared pan.

3. To prepare the topping, stir the sugar, cinnamon, and nuts together. Sprinkle on top of the batter. Bake for 20 to 25 minutes, or until the cake is golden brown and a cake tester inserted in the center comes out clean. Cool on a wire rack. Cut into squares and serve warm, or slice the squares crosswise in half and toast before serving.

Light Touch: This cake gets just 24 percent of its calories from fat; if you omit the nuts you drop 1 gram of fat per serving. If you prefer the cake cholesterol-free, replace the egg with 2 large egg whites plus 1 tablespoon oil. The presence of whole wheat flour and wheat germ boosts dietary fiber to 4 grams per serving.

Nectarine-Raspberry Coffee Cake

◆ ◆ ◆

This moist coffee cake has an attractive topping of nectarine slices and red berries glazed with crunchy sugared pecans. A springform pan is used so the cake can be unmolded easily; if inverted, some of the topping might fall off. I thank Eating Well magazine's test kitchen staff for working with me to develop this recipe.

◆ ◆ ◆

Butter-flavor no stick cooking spray

1 large egg

1 cup nonfat buttermilk

3 tablespoons canola or safflower oil

1 teaspoon vanilla extract

1½ cups unsifted all-purpose flour

½ cup unsifted whole wheat pastry flour

1 tablespoon plus 1 teaspoon baking powder

½ teaspoon salt

1 teaspoon cinnamon

¾ cup granulated sugar

Nutritional Analysis per serving (with optional nuts in topping)

248 calories

7 g protein

7 g fat

0.8 g satfat

42 g carbohydrate

303 mg sodium

24 mg cholesterol

Yield

One 9-inch cake; 10 servings

Advance Preparation

Cake can be baked in advance and kept covered at room temperature for a day or two, but it is best served warm from the oven.

Special Equipment

9-inch springform pan

Temperature and Time

400°F for 40 to 45 minutes

Fruit Topping

    2 nectarines, pitted but unpeeled, cut into ⅛-inch-thick slices (1 cup)

    ½ cup fresh raspberries, or frozen unsweetened whole raspberries

    ¼ cup Grape-Nuts cereal

    3 tablespoons granulated sugar

    2 tablespoons chopped pecans

    ¼ teaspoon cinnamon

Nutritional Analysis per serving

248 calories

5 g protein

6 g fat

0.5 g satfat

45 g carbohydrate

290 mg sodium

21 mg cholesterol

1. Position a rack in the center of the oven and preheat it to 400°F. Coat the springform pan with cooking spray.

2. In a large bowl, whisk together the egg, buttermilk, oil, and vanilla. Set a strainer over the bowl and add both flours, the baking powder, salt, cinnamon, and sugar. Stir and sift the dry ingredients onto the egg mixture. Whisk to blend well. Turn the batter into the prepared pan.

3. To prepare the topping, place the nectarine slices and raspberries on the batter, either scattering them randomly or arranging them in a decorative pattern. Toss together the Grape-Nuts cereal, sugar, pecans, and cinnamon in a small bowl. Sprinkle over the fruit.

4. Bake the cake for 40 to 45 minutes, or until the top of the cake is golden and a cake tester inserted in the center comes out clean. Let the cake cool in the pan on a wire rack for about 10 minutes. Remove the pan sides, leaving the cake on the metal pan bottom. Serve warm.

Light Touch: This rich-tasting cake obtains only 21 percent of its calories from fat. Buttermilk rather than rich sour cream gives flavor as well as moisture and tenderness to the crumb. A small amount of oil blends with the egg to contribute just enough fat to keep the proper texture. The small amount of nuts actually seems like more because they are used in the topping, where they toast during baking to exaggerate their flavor. With the fruit, cereal, nuts, and whole wheat flour, each serving has a little over 2 grams of dietary fiber.

Everyone's Favorite Coffee Cake

❖ · ❖ · ❖ ·

This cake is just the thing for a midsummer brunch. Simply "sugar-up" fresh, ripe berries and top them with a light almond-scented batter. Each bite bursts with flavor and the romance of a berry batch on a country hillside under the hot August sun.

Use whatever combination of berries and/or fruits are available (blueberries and fresh or frozen cranberries, or berries and peach slices, for example). If you use margarine instead of butter in the crumb topping, the cake contains no dairy products, so it is suitable for lactose-intolerant diets.

❖ · ❖ · ❖ ·

Yield

1½ cups batter plus 2 cups fruit; one 10-inch cake (or 8- or 9-inch cake); 10 servings

Advance Preparation

Cake is best fresh from the oven, but it keeps a day or two, covered, at room temperature. Warm before serving.

Special Equipment

10-inch pie plate (or 8- or 9-inch square pan)

Temperature and Time

350°F for 35 to 40 minutes for fresh fruit, 50 minutes for frozen fruit

Butter-flavor no stick cooking spray

1 cup fresh raspberries (or frozen unsweetened whole raspberries)

1 cup fresh blueberries, picked over, rinsed, and patted dry (or frozen unsweetened whole blueberries)

5 tablespoons plus ½ cup granulated sugar, divided

¼ teaspoon cinnamon

2 large egg whites

¼ cup canola or safflower oil

¼ cup unsweetened applesauce

¼ cup apple or orange juice

1 teaspoon almond or orange extract

1 cup unsifted cake flour

1 teaspoon baking powder

½ teaspoon salt

¼ cup toasted wheat germ (optional)

Crumb Topping (optional)

2 tablespoons unsifted cake flour

2 tablespoons granulated sugar

3 tablespoons Grape-Nuts cereal

½ teaspoon cinnamon

2 teaspoons unsalted butter or margarine

1 teaspoon canola oil

1 teaspoon apple or orange juice, or as needed

1. Position a rack in the center of the oven and preheat it to 350°F. Coat the pie plate with cooking spray.

2. Combine the fruit, 5 tablespoons of the sugar, and the cinnamon in the oiled pie plate, and toss together lightly. Set aside.

3. In a large bowl, whisk together the egg whites, the remaining ½ cup sugar, oil, applesauce, juice, and extract. Place a strainer over the bowl and add the flour, baking powder, and salt. Stir and sift the dry ingredients onto the applesauce mixture. Add the wheat germ if using it. Beat the dry ingredients into the wet just to blend; do not overbeat.

4. To make the optional topping, combine the dry ingredients in a small bowl. Add the butter, and use your fingertips to pinch the ingredients together. Add the oil and juice and toss with a fork until crumbly, adding a few more drops of juice if needed.

5. Pour the batter over the fruit in the pan; don't worry if some fruit peeks through. Sprinkle the crumb topping, if using, over the cake. Bake for 35 to 40 minutes, or until the top of the cake is golden brown and springy to the touch and a cake tester inserted in the center of the cake comes out clean. Cool the cake slightly on a wire rack, then cut and serve warm.

Light Touch: I used to make this cake with 2 whole eggs, 1½ cups sugar, ¾ cup melted butter, and ½ cup walnuts; with 58 percent of the total calories from fat, each slice contained 20 grams of fat. Now I find I really prefer my enlightened version, with about half the calories from fat (28 percent) and just a tad of cholesterol (only in the topping). To eliminate cholesterol entirely, make the topping with margarine instead of butter. To achieve the fat reduction, I dropped the nuts in the cake, replacing their texture with the crunchy cereal topping, and eliminated the butter in the cake, replacing it with oil plus some applesauce. The applesauce adds moisture and flavor but weights the crumb slightly. If you prefer a lighter texture, omit the applesauce and use ⅓ cup canola oil (bringing calories from fat up to 34 percent).

This version has become my mother's favorite, and I include it here at her request so we will always know where to find the recipe (out of the shoebox at last). Although it is optional, I do like to add ¼ cup toasted wheat germ; per serving, it adds about 13 calories and 0.4 gram of fat, but it boosts dietary fiber by 1.2 gram per serving. Occasionally, I replace the Grape-Nuts in the topping with 2 tablespoons chopped walnuts to add flavor (as well as 10 calories and 1 gram fat per serving).

Nutritional Analysis per serving (without optional wheat germ but with crumb topping)

206 calories

3 g protein

7 g fat

1 g satfat

36 g carbohydrate

167 mg sodium

2 mg cholesterol

Prune Cake

◆ ◆ ◆

*I*f you like prunes, you will love this fruit-filled cake made with both
prune purée and chopped prunes. The texture is fairly dense, with a
good balance between the sweetness of the prunes and the light blend of
spices. Granulated sugar makes a crackled glaze topping. Serve this with
a spoonful of vanilla yogurt.

As you enjoy the cake, pause a moment to pity the prune, so
maligned and misunderstood. Say the word prune, especially to someone
under ten, and you will get a smile, if not a smirk. Say "prunes and
prisms," however, and you will—if you repeat it often enough—develop
sexy-looking "bee-stung" lips; at least that's what my mother tells me
she and her younger sister believed, practicing each night in front of the
mirror to catch the magical moment of transformation. A prune does
seem to have some kind of transformational magic about it. It is
remarkably delicious although, in fact, it is simply the humble, wrinkled
reduction of a luscious plump fresh plum.

◆ ◆ ◆

Yield

3½ cups batter; one
8-inch square cake;
9 servings

Advance Preparation

Cake can be prepared in
advance, wrapped
airtight, and frozen.

Special Equipment

8 × 8 × 1½-inch pan

Temperature and Time

350°F for 35 to 40
minutes

Butter-flavor no stick cooking spray

1⅓ cups pitted prunes

⅓ cup hot water

1¾ cups sifted cake flour (or use half whole wheat pastry
flour)

1½ teaspoons baking powder

½ teaspoon baking soda

½ teaspoon salt

1½ teaspoons cinnamon

½ teaspoon nutmeg

½ teaspoon ground cloves

1 cup plus 1½ tablespoons granulated sugar

¼ cup canola or safflower oil

2 large egg whites

1 teaspoon vanilla extract

¾ cup nonfat vanilla or plain yogurt

1. Position a rack in the center of the oven and preheat it to 350°F. Coat the baking pan with cooking spray, then dust the pan with flour, and tap out excess flour.

2. In a food processor, combine ⅔ cup of the prunes and the hot water, and process until smooth. Set aside. Using a sharp knife, coarsely chop the remaining ⅔ cup prunes.

3. Sift together the flour, baking powder, baking soda, salt, and spices onto a sheet of wax paper. Stir about 1 tablespoon of this mixture into the chopped prunes. Set aside.

4. In the large bowl of an electric mixer, combine 1 cup of the sugar, the oil, egg whites, vanilla, and yogurt. Beat on medium speed to blend, then beat in the prune purée. In three additions, add the flour-spice mixture to the batter, beating on low speed. Occasionally stop the machine and use a rubber spatula to scrape down the bowl and beaters. Stir in the chopped prunes.

5. Turn the batter into the prepared pan. Sprinkle the remaining 1½ tablespoons sugar evenly over the batter. Bake for 35 to 40 minutes, until the cake is springy to the touch and a cake tester inserted in the center comes out clean. Cool on a wire rack for 10 to 15 minutes. Cut into squares and serve warm.

Light Touch: Prunes contain impressive quantities of dietary fiber, protein, calcium, minerals, and vitamins, and they are very low in fat. In low-fat baking, prune purée can sometimes replicate the viscosity and the hygroscopic (moisture-holding) ability of fat, and so can replace some fat as it does here. This recipe gets 20 percent of its calories from fat, with only a trace of cholesterol. To achieve this, I replaced the butter in the original recipe with a small amount of oil plus the prune purée, omitted egg yolks and nuts, and used yogurt for the moisture and richness that would have come from sour cream. Adding the chopped prunes with the purée underlines the taste, adds texture, and helps boost the dietary fiber to 2 grams per serving.

*Nutritional Analysis
per serving*

283 calories

4 g protein

6 g fat

0.5 g satfat

54 g carbohydrate

247 mg sodium

0 mg cholesterol

Applesauce Cake

◆ ◆ ◆

Apples, cider, cinnamon, cloves, and honey... it's a heady potpourri of aromas that wafts from the oven as this rich, moist holiday cake bakes. One whiff suggests all the romance of a country Christmas.

For the holidays, this cake makes a perfect gift. It is flavorful as well as fruitful, as satisfying for high tea as it is for brunch. Furthermore, this delectable cake is suitable for lactose-free diets. It lacks only one thing—cholesterol!

◆ ◆ ◆

Yield

4 cups batter; one 9-inch tube cake; 14 servings

Advance Preparation

Double-wrapped in plastic and foil, the cake can be kept in a cool place for up to 1 week, or frozen.

Special Equipment

9-inch (6½-cup capacity) tube pan

Temperature and Time

350°F for 55 minutes

Butter-flavor no stick cooking spray

1 medium Granny Smith or other tart apple, peeled, cored, and finely diced (about 1 cup)

½ cup dried apricots, chopped to ¼-inch dice

½ cup seedless raisins

1 cup unsifted all-purpose flour, divided

2 large egg whites, at room temperature

¼ cup canola or safflower oil

3 tablespoons honey

¼ cup apple cider or apple juice

1¼ cups applesauce, preferably unsweetened

1 teaspoon vanilla extract

1 cup light brown sugar, firmly packed

½ cup unsifted whole wheat pastry flour

1 teaspoon baking soda

½ teaspoon salt

1 teaspoon cinnamon

½ teaspoon nutmeg

½ teaspoon ground cardamom (optional)

¼ teaspoon ground cloves

¼ cup toasted wheat germ

3 tablespoons chopped walnuts (optional)

Vanilla Icing Glaze, made with bourbon or skim milk (page 435) or confectioners' sugar (optional)

1. Position a rack in the center of the oven and preheat it to 350°F. Coat the pan with cooking spray. Dust evenly with flour, and tap out excess flour.

2. In a medium bowl, combine the apple, apricots, and raisins. Add ¼ cup of the all-purpose flour and toss to coat.

3. In the large bowl of an electric mixer, combine the egg whites, oil, honey, cider or apple juice, applesauce, and vanilla. Crumble in the brown sugar, and beat well. Set a strainer over the bowl. Add the remaining ¾ cup all-purpose flour, the whole wheat flour, baking soda, salt, and spices. Stir and sift onto the applesauce mixture. Add the wheat germ, and beat on low speed to blend. Using a wooden spoon, stir in the apple mixture and the walnuts, if using them.

4. Spoon the batter into the prepared pan. Bake for about 55 minutes, or until the cake is modestly risen and feels springy to the touch, and a cake tester inserted in the center comes out clean.

5. Cool the cake in the pan on a wire rack for about 10 minutes. Top with a plate or another rack, invert, and lift off the pan. While the cake is still warm, spread on Icing Glaze if using it. Alternatively, sift on a little confectioners' sugar just before serving if desired.

Light Touch: This is the perfect example of a cake that is richly satisfying but just happens to be free of cholesterol, low in fat, full of good things, and good for you. In addition to its other virtues, each slice offers nearly 3 grams of dietary fiber.

My favorite traditional applesauce cake obtains about 40 percent of its calories from fat, and contains 1 whole egg, ½ cup butter, and 1 cup walnuts; one slice delivers 285 calories, 13 grams of fat, and 34 milligrams of cholesterol. In this enlightened version (only 19 percent calories from fat), I have eliminated the cholesterol by replacing the whole egg with 2 whites. I cut two thirds of the total fat by replacing the butter with half the quantity of oil and eliminating the fat from the cup of walnuts by replacing them with fat-free apricots and raisins. If you include the 3 tablespoons optional walnuts, count on 10 extra calories and 1 more gram of fat per serving.

Nutritional Analysis per serving (without optional nuts or icing glaze)

204 calories

3 g protein

4 g fat

0.4 g satfat

39 g carbohydrate

149 mg sodium

0 mg cholesterol

Florida Orange
Kiss-Me Cake

◆ · ◆ · ◆ ·

There are many versions of this divine cake. All the ones I have tasted are moist, chewy, bursting with flavor, and packed with ground whole oranges, raisins, and nuts. I developed this reduced-fat version during many visits to my mother's family in southern Florida, where I could pick the oranges in the backyard. In every taste test for this book, my Kiss-Me Cake was a winner. As a bonus, because the cake is made with orange juice instead of milk, it is safe for those with lactose intolerance.

The flavor of the cake will be affected by the type of orange used. When grinding the orange, you can always use the zest (the bright orange part of the peel), but if the thick white inner pith is very bitter, it will transfer its bitterness to the cake. First cut into the orange peel and taste it—if it is sweet, use it all; if the pith is bitter, grate the zest, then cut away the pith before grinding the rest of the orange.

◆ · ◆ · ◆ ·

Yield

5 cups batter; one
8 × 12-inch cake;
12 servings

Advance Preparation

Cake can be baked
ahead, wrapped airtight,
and frozen.

Special Equipment

Food processor or meat
grinder, 8 × 12-inch
pan, bamboo skewer or
toothpick

Temperature and Time

350°F for 35 to 40
minutes

Butter-flavor no stick cooking spray

2 cups sifted all-purpose flour

½ teaspoon baking powder

1 teaspoon baking soda

½ teaspoon salt

¼ teaspoon nutmeg

¼ teaspoon mace

2 tablespoons toasted wheat germ

1 orange (do not peel), cut into eighths, seeds removed
   (See recipe introduction)

1 cup seedless raisins

¼ cup canola or safflower oil

⅓ cup unsweetened applesauce

1 cup granulated sugar

1 large egg plus 1 large egg white

1 cup orange juice

Orange Glaze

½ cup orange juice

2 tablespoons granulated sugar

Topping

¼ cup granulated sugar

½ teaspoon cinnamon

¼ cup finely chopped pecans

*Nutritional Analysis
per serving*
....
280 calories

4 g protein

7 g fat

0.7 g satfat

53 g carbohydrate

183 mg sodium

18 mg cholesterol

1. Position a rack in the center of the oven and preheat it to 350°F. Coat the pan with cooking spray. Dust with flour, and tap out excess flour.

2. Sift together the flour, baking powder, baking soda, salt, nutmeg, and mace into a bowl or onto a sheet of wax paper. Stir in wheat germ. Set aside.

3. In a food processor, or a meat grinder, pulse to chop, or grind the orange sections and raisins together. If using the processor, be careful not to purée the fruit; pulse just to ⅛-inch bits.

4. In the large bowl of an electric mixer, combine the oil, applesauce, sugar, and egg and egg white. Beat until well blended. Alternately add the flour mixture and the orange juice, beating on low speed, beginning and ending with flour. Stir in the chopped orange-raisin mixture. The batter will be quite thin.

5. Spoon the batter into the prepared pan and level the top. Bake for about 35 to 40 minutes, or until the cake is golden brown on top and springy to the touch and a cake tester inserted in the center comes out clean.

6. While the cake is baking, prepare the glaze and the topping: In a small saucepan set over medium heat, stir together the glaze ingredients until the sugar dissolves. Remove from the heat. In a small bowl, stir together the sugar, cinnamon, and pecans. Set the topping aside.

7. Set the baked cake on a wire rack. Prick the top all over with a toothpick or bamboo skewer and pour over the glaze. Sprinkle on the topping mixture. Allow the cake to sit for about 2 hours to absorb the glaze and cool thoroughly. Cut into squares and serve.

Light Touch: My files hold several slightly different recipes for Kiss-Me Cake; they obtain 33 to 35 percent of their calories from fat and basically are made with ½ cup margarine or solid shortening, at least 2 whole eggs, 1 cup whole milk, and about ½ cup chopped wal-

(continued)

Coffee Cakes and Quick Breads

nuts. Each serving contains about 330 calories, 13 grams of fat, and 2 grams of saturated fat. The good news is that all the fruit contributes nearly 2.5 grams of dietary fiber per serving.

I left the fiber in but reduced the calories from fat to 22 percent by cutting 1 egg yolk and all the solid shortening, substituting a combination of applesauce and canola oil. I replaced the whole milk with orange juice, and the walnuts with half the quantity of pecans (it's a Southern cake, after all), putting them into the topping where they would be more noticeable. If you omit the nuts entirely, it is not a great loss, and you can cut the total calories from fat to 18 percent, dropping 15 calories and 2 grams of fat per serving.

Chopped Apple Cake

◆ · ◆ · ◆ ·

*M*oderately sweet and lightly spiced, this easy-to-prepare tea *cake is filled with chopped apples and currants. Apple butter makes the texture remarkably moist, and a little sugar sprinkled on top gives a sparkling crust.*

◆ · ◆ · ◆ ·

Yield

About 3½ cups batter; one 8-inch square cake; 9 servings

Advance Preparation

Cake can be baked in advance, wrapped airtight, and frozen. Warm before serving.

Special Equipment

8 × 8 × 2-inch pan

Temperature and Time

350°F for 45 to 50 minutes

Butter-flavor no stick cooking spray

2 tablespoons walnut pieces

1 large Granny Smith or Golden Delicious apple, peeled, cored, and cut into ¼-inch dice (1½ cups)

¼ cup dried currants

1 large egg plus 2 large egg whites

½ cup homemade or store-bought apple butter

½ cup dark brown sugar, packed

⅓ cup plus 1½ tablespoons granulated sugar

¼ cup canola or safflower oil

2 teaspoons vanilla extract

¾ cup unsifted all-purpose flour

½ cup unsifted whole wheat pastry flour

1 teaspoon baking powder

½ teaspoon salt

1 teaspoon cinnamon

½ teaspoon nutmeg

Generous pinch of ground ginger

2 tablespoons toasted wheat germ

Nutritional Analysis per serving

....

279 calories

5 g protein

8 g fat

0.8 g satfat

48 g carbohydrate

179 mg sodium

24 mg cholesterol

1. Position a rack in the center of the oven and preheat it to 350°F. Coat the baking pan with cooking spray. Dust the pan with flour, and tap out excess flour.

2. Spread the walnuts in a pie plate and toast them in the oven for 8 to 10 minutes, or until fragrant. Set aside until cool.

3. Coarsely chop the walnuts, and place in a small bowl. Add the chopped apple and currants. Set aside.

4. In a large bowl, combine the egg and egg whites, apple butter, brown sugar, the ⅓ cup white sugar, the oil, and vanilla. Whisk until well blended.

5. Place a strainer over the bowl and add both flours. Then remove a tablespoon or so of the combined flours and toss it with the apple-nut mixture. Set aside. Add the baking powder, salt, and spices to the flour in the strainer. Stir and sift the dry ingredients onto the egg mixture. Add the wheat germ. With an electric mixer on low speed, blend well; do not overbeat. Scrape down the bowl and beaters. Stir in the apple-nut mixture.

6. Turn the batter into the prepared pan and smooth the top. Sprinkle the remaining 1½ tablespoons sugar evenly over the batter. Bake for about 45 to 50 minutes, or until the cake is golden brown on top and springy to the touch, and a cake tester inserted in the center comes out clean. Cool the cake in the pan on a wire rack for about 10 minutes. Cut into squares and serve warm.

Light Touch: This cake obtains 26 percent of its calories from fat. The wheat germ and whole wheat flour add vitamins, minerals, and 2 grams dietary fiber per serving.

Hungarian Plum Cake

◆·◆·◆

Yield

One 8 × 12-inch cake;
12 servings

Advance Preparation

Plum cake is best when
freshly baked. It can be
baked a day in advance
and kept covered at
room temperature, or it
can be wrapped airtight
and frozen. Warm before
serving.

Special Equipment

8 × 12-inch Pyrex
baking dish

Temperature and Time

325°F for 50 to 55
minutes for fresh fruit,
55 to 60 minutes for
frozen fruit

The original version of this recipe was shared with me many years ago by my husband's Hungarian godmother, Maria Peterdi. When Maria made it, the purple plums topped with sugary nut streusel were cradled in the richest, creamiest pound cake that sweet butter, egg yolks, and sour cream could produce. One of the harder, but ultimately most rewarding, tasks of this book has been to lighten this recipe without losing its unique qualities.

I tinkered and fine-tuned this cake through many months and at least two dozen variations. The official word from my husband, who remembers the original better than anyone, is that, at last, I've got it! The cake is still rich in taste and texture, although I have removed more than half the fat.

In our family, this cake became a classic, and today it evokes memories of Maria and her baking as much as it heralds the sharp scents and flavors of fall, when prune plums appear in country markets. Italian prune plums are best for this recipe. I buy in bulk when they are in season; I rinse, dry, halve and pit them, and freeze them in one-pound batches in heavy-duty plastic bags. Frozen plums can be used without being completely thawed, but they are moister than fresh and the cake may take a little longer to bake through.

This recipe works beautifully with many other types of fruit as well, especially sliced peeled apples, peaches, or apricots. I like to use hazelnut oil in both the cake and the streusel topping. It gives a great flavor, and it's low in saturated fat and high in mono-unsaturated fats. If you don't have any, canola or safflower oil can be substituted.

◆·◆·◆

Butter-flavor no stick cooking spray

Topping

    2 tablespoons unsifted cake flour

    3 tablespoons granulated sugar

    3 tablespoons chopped walnuts or hazelnuts

    1 teaspoon hazelnut oil *or* canola or safflower oil

    2 teaspoons unsalted butter, at room temperature

½ teaspoon cinnamon

¼ teaspoon nutmeg

Cake

2 cups plus 3 tablespoons sifted cake flour

1 teaspoon baking powder

¼ teaspoon salt

3 tablespoons light (reduced fat) margarine, at room temperature

3 tablespoons hazelnut oil *or* canola or safflower oil

1 cup plus 2 tablespoons granulated sugar

1 large egg yolk

½ cup nonfat plain or vanilla yogurt

2 teaspoons vanilla extract

1 pound fresh or frozen prune plums (14 to 16), halved and pitted (do not peel)

Nutritional Analysis per serving
....
256 calories

3 g protein

8 g fat

1 g satfat

46 g carbohydrate

94 mg sodium

20 mg cholesterol

1. Position a rack in the center of the oven, and preheat it to 325°F. Coat the baking pan with cooking spray. Dust with flour, and tap out excess flour.

2. Prepare the topping: In a small bowl, combine all the topping ingredients, and pinch them together with your fingertips until they form loose, sandy crumbs. Set them aside.

3. Combine the cake flour, baking powder, and salt on a sheet of wax paper.

4. In the large bowl of an electric mixer, combine the margarine, oil, and sugar and beat on medium speed until light colored. Beat in the egg yolk, yogurt, and vanilla. Add the dry ingredients in 2 batches, beating on low speed. Mix until well blended, but do not overwork.

5. Turn the batter into the prepared pan, and use a rubber spatula to spread it evenly and smooth the top. Arrange the plum halves skin side down in neat rows on top of the batter. Push each plum halfway down into the batter. Sprinkle the topping evenly over the cake.

6. Bake for about 55 minutes, or until the cake is golden brown and firm to the touch at the edges, and a cake tester inserted directly into the cake (not into a plum) comes out clean. (If you have used frozen fruit, you may need to bake the cake slightly longer.) Cool the cake in the pan on a wire rack. Cut it into squares, and serve warm or at room temperature.

(continued)

Light Touch: The original recipe for this cake obtained 48 percent of its calories from fat, and each serving had 345 calories, 19 grams of fat, 11 grams of saturated fat, and 62 milligrams of cholesterol. For both the plum cake and its apple variation following, I have reduced the calories from fat by almost half (to 28 percent), switched from all-purpose to cake flour, which has less protein (to keep the cake tender), replaced sour cream with nonfat yogurt, and, for more flavor, added vanilla extract.

Apple Kuchen

Prepare the recipe as directed, but replace the plums with 1½ medium apples (Rome or Granny Smith, for example), peeled, cored, and thinly sliced. Cover the top of the batter with overlapping rows of apple slices, then sprinkle on the topping. Bake 55 to 60 minutes.

Pineapple-Banana Cake

◆ · ◆ · ◆

The inspiration for this recipe was a confection called Doctor Bird Cake. It was "named for a species of hummingbird in Jamaica," according to the late Helene Brady, who included it as her favorite cake recipe in Roxbury Cookery, *published in 1974 by the Roxbury, Connecticut, Volunteer Fire Department Women's Auxiliary. In the 1920s, Helene served Doctor Bird Cake at a tea shop she had in her country farmhouse in Roxbury.*

My low-fat adaptation retains the unusual and delectable flavor; the large quantity of fruit gives it a moist texture as well as excellent keeping quality. The texture of this cake is best when the batter is beaten by hand rather than in an electric mixer.

◆ · ◆ · ◆

Butter-flavor no stick cooking spray

¼ cup canola or safflower oil

1 large egg, plus 2 large egg whites

1 teaspoon vanilla extract

¾ cup unsifted all-purpose flour

Nutritional Analysis per serving

241 calories

3 g protein

8 g fat

1 g satfat

41 g carbohydrate

94 mg sodium

20 mg cholesterol

Yield

About 4 cups batter; one 8 × 12-inch cake; 12 servings

Advance Preparation

Cake can be baked in advance, wrapped airtight, and frozen. Defrost before adding the confectioners' sugar topping.

Special Equipment

8 × 12-inch pan

Temperature and Time

350°F for 45 to 55 minutes

¾ cup unsifted whole wheat pastry flour (or use a total of 1½ cups unsifted all-purpose flour)

½ teaspoon baking soda

½ teaspoon salt

½ teaspoon cinnamon

¼ teaspoon nutmeg

¾ cup granulated sugar

¼ cup toasted wheat germ (optional)

1 8-ounce can unsweetened crushed pineapple (fruit plus juice)

1 cup mashed ripe bananas (2 medium or 3 small bananas)

Confectioners' sugar

Nutritional Analysis per serving (without the optional wheat germ)

179 calories

3 g protein

5 g fat

0.5 g satfat

31 g carbohydrate

139 mg sodium

18 mg cholesterol

1. Position a rack in the center of the oven and preheat it to 350°F. Coat the baking pan with cooking spray. Dust the pan with flour, and tap out excess flour.

2. In a large bowl, combine the oil, egg and egg whites, and vanilla. Whisk to blend well.

3. Place a strainer over the bowl. Add both flours, the baking soda, salt, cinnamon, and nutmeg. Stir and sift the dry ingredients onto the wet. Add the sugar and wheat germ, if using, and stir with a wooden spoon to blend well. Stir in the pineapple, with its juice, and the bananas, and mix well.

4. Turn the batter into the prepared pan. Bake for 45 to 55 minutes, or until the cake is springy to the touch and a cake tester inserted in the center comes out clean. Cool the cake in the pan on a wire rack for 10 minutes. Then sift a little confectioners' sugar over the top. Cut into squares and serve warm.

Light Touch: The original recipe, made with 3 whole eggs and ¾ cup oil, obtained 47 percent of its total calories from fat; each serving contained 15 grams of fat, 2 grams of which were saturated, plus 53 milligrams of cholesterol. My lightened version cuts the calories from fat almost in half (to 26 percent) by eliminating ½ cup oil and 2 egg yolks—thereby dropping about two thirds of the cholesterol. In addition, I reduced the sugar and slightly increased the spices and fruit to make up for the lack of fat. For extra flavor and dietary fiber, I like to add ¼ cup toasted wheat germ, though it is not essential; it adds 11 calories and 0.3 gram of fat per serving.

Poppy Seed Lemon Cake

•◆•◆•◆•

6 cups batter; one 9-inch
Bundt cake, one 9 × 13-
inch sheet cake, or 2
medium loaf cakes;
Bundt cake serves 14,
loaf cakes serve 12 each,
sheet cake serves 24

Advance Preparation
....

The ground poppy seeds
must soak for at least 1
hour before being used.
Cake can be baked in
advance, wrapped
airtight, and frozen
(without icing).

Special Equipment
....

Electric spice mill or
mini-processor, 9-inch
(8- to 10-cup capacity)
Bundt or tube pan,
9 × 13-inch baking dish
(preferably Pyrex), or 2
medium loaf pans.

Temperature and Time
....

350°F for 45 minutes for
Bundt cake, 30 to 35
minutes for sheet cake,
40 to 45 minutes for
loaves

*T*his recipe was inspired by an elegant Bavarian mohntorte presented on a gilded pedestal tray amidst a dazzling array of cakes at Munich's famed coffeehouse, Kreutzkamm Conditorei. Buttery and rich, a veritable grande dame of a cake, it was laden with poppy seeds, bejeweled with citron and golden raisins, enrobed in a film of marzipan, and glazed with bittersweet chocolate. My notes remind me that on one visit I managed to eat three slices!

Even in this modest incarnation, it remains one of my favorite tea cakes: moist, with a light tender crumb and a delightful flavor balanced between the sweetness of the poppy seeds and the tartness of the lemon. The secret of the rich flavor is to grind the poppy seeds, then soak them in hot milk along with grated lemon zest. Use an electric spice mill or mini-processor to grind the seeds; a blender works but takes longer. A food processor does not work at all.

•◆•◆•◆•

3 tablespoons poppy seeds

Grated zest of 1 lemon (about 2 teaspoons)

1/2 cup skim milk

Butter-flavor no stick cooking spray

1/3 cup canola or safflower oil

1 1/4 cups granulated sugar, divided

1 large egg

2 teaspoons vanilla extract

1 1/8 teaspoons lemon extract

1/3 cup nonfat plain yogurt

1/3 cup unsweetened applesauce

2 1/4 cups sifted cake flour

1 1/8 teaspoons baking powder

1/4 teaspoon baking soda

1/2 teaspoon salt

3 large egg whites

1/8 teaspoon cream of tartar

Confectioners' sugar or 1 recipe Light Cream Cheese Frosting
    (page 444)

1. At least 1 hour in advance, grind the poppy seeds in an electric spice mill or mini-processor. Transfer to a small saucepan and add the lemon zest and milk. Bring to a boil, stir once or twice, and remove from the heat. Allow to stand for at least 1 hour, or up to 12 hours, to infuse the liquid with flavor.

2. Position a rack in the center of the oven and preheat it to 350°F. Coat the baking pan(s) with cooking spray. Dust with flour, and tap out excess flour.

3. In a large bowl, combine the oil, 1 cup of the sugar, the egg, vanilla and lemon extracts, yogurt, applesauce, and the poppy seed–milk mixture, but do not mix at this point. Set aside.

4. In another bowl, stir together the flour, baking powder, baking soda, and salt. Set aside.

5. In a grease-free bowl, combine the egg whites and cream of tartar. Using an electric mixer on medium speed, whip until foamy. Gradually add the remaining ¼ cup of sugar, and whip until medium-stiff. Shake the beaters into the bowl, then return the beaters to the mixer without washing them.

6. With the mixer on medium speed, beat the oil and sugar mixture until well blended. Gradually beat in the flour mixture in several additions. Scrape down the bowl and beaters and mix briefly. Using a rubber spatula, fold in the whipped whites.

7. Turn the batter into the pan(s). Bake a Bundt cake for about 45 minutes, loaves for 40 to 45 minutes, a sheet cake for 30 to 35 minutes, or, in all cases, until the top is springy to the touch and a cake tester inserted in the center comes out clean. Cool the cake(s) in the pan(s) on a wire rack for about 10 minutes. A sheet cake can be sliced and served directly from the pan, but a Bundt cake or loaves should be removed from the pan(s) at this point and cooled on the rack.

8. Just before serving, sift on a light dusting of confectioners' sugar. Or ice with the Cream Cheese Frosting.

Light Touch: My original recipe includes 1 cup poppy seeds, 1 cup whole milk, 1 cup butter, 3 eggs, 1¼ cups sugar, and 2 cups flour. It is no surprise to find it obtains 54 percent of its calories from fat; each slice contains a serious 20 grams of fat, 10 grams of it saturated. One of the difficulties in reducing fat in this recipe is that poppy seeds, like all seeds, contain a large percentage of fat (1 tablespoon has 45 calories and 3.8 grams fat). I tested more than thirty variations while slimming the recipe, replacing the butter with oil, dropping 2 egg yolks

(continued)

Nutritional Analysis per serving (Bundt cake, without icing)
....

204 calories

4 g protein

6 g fat

0.6 g satfat

33 g carbohydrate

143 mg sodium

15 mg cholesterol

Nutritional Analysis per serving (sheet or loaf cakes, without icing)
....

119 calories

2 g protein

4 g fat

0.4 g satfat

19 g carbohydrate

84 mg sodium

9 mg cholesterol

and adding 1 egg white, and altering the proportions of nearly every other ingredient. Finally, I developed a version that retains the cake's characteristic taste and texture but obtains only 28 percent calories from fat. To achieve this, I had to shave the poppy seeds down to 3 tablespoons, replace some of the oil with applesauce, and add yogurt for moisture. To tenderize the crumb and increase the acidity of the batter, I replaced the all-purpose flour with cake flour.

Food scientist, writer, and patient friend Shirley Corriher really saved this recipe as she followed it through innumerable versions, and I gratefully dedicate the cake to her. Originally, I used only the egg yolk in the batter and whipped all the whites into meringue. The cake would rise perfectly in the oven but sink slightly as it cooled. Shirley pointed out that I needed at least 1 white to strengthen the batter; she also suggested adding more flour and changing the proportions of baking powder and baking soda to ensure a nicely domed cake.

Cocoa-Prune Cake

❖ ❖ ❖

This is my adaptation of a cholesterol-free, low-fat recipe for Chocolate Cocoa Cake by Marian Burros published in The New York Times. It is a dark, chocolaty cake with a tender, moist crumb. You cannot actually taste the flavor of the prune butter, but its presence gives the cake a unique texture and makes it slightly sticky on the top. Lekvar prune butter is commercially made and sold in most supermarkets.

❖ ❖ ❖

Yield

3½ cups batter; one 8-inch square cake; 12 servings

Advance Preparation

Cake can be prepared in advance, wrapped airtight, and frozen. Defrost, still wrapped, overnight in the refrigerator before serving.

Special Equipment

8 × 8 × 2-inch pan

Temperature and Time

350°F for 30 to 35 minutes

Butter-flavor no stick cooking spray

1¼ cups granulated sugar

2 large egg whites

⅔ cup warm water

½ cup prune butter (lekvar)

1¼ cups sifted cake flour

½ cup nonalkalized unsweetened cocoa

1 teaspoon baking powder

½ teaspoon baking soda

½ teaspoon salt

1. Position a rack in the center of the oven and preheat it to 350°F. Coat the baking pan with cooking spray. Dust evenly with cocoa, and tap out excess cocoa.

2. In the large bowl of an electric mixer, combine the sugar, egg whites, and warm water, and mix well on low speed. Add the prune butter and blend well.

3. Place a strainer over the bowl and add the flour, cocoa, baking powder, baking soda, and salt. Stir and sift the dry ingredients onto the prune mixture. With the mixer on low speed, blend well.

4. Turn the batter into the prepared pan, and smooth the top. Bake for about 30 to 35 minutes, or until a cake tester inserted in the center comes out clean. Cool for about 10 minutes in the pan on a wire rack, then invert onto a serving plate. Or serve directly from the pan.

Light Touch: Marian Burros started with a recipe in which corn syrup replaced the fat; she then substituted baby-food prunes, and in place of 1 whole egg, used 1½ egg whites. In my tests, I found the baby-food prunes too soft, and so I replaced them with the bottled prune butter called lekvar (sold in supermarkets). Instead of the 1½ whites, I used 2—it's easier to measure whole whites.

Nutritional Analysis per serving

138 calories

2 g protein

1 g fat

0.4 g satfat

33 g carbohydrate

161 mg sodium

0 mg cholesterol

Cinnamon-Cider-Cranberry Cake

◆ ◆ ◆

This lightly spiced, cranberry-studded cake is filled with the perfumes and flavors of the holiday season. Serve it warm on Christmas morning, the perfect treat to nibble on while opening presents and drinking mugs of steaming coffee or hot cider.

◆ ◆ ◆

Yield

4 cups batter; one 9-inch Bundt cake; 12 servings

Advance Preparation

Cake is best when fresh from the oven, but it may be made in advance, wrapped airtight, and frozen. Thaw and warm before serving.

Special Equipment

9-inch Bundt pan, preferably nonstick Pyrex

Temperature and Time

350°F for 45 to 50 minutes

Butter-flavor no stick cooking spray

2 cups sifted all-purpose flour

1 teaspoon baking soda

1 teaspoon cinnamon

½ teaspoon salt

1 cup fresh cranberries or frozen whole cranberries, picked over, rinsed, and patted dry

1 cup granulated sugar

2 tablespoons canola or safflower oil

2 tablespoons unsalted butter, at room temperature (see Light Touch)

1 large egg

1 cup apple cider or apple juice

½ cup unsulfured molasses

1. Position a rack in the center of the oven and preheat it to 350°F. Generously coat the baking pan with cooking spray. Dust with flour, and tap out excess flour. (Be sure to grease and flour the pan very thoroughly so the cranberries do not stick.)

2. Sift together the flour, baking soda, cinnamon, and salt onto a sheet of wax paper or into a bowl. Combine about 3 tablespoons of the flour mixture with the cranberries in another bowl, and toss well. Set aside.

3. In the large bowl of an electric mixer, beat together the sugar, oil, and butter until well blended. Add the egg and beat well.

4. In a small saucepan, bring the cider or apple juice to a boil. Remove from the heat and add the molasses, stirring until it dissolves.

5. With the mixer on very low speed, alternately add the dry ingredients and the molasses mixture to the beaten sugar-egg mixture, beginning and ending with the dry ingredients. Stir in the cranberries. The batter will be quite thin.

6. Spoon the batter into the prepared pan. Bake for 45 to 50 minutes or until the top is springy to the touch and a cake tester inserted in the center comes out clean. Cool the cake in the pan on a wire rack for 15 minutes, then invert onto another rack and let cool.

Light Touch: The texture of this rich, moist cake really varies depending upon the type of fat used. I have tried making it with all oil, but find it is appreciably better with a small amount of solid fat. My personal preference is for the butter-oil combination, which weighs in with 20 percent of its total calories from fat. To reduce the calories from fat to 18 percent, substitute 4 tablespoons hard stick corn oil margarine for the butter and oil; this cuts 4 calories, 1 gram of fat, and 0.7 gram saturated fat from each serving.

Nutritional Analysis per serving

221 calories

3 g protein

5 g fat

1.5 g satfat

43 g carbohydrate

166 mg sodium

23 mg cholesterol

Spicy Apple Corn Bread

❖ ◆ ❖ ◆

I first encountered this prizewinning corn bread when I was one of the judges at the Third Annual Apple Bake-Off in Essex, Vermont. Sponsored by the New England Culinary Institute and the Vermont Apple Marketing Board, the contest inspired many creative efforts, including a Spicy Apple Raisin Corn Bread made by Karen Lanzer of Claremont, New Hampshire. Taking a blue ribbon in the "bread and muffin" category, this was traditional corn bread with a twist: apples, raisins, and spices complemented the flavor of the corn.

The concept of that recipe intrigued me; after the contest, I began to experiment with my own variations on Karen's theme. My first kitchen notes read: "Add apples, applesauce, and yogurt, up the moisture, down the satfat, enhance spices, cut breadiness." I did. Six versions later, I had what I was looking for, a cinnamon-sugar-glazed moist coffee cake in which the spiced apples predominate without overwhelming the flavor and texture of the cornmeal. Serve it warm right from the pan for breakfast or brunch.

❖ ◆ ❖ ◆

Yield

4½ cups batter; one 8- or 9-inch square cake; 9 servings

Advance Preparation

Cake can be made a day or two in advance and rewarmed before serving. Wrapped airtight, it can be frozen for up to 2 weeks.

Special Equipment

8 × 8 × 1½-inch or 9 × 1½-inch baking pan

Temperature and Time

400°F for 30 minutes

Butter-flavor no stick cooking spray

2 medium apples, such as Golden Delicious or Rome, peeled, cored, and cut into ¼-inch dice

½ cup golden raisins

1 cup skim milk

¼ cup canola or safflower oil

2 large egg whites

¼ cup unsweetened applesauce

¼ cup nonfat plain yogurt

⅓ cup plus 2 tablespoons granulated sugar, divided

1 cup unsifted all-purpose flour

¾ cup yellow cornmeal

2½ teaspoons baking powder

½ teaspoon salt

1¼ teaspoons cinnamon, divided

1 teaspoon nutmeg

½ teaspoon allspice

½ teaspoon ground ginger

⅛ teaspoon ground cloves

266 calories

5 g protein

7 g fat

0.6 g satfat

48 g carbohydrate

243 mg sodium

1 mg cholesterol

1. Position a rack in the center of the oven and preheat it to 400°F. Coat the baking pan with cooking spray.

2. In a small bowl, toss together the chopped apples and raisins.

3. In a large bowl, whisk together the milk, oil, egg whites, applesauce, and yogurt. Add ⅓ cup of the sugar, the flour, cornmeal, baking powder, salt, 1 teaspoon of the cinnamon, the nutmeg, allspice, ginger, and cloves. Whisk to blend well. Stir in the apple-raisin mixture. Turn the batter into the prepared pan and smooth the top.

4. Combine the remaining 2 tablespoons sugar and ¼ teaspoon cinnamon, and sprinkle evenly over the batter. Bake for 30 minutes, or until the top of the cake feels springy to the touch and a cake tester inserted in the center comes out clean. Cool the cake in the pan on a wire rack for 10 minutes. Cut into squares and serve warm.

Light Touch: Karen's prizewinning recipe included 1 whole egg, 1 cup whole milk, and 3 tablespoons butter. The butter and egg yolk gave each serving 3 grams of saturated fat and 38 milligrams of cholesterol, but the cake obtained only 23 percent of its total calories from fat. In my opinion, it was a little too dry and could have used more fat, but less of it saturated, as well as more moisture. My variation gets 22 percent of its total calories from fat, but the saturated fat drops to 0.6 gram per serving. I used a small amount of oil plus some applesauce and yogurt to retain moisture and give flavor; in addition, I doubled the original quantity of diced apple. To lower cholesterol, I replaced the egg yolk with another egg white. I replaced the whole milk with skim, and to spark up the flavor, adjusted the proportions of the spices Karen used and added nutmeg and cloves.

Blueberry Gingerbread

-◆-◆-◆-

An old-fashioned favorite has a new tempo . . . juicy sweet blueberries playing counterpoint to the rich snap of ginger and spice. This moist, tender cake is also nutritious, with whole wheat flour, molasses, and yogurt. Serve it warm from the oven, with plain or vanilla yogurt alongside, or bake it into cupcakes and freeze them, to take out one at a time for a lunch-box treat. For variety, try the cranberry gingerbread variation, or make old-fashioned plain gingerbread, without any fruit, using the basic recipe.

-◆-◆-◆-

Yield

3¾ cups batter; one 8-inch square cake; 9 servings

Advance Preparation

Cake can be baked in advance, wrapped airtight, and frozen. Thaw and warm before serving.

Special Equipment

8 × 8 × 2-inch pan, 2-cup Pyrex measure

Temperature and Time

350°F for 35 to 45 minutes for fresh berries, about 50 minutes for frozen berries

Butter-flavor no stick cooking spray

1½ cups unsifted cake flour

1 cup unsifted whole wheat pastry flour

1 teaspoon baking powder

1 teaspoon baking soda

¾ teaspoon salt

1 teaspoon cinnamon

2 teaspoons ground ginger

½ cup plus 2 tablespoons dark brown sugar, packed

⅓ cup canola or safflower oil

1 large egg

½ cup nonfat plain or vanilla yogurt

¼ cup plus 2 tablespoons unsulfured molasses

1 cup very hot water

1 cup fresh blueberries, picked over, rinsed, and gently dried, or frozen unsweetened whole blueberries (do not thaw)

1. Position a rack in the center of the oven and preheat it to 350°F. Coat the pan with cooking spray. Dust with flour, and tap out excess flour.

2. Sift together both flours, the baking powder, baking soda, salt, and spices into a bowl or onto a sheet of wax paper.

3. In the large bowl of an electric mixer, beat together the sugar, oil, egg, and yogurt.

4. In a 2-cup Pyrex measure, combine the molasses and hot water; stir well to blend. With the mixer on low speed, alternately add the dry ingredients and molasses to the egg-yogurt mixture. Stir in the blueberries. The batter will be thin.

5. Turn the batter into the prepared pan. Bake for 35 to 45 minutes, or until the top is springy to the touch and a cake tester inserted in the center comes out clean. Cool the cake in the pan on a wire rack. Cut into squares and serve.

Light Touch: My favorite traditional gingerbread recipe contains ½ cup butter and ½ cup regular sour cream; it obtains 37 percent of its total calories from fat and each serving weighs in at 345 calories, 14 grams of fat (of which 9 grams are saturated), and 59 milligrams of cholesterol. Made with all white flour, it contains less than 1 gram of dietary fiber. By replacing the sour cream with nonfat yogurt, and the butter with ⅓ cup canola oil, I eliminated over 5 grams of total fat and 8 grams of saturated fat per serving, and dropped the cholesterol to less than half the original amount; 27 percent of the calories come from fat. To enhance the nutritional content, I replaced some of the all-purpose flour with whole wheat flour, which also contributes 2 grams of dietary fiber per serving. To eliminate the cholesterol, you can substitute 2 egg whites for the whole egg.

I have tinkered endlessly with this recipe, whittling down the fats while trying to save flavor and texture. In the end, I prefer the results using 1 whole egg and ⅓ cup of oil as in the version above. However, it is possible to cut the recipe down to 20 percent total calories from fat, with 283 calories and 6 grams fat per serving, by substituting 2 egg whites for the whole egg, and using all white flour and only ¼ cup oil.

Cranberry Gingerbread

Prepare the recipe as directed but substitute 1 cup fresh or frozen (unthawed) whole cranberries, picked over, rinsed, and patted dry, for the blueberries. Coarsely chop or halve ¾ cup of the cranberries, then dredge all the cranberries with 2 tablespoons of the all-purpose flour. Stir the cranberries into the batter just before baking.

Nutritional Analysis
per serving

310 calories

5 g protein

9 g fat

1 g satfat

53 g carbohydrate

331 mg sodium

24 mg cholesterol

Nutritional Analysis
per serving

307 calories

5 g protein

9 g fat

1 g satfat

52 g carbohydrate

330 mg sodium

24 mg cholesterol

Carrot-Rosemary Bread

◆ ◆ ◆

"Rosemary is for remembrance," according to herbalists. You will remember this tea bread with pleasure. Though related to carrot cake, it is less sweet, but equally moist, with a delightfully subtle overtone of rosemary.

I have always loved the complex perfume of oven-roasted carrots sprinkled with rosemary, but never thought to use the combination in baking until I began creating variations on carrot cake for this book. Then, I came across Rosemary-Carrot Bread as a variation on Zucchini Bread in Marion Cunningham's impressive revision of The Fannie Farmer Baking Book. I took this as a sign and decided to pursue the notion. I adapted this recipe from the basic Carrot Cake in my book A Piece of Cake.

◆ ◆ ◆

Yield

2¾ cups batter; 1 loaf cake; 10 servings

Advance Preparation

Bread can be made in advance, wrapped airtight, and frozen for up to 2 months without losing flavor. Thaw, still wrapped, overnight in the refrigerator, and warm before serving. Bread stays fresh for about a week, wrapped airtight, stored at room temperature or refrigerated.

Special Equipment

9 × 5 × 3-inch loaf pan or 8½ × 4½ × 2¾-inch loaf pan

Temperature and Time

350°F for 45 to 50 minutes

Butter-flavor no stick cooking spray

3 large egg whites, at room temperature

½ cup dark brown sugar, packed

⅓ cup granulated sugar

¼ cup canola or light olive oil

⅓ cup unsweetened applesauce

1 tablespoon vanilla extract

1½ cups sifted all-purpose flour

¾ teaspoon baking soda

½ teaspoon baking powder

½ teaspoon salt

1 teaspoon cinnamon

½ teaspoon nutmeg

⅛ teaspoon ground cloves

2 teaspoons dried rosemary, finely ground (with a mortar and pestle or in an electric herb mincer), or 1½ tablespoons fresh rosemary, minced

3 to 4 medium carrots, peeled, and grated in a food processor or on medium-sized holes of a box grater (2 cups grated carrots, do not pack)

2 tablespoons chopped walnuts (optional)

1. Position a rack in the center of the oven and preheat it to 350°F. Coat the loaf pan with cooking spray. Dust evenly with flour, and tap out excess flour.

2. In the large bowl of an electric mixer, beat together the egg whites and both sugars until well blended. Add the oil, applesauce, and vanilla and beat to blend.

3. Set a large strainer over the bowl and add the flour, baking soda, baking powder, salt, spices, and rosemary. Stir and sift the dry ingredients onto the applesauce mixture. With the mixer on low speed, beat until well blended. Stir in the grated carrots and blend well.

4. Turn the batter into the prepared pan, and smooth the top. If using the nuts, sprinkle them evenly over the top. Bake for about 45 to 50 minutes, until a cake tester inserted in the center comes out clean. Cool the bread in the pan on a wire rack for about 10 minutes. Then invert onto another rack, lift off the pan, and invert again onto the rack. Cool completely before slicing with a serrated knife.

Light Touch: My original carrot cake contains 2 whole eggs, ¾ cup oil, and ½ cup walnuts; it gets about 56 percent calories from fat. In my first pass at lightening the recipe, I replaced 1 whole egg with 2 whites, dropped the oil to ½ cup, and cut the nuts to 3 tablespoons— and was dismayed to find I still had 48 percent calories from fat. To reach the present level of 26 percent and still retain all the moisture and flavor, I needed to drop the remaining yolk and the nuts and find a creative substitution for part of the oil: Applesauce did the trick. And now it is cholesterol-free as well.

If you do include the nuts, sprinkling them on top of the loaf so they toast and become more flavorful during baking, the total calories from fat rises to 28 percent—just a fraction more per serving.

Nutritional Analysis per serving (without the optional nuts)

200 calories

3 g protein

6 g fat

0.4 g satfat

34 g carbohydrate

213 mg sodium

0 mg cholesterol

Irish Soda Bread

❖ ・ ❖ ・ ❖ ・

Every Saint Patrick's Day, my Irish aunt, Winifred Tunney Gold, makes her famous soda bread to accompany a traditional holiday dinner. Winnie was born in the town of Balla, County Mayo, and came to the United States at age fourteen, carrying her grandmother's recipe with her. Winnie's personal touch is to blend both currants and raisins into the dough before shaping a round loaf, cutting a cross in the top surface, and brushing it with egg glaze to bake into a golden finish.

Soda bread is traditional in Ireland because the climate favors the cultivation of fine soft wheat, good for quick breads risen with baking soda rather than hard wheat breads risen with yeast. Buttermilk is used in combination with baking soda, and sometimes baking powder as well, for leavening. To achieve a properly tender crumb, handle the dough as lightly as possible so the gluten in the flour is not overly developed.

❖ ・ ❖ ・ ❖ ・

Butter-flavor no stick cooking spray
4 cups unsifted all-purpose flour
1 tablespoon baking powder
1 teaspoon baking soda
1 teaspoon salt
2½ tablespoons granulated sugar
2 tablespoons unsalted butter, at room temperature
¾ cup seedless raisins
½ cup dried currants
1 large egg
1½ cups plus 2 tablespoons nonfat buttermilk

1. Position a rack in the center of the oven and preheat it to 375°F. Coat the cookie sheet or baking pan with cooking spray. Dust with flour, and tap out excess flour.

2. In a large bowl, stir together the flour, baking powder, baking soda, salt, and sugar. Add the butter, and use your fingertips to pinch it into the flour until it is in very small flakes and no large lumps remain. Stir in the raisins and currants.

Yield

1 round loaf; 16 slices

Advance Preparation

Soda bread is best freshly baked, but will keep a few days wrapped airtight. It may be also baked in advance, double-wrapped, and frozen for up to 2 months. Thaw and serve warm.

Special Equipment

Cookie sheet or 8 × 1-inch round cake pan, pastry brush

Temperature and Time

375°F for 40 to 45 minutes

3. Beat the egg in a cup or small bowl. Make a well in the center of the dry ingredients and add the buttermilk and all but 1 tablespoon of the beaten egg (reserving the rest for glaze). With a wooden spoon, blend thoroughly, but do not overbeat. The dough will be sticky.

4. Turn the dough onto a lightly floured work surface, and knead with floured hands for 2 or 3 minutes. The dough should be neither wet nor totally dry to the touch; the surface will be bumpy. Add a little more flour if necessary. Form the dough into a ball about 8 inches in diameter.

5. Set the dough on the prepared cookie sheet or in the pan. Use a sharp knife to cut a cross about ½ inch deep in the top. Using a pastry brush, brush the reserved beaten egg over the top of the dough. Bake for about 40 to 45 minutes, until the bread is well risen and golden brown on top, and a long skewer inserted in the center comes out dry.

6. Traditionally, the bread is cooled on a rack, then covered with a cloth towel, which softens the crust and keeps the interior moist. Alternatively, the loaf can be cooled and stored in an airtight tin or plastic bag. To serve, cut into wedges with a serrated knife. Serve freshly baked bread as is, day-old bread toasted.

Light Touch: Because it is made with buttermilk and a minimum of added fat, Irish soda bread is traditionally low in fat. While some classic recipes use 4 tablespoons butter, this version contains half that to cut calories from fat to barely 12 percent.

Nutritional Analysis per slice

173 calories

5 g protein

2 g fat

1 g satfat

34 g carbohydrate

278 mg sodium

17 mg cholesterol

Cakes

Bake a cake and you make a party! There is no doubt that the appearance of a cake—be it a simple layer cake or a Bundt—can transform an ordinary meal into a festive occasion, while the presentation of a smashing *gâteau* can become the centerpiece of a gala.

The cakes in this chapter divide naturally into two categories: classics for your basic repertoire, and elegant, festive party cakes and pastries. This division is, of course, somewhat arbitrary; basic layer cakes can be party cakes and chiffon cakes really are basic. Enjoy them all.

To begin, there is traditional Classic Angel Food Cake with variations, plus several layer cakes, including Old-Fashioned Silver Cake and a divine Chocolate Buttermilk Cake. Bundt and tube cakes include a moist, virtually fat-free Cocoa Bundt, plus Carrot Cake and Spice Cake; all of these can also be baked in layer or sheet pans with adjustments in timing. Add an unusual note to a brunch or casual dinner party with new interpretations of the always popular upside-down cakes, such as Blueberry and Pear-Gingerbread. For a Fourth of July picnic, prepare everyone's favorite, Strawberry Shortcake.

Cakes in the "special" category are not necessarily more difficult to make than the basic cakes, but some require more time. Most, however, can be made in advance. All share the remarkable qualities of being low in fat, great tasting, and elegant in presentation.

To dazzle guests at a chic dinner party, serve Burgundy Cherry Mousse Cake with Cassis Glaze, an impressive, do-ahead six-layer confection; two-cakes-in-one Blitz Torte topped with nut-sprinkled meringue and filled with strawberries and cream; Double-Chocolate Meringue Cake, crisp cocoa-meringue layers filled with Chocolate Mousse; Mandarin Orange Charlotte, a ladyfinger-lined mold filled with a rich orange mousse; Lemon Roulade with Lemon Curd and Fresh Berries, or Cocoa Roulade filled with Raspberry Cream. For a dessert party buffet, be sure to include Panatela Borracha, a simple but inspired concoction of angel food cake squares soaked in spiced orange-rum syrup.

Holidays call for special ingredients and remarkable recipes. For Passover, serve the light, moist Orange Sponge Cake made with matzo meal and potato starch. At Christmastime, serve the first and only fruitcake your friends will honestly like: Fabulous Holiday Fruitcake, a rich applesauce cake filled with plump dried fruits such as peaches, apricots, and mangoes, with nary a glacéed red morsel to be found.

Chiffon cakes go with any holiday...my five flavors give you lots of choices. They are easy to make and turn any dinner party into a festive occasion.

Cheesecakes are a class unto themselves, cream desserts guaranteed to please. Here are ten recipes, varying from simple to extravagant.

Classic Angel Food Cake

◆ ･ ◆ ･ ◆

Angel food cake is basically a sponge cake without egg yolks or fat. This traditional recipe makes a tender, but not overly sweet cake, a perfect blank canvas for your own creative touches. Cover slices with warm *Spiced Blueberry Sauce* (page 415) or soak them in *Yogurt Rum Sauce* (page 417). You can make an "ice cream" cake by hollowing out a whole cake, filling it and frosting it with low-fat frozen yogurt, then freezing it. Or, bake angel food batter in a jelly-roll pan, fill it with any number of fillings, and roll it up.

For successful angel food cakes, keep these tips in mind:

Angel food cake contains no chemical leavening (baking powder or soda); its rise depends entirely on egg white foam and the steam that forms as the cake bakes. The success of the cake thus depends upon understanding how to handle and whip egg whites (see page 20). Use grease-free utensils and be sure the egg whites are at room temperature before whipping. Test the temperature of the egg whites before you begin beating; if they feel cold, warm them by pouring them into a bowl, and placing it in a pan of very warm water. Stir the whites until they no longer feel cool.

Cake flour is best because it contains less gluten and produces a more tender cake than all-purpose flour. Superfine and confectioners' sugar are preferred because they dissolve quickly. To maintain the light texture, fold the dry ingredients into the whipped whites very gently; professional chefs often do this with the flat of their bare hands to control the technique. You can use a spatula, but be sure to lift and turn as you fold; do not stir or deflate the foam.

Bake the cake as soon as the batter is in the pan; if the batter stands, it will deflate and fall.

Bake the cake at the correct heat. Egg whites are protein and will toughen and shrink if overheated. In this case, it's mandatory to have an accurate oven thermometer.

If the baked cake looks flat and dense, the cake was not inverted to cool, and gravity made it sink. If the top is concave, the whites were overwhipped.

◆ ･ ◆ ･ ◆

(continued)

One 10-inch cake;
12 servings

Cake can be made in advance, wrapped airtight, and stored at room temperature for several days. It can also be wrapped airtight and frozen, but its flavor starts to deteriorate after 2 or 3 weeks.

10 × 4-inch angel food cake pan with raised "feet" (or a tall bottle or large funnel), serrated knife or pronged angel food cake cutter

325°F for 45 to 50 minutes

1 cup sifted cake flour

½ cup sifted confectioners' sugar (or substitute ½ cup superfine sugar)

½ teaspoon salt

¾ cup superfine sugar

1½ cups egg whites (10 to 12 large egg whites), at room temperature

1 teaspoon cream of tartar

1 teaspoon vanilla extract

1 teaspoon orange, lemon, or almond extract (optional)

1. Position a rack in the center of the oven and preheat it to 325°F. (Do not grease the cake pan.)

2. Sift the flour onto a sheet of wax paper, then resift it with the confectioners' sugar and salt. Sift the superfine sugar onto another sheet of wax paper, then transfer it to a cup.

3. In a large grease-free bowl, combine the egg whites and cream of tartar. With an electric mixer on medium speed, whip until foamy. Gradually add the superfine sugar, and whip until the whites are nearly stiff but not dry. They should look glossy and satiny smooth, and you should be able to invert the bowl without having the mass of whites move or slide. Sprinkle the vanilla and the orange or other extract, if using, over the beaten whites and whisk once or twice by hand to blend.

4. Using a rubber spatula or flat whisk, fold in the flour mixture about 3 tablespoons at a time. Sprinkle the dry mixture lightly over the whites, or sift it on, and then fold with a light touch. Cut down through the center of the whites to the bottom of the bowl, then turn the spatula as you bring it back up while giving the bowl a quarter turn. Repeat until the dry ingredients are just barely incorporated. Do not stir the batter.

5. Very gently turn the batter into the ungreased tube pan, and smooth the top lightly. Cut down through the batter one time with the spatula to be sure there are no large air pockets. Immediately place the cake in the oven. Bake for about 45 minutes, or until well risen and golden on top, and a cake tester (such as a long thin bamboo skewer) comes out clean.

6. As soon as the cake is baked, invert the cake pan onto its raised feet or hang the pan upside down over the neck of a bottle or funnel. Allow the cake to hang upside down for several hours (or overnight), until completely cool.

7. To remove the cake from the pan, slide the blade of a long thin knife between the cake and the pan sides, and center tube, to loosen it. Top the cake with a plate, invert, and lift off the pan. (If the pan has a removable bottom, remove the sides first, then slide the knife between the pan bottom and cake to release it.) Leave the cake upside down on the plate, or invert it onto another plate. To serve, cut with a serrated knife or pronged angel-food cake cutter.

Light Touch: Angel cake obtains less than 1 percent of its calories from fat and contains zero cholesterol.

Nutritional Analysis per serving
....
113 calories

4 g protein

0 g fat

0 g satfat

24 mg carbohydrate

144 mg sodium

0 mg cholesterol

Nut Angel Cake

Prepare the recipe as directed, adding 1 teaspoon almond extract. Because the cake contains no other fat, you can add some nuts. Toast ½ cup hazelnuts or blanched almonds (page 47), and grind them in the food processor with ¼ cup of the sifted confectioners' sugar. Sift the flour together with the remaining ¼ cup confectioners' sugar and the salt as directed, and then combine the ground nuts with the flour mixture for folding into the batter. Almonds raise the total calories from fat to 16 percent, hazelnuts to 19 percent. Both add slightly less than 30 calories, as well as 3 grams of fat and 0.2 gram saturated fat per serving—not enough to worry about.

Orange Angel Cake

Prepare the recipe as directed, adding 1 teaspoon orange extract and the grated zest of 2 oranges. Toss the zest with the flour-sugar mixture before folding into the batter. Frost with Orange Icing Glaze (page 437).

The orange additions do not change the fat content of the cake.

Cocoa Angel Cake

This recipe uses the same number of egg whites as the basic recipe but it must be baked in a smaller pan, an ungreased 9 × 4-inch angel cake tube. That is because the cocoa powder contains a small amount of butterfat, which weighs down the meringue foam and slightly reduces the volume of the cake.

Prepare the recipe with the following changes: Omit the confectioners' sugar, and use a total of 1¼ cups superfine sugar. Add ¼ cup Dutch-processed unsweetened cocoa and ½ teaspoon cinnamon, and sift with the flour; reduce the salt to a pinch. Bake for about 55 minutes. Frost the cake with Boiled Icing (page 441). Adding cocoa scarcely raises the calories from fat at all, just to 2 percent.

Old-Fashioned Silver Cake

◆ ◆ ◆

I n the 1920s, yolk-free "silver" cakes were the height of fashion, served with warm fruit sauces or layered with rich foamy icing. Today, the same cake is appreciated for its cholesterol-free virtues as well as its fine grain and not-too-sweet flavor. It is fine as a plain vanilla cake, but gains some pizzazz when almond or citrus flavoring is used as well. Consider this a basic white cake and serve it the old-fashioned way, piled high with Seven-Minute or Boiled Icing (pages 439 and 441), or spread fruit preserves between the layers and sift confectioners' sugar or cocoa on top. My favorite presentation is slices of plain cake accompanied by warm fruit compote or warm berry sauce.

◆ ◆ ◆

Yield

4½ cups batter; one 2-layer 8-inch cake; 10 servings

Advance Preparation

Cake can be prepared ahead, wrapped airtight, and frozen for up to 3 months.

Special Equipment

Two 8 × 1½-inch round pans

Temperature and Time

350°F for 20 minutes

Butter-flavor no stick cooking spray

2 cups sifted cake flour

1 tablespoon baking powder

½ teaspoon salt

4 large egg whites, at room temperature

¾ cup plus 2 tablespoons granulated sugar, divided

⅓ cup canola or safflower oil

½ cup skim milk

2 teaspoons vanilla extract

1 teaspoon almond or orange extract

1. Position a rack in the center of the oven and preheat it to 350°F. Coat the baking pans with cooking spray. Dust the pans evenly with flour, and tap out excess flour.

2. Sift together the flour, baking powder, and salt onto a sheet of wax paper.

3. In a large grease-free bowl, whip the whites until foamy. Slowly add ¼ cup plus 2 tablespoons of the sugar, and whip until the whites are stiff but not dry. Remove the bowl of whites from the stand. Shake off beaters and, without washing them, return them to the mixer.

4. In another large mixer bowl, combine the oil, the remaining ½ cup sugar, the milk, vanilla, and almond or orange extracts, if using. Beat until well blended. Remove the bowl from the mixer stand. Whisk in about half of the flour mixture. Then alternately fold in the remaining flour with the whipped whites.

5. Divide the batter evenly between the prepared pans. Bake for about 20 minutes, or until the cake is springy to the touch and a cake tester inserted in the center of a layer comes out clean. Cool the cake in the pans on a wire rack for 10 minutes. Top each layer with another rack, invert, and remove the pans. Cool completely.

Light Touch: While this simple cake has always been low in cholesterol, it was originally made with whole milk, or even cream, so there was some cholesterol present. The classic recipe contains, in addition to the milk, ½ cup butter and 1 cup sugar. With 38 percent of its calories from fat, each serving contains 9 grams of fat, 5 of which are saturated. I have replaced the butter with a reduced quantity of oil, switched from whole to skim milk, cut the sugar, and substituted cake flour, which contains less gluten than all-purpose flour, to give a finer, more tender crumb. Since the meringue contributes leavening, I have strengthened it by increasing the proportion of sugar whipped with the whites. The only fat comes from the ⅓ cup oil, giving the recipe 30 percent of its calories from fat. The following variation has only 28 percent fat because the milk is replaced by juice plus an orange soaking glaze.

Orange Cake with Orange Glaze

Prepare the cake as directed, but with the following changes: After coating the baking pans, line them with wax paper or baking parchment, then spray the paper (this facilitates removal of the glaze-soaked cakes); do not dust the pans with flour. Replace the milk with orange juice. In addition to the vanilla extract, add 1½ teaspoons orange extract plus the grated zest of 1 orange (about 4 teaspoons).

While the cake bakes, prepare an Orange Glaze: In a small saucepan, stir together ½ cup orange juice, 2 tablespoons sugar, and the grated zest of ½ orange (2 teaspoons). Bring to a boil, stirring until the sugar dissolves. Remove pan from the heat. Rewarm the glaze just before using it if necessary.

As soon as the pans of hot cake are set on the cooling rack, prick each layer all over with a toothpick. Brush on the warm glaze, dividing it between the layers. Allow them to cool, then invert the layers onto flat plates and peel off the paper.

Slice the cake and serve it plain or fill the layers with warmed orange marmalade stirred with a couple of tablespoons of orange liqueur. Cover the filled cake with Boiled Icing (page 441).

Nutritional Analysis per serving

222 calories

4 g protein

7 g fat

0.6 g satfat

35 g carbohydrate

234 mg sodium

0 mg cholesterol

Nutritional Analysis per serving (without filling or icing)

235 calories

3 g protein

7 g fat

0.5 g satfat

40 g carbohydrate

162 mg sodium

0 mg cholesterol

Chocolate
Buttermilk Cake

◆·◆·◆

This is the perfect all-purpose chocolate layer cake. It is not too sweet, has a moist, tender crumb, and is absolutely reliable and easy to prepare. In taste tests, this cake was the hands-down favorite, easily as popular as a classic version with twice the amount of fat. You can bake this as a sheet cake or in layers filled with raspberry or apricot preserves and sift confectioners' sugar over a paper doily set on top to create a decorative pattern. Or, for a gala occasion, frost the cake with great swirls of satiny Seven-Minute Icing (page 439) or Seafoam Icing (page 440), and pass a bowl of fresh raspberries. I prefer to use the European-style Dutch-processed cocoa for this cake as it does not have the slightly bitter aftertaste of natural cocoa.

◆·◆·◆

Butter-flavor no stick cooking spray

1¼ cups dark brown sugar, packed

1 cup nonfat buttermilk

½ cup water

⅓ cup canola or safflower oil

3 tablespoons dark corn syrup

1 large egg, separated, plus 2 large egg whites

1 tablespoon vanilla extract

1½ cups sifted all-purpose flour

2 tablespoons cornstarch

¾ cup unsweetened Dutch-processed cocoa

1¼ teaspoons baking powder

½ teaspoon baking soda

Scant teaspoon salt

¼ teaspoon cinnamon

2 tablespoons granulated sugar

1. Position a rack in the center of the oven and preheat it to 350°F. Lightly coat the baking pan(s) with cooking spray. Line the pan(s) with wax paper or parchment, and spray or oil the paper. Dust evenly with sifted cocoa, and tap out excess cocoa.

Yield

About 7 cups batter; one 2-layer 9-inch cake or 9 × 13-inch sheet cake; 12 servings

Advance Preparation

Cake can be prepared ahead, wrapped airtight, and frozen (without icing).

Special Equipment

Two 9 × 1½-inch round cake pans or one 9 × 13-inch baking pan, wax paper or baking parchment

Temperature and Time

350°F for 30 to 35 minutes for layers, 35 to 40 minutes for sheet cake

Have Your Cake and Eat It, Too

2. In a large bowl, combine the brown sugar, buttermilk, water, oil, corn syrup, egg yolk, and vanilla. Using an electric mixer, beat on low speed until well blended.

3. Place a strainer over the bowl and add the flour, cornstarch, cocoa, baking powder, baking soda, salt, and cinnamon. Stir and sift the dry ingredients onto the wet ingredients. With the mixer on low speed, blend well. Set aside.

4. In a large grease-free bowl, using clean beaters, whip the egg whites until foamy. Add the granulated sugar and whip on medium speed until stiff but not dry.

5. Fold about one quarter of the whites into the chocolate batter to lighten it, then gradually fold in the remaining whites. Don't worry if a few traces of white remain. Divide the batter evenly between the prepared layer pans or spread it into the sheet pan. Bake layers for about 30 to 35 minutes, a sheet cake for 35 to 40 minutes, or until the cake feels springy to the touch and a cake tester inserted in the center comes out clean. Cool the cake in the pan(s) on a wire rack for about 10 minutes. Top with another rack, invert, and remove the pan(s) and paper. Let cool completely.

Light Touch: My grandmother's recipe for traditional chocolate buttermilk cake, made with 4 whole eggs, 1 cup sweet butter, and 4 ounces unsweetened solid chocolate, gets, to no one's great surprise, 50 percent of its calories from fat. Just one slice sets you back 23 grams of fat, 11 of which are saturated. I can honestly say this enlightened version tastes good, with half the calories from fat (26 percent). While keeping the fine grain and rich chocolate taste, I achieved the reductions by using only 1 egg yolk and 3 whites, replacing the butter with much less oil, substituting cocoa for the chocolate, and substituting brown sugar, which adds moisture, for most of the white. Unlike other low-fat cakes, this one works better with all-purpose flour and a little cornstarch instead of softer cake flour.

253 calories

4 g protein

8 g fat

1 g satfat

44 g carbohydrate

287 mg sodium

18 mg cholesterol

Cocoa Bundt Cake

◆ ◆ ◆

*D*ark corn syrup replaces all the oil in this nearly fat-free but remarkably good chocolate cake. The taste is rich and satisfying and even chocoholics will never guess that it is missing cholesterol as well as fat. I developed this recipe while preparing a group of fat-free cakes for Best Foods, the makers of Karo Syrup. The flavor is not too sweet, the crumb is soft and moist, and the taste chocolaty. When freshly baked, the crust is slightly chewy (a characteristic of fat-free cakes), but by the second day, it softens and is as soft and moist as the interior.

Top this cake with a light dusting of confectioners' sugar, or add Cocoa Icing Glaze (page 436). Serve the cake plain, or with fresh raspberries and a little Vanilla Custard Sauce (page 410).

◆ ◆ ◆

Yield

6 cups batter; one 9-inch Bundt cake; 14 servings

Advance Preparation

Cake can be made a day or two in advance and kept, covered, at room temperature. Wrapped airtight, it freezes well.

Special Equipment

9-inch Bundt pan (6 to 8-cup capacity), preferably nonstick

Temperature and Time

350°F for 45 minutes

Butter-flavor no stick cooking spray

1⅓ cups unsifted cake flour

2 tablespoons cornstarch

2 teaspoons baking powder

½ teaspoon baking soda

¼ teaspoon salt

⅛ teaspoon cinnamon

½ cup plus 2 tablespoons unsweetened cocoa, preferably nonalkalized

1 cup plus 2 tablespoons granulated sugar, divided

½ cup dark or light corn syrup

½ cup plus 2 tablespoons warm water

2 teaspoons vanilla extract

4 large egg whites

Pinch of cream of tartar

Icing

Cocoa Icing Glaze (page 436) or Mocha Icing Glaze (page 436)

1. Position a rack in the center of the oven and preheat it to 350°F. Coat the Bundt pan with cooking spray. Dust the pan with sifted cocoa, and tap out excess cocoa.

2. Sift the flour, cornstarch, baking powder, baking soda, salt, cinnamon, and cocoa into a large bowl. Make a well in the center of the dry ingredients and add 1 cup of the sugar, the corn syrup, water, and vanilla, but do *not* blend together at this point. Set aside.

3. In another large bowl, with an electric mixer, whip the egg whites with cream of tartar until foamy. Add the 2 remaining tablespoons sugar, and whip the whites until stiff but not dry. Remove the bowl of whites from the stand. Shake off the beaters, and without washing them, return them to the mixer.

4. With the mixer on low speed (it's not necessary to wash the beaters), beat the cocoa and corn syrup mixture until well blended. Stir about 1 cup of the whipped whites into the chocolate batter to lighten it. Then gently fold in the remaining whites.

5. Turn the batter into the prepared pan. Bake for about 45 minutes, or until the top is springy to the touch and a cake tester inserted in the center comes out clean. Cool the cake in the pan on a wire rack for about 5 minutes, then top with another rack or a plate and invert. Lift off the pan. Cool, then add glaze.

Light Touch: This cake has many virtues: It receives only 5 percent of its total calories from fat, and it is not only cholesterol-free, but lactose-free as well. In my experience, it is rare for a cake to have a good texture without any added fat, but the balance between the ingredients in this recipe was carefully adjusted, and it works.

Nutritional Analysis per serving

151 calories
2 g protein
1 g fat
0.4 g satfat
35 g carbohydrate
141 mg sodium
0 mg cholesterol

Spice Cake

◆ · ◆ · ◆ ·

An old-fashioned, moderately sweet spice cake with a fine moist crumb that is perfect for mid-afternoon tea or Sunday brunch. Serve it plain, glazed with icing, or dressed up for company dessert with warm Bourbon Sauce (page 418) or a dollop of Apple Snow (page 382).

◆ · ◆ · ◆ ·

Butter-flavor no stick cooking spray

1½ cups all-purpose flour

¼ cup cornstarch

1 teaspoon baking powder

½ teaspoon baking soda

¼ teaspoon salt

1 teaspoon cinnamon

½ teaspoon nutmeg, preferably freshly grated

¼ teaspoon ground cloves

⅛ teaspoon ground ginger

1 cup granulated sugar, divided

2 tablespoons canola or safflower oil

⅓ cup dark corn syrup

½ cup apple or orange juice

½ cup unsweetened applesauce

1½ teaspoons vanilla extract

3 large egg whites, at room temperature

Pinch of cream of tartar

Confectioners' sugar or Vanilla Icing Glaze (page 435) (optional)

1. Position a rack in the center of the oven and preheat it to 350°F. Coat the baking pan with cooking spray. Dust with flour, being sure to coat the tube and tap out excess flour.

2. Sift together the flour, cornstarch, baking powder, baking soda, salt, and spices into a large bowl. Stir in ¾ cup of the sugar.

3. In a small saucepan, combine the oil, corn syrup, and fruit juice, and stir over medium heat just until well blended. Remove from the heat.

4. Make a well in the center of the flour mixture, and pour in the warmed corn syrup mixture. Whisk to combine, then beat in the applesauce and vanilla extract.

5. In a grease-free bowl, combine the egg whites and cream of tartar, and whip with an electric beater on medium speed until foamy. Gradually add the remaining ¼ cup sugar, and whip until the whites are stiff but not dry. Stir about 1 cup of the whipped whites into the spice batter to lighten it. Then gently fold in the remaining whites.

6. Spoon the batter into the prepared pan, and smooth the top. Bake for about 35 minutes, or until the top feels springy to the touch and a cake tester inserted in the center comes out clean. Do not overbake.

7. Cool the cake in the pan on a wire rack, for about 10 minutes, then top with another rack, invert, and remove the pan. Allow the cake to cool completely. Serve it plain, or sift on a little confectioners' sugar or top with Vanilla Glaze.

Light Touch: This cake has a long history. It began as a totally cholesterol- and fat-free recipe, in which corn syrup was supposed to substitute for oil, replacing all the fat. The resulting cake was acceptable in flavor, but—as with all totally fat-free baked products—the crust was hard, the inner texture dry (and a little odd). But something kept me from adding this to the collection on the cutting-room floor...instead, I started making changes. Ultimately, I replaced some of the fat, in the form of oil, plus applesauce, to provide and retain moisture; I also cut the corn syrup by two thirds. The original used 4 egg whites, which probably contributed to the dryness, so I dropped 1 white and adjusted the liquid accordingly. The resulting cake has an excellent moist texture and well-balanced spicy flavor. It is neither dry nor tough; judged a success by testers, it obtains only 12 percent calories from fat.

Nutritional Analysis
per serving
....

225 calories

3 g protein

3 g fat

0.2 g satfat

47 g carbohydrate

152 mg sodium

0 mg cholesterol

Carrot Cake

◆ ◆ ◆

This old favorite is just as moist and rich-tasting as ever, enhanced with raisins and pineapple. It is topped with a pineapple glaze; for diehards who cannot do without the traditional cream cheese topping, use Light Cream Cheese Frosting (page 444).

◆ ◆ ◆

Yield

About 3½ cups batter; one 8-inch square or 9-inch tube cake; 10 servings

Advance Preparation

Cake can be baked ahead and stored at room temperature, well wrapped, for about 1 week. Or it can be wrapped airtight and frozen.

Special Equipment

8 × 8 × 2-inch baking pan or 9-inch (6½-cup) tube pan

Temperature and Time

400°F for 40 to 45 minutes

Butter-flavor no stick cooking spray

2 large egg whites, at room temperature

½ cup nonfat plain yogurt

3 tablespoons canola or safflower oil

½ cup dark brown sugar, packed

2 teaspoons vanilla extract

1 cup unsifted all-purpose flour

½ cup plus 2 tablespoons unsifted whole wheat pastry flour

1¼ teaspoons baking powder

½ teaspoon baking soda

Generous ¼ teaspoon salt

1 teaspoon cinnamon

½ teaspoon nutmeg

2 tablespoons toasted wheat germ

1 cup grated or shredded carrots, lightly packed (about 2 carrots, peeled and grated on medium-size holes of a box grater)

¾ cup drained sweetened crushed pineapple

½ cup dried currants or seedless dark raisins

Pineapple Glaze

1½ cups sifted confectioners' sugar

3 to 5 tablespoons pineapple juice

1. Position a rack in the center of the oven and preheat it to 400°F. Coat the baking pans with cooking spray. Dust with flour, and tap out excess flour.

2. In a large bowl, whisk together the egg whites, yogurt, oil, brown sugar, and vanilla. Set a strainer over the bowl and add both flours, the baking powder, baking soda, salt, and spices. Stir and sift the dry ingredients onto the yogurt mixture. Blend lightly. Add the wheat germ, carrots, pineapple, and currants or raisins and stir to blend well.

3. Turn the batter into the prepared pan. Bake for 40 to 45 minutes, or until a cake tester inserted in the center comes out clean. Cool the cake on a wire rack for about 10 minutes, then slide a knife blade between the cake and sides of the pan as well as top edge of center tube to loosen it. Invert the cake onto a platter and cool completely.

4. For the topping, blend the sugar and juice together in a small bowl, adding liquid just until the consistency of cream. Spread over the cooled cake, letting glaze run down the sides.

Light Touch: My classic carrot cake recipe, made with ¾ cup oil, 2 whole eggs, 1 cup sugar, and ½ cup walnuts, gets a generous 56 percent of its calories from fat, with 338 calories, 21 grams fat (of which 3 grams are saturated), and 43 milligrams of cholesterol per serving. Adding the traditional rich cream cheese icing (48 percent total calories from fat) piles on an extra 322 calories and 18 grams of fat (11 of them saturated) per slice!

You can bask in a virtuous glow as you enjoy this lightened version, which gets only 15 percent of its calories from fat. It has one fourth the fat per serving, and zero cholesterol. I have achieved this by cutting the oil to only 3 tablespoons, removing the egg yolks and all the nuts, and reducing the sugar by ¼ cup. Using a pineapple glaze instead of the rich cream cheese frosting keeps the final results light.

*Nutritional Analysis
per serving with glaze*

267 calories

5 g protein

5 g fat

0.4 g satfat

53 g carbohydrate

164 mg sodium

0 mg cholesterol

Strawberry Shortcake

◆ ◆ ◆

*T*his all-American classic is traditionally made with buttery baking powder biscuits embracing clouds of whipped heavy cream and sweetened ripe berries. To lighten the clouds while keeping the luxurious vision and rich taste, I have replaced the cream with frozen vanilla yogurt. The quantity of fruit in this recipe is very generous because I love lots of strawberry sauce soaking into the cake in addition to whole berries for a garnish on top. I add a little sugar to plain biscuits when I'm baking them for shortcake, but many purists prefer none; suit yourself.

◆ ◆ ◆

Yield

10 servings

Advance Preparation

Biscuits have the lightest texture when freshly baked. However, they can be made in advance, double-wrapped, and frozen for up to 1 month. The strawberries can be sliced and sugared several hours in advance. Assemble the shortcakes just before serving.

1 recipe Basic Biscuits (page 92), prepared as directed below, with 2 tablespoons granulated sugar if desired

1½ quarts ripe strawberries, rinsed and dried

¼ to ½ cup granulated sugar, to taste

About 1 quart nonfat frozen vanilla yogurt

1. Prepare the biscuit dough following instructions on page 92, adding 2 tablespoons sugar along with the dry ingredients if you wish. Pat the dough into a rectangle about ½ inch thick and cut out 10 biscuits with a 2½-inch round cutter. Bake as directed. Let cool.

2. To prepare the filling, set aside 10 perfect whole strawberries for garnish. Hull and slice the remaining berries, place in a bowl, and stir in sugar to taste. Refrigerate until ready to assemble the shortcakes.

3. About 15 minutes before you are ready to assemble the shortcakes, if the frozen yogurt is very hard, remove from the freezer to soften slightly.

4. With a serrated knife, slice each biscuit in half. To assemble the shortcakes, set the bottom half of each biscuit on a dessert plate and top with a generous spoonful of sliced berries and a dollop of frozen yogurt. Cover with the top of the biscuit, spoon a little more strawberry sauce over, and top with a spoonful of yogurt and a reserved whole berry, stem up. Pass any remaining berry sauce and yogurt at the table.

Light Touch: Although rich in taste, these shortcakes contain very little cholesterol and obtain just 29 percent of their calories from fat, nearly all of which comes from the biscuits. To cut the fat further, use only half a biscuit per serving. To enhance your sense of moral superiority while savoring the rich taste and texture, compare these shortcakes with a traditional recipe that uses biscuits made with ¼ cup butter and topped with berries and whipped heavy cream—weighing in at 65 percent calories from fat (more than twice as much) and with a hefty 62 milligrams cholesterol in each serving.

Nutritional Analysis per serving (includes yogurt plus optional sugar in biscuits and sugar on berries)

....

280 calories

5 g protein

9 g fat

2.4 g satfat

45 g carbohydreate

304 mg sodium

2 mg cholesterol

Blueberry Upside-Down Cake

· ◆ · ◆ · ◆ ·

R emember pineapple upside-down cake, sweet, golden pineapple rings coated with buttery caramel syrup, at once gilding and glazing the buttery cake held in their embrace? You will be admitting your age if you long for this darling of the 1950s, but don't be shy. This updated blueberry version is a cake for the 90s: light, filled with flavor and fruit, quick and easy to make. Serve it warm, with a spoonful of vanilla yogurt.

A blend of sweetened fruit and syrup is cooked briefly in a skillet, then topped by a slightly spiced, cholesterol-free batter and baked. When done, the cake is inverted (to fanfare), and the glazed fruit becomes the topping. The surprise of seeing the downside turn up is fun, especially if there is a child around to help with preparation and celebrate the finale with a cheer.

Don't wait until summer to try this delectable cake. Out of season, use frozen unsweetened berries, or any blend of fresh, frozen, or canned fruit you desire—thinly sliced pears and Golden Delicious apples; golden raisins, cranberries, and pecans; dried fruits such as prunes, apricots, and peaches—be creative, this cake can take it.

· ◆ · ◆ · ◆ ·

(continued)

Butter-flavor no stick cooking spray

Topping

⅓ cup plus 1 tablespoon dark brown sugar, packed

3 tablespoons light corn syrup

1½ tablespoons fresh lemon juice

1 teaspoon grated lemon or orange zest

2 cups fresh blueberries, picked over, rinsed, and patted dry, or frozen unsweetened whole berries, unthawed

Cake

⅓ cup canola or safflower oil

½ cup granulated sugar

⅓ cup honey

2 large egg whites

1 teaspoon vanilla extract *or* ½ teaspoon almond or orange extract

⅓ cup skim milk *or* orange or apple juice

1½ cups sifted cake flour

1 teaspoon baking powder

¼ teaspoon baking soda

⅛ teaspoon salt

½ teaspoon cinnamon

½ teaspoon nutmeg

1. Position a rack in the center of the oven and preheat it to 325°F.

2. Prepare the fruit topping: Coat the frying pan or pie plate generously with cooking spray. Add the brown sugar, corn syrup, and lemon juice. Stir, then place the pan over medium heat for about 1 minute, stirring with a wooden spoon to partially melt the sugar. Remove the pan from the heat. Add the zest and blueberries, spreading them in a single layer. Set aside.

3. In a large bowl, combine the oil, granulated sugar, honey, egg whites, extract, and milk or juice. Whisk lightly to combine. Set a strainer over the bowl and add the flour, baking powder, baking soda, salt, cinnamon, and nutmeg. Stir and sift the dry ingredients onto the wet. With an electric mixer on low speed, beat until well blended, scraping down the bowl and beaters several times. The batter will be runny.

4. Pour the batter evenly over the blueberries in the pan. Bake for 30 to 35 minutes, or until a cake tester inserted in the center comes

---

2½ cups batter; one 10-inch cake; 10 servings

Advance Preparation

Cake can be baked ahead and kept a day, but its texture is best when fresh from the oven, while the glaze is still a runny sauce. On standing, the glaze permeates and moistens the cake; not bad, just different.

Special Equipment

10-inch heavy ovenproof skillet, such as cast-iron or enameled iron, or 10-inch deep-dish Pyrex pie plate; 12-inch or larger flat serving platter

Temperature and Time

325°F for 30 to 35 minutes; if using frozen berries, increase baking time slightly

Have Your Cake and Eat It, Too

out clean and the cake top is golden and springy to the touch. Don't forget to use a potholder when handling the skillet; it is hot!

5. Cool the cake in the pan on a wire rack for 3 or 4 minutes, until the glaze stops bubbling. Top the pan with a large flat serving platter. Holding the plate and pan together with potholders, invert. Lift off the skillet. Reposition any fruit that may have stuck to the pan.

Light Touch: In its traditional form, upside-down cake is usually made with a 2-egg butter cake batter (about 34 percent calories from fat) and a glaze of sugared fruit cooked in about ⅓ cup of butter. I have cut total calories from fat down to 20 percent by reducing the amount of fat in the batter, substituting oil for butter, and dropping 2 egg yolks. In the glaze, the melted sugar plus corn syrup and fruit juice provide the liquid instead of melted butter.

In the variations, the fruit changes, but the total fat is not significantly altered.

Nutritional Analysis per serving

255 calories

2 g protein

6 g fat

0.4 g satfat

50 g carbohydrate

102 mg sodium

0 mg cholesterol

Blueberry-Peach Upside-Down Cake

Prepare the cake as directed, but, use 1 cup blueberries and ¾ cup thinly sliced peeled peaches, either fresh, or frozen or canned (drained and dried), in the glaze.

Cherry-Raspberry Upside-Down Cake

Prepare the cake as directed but use 1 cup fresh sweet dark cherries, pitted and halved, plus 1 cup fresh raspberries or frozen whole unsweetened raspberries in the glaze.

Pear-Gingerbread
Upside-Down Cake

◆ · ◆ · ◆

Sugar-glazed pear slices fanned out in a glistening pattern are edged with golden-brown gingerbread when this moist, aromatic cake is unmolded. It tastes as good as it looks, the spices perfectly balanced by the mildly sweet fruit. Serve it warm from the oven and pass vanilla yogurt to spoon alongside.

The texture of this cake is best when the batter is mixed with a wooden spoon rather than an electric mixer. This recipe was developed in conjunction with Eating Well magazine.

◆ · ◆ · ◆

Yield

About 2½ cups batter; one 8-inch square cake; 9 servings

Advance Preparation

Cake should be made on the day it is to be served. It is best warm from the oven, when the glazing is still runny.

Special Equipment

8 × 8 × 1½-inch baking pan

Temperature and Time

375°F for 45 to 50 minutes (15 minutes for the pears alone, then 30 to 35 minutes longer to bake the cake)

Topping

    1 tablespoon unsalted butter

    3 tablespoons light brown sugar, packed

    3 ripe but firm pears, such as Bosc or Bartlett

    1 tablespoon fresh lemon juice

Cake

    2 large egg whites

    ½ cup nonfat buttermilk

    ¼ cup unsulfured molasses

    2 tablespoons canola or safflower oil

    1¼ cups sifted cake flour

    ¾ teaspoon baking powder

    ¼ teaspoon baking soda

    ½ teaspoon salt

    2 teaspoons cinnamon

    1 teaspoon ground ginger

    ½ teaspoon allspice

    ¼ teaspoon nutmeg

    ½ cup granulated sugar

1. Position a rack in the lower third of the oven and preheat it to 375°F. Coat the baking pan with cooking spray.

2. Prepare the fruit topping: Add the butter to the prepared pan and melt it over low heat. Remove from the heat and stir in the brown sugar.

3. Peel, halve, and core the pears, and brush them with the lemon juice to avoid discoloration. Set each pear half cut side down on a cutting board and cut crosswise into $\frac{1}{8}$-inch-thick slices. Keeping the slices together, slide a metal spatula underneath and invert a sliced pear half onto your hand, pressing on it so it fans out slightly. Place it cut side up (with the narrower top part in the center) in the brown sugar mixture in the pan. Repeat with the remaining pear halves. Bake, uncovered, for 15 minutes.

4. While the pears are baking, combine the egg whites, buttermilk, molasses, and oil in a large bowl. Whisk to blend well. Place a strainer over the bowl and add the flour, baking powder, baking soda, salt, spices, and sugar. Stir and sift the dry ingredients onto the buttermilk mixture. With a wooden spoon, stir until just blended; do not overbeat.

5. When the pears have baked for 15 minutes, remove them from the oven and pour the batter evenly over them. Bake for 30 to 35 minutes longer, or until the top of the cake is springy to the touch and a cake tester inserted in the center comes out clean.

6. Let the cake sit for 2 to 3 minutes on a wire rack. Run a knife between the cake and the sides of the pan to loosen the edges. Invert a serving platter over the baking pan. Holding the pan and platter together with potholders, invert, using a sharp downward motion. Lift off the baking pan. Remove any pear slices that have adhered to the pan and replace them on top of the cake. Let cool for 5 to 10 minutes, then cut into squares and serve warm.

Light Touch: This recipe obtains only 20 percent of its calories from fat. It has just a touch of cholesterol from the butter used to flavor the glaze; margarine may be substituted to omit cholesterol entirely. The fruit contributes 2 grams of dietary fiber per serving.

*Nutritional Analysis
per serving*
....

213 calories

3 g protein

5 g fat

1.1 g satfat

41 g carbohydrate

199 mg sodium

4 mg cholesterol

Blitz Torte with Strawberries and Cream

◆ ◆ ◆

T his unusual cake is a delightful blend of contrasts and surprises. It is lovely to look at yet relatively easy to prepare; it is made with a "butter" cake layer and a meringue layer baked right on top of each other; and it is filled with cream, strawberries, toasted almonds, and cinnamon sugar and would seem to be heavy and rich, yet is refreshing and light. Ripe peaches, peeled and sliced, or other berries can be substituted for the strawberries.

A pleasure for the eye and the palate, this cake has been a hit at every dinner party and dessert tasting. I even served it once as the grand finale after a banquet of whole roast suckling pig, proving it is the perfect light ending to a heavy meal.

◆ ◆ ◆

Yield

One 2-layer 8-inch cake; 10 servings

Advance Preparation

Cake can be prepared a day or two in advance and wrapped airtight; it is best not to freeze it, or the meringue layer will soften. Cream filling can be prepared a day or two in advance and stored, covered, in the refrigerator. Cake can be assembled about 4 hours in advance of serving and refrigerated; if stored longer, the meringue will begin to soften slightly, but that is not fatal.

Special Equipment

Two 8 × 1½-inch round pans, wax paper or baking parchment, pastry brush

Temperature and Time

350°F for about 30 minutes

Butter-flavor no stick cooking spray

Cake

1¼ cups sifted cake flour

1¼ teaspoons baking powder

⅛ teaspoon salt

¼ cup plus 2 tablespoons skim or 1% milk

1 large egg yolk

1 teaspoon vanilla extract

1 teaspoon almond extract

¾ cup granulated sugar, divided

2 large egg whites

Meringue Layer

4 large egg whites, at room temperature

¼ teaspoon cream of tartar

1 cup plus 1 tablespoon superfine sugar, divided

1 teaspoon cinnamon

¼ cup sliced almonds

Have Your Cake and Eat It, Too

Vanilla Cream Filling

    4 ounces low-fat cream cheese, at room temperature

    ½ cup low-fat vanilla yogurt, drained in a strainer for 15 minutes

    1 tablespoon granulated sugar, or to taste

    1 teaspoon vanilla extract

Fruit

    2 tablespoons hazelnut or orange liqueur

    3 cups fresh strawberries, rinsed, hulled, dried, and sliced

    1 tablespoon granulated sugar

Nutritional Analysis per serving

284 calories

6 g protein

4 g fat

1.5 g satfat

56 g carbohydrate

181 mg sodium

25 mg cholesterol

1. Position a rack in the center of the oven and preheat it to 350°F. Coat the baking pans with cooking spray. Line the pans with wax paper or parchment, and spray the paper. Dust the pans with flour, and tap out excess flour.

2. Prepare the cake batter: Sift together the flour, baking powder, and salt onto a sheet of wax paper or into a bowl. Set aside.

3. In a small saucepan, heat the milk to just below a simmer. Remove from the heat and let cool until tepid.

4. In a medium bowl, using an electric mixer, beat the egg yolk and vanilla and almond extracts until blended. Add ½ cup of the sugar and beat until light in color. Scrape down the bowl and beaters. With the mixer on low speed, gradually add the warm milk. Increase the speed to medium and whip until the sugar is completely dissolved. Scrape down the bowl and beaters.

5. In a clean bowl, with clean beaters, whip the egg whites until foamy. Gradually add the remaining ¼ cup sugar and whip until the whites are stiff but not dry. Fold about one third of the whipped whites into the egg yolk mixture. Then alternately fold in the flour mixture and the remaining whites. Divide the batter equally between the prepared baking pans, and smooth the tops. Set aside.

6. Prepare the meringue layer: In a clean bowl, using the electric mixer, whip the egg whites with the cream of tartar until foamy. Gradually add the 1 cup sugar and whip until the whites are stiff but not dry.

7. Divide the meringue between the cake pans, spreading it evenly over the cake batter. Combine the cinnamon and the remaining 1 tablespoon sugar and sprinkle it over the meringue layers. Then sprinkle the sliced almonds over each layer. Bake for about 30 minutes, until the meringue top is ivory-colored and crisp to the touch.

(continued)

8. Cool the layers in the pans on wire racks for about 10 minutes. Run a knife blade between the cakes and the sides of the pans, top each layer with a plate covered with foil, and invert. Remove the pans and papers, invert the layers again onto racks, and cool completely.

9. Prepare the filling: Combine all the ingredients in a mixer or a food processor and process until completely smooth. Refrigerate until needed.

10. To assemble the cake, place 1 cake layer, meringue side down, on a flat plate. Brush the hazelnut or orange liqueur over the cake. Spread the cream filling on top, then cover it with a generous layer of sliced strawberries. Add the second layer, meringue side up. Refrigerate until serving time. Place the remaining berries in a bowl, sprinkle them with the sugar, and toss lightly.

11. To serve, place a spoonful of berries alongside each slice of cake.

Light Touch: This cake is German in origin. I suspect the title comes from the fact that *blitz* means "wink," referring to the fact that, in a wink, you have baked two cakes at once. Naturally, the cake layer of the original was butter-laden, and although the meringue was fat-free, the cake was filled with a 3-yolk pastry cream, bringing the total calories from fat to about 40 percent. And as if that weren't enough, a little whipped cream often adorned each serving.

I consider my Blitz Torte a shining example of the fact that a marvelous pastry creation can also be low in fat. By removing all the butter and 2 of the yolks from the batter, I have eliminated the majority of the fat from the cake layers. By replacing the classic pastry cream with an equally tasty blend of light cream cheese and yogurt, I cut about two thirds of the total fat. This version weighs in with only 13 percent of its calories from fat. Finally, I skip the *schlagobers* (whipped cream) and garnish each serving with sugared ripe berries.

Double-Chocolate Meringue Cake

◆ · ◆ · ◆ ·

hree crisp cocoa-meringue layers are filled with a rich chocolate peppermint mousse in this easy-but-elegant recipe. A chocolate lover's party cake, it is practical for entertaining because it can be prepared well in advance. The meringue cake is a basic formula; the filling can be anything you wish. Try any of the other mousses in the book (Cappuccino, page 306, Mandarin Orange, page 186, or Burgundy Cherry, page 204). For an easier but still divine variation, forget assembling the layers in a springform pan: Blend Vanilla Cream (page 402) with a pint of fresh raspberries and spread half over the bottom cake layer, then half over the second layer, and top with the third meringue disk; sift a little unsweetened cocoa on top and garnish with a ring of fresh berries.

◆ · ◆ · ◆ ·

Chocolate Meringue Layers

    Butter-flavor no stick cooking spray

    1¼ cups sifted superfine sugar, divided

    2 tablespoons sifted cornstarch

    2 tablespoons sifted unsweetened cocoa, preferably Dutch-processed

    6 large egg whites (¾ cup), at room temperature

    ¼ teaspoon cream of tartar

    ⅛ teaspoon salt

    1 teaspoon vanilla extract

    ¾ teaspoon almond extract (optional)

    1 recipe Chocolate Mousse (page 304; if you prefer, substitute 1 teaspoon almond or orange extract for the peppermint flavoring), prepared through step 8, combining meringue with chocolate

    Unsweetened cocoa

1. Position 2 racks to divide the oven in thirds and preheat it to 300°F. Line the cookie sheets with parchment or foil, dabbing each sheet in a few spots with solid shortening or margarine to anchor the parchment or foil. Spray with cooking spray, dust generously with flour,

(continued)

One 3-layer 9-inch cake; 12 servings

Meringue layers can be made up to a week in advance and stored in an airtight container at room temperature, or they can be frozen. If they soften in humid weather, recrisp them in a 300°F oven for a few minutes, then cool before filling. Once the cake is assembled, it needs at least 3 hours to set. The meringue softens slightly after standing more than 6 hours.

2 large cookie sheets, baking parchment or foil, 8-inch pot lid or plate to use as template, 16- to 18-inch pastry bag, ½-inch (#6) round tip, 9-inch springform pan, 8-inch cardboard cake disk (optional)

300°F for 40 to 50 minutes

and tap out excess flour. Use a toothpick or pencil to draw around an 8-inch-diameter template to mark 2 rounds, set well apart, on one sheet; mark a third round on the second sheet.

2. Sift together ¾ cup of the sugar, the cornstarch, and cocoa onto a sheet of wax paper.

3. In a large grease-free bowl, combine the egg whites, cream of tartar, and salt. Using an electric mixer on medium speed, whip until foamy. Gradually add the remaining ½ cup sugar, and whip until the whites are satiny and nearly stiff, but not dry.

4. Sprinkle a few tablespoons of the cornstarch-cocoa mixture over the whipped whites, and fold in gently with a rubber spatula or flat whisk. Fold in the remaining dry ingredients by hand in several additions. Finally, fold in the extract(s). Don't worry if a few streaks of white remain visible.

5. Set out a large measuring cup or mug to serve as a stand for the pastry bag: Fit a ½-inch tip to the bag, fold back a generous 4- to 5-inch cuff, and set the bag tip-down in the cup. Spoon in the meringue, and twist the bag closed.

6. To make the meringue disks, first pipe meringue around the outside of each ring traced on the baking sheets, then pipe the meringue in a spiral in the center, completely filling the circle. If there are any spaces, use an icing spatula or your fingertip to spread the meringue. (Depending upon how much volume you achieved whipping the whites, you may be able to make several small meringue cookies with the remaining meringue.)

7. Bake for 40 to 50 minutes, or until the meringue is thoroughly set and a very light beige. Check after about 25 minutes; if the meringue appears to be darkening too quickly, lower the heat to 275°F.

8. Set the pans on a wire rack, and let the meringue layers cool and crisp completely. Then use a flat spatula to slide them off the sheets; if you used foil, peel it off the back of the layers if they do not lift off easily. If the layers are not crisp when completely cool, set them back on parchment- or foil-lined baking sheets and return to the 275°F oven for another 10 to 20 minutes.

9. To assemble the cake, first trim the meringue layers to a uniform size: Place the pot lid or plate you used as a template against each baked meringue and trim the edges with a sharp paring knife. Reserve the trimmings to crumble and blend into the filling if you wish. Set aside the best looking meringue layer for the top.

10. If using a cardboard cake disk, cover it with foil and place it in the bottom of the springform pan. Dab a little of the mousse in the center of the disk, or on the pan bottom, and center a meringue layer in the pan. Spread about 1¼ cups of the mousse over the meringue layer, top it with a second layer, and cover it with about 1¼ cups mousse. Spoon the remaining mousse around the edges, filling the space between the layers and the sides of the pan. Slide the blade of a table knife into the gap and run it around the cake to smooth the sides. Top the cake with the reserved meringue layer, right side up. Carefully slide the table knife between the cake and the pan sides and work some of the mousse up so it just touches the outer edge of the top layer; keep the top free of mousse. Cover the cake with foil or plastic wrap and refrigerate for at least 3 hours, or overnight.

11. To unmold the cake, dip a towel into very hot water, wring it out, and wrap it around the pan sides for several seconds. Then loosen the spring and jiggle the pan sides to detach them. Lift off the sides, and place the cake, on the cardboard disk or the pan bottom, on a serving plate. Sift a light dusting of cocoa over the top.

Light Touch: The filling tastes so rich and chocolaty, you would never guess that this cake gets just 12 percent of its calories from fat. Compare this to a meringue cake filled with a classic chocolate mousse loaded with eggs, butter, solid chocolate, and whipped cream: nearly 50 percent calories from fat and about 120 milligrams more cholesterol per serving!

*Nutritional Analysis
per serving*
....
233 calories

6 g protein

3 g fat

0.2 g satfat

50 g carbohydrate

115 mg sodium

20 mg cholesterol

Mandarin Orange Charlotte

◆ ◆ ◆

A charlotte is a molded dessert made in a pan lined with ladyfingers, cake slices, or bread and filled with a mousse, pudding, Bavarian cream, or a mélange of fruit. This version combines homemade ladyfingers (store-bought can be substituted) with a richly flavored, fruit-filled orange mousse. You can use this recipe as a model for your own inventions; substitute a different mousse (Chocolate, page 304, Cappuccino, page 306, or Raspberry, page 302) or your own gelatine-set fruit fillings. You can also serve the mousse alone as a dessert, spooning it into individual serving dishes or goblets to set.

Serve the charlotte plain, or gild it with Apricot-Orange Sauce (page 413) or Raspberry Sauce (page 412).

◆ ◆ ◆

Advance Preparation

The yogurt must drain through a strainer for about 30 minutes before using. Mousse needs a minimum of 3 hours to set before serving. Charlotte can be assembled a day in advance and refrigerated until shortly before serving.

Special Equipment

1½-quart French charlotte mold or soufflé dish or similar-sized container (such as a plastic bucket or freezer container)

Butter-flavor no stick cooking spray

1 recipe Ladyfingers (page 326) or approximately 24 store-bought ladyfingers (number depends upon size)

Mandarin Orange Mousse

1¼ cups (10 ounces) low-fat orange yogurt *or* nonfat vanilla or plain nonfat yogurt

1 15-ounce can mandarin orange segments in light syrup

¾ cup (6 ounces) nonfat cottage cheese

¾ cup (6 ounces) low-fat cream cheese

¾ cup granulated sugar

1½ teaspoons pure orange extract

3 tablespoons orange-flavored liqueur (such as Grand Marnier) or reserved syrup from canned oranges

Grated zest of 1 large orange

¼ cup plus 1 tablespoons frozen orange juice concentrate

3 tablespoons fresh lemon juice

Scant 3½ teaspoons Knox unflavored gelatine

Confectioners' sugar

1. Cut a round of wax paper to fit the bottom of the charlotte mold. Lightly coat the inside of the mold with cooking spray, and press the round of wax paper onto the bottom (don't oil the paper).

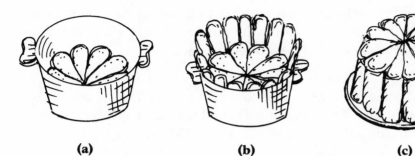

(a)   (b)   (c)

Nutritional Analysis
per serving
....

328 calories

11 g protein

5 g fat

0.4 g satfat

62 g carbohydrate

272 mg sodium

63 mg cholesterol

2. To line the mold, cut some of the ladyfingers into wedges and fit them side by side in the bottom of the mold to make a flower-shaped disk (a). Fill in any empty spaces with scraps of ladyfingers.

Line the sides of the mold with ladyfingers on end, placing them side by side (b). If necessary, trim the ladyfingers to fit. Trim off any ends that protrude beyond the top of the mold. Reserve the remaining ladyfingers and all scraps.

3. Prepare the mousse: Place the yogurt in a strainer set over a bowl and allow to drain for 30 minutes. Then transfer the yogurt to a bowl.

4. Drain the canned oranges (reserve 3 tablespoons of the juice if using it instead of orange liqueur). Spread the orange segments on a double thickness of paper towels and allow to drain completely. Gently pat the fruit dry.

5. Place the cottage cheese in a strainer set over a bowl. Cover the cheese with a piece of wax paper or plastic wrap and press down on it to force out excess liquid. Transfer the cottage cheese to a food processor. Add the cream cheese and sugar and process for 3 minutes, or until the mixture is absolutely smooth without a trace of graininess. Add the orange extract, orange liqueur (or reserved syrup), orange zest, and drained yogurt, and pulse to blend well.

6. In a small saucepan, combine the orange juice concentrate and lemon juice. Sprinkle on the gelatine and allow to sit for about 3 minutes to soften. Then set the pan over low heat and stir until the gelatine is dissolved; do not boil.

7. With the processor running, pour the dissolved gelatine mixture through the feed tube, using a rubber spatula to scrape out all the gelatine, and process until blended. Remove the bowl from the processor, add the drained orange segments, and stir gently to distribute them. Pour the mousse into the prepared mold.

(continued)

8. Use the reserved ladyfingers and scraps to cover the top of the mousse. (Forget symmetry of design here; this will be the bottom when the dessert is unmolded.) Cover the mold with wax paper or plastic wrap and refrigerate for at least 3 hours to set.

9. To unmold the charlotte, unwrap it and top it with a flat serving plate. Invert the mold and plate, and give a sharp jerk as you lift the mold straight up off the charlotte. Peel off the wax paper (c). Sift on a very light dusting of confectioners' sugar and serve.

Light Touch: The homemade ladyfingers have only 10 percent calories from fat, so they are a good choice for lining the charlotte mold. A conventional version of orange mousse enriched with 1 cup whipped heavy cream gets 31 percent calories from fat but has 7 grams of saturated fat and 94 milligrams of cholesterol per serving. By substituting a blend of yogurt, nonfat cottage cheese, and low-fat cream cheese for the cream, I have reduced the calories from fat to just 13 percent, and dropped virtually all the saturated fat and 31 milligrams of cholesterol per serving. The ladyfingers contain nearly all the cholesterol in this recipe; to avoid cholesterol almost entirely, serve only the mousse, spooning it into dessert glasses.

Lemon Roulade with
Lemon Curd and Fresh Berries

◆·◆·◆·

This light sponge cake has a tender, fine grain and is flexible enough to roll without cracking. In this recipe, Light Lemon Curd is paired with fresh strawberries for an elegant summer dessert. But go ahead and experiment: Change the flavor of the cake (to orange or almond by changing the extract) to complement any filling such as Ricotta Cream, Vanilla Pastry Cream, or Vanilla Cream with sliced berries, or any type of mousse (see Index).

◆·◆·◆·

Cake

Butter-flavor no stick cooking spray

½ cup sifted cake flour

¼ cup sifted cornstarch

1 teaspoon baking powder

2 large eggs, separated, plus 2 large egg whites

Pinch of salt

½ cup plus 2 tablespoons granulated sugar, divided

1 tablespoon canola or safflower oil

1 teaspoon lemon extract *or* orange or vanilla extract

¼ cup plus 2 tablespoons confectioners' sugar, divided

1 recipe Light Lemon Curd (page 404)

1½ cups fresh strawberries, rinsed, hulled, dried, and thinly sliced

1 cup fresh whole berries for garnish (optional)

1. Position a rack in the center of the oven and preheat it to 350°F. Line the bottom of the jelly-roll pan with baking parchment or wax paper. Lightly coat the paper with cooking spray. Dust with flour, and tap out excess flour.

2. Sift together the flour, cornstarch, and baking powder.

3. Place the egg whites in a grease-free medium bowl. Add the salt. With an electric mixer on medium speed, whip the whites until

(continued)

Yield

One 10-inch roll; 12 servings

Advance Preparation

Cake can be baked in advance, rolled up in the towel, and left to cool for several hours or overnight. Or, left in the towel, it can be wrapped in a heavy-duty plastic bag and frozen for up to 1 week. Thaw, still wrapped, overnight in the refrigerator. Lemon Curd can be prepared up to 2 days in advance and refrigerated. Filled cake can be refrigerated for up to 24 hours, but it really is best served the day it is assembled. (Do not freeze a roulade filled with curd or custard.)

Special Equipment

15½ × 10½-inch jelly-roll pan, baking parchment or wax paper, tea towel at least 18 × 10 inches, serrated knife

Temperature and Time

350°F for 11 to 13 minutes

Nutritional Analysis per serving (filled with curd and sliced berries but without garnish berries)

....

151 calories

2 g protein

3 g fat

0.9 g satfat

30 g carbohydrate

95 mg sodium

39 mg cholesterol

foamy. Gradually add ¼ cup plus 2 tablespoons of the granulated sugar, and whip until the whites are stiff but not dry. Set the whipped whites aside. Shake off the beaters, and without washing them, return them to the mixer.

4. In a large bowl, combine the egg yolks, oil, and the remaining ¼ cup granulated sugar. With the electric mixer, whip until thick and light-colored. Scrape down the bowl and beaters. Add the extract and whip on high speed for 3 to 4 minutes, until the batter forms a ribbon falling back on itself when the machine is turned off and the beater is lifted.

5. Fold about one third of the beaten whites into the batter, then fold in a few tablespoons of the flour mixture. Gently fold in the remaining whites and flour in several additions. The batter should remain light, airy, and smooth. Turn the batter into the prepared pan, smoothing the top and spreading it to the edges of the pan with a rubber spatula. Bake for 11 to 13 minutes, or until the top of the cake is golden and feels springy to the touch and the edges begin to pull away from the sides of the pan. Do not overbake.

6. Meanwhile, spread out the tea towel on a work surface and sift ¼ cup of the confectioners' sugar over it, covering an area roughly 10 by 15 inches.

7. As soon as the cake is baked, invert the pan over the sugared area of the towel. Lift off the pan, and peel off the paper. With a serrated knife, trim off a scant ⅛-inch edge all around the cake. Fold one end of the towel over a short end of the cake, and roll up together. Set the roll seam side down on a rack to cool.

8. When the cake is completely cool, unroll it. Spread the lemon curd evenly over the cake. Spread the sliced strawberries over the filling. Roll up the cake and place it seam side down on a serving platter. Sift the remaining 2 tablespoons confectioners' sugar over the top of the cake. Refrigerate until about 20 minutes before you are ready to serve.

9. Just before serving, arrange the whole berries, if using, around the cake for garnish. Slice the cake with the serrated knife.

Light Touch: The classic jelly-roll recipe uses 4 whole eggs, and obtains 15 percent of its calories from fat. By dropping 2 yolks and substituting 1 tablespoon of canola oil, I actually raised the number of calories from fat to 18 percent but lowered cholesterol. What happened? Yolks have less fat than oil—but, oil has no cholesterol: The change cuts approximately half the cholesterol, altering the total fat distribution very slightly. Baking powder is added to bolster the leavening power of the yolk-reduced egg foam. When this cake is filled with light lemon curd and berries it still gets only 18 percent of its calories from fat. Remember the days when we filled roulades with whipped cream (42 percent calories from fat)?

Cocoa Roulade
with Raspberry Cream

◆ ◆ ◆

I magine a velvety chocolate sponge cake rolled around a luxurious silken raspberry cream . . . the stuff dreams are made of? But you can have this cake and eat it too, because the cream filling is primarily meringue, enriched with just a touch of real cream blended with fresh berries and a dash of raspberry liqueur. This is a festive cake to serve on gala occasions. The roll is iced with meringue but it can be left plain and simply dusted with a little cocoa; either way, garnish it with fresh raspberries.

The cocoa roulade is a good basic cake that stays moist, rolls without cracking, and has a strong chocolate flavor. Use it with other fillings such as Light Lemon Curd (page 404) or Shortcut Vanilla Pastry Cream Filling (page 401) and complementary fruits and berries. Or fill with a mousse such as the Cappuccino Mousse Filling (page 306).

The raspberry meringue filling contains uncooked egg whites. To ensure safety, they are prepared with a boiled sugar syrup that heats them enough to destroy any bacteria (see page 23).

◆ ◆ ◆

(continued)

One 10-inch roulade;
12 servings

Cake can be baked up to
1 month in advance,
rolled up in the tea
towel, wrapped airtight
in a heavy-duty plastic
bag, and frozen. Thaw,
still wrapped, overnight
in the refrigerator or for
at least 2 hours at room
temperature before
unrolling. Finished cake
must be refrigerated for
at least 1 hour to set the
filling, but it should be
served the day it is
assembled.

10½ × 15½-inch jelly-
roll pan, baking
parchment or wax paper,
tea towel at least 18 ×
10 inches, serrated knife,
candy thermometer
(optional)

350°F for 15 minutes

Cake

Butter-flavor no stick cooking spray

⅔ cup sifted unsweetened Dutch-processed cocoa, divided

5 tablespoons sifted cake flour

2 tablespoons sifted cornstarch

½ teaspoon baking powder

¼ teaspoon baking soda

¼ teaspoon salt

⅛ teaspoon cinnamon

2 large eggs, separated, plus 3 large egg whites, at room temperature

¾ cup granulated sugar, divided

1 teaspoon vanilla extract

Filling

¼ cup plus 3½ tablespoons water, divided

½ cup granulated sugar, divided

⅛ teaspoon cream of tartar

2 large egg whites, at room temperature

1¼ teaspoons Knox unflavored gelatine

3 tablespoons Chambord or Framboise

⅓ cup heavy cream, chilled

1½ cups fresh raspberries

1. Position a rack in the center of the oven and preheat it to 350°F. Line the bottom of the jelly-roll pan with parchment or wax paper. Lightly coat the paper with cooking spray. Dust the paper with sifted cocoa, and tap out excess cocoa.

2. Sift together ⅓ cup of the cocoa, the flour, cornstarch, baking powder, baking soda, salt, and cinnamon into a medium bowl.

3. In a large grease-free bowl, using an electric mixer, whip the 5 egg whites until foamy. Gradually add ½ cup of the sugar, and whip until the whites are stiff but not dry. Shake off the beaters, and without washing them, return them to the mixer. Set the whites aside.

4. In another large bowl, combine the egg yolks and vanilla. With the electric mixer on medium speed, whip until pale yellow, about 1 minute. Add the remaining ¼ cup sugar and whip for 3 or 4 minutes longer, or until the batter forms a ribbon falling back on itself when the mixer is turned off and the beaters are lifted.

5. Fold about one third of the beaten whites into the batter, then fold in one third of the flour-cocoa mixture. Fold in the remaining whites and dry ingredients in 2 additions each. Turn the batter into the prepared pan, spreading it to the edges and smoothing the top. Bake for about 15 minutes, or until the top of the cake feels springy to the touch and the sides begin to shrink from the pan. Do not overbake.

6. Meanwhile, spread out the tea towel on a work surface and sift the remaining ⅓ cup cocoa over it, covering an area roughly 10 by 15 inches.

7. As soon as the cake is baked, invert the pan over the towel so the cake falls onto the cocoa. Lift off the pan, and peel off the paper. With a serrated knife, trim away a scant ⅛-inch edge all around the cake. Fold one end of the towel over a short end of the cake and roll up together. Set the roll seam side down on a rack to cool.

8. Make the filling: Combine 3½ tablespoons of the water, 7 tablespoons of the sugar, and the cream of tartar in a heavy medium saucepan. Cook over medium heat, swirling the pan gently, until the sugar dissolves. If you have a candy thermometer, clip it to the pan. To prevent crystallization, wash down the sides of the pan with a pastry brush dipped in cold water. Increase the heat to medium high, and cook for 3 to 5 minutes, until the thermometer registers 239° to 242°F, the soft-ball stage (a drop of the syrup should form a soft ball if dropped in ice water).

9. While the syrup is cooking, begin whipping the egg whites: In a medium bowl, with the electric mixer on medium-low speed, whip the whites until soft peaks form. Add the remaining 1 tablespoon sugar, and whip until *nearly* stiff but not dry.

10. As soon as the sugar syrup reaches the desired temperature, remove it from the heat and gradually pour it over the whites while whipping them on medium-low speed. Pour the syrup in a steady stream between the sides of the bowl and the beater. (Do not scrape in the hardened bits of syrup.) Continue whipping until the whites are stiff, satiny, and cool, about 5 minutes. Set aside.

11. Pour the ¼ cup water into a small saucepan, sprinkle on the gelatin, and allow to sit for about 3 minutes to soften. Then stir over low heat just until the gelatine is dissolved. Do not boil. Remove from the heat, and cool to room temperature. Stir in the raspberry liqueur.

12. In a medium bowl, whip the cream until soft peaks form. Whisk in the cooled gelatine mixture. Fold in half the cooled meringue, then fold in 1 cup of the berries.

(continued)

158 calories

4 g protein

4 g fat

1.7 g satfat

28 g carbohydrate

115 mg sodium

44 mg cholesterol

13. Unroll the cake on a work surface. Spread the filling evenly over the cake. Roll up the cake and place it seam side down on a serving platter. Spread the remaining meringue over the cake, and garnish with a row of the remaining berries down the top. Refrigerate for about 1 hour to set the filling before serving.

Light Touch: For years, I baked a classic cocoa roulade made with 4 whole eggs; for the filling and icing, I whipped 1 cup of heavy cream. The fat content was a resounding 45 percent, with each serving offering 9 grams of fat, 5 of them saturated, and 98 milligrams of cholesterol.

Without losing any of this dessert's world-class flavor or texture, I cut 53 percent of the calories from fat (to 21 percent) by dropping 2 yolks from the cake and adding another white and by substituting meringue for most of the cream in the filling. Only a little cream is retained, to add flavor and smooth out the texture. These changes dropped 20 calories, 5.8 grams of fat, 3.3 grams saturated fat, and 54 milligrams cholesterol per serving.

Fabulous
Holiday Fruitcake

◆ ◆ ◆

This recipe is your special reward for buying this book. You will thank me, I promise. This is a fruitcake you can, and will, love. You will make it, serve it, and eat it with pleasure. This fruitcake never has been, and never will be, recycled, used to fill a pothole, used to pound nails, used as an anchor. The recipe, rather than the fruitcake itself, will become an heirloom you will pass to your child as I have to mine.

There are two secret ingredients here: the cake and the fruit. A moist, lightly spiced applesauce cake with a fine, flavorful crumb binds a cornucopia of naturally sweet (not candied) dried fruits. Not a red or green one in the lot. Just natural, organic, dried fruits from the natural food store or fine grocery cut up with kitchen shears or chopped with a knife. Try apples, apricots, pears, peaches, pineapple, prunes, dates, black and golden raisins, and currants. Not creative enough? Add dried mango or papaya, or dried cherries, cranberries, or blueberries. Candied pineapple is neither medicinal nor chemical in taste; it is the one holdover I occasionally use. I have avoided nuts because they are so high in fat, and with the great variety of ingredients, I don't miss them. If you wish, you can use halved nuts to garnish the cake top along with the Vanilla Icing Glaze.

A perfect Christmas gift cake, this makes one-stop shopping: You get eight small loaves with this recipe. Because the recipe does not halve (or double) exactly, I have also included a smaller version that makes four small loaves.

Don't be put off by the long list of ingredients; fruitcake is supposed to have a lot of stuff in it.

◆ ◆ ◆

(continued)

Fruit

1 cup (6 ounces) cut-up dried pears, packed

1 cup (6 ounces) cut-up dried peaches, packed

1 cup (6 ounces) cut-up dried apricots, packed

1 cup (6 ounces) cut-up dried pitted prunes, packed

1 cup (6 ounces) cut-up dried pitted dates, packed

1¾ cups (6 ounces) cut-up dried apple slices, packed

1 cup (5 ounces) seedless raisins, packed

1 cup (5 ounces) golden raisins, packed

½ cup (2½ ounces) dried currants, packed

½ cup (4 ounces) candied yellow pineapple, chopped (optional)

1 cup dark rum or brandy

Cake

Solid shortening

Butter-flavor no stick cooking spray

1 large egg plus 3 large egg whites

1¾ cups light brown sugar, packed

½ cup canola or safflower oil

½ cup honey

⅓ cup apple or orange juice

2 cups unsweetened applesauce

2 teaspoons vanilla extract

2 tablespoons grated orange zest or ½ teaspoon pure orange
    oil or orange extract

2¼ cups unsifted all-purpose flour

1 cup unsifted whole wheat pastry flour (or use a total of
    3¼ cups all-purpose white flour)

1½ teaspoons baking powder

½ teaspoon baking soda

¾ teaspoon salt

1½ teaspoons cinnamon

1 teaspoon nutmeg

½ teaspoon ground cloves

⅓ cup toasted wheat germ

Dark rum or brandy for soaking cakes (optional)

2 recipes Vanilla Icing Glaze (page 435), substituting apple juice,
    strained orange juice, dark rum, or brandy for the liquid

Pecan or walnut halves or whole blanched almonds (optional),
    for garnish

Version #1 makes 14 cups batter; 8 small loaves (5½ × 3 × 2⅛), 8 servings each, or 4 average-size loaves (8½ × 4½ × 2¾), 16 servings each. Version #2 makes about 6½ cups batter; 4 small loaves, 8 slices each, or 2 average-size loaves, 16 slices each.

Advance Preparation

If you have the time, the fruit benefits from macerating for 24 hours in rum or brandy; otherwise, mix up the fruit before you make the cakes. Cakes can be wrapped in cloths soaked with brandy or dark rum and stored in tins for (theoretically) several months. I have only kept them soaking for up to 1 month because I prefer to freeze the cakes after aging them in spirit-soaked cloths for 1 week. At holiday time, I am usually rushed, so I often forget the soaking and aging and just bake the cakes, glaze them, wrap airtight in several layers of plastic wrap and a heavy-duty plastic zip-lock bag, and freeze. Then you can remove from the freezer, add a ribbon and a recipe card (and, if you are feeling expansive, a new loaf pan), and give as gifts.

Version #2

Fruit

½ cup (3 ounces) cut-up dried pears, packed

½ cup (3 ounces) cut-up dried peaches, packed

½ cup (3 ounces) cut-up dried apricots, packed

½ cup (3 ounces) cut-up dried pitted prunes, packed

½ cup (3 ounces) cut-up dried pitted dates, packed

1 cup (3¼ ounces) cut-up dried apple slices, packed

½ cup (2½ ounces) seedless raisins, packed

½ cup (2½ ounces) golden raisins, packed

¼ cup (1¼ ounces) dried currants

¼ cup (2 ounces) candied pineapple, chopped (optional)

½ cup dark rum or brandy

Cake

Solid shortening

Butter-flavor no stick cooking spray

2 large egg whites

1 cup light brown sugar, packed

¼ cup canola or safflower oil

¼ cup honey

¼ cup apple or orange juice

1 cup unsweetened applesauce

1 teaspoon vanilla extract

1 tablespoon grated orange zest or ½ teaspoon orange oil or orange extract

1 cup unsifted all-purpose flour

½ cup unsifted whole wheat pastry flour (or use a total of 1½ cups all-purpose flour)

1 teaspoon baking powder

½ teaspoon baking soda

½ teaspoon salt

1 teaspoon cinnamon

½ teaspoon nutmeg

¼ teaspoon ground cloves

¼ cup toasted wheat germ

Dark rum or brandy for soaking cakes (optional)

1 recipe Vanilla Icing Glaze (page 435), substituting apple juice, strained orange juice, dark rum, or brandy for the liquid

Pecan or walnut halves or whole blanched almonds (optional), for garnish

(continued)

Temperature and Time

350°F for 60 to 65 minutes for small loaves, 1 hour and 15 to 20 minutes for average loaves

1. Twenty-four hours before baking the cakes (or as early on the baking day as possible), assemble all the fruit in a large bowl. Stir in the dark rum or brandy, cover with plastic wrap, and set aside.

2. Position 2 racks to divide the oven in thirds, and preheat the oven to 350°F. Lightly grease the pans with solid shortening. Cut wax paper or parchment liners to fit inside, and press the papers against the greased pan bottom and sides. Lightly coat the paper with cooking spray.

3. In a large bowl, combine the egg and egg whites (or just whites in version #2), brown sugar, oil, honey, juice, applesauce, vanilla, and grated zest or orange flavoring. Whisk, or beat with an electric mixer on low, to blend well. Set a large strainer over the bowl and add both flours, the baking powder, baking soda, salt, and spices. Stir and sift the dry ingredients onto the wet. Add the wheat germ. With the whisk, or the mixer on low speed, mix just until blended. Do not overbeat.

4. Stir the spirit-soaked fruit into the batter and blend well. Divide the batter among the prepared pans, filling them about three quarters full. (The batter is very heavy, and while it does rise, it will not overflow the pans.) Bake small loaves for about 60 to 65 minutes and regular loaves for about 1 hour and 15 to 20 minutes, or until the cakes are risen and golden brown on top, and a cake tester inserted in the center comes out clean.

5. Cool the cakes in the pans on wire racks for about 10 minutes. Then tip them gently from the pans, peel off the paper, and set them right side up on wire racks to cool completely.

6. When the cakes are completely cool, if you like, wrap them in rum- or brandy-soaked cloths, place in heavy-duty zip-lock bags or plastic boxes, and set in a cool dark location to age for about 1 month. Renew the spirits when they dry out. (Do not attempt to substitute fruit juice for spirits; only alcohol will preserve the cakes.)

7. To glaze the cakes, set them on racks over wax paper. Drizzle some of the glaze on top of each cake, letting it run down the sides. If you wish, place a few nuts in the glaze before it dries. Let sit until the glaze is dried and set, about 30 minutes. When the glaze is hard, you can wrap the cakes in plastic wrap and freeze them, or give them as gifts, or slice and serve.

Light Touch: This cake tastes rich and moist, yet the large recipe gets only 12 percent calories from fat and the smaller recipe only 11 percent. Compare this with my classic English Fruitcake in my book

A Piece of Cake: It gets about 34 percent calories from fat—not overwhelming, but still about three times as much as this lighter version.

I cut the fat by substituting egg whites for whole eggs (leaving 1 yolk in the larger recipe), replacing 1 cup butter with ¼ cup oil plus 1 cup applesauce, and eliminating the nuts. Yet the point is not only that I have cut the saturated fat, but that the taste and texture are every bit as good. The new cake received rave reviews from all recipients last Christmas... it is now known as "The Friendly Fruitcake." And it keeps, and mails, well.

As noted above, nuts are omitted because they contain up to 81 percent fat; however, if you want to add a row of halved walnuts or pecans or blanched almonds across the top of the glazed cakes to give a festive air, they will add a scant 8 to 10 calories and ¾ to 1 gram of fat per serving. Remember that in addition to natural sugars, dried fruits are full of vitamins, minerals, and fiber: Each slice of this fruitcake provides 2.1 grams of dietary fiber. If you substitute other dried fruits, the fat content will remain practically unchanged; since it is so low, you can experiment freely as long as you leave the cake formula as is.

Nutritional Analysis per serving (Version #2, without the optional nuts)

158 calories

2 g protein

2 g fat

0.2 g satfat

33 g carbohydrate

67 mg sodium

0 mg cholesterol

Passover
Orange Sponge Cake

◆ ‧ ◆ ‧ ◆ ‧

T his citrus-flavored sponge cake is the perfect finale for a traditional Passover seder, or for any occasion where a light-textured cake is desired. Serve it plain or with Apricot-Orange Sauce (page 413) or Dried Fruit Compote (page 397). Instead of cake flour, this recipe uses potato starch (also called potato flour) and matzo meal; both ingredients are available in large supermarkets, many gourmet shops, and natural food stores.

◆ ‧ ◆ ‧ ◆ ‧

Yield

8½ cups batter; one 10-inch tube cake; 12 servings

Advance Preparation

Cake will keep for several days at room temperature if wrapped airtight. It can be double-wrapped and frozen, but it tends to dry out after about a week.

Special Equipment

10 × 4-inch angel food cake pan with raised feet (or a tall bottle or large funnel), serrated knife

Temperature and Time

350°F for 50 to 55 minutes

¾ cup matzo meal

½ cup potato flour

½ teaspoon salt

1 cup granulated sugar, divided

⅓ cup canola or safflower oil

1 large egg, separated, plus 5 large egg whites, at room temperature

¾ cup fresh orange juice

Grated zest of 1 large orange (2 to 3 tablespoons)

3 tablespoons fresh lemon juice

Grated zest of 1 lemon (2 to 3 teaspoons)

1 teaspoon pure orange or lemon extract

1. Position a rack in the center of the oven and preheat the oven to 350°F. Do not grease the tube pan.

2. Sift together the matzo meal, potato flour, salt, and ½ cup of the sugar into a large bowl. Stir these ingredients together. Make a well in the center and add the oil, egg yolk, orange juice and zest, lemon juice and zest, and extract, but do not blend together at this point. Set aside.

3. In a large grease-free bowl, whip the egg whites until foamy. Gradually add the remaining ½ cup sugar, and whip until the whites are satiny and nearly stiff, but not dry; do not overbeat. Shake off the beaters into the bowl, and without washing them, return them to the mixer.

4. With the mixer on low speed, beat the dry and liquid ingredients in the first bowl until well blended. Gradually fold in the whipped whites by hand. Don't worry if there are some streaks of white remaining.

Turn the batter into the ungreased cake pan. Bake for about 50 minutes, or until the top of the cake is golden brown and feels springy to the touch, and a cake tester comes out clean. Invert the pan so it stands upside down on its own feet, or hang the pan upside down over the neck of a bottle or large funnel. Let cool completely.

6. To remove the cake from the pan, slide the blade of a long thin knife between the cake and the sides of the pan to loosen it. Run the knife around the center tube. Top the cake with a platter, then invert and lift off the pan. (If the pan has a removable bottom, remove the sides first, then slide the knife between the pan bottom and cake to release it.) To serve, cut with a serrated knife.

Light Touch: Though it was never high in saturated fat, the traditional version of this cake includes 6 whole eggs and ½ cup vegetable oil, bringing the total calories from fat to 44 percent, with 107 milligrams of cholesterol per serving.

By cutting back the oil and dropping all but 1 egg yolk, I dropped the calories from fat to 30 percent and eliminated 89 milligrams cholesterol and 5.3 grams fat per serving, for a low-cholesterol as well as low-fat cake.

Nutritional Analysis per serving

192 calories

4 g protein

7 g fat

0.6 g satfat

31 g carbohydrate

120 mg sodium

18 mg cholesterol

Panatela Borracha
(Drunken Cake)

◆ · ◆ · ◆ ·

This recipe for "Drunken Cake" raises the virtually fat-free but bland angel food cake to glorious heights. Drenched in spiced orange-rum syrup and topped with a dab of orange-flavored real whipped cream, it's a guaranteed party favorite. Make it with a homemade or store-bought cake and be sure to prepare it several hours in advance, so the cake—as well as the guests—can imbibe the spirits.

◆ · ◆ · ◆ ·

Classic Angel Food Cake (page 161) or one 10 × 4-inch store-bought cake

Spiced Orange-Rum Syrup

2 cups granulated sugar

1 cup water

2 teaspoons grated orange zest

1 cup fresh orange juice (about 3 oranges)

1½ teaspoons grated lemon zest

¼ cup fresh lemon juice (1 large lemon)

½ teaspoon ground cinnamon

1 2- to 3-inch-long cinnamon stick

½ to ¾ cup dark rum, to taste

2 teaspoons vanilla extract

Orange Cream Topping

⅓ cup heavy cream

2 teaspoons sifted confectioners' sugar

2 teaspoons orange-flavored liqueur (such as Grand Marnier) or 1 teaspoon pure orange extract

2 tablespoons low-fat plain yogurt

Ground cinnamon

1. Cut the cake into 10 slices. Slice each piece in half crosswise. Cover the slices with plastic wrap while you prepare the syrup.

Yield

20 servings

Advance Preparations

Cake alone can be made in advance and stored at room temperature for several days or frozen. Cake should soak at least 2 hours, or overnight, in the syrup before serving.

Special Equipment

Large glass baking pan for soaking cake, serving platter with lip, broad spatula or cake server

Have Your Cake and Eat It, Too

2. In a large nonreactive saucepan, combine the sugar, water, orange zest and juice, lemon zest and juice, ground cinnamon, and cinnamon stick. Bring slowly to a boil, stirring, over low heat. Boil gently for about 5 minutes, until the sugar is dissolved. Remove from the heat and allow the syrup to cool. Stir in the rum and vanilla; discard the cinnamon stick.

3. Arrange the cake slices in a single layer in a glass baking pan. Pour the syrup over the cake, and turn the pieces, to coat with syrup. Cover the pan with plastic wrap and set in a cool place, or in the refrigerator, for at least 2 hours, or overnight, turning the pieces gently from time to time.

4. Shortly before serving, whip the cream until nearly stiff. Add the confectioners' sugar and orange liqueur or extract and whip to blend. Fold in the yogurt. Place the cream in a serving bowl and sprinkle a little cinnamon on top.

5. With a spatula or cake server, carefully transfer the soaked cake slices to a serving platter with a lip to catch the syrup. Serve each slice with a dab of the orange cream on top.

Light Touch: This is an ideal low-fat party cake. The syrup-saturated cake gets only 1 percent of the total calories from fat. Because it is so virtuous, you are allowed the indulgence of a dab of whipped cream to gild the lily. It is not too scandalous, as some low-fat yogurt is folded into the small amount of flavored whipped cream. However, it's the little dab that did it, pushing the total calories from fat to a wild 7 percent. Have a second helping.

Nutritional Analysis per serving with cream topping

174 calories

3 g protein

1 g fat

0.7 g satfat

35 g carbohydrate

90 mg sodium

4 mg cholesterol

Burgundy Cherry Mousse Cake
with Cassis Glaze

❖ ◆ ❖

When the occasion calls for big flavors, sophisticated, luxurious textures, and bright colors, serve this showpiece topped with a dazzling wine-red cassis glaze.

This cake is as bright as it is beautiful, letting you prepare it in stages well in advance. The longer it stands, the more the flavors of the filling permeate the cake. This is a bit of a production, but well worth the effort.

❖ ◆ ❖

Yield

One 6-layer 9½-inch cake; 16 servings

Advance Preparation

Cake layers can be baked up to 1 month ahead, wrapped airtight, and frozen. Thaw, still wrapped, overnight in the refrigerator before using. Assembled cake, without the cassis glaze, can be wrapped in a double layer of heavy-duty foil and frozen for up to 2 weeks or refrigerated for 1 week. Add the cassis glaze and refrigerate no more than 24 hours before serving.

Note that the yogurt for the mousse filling needs to drain for 1 hour before being used. The cake and mousse must be assembled and refrigerated for a minimum of 3 hours, or overnight, to set before the cassis glaze can be added. Then the glaze needs an additional 3 hours to set. Thus, it is best to make the cake in stages, starting 2 days ahead.

Cake

Butter-flavor no stick cooking spray
¼ cup plus 2 tablespoons 1% or skim milk
1¼ cups sifted cake flour
1¼ teaspoons baking powder
⅛ teaspoon salt
1 large egg, separated, plus 1 large egg white
2 teaspoons vanilla extract
¾ cup granulated sugar

Burgundy Cherry Mousse

2¾ cups low-fat vanilla yogurt
2 17-ounce cans dark sweet pitted cherries in heavy syrup
1 tablespoon Knox unflavored gelatine
¼ cup crème de cassis (black currant liqueur)
¼ cup granulated sugar
2 tablespoons fresh lemon juice
Pinch of salt

Cake Glaze

3 tablespoons crème de cassis

Cassis Glaze

1⅛ teaspoons Knox unflavored gelatine
3 tablespoons cold water
¾ cup reserved syrup from canned cherries (above)
3 tablespoons crème de cassis
1 teaspoon fresh lemon juice

1. Prepare the cake: Position a rack in the center of the oven and preheat it to 350°F. Coat the 9½-inch round baking pans with cooking spray. Line the bottoms of the pans with parchment or wax paper, and spray the paper. Dust the pans with flour, and tap out excess flour.

2. In a small saucepan, bring the milk to a simmer over low heat. Remove from the heat and cool to lukewarm.

3. In a small bowl, sift together the flour, baking powder, and salt.

4. In a medium bowl, combine the egg yolk and vanilla. With an electric mixer, beat lightly. Add ½ cup of the sugar and beat until pale yellow, 3 to 4 minutes. Scrape down the bowl and beaters. Beating at low speed, gradually add the lukewarm milk. Increase the speed to medium and whip until the sugar is completely dissolved, about 10 to 12 minutes.

5. In a large grease-free bowl, using clean beaters, whip the egg whites with the mixer on medium speed until foamy. Gradually add the remaining ¼ cup sugar, and whip until stiff but not dry. Fold half the whites into the yolk mixture. Then fold in the flour mixture alternately with the remaining whites.

6. Spoon about 1 cup batter into one of the prepared pans, and spoon the remaining batter into the second pan. Smooth the tops. Bake for 12 to 14 minutes, or until the cakes are a light golden color and a cake tester inserted in the center comes out clean. Cool the cakes in the pans on wire racks for 10 minutes, then invert onto other racks, remove the pans, and peel off the paper. Cool completely. With a serrated knife, slice the thicker cake in half into 2 layers. Wrap the cool cake layers in plastic wrap and set aside while you prepare the filling.

7. Prepare the mousse: Measure the yogurt into a cheesecloth-lined strainer set over a bowl and let it sit in the refrigerator for about 1 hour to drain off excess liquid; you should end up with about 1¾ cups.

8. Drain the canned cherries and reserve the syrup. Cut 1 cup of the cherries into quarters and set aside. In a food processor or blender, purée the remaining cherries.

9. Measure ¾ cup of the reserved cherry syrup into a small saucepan. Sprinkle on the gelatine and allow to sit for about 3 minutes to soften. Then stir the mixture over low heat just until the gelatine is dissolved; do not boil. Remove from the heat and stir in the crème de cassis, sugar, lemon juice, salt, cherry purée, and quartered cherries. Transfer to a bowl.

(continued)

Special Equipment

Two 9 × 1½-inch round baking pans, baking parchment or wax paper, serrated knife, cheesecloth, 9½-inch springform pan, pastry brush

Temperature and Time

350°F for 12 to 14 minutes

Nutritional Analysis
per serving
....

168 calories

5 g protein

1 g fat

0.1 g satfat

34 g carbohydrate

103 mg sodium

13 mg cholesterol

10. Set the bowl in a larger bowl of ice water. Let sit, stirring occasionally, for about 10 to 12 minutes, or until the mixture thickens to the consistency of raw egg whites. Then whisk in 1¾ cups of the drained yogurt (reserve any remaining yogurt for another use), and continue stirring over the ice water for about 10 minutes longer, until thickened but not completely set. Remove from the ice water.

11. Assemble the cake: Dab a little mousse in the center of the 9½-inch springform pan. Place 1 cake layer on top. Brush the cake with 1½ tablespoons of the crème de cassis. Top with about 1 cup of the cherry mousse, smoothing the top with a rubber spatula. Add another cake layer, brushing it with the remaining 1½ tablespoons liqueur and spreading it with another 1 cup mousse. Top with the third cake layer. Press down gently to compress the layers slightly.

12. Spoon some of the remaining mousse around the edge of the cake, filling in the gap between the cake and the pan. Slide a long thin knife blade into the gap and run it around the outside of the cake to smooth the mousse. Spread the remaining mousse evenly over the cake top. (This layer doesn't have to be perfectly smooth because it will be covered with the glaze.)

13. Wipe the edges of the pan clean, and cover the cake with a sheet of foil, pulling it taut so it doesn't sag onto the mousse. Refrigerate the cake for at least 3 hours, or overnight.

14. Prepare the glaze: In a small saucepan, sprinkle the gelatine over the cold water. Allow to sit for about 3 minutes to soften. Then stir the mixture over low heat just until the gelatine is dissolved; do not boil. Remove from the heat. Stir in the ¾ cup reserved cherry syrup, the crème de cassis, and lemon juice. Let cool to room temperature. You can refrigerate for a few minutes to speed the process, but do not let the syrup set. (If it does, stir over a bowl of warm water for a few seconds to soften the gelatine.)

15. Carefully pour the cooled syrup over the chilled cake. Refrigerate the cake, uncovered, for 2 to 3 hours, or until the glaze is set. (If not serving immediately, refrigerate for up to 24 hours. To hold longer, cover the cake with a taut piece of foil, taking care that the foil stays well above the glaze.)

16. To unmold the cake, dip a towel into very hot water, wring it out, and wrap it around the springform pan sides for several seconds. Then loosen the spring and jiggle the pan sides to detach them. Lift off the sides and place the cake, still on the pan bottom, on a serving plate.

Light Touch: Although based on a French gâteau miroir, the recipe for the cake layers builds on a traditional American-style sponge cake that includes baking powder as a leavener. My classic recipe uses 3 whole eggs; I scaled the recipe down to 1 whole egg plus 1 white. The primary reduction in fat comes from substituting drained low-fat yogurt for the traditional heavy cream whipped into the mousse. In its original form, this cake gets 30 percent calories from fat. The enlightened version plummets to 4 percent calories from fat, yet retains all the elegance, texture, and flavor of the original.

Chiffon Cakes

In the history of cakes, the chiffon is unique because we actually know its birthday. In 1927, a Los Angeles insurance salesman/caterer named Henry Baker created an exceptionally light, moist cake using what he called a mystery ingredient—vegetable oil. Baker guarded his secret formula for twenty years, before selling the recipe to General Mills in 1947. By 1948, the "glamorous cake made with salad oil" was heavily promoted by that flour company. Christened *chiffon* from the French word for a light, fragile scrap of fabric, a good description of the cake's airy texture, it was an immediate hit with the vegetable oil producers.

At first, the popularity of the cake was due to its novelty. However, its exceptionally light, tender texture and moist crumb, from the presence of oil instead of solid shortening or butter, quickly made it a favorite.

Chiffon is light like an angel food cake, but has a more satisfying, cakelike crumb, closer to that of a butter cake. Today, chiffon cake deserves attention for its ability to satisfy our craving for a moderately sweet cake while accommodating our need for a dessert that is not dependent upon saturated fat.

The procedure for making a chiffon cake is streamlined and easy. First, the dry ingredients are combined and a well is scooped out in the center. Liquid, oil, and flavorings are added, and finally folded with stiffly beaten egg whites.

Chiffon cakes can be baked in layers or in a tube pan, which I prefer, because the central column conducts the heat to the center of the cake so it bakes quickly and evenly. The tube pan can be left ungreased, as for an angel food cake, and after baking, hung upside down while the cake cools. Or, a chiffon cake can be prepared like a butter cake, baked in a greased and floured tube, layer, or sheet pan, or even cupcake tins and cooled right side up. Follow the method in each recipe.

Because the basic formula is simple, it is easy to improvise your own chiffon variations. Substitute fruit flavors of your own, or use a fruit liqueur or Madeira wine. Add chopped fresh fruit or dried cherries or dried cranberries soaked in water or wine. Fresh fruit or berries, a puréed fruit sauce, a scoop of fruit-flavored yogurt, or a fruit compote are good accompaniments to chiffon cakes.

I rarely add icing, preferring to top a chiffon cake with a light sugar-and-fruit-juice glaze or a dusting of confectioners' sugar or cocoa. For festive occasions I sometimes make a "faux ice cream cake," filling and frosting the chiffon with frozen yogurt. The chiffon crumb never completely hardens in the freezer, so you can serve it frozen—a fine summer dessert. For a gala occasion, old-fashioned Seven Minute Icing provides a luxurious meringue coating without any cholesterol.

Light Touch: In its classic form, the chiffon is a relatively high-cholesterol, rather than high-fat, cake. Because it is traditionally made with 6 whole eggs and ½ cup vegetable oil, it gets about 35 to 38 percent of its calories from fat, with only 9 grams of fat—but 80 milligrams of cholesterol—per serving. When the yolks are replaced by whites, or, for a richer version, whites and a single yolk, the total fat is reduced almost 25 percent, and when all whites are used, the cholesterol is totally eliminated.

It should be noted that the chiffon cakes here range from 28 to 39 percent total calories from fat, but all are low in saturated fat and, with two exceptions, are cholesterol-free. While at first they appear to have a high proportion of fat, you will see that, with the exception of the cocoa cake which has a yolk added, the only added fat is ½ cup canola oil.

Chiffon Basics

- Prepare baking pans in advance, and preheat the oven so the cake can be baked as soon as the batter is ready; a batter made with meringue begins to deflate quickly on standing, resulting in a dense cake.

- To avoid dry lumps in the cake, sift the dry ingredients together. Remember to scrape down the bowl and beaters often to incorporate and evenly blend all the ingredients. Fold in the whites gently but thoroughly.

- Treat the egg whites with care: They leaven the cake. Remember that eggs separate most easily when cold but whip to greater volume when at room temperature. The bowl and beaters must be completely free of fat; wipe them clean with a paper towel dampened with white vinegar.

- Whip the whites until foamy before adding the sugar. Then whip until stiff but not dry; at this point, the peaks will be glossy and hold their shape. Continue to whip just until peaks no longer droop.

- Lightly fold the batter into the whipped whites; stirring deflates the fragile structure. Troubleshooting: If the texture of the baked cake is tight and rubbery or tough and springy, the egg whites were under-whipped. If the cake sinks after baking, the whites were overwhipped.

- To bake chiffon cupcakes using these recipes, spray $2\frac{1}{2}$-inch muffin cups with cooking spray; bake for 15 to 17 minutes.

- To serve, cut chiffon cakes with a serrated knife, using a sawing motion.

- Low-fat chiffon cakes are not ideal candidates for long-term freezer storage because they dry out and lose flavor. They can, however, be frozen for up to a week if wrapped airtight.

Cocoa Chiffon Cake

◆ ◆ ◆

This cake is not too sweet, with a light, soft crumb and a satisfyingly deep chocolate flavor. It is made with one egg yolk, which adds richness and moisture; it can be made without any yolks to eliminate the cholesterol, but it will have a slightly drier texture.

As a variation you can make a four-layer Chocolate-Raspberry Cake. Bake the cake in two 8- or 9-inch round cake pans (for about 20 minutes at 350°F). Then slice each cooled layer in half with a serrated knife, and spread raspberry preserves between the layers.

◆ ◆ ◆

Butter-flavor no stick cooking spray

1½ cups sifted cake flour

⅓ cup plus 1 tablespoon sifted unsweetened Dutch-processed cocoa

1¼ cups granulated sugar

2 teaspoons baking powder

¼ teaspoon salt

¼ teaspoon cinnamon

½ cup canola or safflower oil

½ cup plus 2 tablespoons warm water

2 teaspoons vanilla extract

1 large egg, separated, plus 4 large egg whites

Pinch of cream of tartar

2 tablespoons sifted confectioners' sugar

Confectioners' sugar or unsweetened cocoa

1. Position a rack in the center of the oven and preheat it to 350°F. Coat the baking pan with cooking spray. Lightly sift on unsweetened cocoa, and tap out excess cocoa.

2. Sift together the cake flour, cocoa, sugar, baking powder, salt, and cinnamon into a large bowl. Make a well in the center of the dry ingredients and add the oil, water, vanilla, and egg yolk. Do not mix at this point; set aside.

3. Place the egg whites in a large grease-free bowl, and add the cream of tartar. Using an electric mixer on medium speed, whip the whites until foamy. Add the 2 tablespoons confectioners' sugar and

Yield

7 cups batter; one 9-inch tube cake; 16 servings

Advance Preparation

Cake can be baked in advance, wrapped airtight, and frozen for up to 1 week. It will keep fresh at room temperature for several days.

Special Equipment

9-inch (8- to 9-cup) Bundt pan

Temperature and Time

350°F for 40 to 45 minutes

whip until stiff but not dry. Scrape the beaters into the bowl. Set the whites aside and, without washing beaters, return them to the mixer.

4. With the mixer on low speed, beat the flour and oil mixture just until well blended. In several additions, gently fold the chocolate batter into the whipped whites. Don't worry if a few streaks of white remain.

5. Turn the batter into the prepared pan and smooth the top with a rubber spatula. Tap the pan sharply once on the counter to remove large air bubbles. Bake for about 40 to 45 minutes, or until the cake is well-risen and slightly springy to the touch, and a cake tester inserted in the center comes out clean. (The top of the cake will be slightly cracked.)

6. Cool the cake in the pan on a wire rack for 10 minutes. Use the tip of a long thin knife to loosen the cake from the sides and center tube of the pan. Top the cake with a wire rack or plate and invert. Lift off the pan, and cool completely.

7. To serve, dust the top of the cake with a light sifting of confectioners' sugar or unsweetened cocoa. Slice the cake with a serrated knife.

Light Touch: See page 208. Thirty-nine percent calories from fat.

Nutritional Analysis per serving

172 calories

2 g protein

8 g fat

0.8 g satfat

25 g carbohydrate

110 mg sodium

13 mg cholesterol

Pineapple Chiffon Cake

◆ ‧ ◆ ‧ ◆

A generous quantity of crushed pineapple contributes texture, flavor, and color to this unusual, cholesterol-free cake. It is a delightful summer dessert on its own or paired with fresh berries.

◆ ‧ ◆ ‧ ◆

Yield

Approximately 6 cups batter; one 9-inch tube cake; 16 servings

Advance Preparation

Cake is best when served fresh, but it can be wrapped and stored at room temperature for several days.

Special Equipment

9-inch (8-cup) Bundt pan or springform tube pan

Temperature and Time

350°F for 35 minutes

Cake

   Butter-flavor no stick cooking spray

   1½ cups sifted cake flour

   1 cup granulated sugar

   2 teaspoons baking powder

   ¼ teaspoon salt

   ½ cup canola or safflower oil

   ½ cup frozen pineapple juice concentrate, at room temperature

   1 teaspoon vanilla extract

   6 large egg whites, at room temperature

   2 tablespoons sifted confectioners' sugar

   1 20-ounce can unsweetened crushed pineapple, very well drained

Pineapple Glaze

   1½ cups sifted confectioners' sugar, or more to taste

   ¼ cup frozen pineapple juice concentrate, at room temperature

   1 teaspoon fresh lemon juice, or more to taste

1. Position a rack in the center of the oven and preheat it to 350°F. Coat the baking pan with cooking spray. Dust the pan with flour, and tap out excess flour.

2. Sift together the flour, sugar, baking powder, and salt into a large bowl. Make a well in the center of the dry ingredients and add the oil, pineapple juice concentrate, and vanilla. Do not mix at this point; set aside.

3. In another large bowl, using an electric mixer, beat the egg whites until foamy. Add the confectioners' sugar and whip until stiff but not dry. Scrape the beaters into the bowl. Set the whites aside and, without washing beaters, return them to the mixer.

4. With the mixer on medium-low speed, beat the flour and oil mixture until well blended. In several additions, gently fold the batter and the drained crushed pineapple into the beaten whites.

5. Turn the batter into the prepared pan and smooth the top with a rubber spatula. Bake for about 35 minutes, or until the cake feels springy to the touch and a cake tester inserted in the center comes out clean. Cool the cake in the pan on a wire rack for 10 minutes. Use the tip of a long thin knife to loosen the cake from the sides and center tube of the pan. Then invert onto a wire rack and lift off the pan.

6. Make the glaze: Combine the confectioners' sugar, pineapple juice concentrate, and lemon juice in a bowl and beat until smooth and thick but pourable. Adjust for flavor and consistency by adding more sugar or juice if desired.

7. Spread the glaze over the top of the warm cake, letting it drip down the sides.

Light Touch: See page 208. Twenty-eight percent calories from fat.

Nutritional Analysis per serving

220 calories

2 g protein

7 g fat

0.5 g satfat

38 g carbohydrate

96 mg sodium

0 mg cholesterol

Orange Chiffon Cake

◆ · ◆ · ◆ ·

Everyone's favorite, this light, tart, cholesterol-free cake is topped with an orange glaze. Serve it with a colorful splash of Fresh Orange-Raspberry Compote (page 396), made with mandarin oranges and raspberries.

◆ · ◆ · ◆ ·

Yield

Approximately 6 cups batter; one 9-inch Bundt or tube cake; 16 servings

Advance Preparation

Cake can be baked in advance, wrapped airtight, and frozen for up to 1 week. It will keep fresh at room temperature for several days.

Special Equipment

9-inch (8-cup) Bundt pan or springform tube pan

Temperature and Time

350°F for 35 minutes

Cake

Butter-flavor no stick cooking spray

1½ cups sifted cake flour

¾ cup granulated sugar

2 teaspoons baking powder

¼ teaspoon salt

½ cup canola or safflower oil

½ cup fresh orange juice

1 teaspoon orange extract

Grated zest of 2 oranges (about 3½ tablespoons)

6 large egg whites, at room temperature

2 tablespoons sifted confectioners' sugar

Orange Glaze

1½ cups sifted confectioners' sugar

1½ tablespoons fresh orange juice, or more as needed

2 teaspoons fresh lemon juice, or more as needed

1 recipe Fresh Orange-Raspberry Compote (page 396)

1. Position a rack in the center of the oven and preheat it to 350°F. Coat the baking pan with cooking spray. Dust the pan with flour, and tap out excess flour.

2. Sift the flour, sugar, baking powder, and salt into a large bowl. Make a well in the center and add the oil, orange juice, extract, and 3 tablespoons of the orange zest. (Reserve the remaining zest for garnish.) Do not mix at this point; set aside.

3. In another large bowl, using an electric mixer, whip the whites until foamy. Add the confectioners' sugar and whip until the whites are stiff but not dry. Set the whipped whites aside, shake off the beaters, and, without washing beaters, return them to the mixer.

214   **Have Your Cake and Eat It, Too**

4. With the mixer on medium-low, beat the flour and oil mixture until well blended. In several additions, gently fold the batter into the whites.

5. Turn the batter into the prepared pan and smooth the top with a rubber spatula. Rap the pan sharply on the counter once to remove any large air bubbles. Bake for about 35 minutes, or until the top of the cake is golden brown and springy to the touch and a cake tester inserted in the center comes out clean. Cool the cake in the pan on a wire rack for 10 minutes. With a long, thin knife, loosen the cake from the sides and center tube of the pan. Top the cake with a rack, invert, and lift off the pan.

6. Make the glaze: Combine the confectioners' sugar, orange juice, and lemon juice in a bowl and beat until smooth. Adjust the consistency by adding more sugar or juice if needed; the glaze should be thick but pourable. Spread the glaze over the top of the warm cake, letting it drip down the sides. Sprinkle the reserved orange zest on top of the glaze. Serve with the Fresh Orange-Raspberry Compote.

Light Touch: See page 208. Thirty-three percent calories from fat.

Nutritional Analysis
per serving

182 calories

2 g protein

7 g fat

0.5 g satfat

29 g carbohydrate

96 mg sodium

0 mg cholesterol

Frozen Framboise Chiffon Cake

◆ ◆ ◆

A light and refreshing summer dessert, this layer cake is flavored with Framboise or Chambord and filled and frosted with frozen berry yogurt.

If you use Chambord, the batter will be a light pink.

◆ ◆ ◆

Yield

About 6 cups batter; one 2-layer 9-inch cake; 16 servings

Advance Preparation

Cake layers can be baked in advance, wrapped airtight, and frozen for up to 1 week. The assembled cake must be frozen for at least 4 hours, or overnight, before serving.

Special Equipment

Two 9-inch round cake pans, baking parchment or wax paper, 9-inch springform pan

Temperature and Time

350°F for 22 to 25 minutes

Cake

Butter-flavor no stick cooking spray

1½ cups sifted cake flour

¾ cup granulated sugar

2 teaspoons baking powder

¼ teaspoon salt

½ cup corn, safflower, or canola oil

¼ cup water

¼ cup Framboise or Chambord

1 teaspoon vanilla extract

6 large egg whites, at room temperature

2 tablespoons sifted confectioners' sugar

1 quart low-fat frozen vanilla yogurt

2¼ cups fresh raspberries or 1½ cups frozen whole unsweetened raspberries

3 tablespoons Framboise or Chambord, or to taste

1. Position a rack in the center of the oven and preheat it to 350°F. Coat the layer pans with cooking spray. Line each pan with baking parchment or wax paper, and oil the paper. Dust the pans with flour, and tap out excess flour.

2. Sift together the flour, sugar, baking powder, and salt into a large bowl. Make a well in the center of the dry ingredients and add the oil, water, Framboise or Chambord, and vanilla. Do not mix at this point; set aside.

3. In another large bowl, using an electric mixer, whip the whites until foamy. Add the confectioners' sugar and whip until the whites are stiff but not dry. Set the whipped whites aside. Shake off the beaters, and, without washing them, return them to the mixer.

4. With the mixer on medium-low speed, beat the flour and oil mixture until well blended. Gently stir about 1 cup of the whites into the batter to lighten it. Fold in the remaining whites in several additions.

5. Divide the batter evenly between the prepared pans and smooth the tops. Bake for 22 to 25 minutes, or until the cakes are pale beige in color and feel springy to the touch, and a cake tester inserted in the center comes out clean. Cool the layers in the pans on a wire rack for 5 minutes. Then invert onto a rack, remove the pans, and peel off the paper. Cool completely.

6. About 30 minutes before filling and frosting the cake, transfer the frozen yogurt from the freezer to the refrigerator to soften to a spreadable consistency.

7. Meanwhile, purée 1½ cups of the fresh raspberries, or all the frozen berries, in a food processor or blender. Strain to remove the seeds, if desired.

8. In a bowl, stir together the softened frozen yogurt, the Framboise or Chambord, and raspberry purée. Place a dab of the frozen yogurt in the center of the springform pan. Center a cake layer in the bottom of the pan. Add slightly less than half the frozen yogurt, spreading it over the top and down the sides of the cake to fill the space between the cake and the sides of the pan. Run a table knife or icing spatula between the cake and the pan to be sure the yogurt fills the space. Spoon a little more yogurt over the cake if filling looks thin, then add the second cake layer. Spoon on more yogurt, again filling the space between the cake and the sides of the pan. Then smooth the remaining yogurt over the top. Smooth the top with a spatula. Cover with a sheet of plastic wrap, then foil. Freeze for at least 4 hours, or overnight.

9. About 20 to 30 minutes before serving time, soak a towel with hot water, wring it out, and wrap it around the sides of the springform pan for about 5 seconds. Then remove the sides of the pan, leaving the cake on the pan bottom, and place it on a serving platter. If necessary, smooth the yogurt frosting on cake sides with an icing spatula dipped in warm water. To garnish, place a ring of the remaining fresh berries around the top edge of the cake. Then place the cake in the refrigerator to soften slightly before serving.

Light Touch: See page 208. Thirty-five percent calories from fat.

Nutritional Analysis per serving

226 calories

4 g protein

9 g fat

1.7 g satfat

31 g carbohydrate

127 mg sodium

1 mg cholesterol

Spiced Apple
Chiffon Cake

◆ · ◆ · ◆

*C*hopped apples, freshly grated ginger, and orange zest fill the kitchen with the scent of an old-fashioned coffee cake. Baked in a tube pan, this is perfect to serve a crowd for brunch or afternoon tea. Top it with maple syrup glaze or a simple dusting of confectioners' sugar.

◆ · ◆ · ◆

Yield

5½ cups batter; one 9-inch Bundt or tube cake; 16 servings

Advance Preparation

Cake can be baked in advance, wrapped airtight, and frozen for up to a week. It will keep fresh at room temperature for several days.

Special Equipment

9-inch (8-cup) Bundt pan or springform tube pan

Temperature and Time

350°F for about 40 to 45 minutes

Cake

Butter-flavor no stick cooking spray

1½ cups sifted cake flour

½ cup peeled and finely diced Granny Smith, Greening, or other tart apple

2 teaspoons baking powder

¼ teaspoon baking soda

¼ teaspoon salt

¾ cup plus 2 tablespoons granulated sugar

2 tablespoons dark brown sugar, packed

1 teaspoon cinnamon

1 teaspoon ground cardamom

½ teaspoon freshly grated nutmeg

¼ teaspoon ground cloves

1 teaspoon grated fresh ginger or ¼ teaspoon ground ginger

2 teaspoons grated orange zest or 1 teaspoon dried ground orange peel

½ cup canola or safflower oil

½ cup apple cider or apple juice

1 teaspoon vanilla extract

5 large egg whites, at room temperature

2 tablespoons sifted confectioners' sugar

Maple Syrup Glaze

5 tablespoons pure maple syrup, or more as needed

1½ cups sifted confectioners' sugar, or more as needed

Dash of fresh lemon juice, or to taste

1. Position a rack in the center of the oven and preheat it to 350°F. Coat the baking pan with cooking spray. Dust the pan with flour, and tap out excess flour.

2. Sift the flour into a large bowl. Place the diced apples in a small bowl and toss with 2 tablespoons of the flour; set aside. Sift the baking powder, soda, and salt into the bowl of flour. Add both sugars, the spices, ginger, and orange zest. Make a well in the center of the dry ingredients and add the oil, apple cider, and vanilla. Do not mix at this point; set aside.

3. In a large bowl, using an electric mixer, whip the egg whites until foamy. Add the confectioners' sugar and whip until the whites are stiff but not dry. Scrape the beaters into the bowl. Set the whites aside and, without washing the beaters, return them to the mixer.

4. With the mixer on medium-low speed, beat the flour and oil mixture until well blended. In several additions, gently fold the batter into the whites. Fold in the diced apples.

5. Turn the batter into the prepared pan, and smooth the top with a rubber spatula. Bake for about 40 minutes, or until the top of the cake feels springy to the touch and a cake tester inserted in the center comes out clean. Cool the cake in the pan on a wire rack for 10 minutes, then top with another rack and invert. Lift off the pan, and cool completely, about 10 minutes. While still warm, coat the top with Maple Syrup Glaze. Or cool completely and sift on about 2 tablespoons confectioners' sugar just before serving.

6. Make the glaze: In a small pan, warm the maple syrup just until comfortable to touch. Remove from the heat, and beat in the confectioners' sugar. Add lemon juice to taste. Adjust the consistency if necessary by adding more sugar or syrup; the glaze should be thick but pourable.

7. Spoon the glaze over the warm cake, letting it drip down the sides.

Light Touch: See page 208. Twenty-nine percent calories from fat.

Nutritional Analysis per serving (including Maple Syrup Glaze)
....
212 calories

2 g protein

7 g fat

0.5 g satfat

37 g carbohydrate

112 mg sodium

0 mg cholesterol

Cheesecakes

S ay the word *cheesecake* and rich, creamy, mouth-watering adjectives leap to mind. Can you actually remove butterfat and leave anything worth eating? Em*phat*ically, yes!

All the recipes in this chapter have been tested and tasted to rave reviews many times. These are not deprivation desserts. Ingredients have been adjusted, reduced, substituted. Some fat, eggs, and cream have been left in, making these among the higher calories-from-fat recipes in the book. As my friend Myra Chanin says in her book *Mother Wonderful's Cheesecakes,* "If God had wanted cheesecake to be a diet aid, he would have made butterfat noncaloric."

Consider one of the richest classic cheesecakes, New York Cheesecake. The crust is butter pastry. The batter contains 2½ pounds regular cream cheese, 1¾ cups sugar, 5 eggs plus 2 extra yolks, and ¼ cup heavy cream, plus flavoring. It's no surprise that this recipe gets 67 percent of its calories from fat; each serving contains 525 calories, 40 grams of fat (24 of them saturated), and 236 milligrams of cholesterol!

In a reduced-fat cheesecake, regular cream cheese is replaced by low-fat cream cheese. Sometimes low-fat or nonfat cottage cheese is added for bulk and creaminess. The cottage cheese must be strained and pressed in a sieve to remove as much whey (liquid) as possible; the dry curds are then puréed in a blender or food processor. Fewer eggs are used, and more whites are used in proportion to yolks. Often egg whites are stiffly whipped to contribute leavening to the cake (see page 20).

Many classic cheesecakes contain sour cream, either in the cake or topping or both. I use low-fat or nonfat sour cream or substitute drained plain or vanilla yogurt in the cake and eliminate the creamy toppings. Yogurt that has been drained for twenty-four hours makes a smooth rich spread with a cream cheese texture, and is a good substitute in some recipes.

Because cheesecake batters are so rich, they don't need a pastry crust. In fact, they really don't even need a nut/crumb crust held together with melted butter, except to prevent the batter from sticking to the pan and to provide textural contrast. Instead of crust I prefer a simple dusting of ground nuts or cookie or cereal crumbs between the cake and the pan; they give a good appearance and provide some textural change without adding unnecessary calories or fat.

When fat is removed from the batter, moisture tends to leak out as the cake bakes; occasionally, the crumb crust gets wet. To prevent this problem and to keep moisture in the batter, flour and/or cornstarch is added.

There are a few basic techniques that ensure success when making cheesecakes. Tinned steel and nonstick springform pans are nonreactive. Some aluminum pans may react and discolor cheesecakes. To prevent this, line aluminum pan bottoms with baking parchment or wax paper.

Cheesecake batter generally does not need air whipped into it. If your electric mixer has a paddle attachment, use it to blend the ingredients. Bake cheesecakes at a moderate heat, usually 300° to 325°F, so the proteins in the batter set slowly and remain creamy. If the heat is too high, the texture will change and toughen.

Many cheesecakes crack on top when they cook or cool. Most cracks occur because the cake has released its moisture or steam too quickly, causing fissures in the delicate, warm structure. Sometimes cracks that appear during baking close up as a cake cools. Other cracks appear when the cake cools, if it is exposed to drafts or extreme temperature changes. Leave the cake in the oven after baking, with the heat turned off. This allows the cake to cool very slowly away from drafts. Another technique for minimizing cracks (by minimizing drafts) is to set a cardboard cake disk over the cake after it is removed from the oven. Or, run the blade of a long thin knife between the baked cake and the pan to allow steam to escape as the cake cools. Sometimes, no matter what, cracks happen. If you think they look unsightly, top the cake with Strawberry Topping and Glaze (page 434) or Any-Berry Sauce (page 414). Or, toss a cup or two of fresh berries with some warm apricot jam and pile them on top of the cake to hide a multitude of sins.

How do you cut cheesecake? I learned the best way from my father who was a dentist: Use dental floss. Simply cut a long piece, wrap one end around each hand, pull it taut, and press it down through the cake. Release one end and pull the floss out. It gives your guests something to talk about and takes care of the sticky knife problem at the same time. Alternatively, use a cake knife dipped into hot water between slices.

Vanilla Cheesecake
with Strawberry Glaze

◆ • ◆ • ◆

T his is a remarkably rich and creamy cake with a relatively high proportion of cream cheese, albeit the reduced-fat variety. It achieves its light texture from stiffly whipped egg whites. The vanilla flavor is the perfect foil for a topping and glaze of fresh strawberries. If your berries are deep red and very ripe, use Strawberry Topping and Glaze (page 434). Out of season, make the topping with strawberries plus red currant jelly, per the recipe, to achieve a ruby-hued glaze.

You can change the flavor of the cake by adding (in addition to the vanilla) a teaspoon of maple, almond, or orange extract; select a fruit topping to complement the flavor.

◆ • ◆ • ◆

Yield

7 cups batter; one 9-inch cake; 12 servings

Advance Preparation

After baking, the cake needs about 3 hours to cool completely, then at least 4 hours to chill and firm in the refrigerator before serving. Ideally, bake this cake a day in advance, as it benefits from mellowing overnight. Or bake it in advance and when cold, but before it is glazed, wrap it airtight, and freeze for up to 2 weeks. Defrost, still wrapped, overnight in the refrigerator.

Special Equipment

9-inch springform pan, baking parchment or wax paper, optional sturdy baking sheet

Temperature and Time

300°F for 1 hour plus 1 hour in oven with heat off and door closed

Crust

Butter-flavor no stick cooking spray

3 tablespoons Grape-Nuts or finely crumbled Shredded Wheat

1 tablespoon granulated sugar

Filling

¼ cup plus 2 tablespoons unsifted all-purpose flour

¼ teaspoon salt

1½ cups (12 ounces) low-fat cream cheese, at room temperature

1¼ cups granulated sugar, divided

2 large eggs, separated

1 tablespoon vanilla extract

2 cups low-fat vanilla yogurt

1 quart ripe strawberries, rinsed and hulled

½ cup red currant jelly

1. Position a rack in the center of the oven and preheat it to 300°F. Coat the springform pan with cooking spray. If using an aluminum pan, line the bottom with baking parchment or wax paper and spray.

Combine the cereal and sugar and add to the prepared pan. Tilt and rotate the pan until evenly dusted with crumbs; spread the loose crumbs evenly over the bottom.

2. Sift together the flour and salt into a small bowl or onto a sheet of wax paper.

3. In a large bowl, beat the cream cheese with an electric mixer until smooth. Beat in 1 cup of the sugar, the egg yolks, and vanilla until well blended. Reduce the speed to low and alternately add the flour mixture and yogurt. Beat until smooth.

4. In a clean grease-free bowl, using clean beaters, whip the egg whites until foamy. Gradually add the remaining ¼ cup sugar, and whip until the whites are stiff but not dry. Fold the whites into the batter in several additions.

5. Turn the batter into the prepared pan and set it on a heavy baking sheet for ease in handling. Bake for about 1 hour, or until the edges of the cake are slightly puffed up and the center is dry to the touch but slightly wobbly. Turn off the heat, leaving the cake in the oven with the door closed for 1 hour. Set the cake on a wire rack away from drafts until thoroughly cool. Cover and refrigerate for a minimum of 4 hours, or overnight, to firm.

6. To unmold the cake, run the top of a paring knife between the top edge of the cake and the pan. Loosen the spring and lift off the pan sides, leaving the cake on the pan bottom. Cover with plastic wrap and refrigerate.

7. At least 1½ hours before serving, add the strawberries and glaze, if using, to the cold, chilled cake. If using the Strawberry Topping and Glaze, arrange whole berries on top of the cold cake and spoon on ⅔ cup of glaze. Pass the remaining glaze at the table. Or, prepare the topping as follows: Slice 1 cup of the berries and combine in a medium heavy-bottomed saucepan with the jelly. Heat to simmer, cover 3 minutes to soften the berries, uncover, and cook 3 minutes longer. Strain through a coarse sieve. Arrange 3 cups of whole berries on the cake top, then spoon on glaze. Refrigerate cake for about 1 hour to set the glaze. About 30 minutes before serving, remove the cake from the refrigerator to take the chill off.

Light Touch: The model for this recipe is a classic cheesecake with a buttery hazelnut crust and a filling that includes 18 ounces rich cream cheese, 6 whole eggs, and 2 cups sour cream. Although the texture is "lightened" with a meringue, the calories from fat weigh in at a

(continued)

Nutritional Analysis per serving (including optional strawberry topping and glaze)

259 calories

7 g protein

6 g fat

0.3 g satfat

46 g carbohydrate

212 mg sodium

45 mg cholesterol

whopping 61 percent. I have dropped them to 21 percent by replacing the crust with a thin coating of crumbs, cutting 1 yolk, and replacing all the cream cheese with a smaller quantity of low-fat cream cheese. I substitute an equal amount of low-fat vanilla yogurt (not the nonfat type, which has somewhat less flavor) for the sour cream.

Raspberry Marble Cheesecake

◆ ◆ ◆

*T*his is a showstopper! With a stunning design of red raspberry sauce swirled through silken vanilla batter, it is as dazzling to admire as it is to eat.

The sauce can be flavored with either raspberry liqueur (Chambord) or raspberry eau-de-vie (Framboise).

Small cracks may appear along the marbleizing lines on top as the cake cools. Ignore them or fill them in with raspberry jam. The whipped egg whites leaven the cake and must be properly beaten; be sure to read page 20 before starting.

◆ ◆ ◆

be sure to read page 20 before starting.

Yield

7 cups batter; one 9-inch cake; 14 servings

Advance Preparation

After baking and cooling, the cake needs at least 4 hours to firm before serving. Ideally, bake this a day before serving.

Special Equipment

9-inch springform pan, baking parchment or wax paper (optional)

Temperature and Time

300°F for 1 hour plus 1 hour in oven with heat off and door propped open

Filling

2 cups low-fat vanilla yogurt

1½ cups (12 ounces) low-fat cream cheese, at room temperature

1 large egg, separated, plus 1 large egg white

1½ tablespoons vanilla extract

1 cup granulated sugar, divided

¼ cup plus 2 tablespoons unsifted all-purpose flour

¼ teaspoon salt

Crust

Butter-flavor no stick cooking spray

3 tablespoons Grape-Nuts

1 tablespoon walnuts

1 tablespoon granulated sugar

Raspberry Topping and Sauce

   1 12-ounce jar best-quality seedless raspberry jam

   2 tablespoons fresh lemon juice

   1 tablespoons Framboise or Chambord

   1 cup fresh or frozen whole raspberries

Nutritional Analysis per serving

240 calories

6 g protein

5 g fat

0.1 g satfat

44 g carbohydrate

218 mg sodium

24 mg cholesterol

1. Place a fine-mesh sieve over a bowl, put the yogurt in the sieve, and allow it to drain for about 30 minutes to remove excess liquid.

2. Coat the springform pan with cooking spray. If using an aluminum pan, line the bottom with baking parchment or wax paper and spray. To make the crust, combine the Grape-Nuts, walnuts, and sugar in a food processor and blend until fine crumbs. Add the crumbs to the prepared pan, and tilt and rotate pan until evenly dusted with crumbs. Set the pan flat on a table and tap so any loose crumbs are spread more or less evenly over the bottom.

3. To prepare the topping, place the jam in a small saucepan and set it over medium-low heat. Stir for 3 to 4 minutes, until completely smooth and warm to the touch; do not boil. The jam should generously coat the back of a spoon and form ribbons as it drips from the spoon's edge. Remove 7 tablespoons of jam to a cup and set aside to use for marbleizing the cake.

4. To complete the sauce, stir the lemon juice, raspberry liqueur, and raspberries into the remaining jam. Set aside. (If the sauce thickens too much after standing, stir over a very low heat just before serving.)

5. Position a rack in the center of the oven and preheat it to 300°F.

6. In a large bowl, combine the cream cheese, egg yolk, vanilla, and ¾ cup of the sugar. With an electric mixer on medium speed, beat well to blend. Beat in the drained yogurt. Set a fine-mesh sieve over the bowl add the flour and salt. Stir and sift onto the cheese mixture. With the mixer on low, beat until very smooth.

7. In a clean, grease-free bowl, using clean beaters, whip the egg whites until foamy. Gradually add the remaining ¼ cup sugar and whip until the whites are stiff but not dry. Fold the whites into the cheese batter in three additions.

8. Pour half the batter into the prepared pan. Using ¼ cup of the reserved jam, make a pattern of stripes across the batter in the pan. Gently spoon on the remaining batter, covering the sauce. Using a spatula, smooth the top.

(continued)

Cheesecakes   **227**

(a)   **(b)**

9. To marbleize the cake top, spoon lines of the remaining reserved jam across the cake top more or less as shown (a). Draw long swirls with the tip of a knife, pulling through the jam to create an allover marbleized pattern of red and white lines (b). (The simpler the design, the better.)

10. Bake for about 1 hour. The top of the cake should be set but neither darkened nor browned in color; the center will be somewhat soft. The cake will rise slightly and some cracks may appear; they will close up when the cake cools. Turn off the oven and prop open the oven door slightly, leaving the cake inside to cool slowly for 1 hour. Remove the cake from the oven and place it on a wire rack away from drafts. Run a long, thin knife blade between the cake and the pan sides to release some steam. Then place a piece of cardboard on top and allow it to cool completely. Refrigerate for at least 4 hours, or overnight, to firm and mellow.

11. To unmold the cake, run the blade of a long thin knife between the top edge of the cake and the pan. Loosen the spring and carefully lift off the pan sides, leaving the cake on the pan bottom.

Light Touch: My goal was to create an even lighter version of my mother's famous "light" cheesecake; hers was considered light because 6 stiffly whipped egg whites were added to breathe some air into a batter weighed down by 18 ounces cream cheese, 6 egg yolks, and 2 cups sour cream. Divine, yes, but with 61 percent of its calories from fat, each serving carried 386 calories and 27 grams of fat, 15 grams of which were saturated. My *really* light version cuts fat dramatically, dropping to 18 percent calories from fat and cutting out 22 grams of fat per serving. To achieve this, I replaced the cream cheese with a combination of drained low-fat vanilla yogurt and low-fat cream cheese. I used 1 yolk plus 2 egg whites and eliminated the rich nut crust, replacing it with low-fat but crunchy cereal and a small amount of walnuts. To compensate for the flavor lost with the fat, I increased the vanilla and added the raspberry sauce with berries.

Café au Lait Cheesecake

◆ · ◆ · ◆

With its rich coffee flavor and velvety texture, this remarkable cheesecake—which does not crack on top—is an elegant dinner party dessert.

Because the cake itself is so flavorful, there is no need for a rich crust, other than a light dusting of crumbs to prevent the cake from sticking to the pan. For a finishing touch, decorate the top with chocolate-covered espresso beans or a sprinkling of instant coffee granules.

◆ · ◆ · ◆

Crust

    Butter-flavor no stick cooking spray

    3 tablespoons Grape-Nuts or Shredded Wheat

    1 tablespoon chopped walnuts

    1 tablespoon granulated sugar

Filling

    2 cups (16 ounces) nonfat cottage cheese

    1½ cups (12 ounces) low-fat cream cheese, at room temperature

    1¼ cups granulated sugar

    1⅓ cups low-fat sour cream

    2 large eggs plus 2 large egg whites

    6 tablespoons sifted all-purpose flour

    2½ tablespoons espresso coffee powder (such as Medaglia d'Oro brand or substitute regular instant coffee)

    2½ tablespoons coffee liqueur (such as Kahlúa)

    1½ tablespoons nonalkalized unsweetened cocoa

    ⅛ teaspoon cinnamon

    ¼ teaspoon salt

    16 chocolate-covered espresso beans, or instant coffee granules

(continued)

Yield

6 cups batter; 9-inch cake; 14 servings

Advance Preparation

After baking, the cake needs about 3 hours to cool completely, then at least 4 hours to chill and firm in the refrigerator before serving. For best results, bake a day in advance and refrigerate. Bring to room temperature before serving. Or wrap the cake airtight and freeze for up to 3 weeks. Thaw, still wrapped, overnight in the refrigerator.

Special Equipment

9-inch springform pan; baking parchment or wax paper (only for use with aluminum pan)

Temperature and Time

300°F for 65 to 70 minutes plus 30 minutes in oven with heat off and door closed

....

217 calories

9 g protein

7 g fat

0.3 g satfat

31 g carbohydrate

316 mg sodium

42 mg cholesterol

1. Position a rack in the center of the oven and preheat it to 300°F. Coat the springform pan with cooking spray or brush with vegetable oil. If using an aluminum pan, line the bottom with baking parchment or wax paper and spray.

2. To make the crust, combine the cereal, walnuts, and sugar in a food processor and blend to fine crumbs. Add the crumbs to the prepared pan and tilt and rotate the pan to coat with crumbs. Set the pan flat on a table and tap so any loose crumbs are spread more or less evenly over the bottom. With a dampened paper towel, wipe all the crumbs from the food processor.

3. To make the filling, place the cottage cheese in a fine-mesh sieve over a bowl. Place a piece of plastic wrap on the cheese and with your hand, press down firmly on the cheese to force out as much liquid as possible, making relatively dry curds. (Some brands contain gums which make draining difficult; nevertheless, remove what you can.)

4. Place the drained cottage cheese in the food processor and process about 2 full minutes, or until the curds are absolutely smooth, without a trace of graininess. Halfway through, stop the machine and scrape down the bowl.

5. Add the cream cheese, sugar, sour cream, eggs and egg whites, and flour. Process about 15 seconds to blend well. Scrape down the bowl.

6. In a small bowl, dissolve the espresso powder in the coffee liqueur, then add to the processor along with the cocoa, cinnamon, and salt. Process 10 to 15 seconds to blend well.

7. Turn the batter into the prepared pan and bake for 1 hour and 5 to 10 minutes, until set on top, slightly risen, and the center is slightly wobbly when the pan side is tapped. Turn off the oven heat and leave the cake inside for 30 minutes.

8. Remove the cake to a wire rack. Run the blade of a long, thin knife between the cake and the pan side to release steam. Let the cake cool completely (about 3 hours), then top with foil or plastic wrap and refrigerate at least 4 hours, or overnight, to firm before serving.

9. About 30 minutes before serving, remove the cake from the refrigerator and bring it to room temperature. To unmold the cake, release the spring and lift off the sides, leaving the cake on the pan bottom.

10. If desired, garnish the cake with a ring of chocolate-covered espresso beans around the outside edge or sprinkle on a few granules of instant coffee.

Light Touch: My favorite full-fat coffee cheesecake is made with 1 pound cream cheese, 3 eggs, 1 cup sour cream, and almost ½ cup butter; it gets, not surprisingly, 68 percent of its calories from fat. Each serving has 15 grams saturated fat and 110 milligrams cholesterol.

I have reduced the calories from fat to 28 percent (eliminating nearly all the saturated fat and almost two thirds of the cholesterol) by dropping the butter and an egg yolk and using a blend of low-fat and nonfat cheeses. The flavor of the cake is strong enough to do without a rich nut crust, so it is replaced by a light dusting of cereal and nuts.

Brown Sugar Cheesecake with Spiced Blueberry Sauce

-◆-◆-◆-

I created this recipe after tasting a caramel cheesecake in an Atlanta restaurant; the use of brown sugar in baking is a Southern trademark. The light caramel flavor of this extra-creamy cheesecake is delightfully accented by the Spiced Blueberry Sauce.

The high proportion of cheese in the cake is made possible by the use of some nonfat cottage cheese, which must be blended until absolutely smooth to achieve the correct cake texture. During baking, this cake rises fairly high and may crack around the edges; as it cools and sinks down, the cracks compress and most will disappear.

-◆-◆-◆-

Yield

7 cups batter; one 9-inch cake; 12 servings

Advance Preparation

After baking, the cake needs about 3 hours to cool completely, then at least 4 hours to chill and firm in the refrigerator before serving. Ideally, bake the cake a day in advance. Because of the nonfat cottage cheese, this cake is not recommended for freezing.

Special Equipment

9-inch springform pan, baking parchment or wax paper (optional), sturdy baking sheet

Temperature and Time

325°F for 1 hour and 20 minutes plus 1 hour in oven with heat off and door closed

Crust

Butter-flavor no stick cooking spray

2½ tablespoons Grape-Nuts or Honey-Nut Cheerios cereal

1 tablespoon chopped walnuts or pecans

1 tablespoon granulated sugar

Filling

¼ cup unsifted all-purpose flour

2 teaspoons cornstarch

Scant ⅛ teaspoon salt

3 cups (24 ounces) nonfat cottage cheese

1½ cups (12 ounces) low-fat cream cheese, at room temperature

1 large egg

2 large egg whites

¾ cup dark brown sugar, packed

1 tablespoon vanilla extract

1 recipe Spiced Blueberry Sauce (page 415), warmed (optional)

1. Position a rack in the center of the oven and preheat it to 325°F. Coat the springform pan with cooking spray. If using an aluminum pan, line the bottom with baking parchment or wax paper and spray.

2. To make the crust, combine the cereal, nuts, and sugar in a food processor and pulse to medium-fine crumbs. Add the crumbs to the prepared pan, and tilt and rotate the pan to coat with crumbs. Set the pan flat on a table and tap so any loose crumbs are spread more or less evenly over the bottom. Set the pan aside. With a dampened paper towel, wipe all the crumbs from the food processor.

3. Sift together the flour, cornstarch, and salt into a bowl or onto a sheet of wax paper.

4. Place the cottage cheese in a fine-mesh sieve over a bowl. Place a piece of plastic wrap on the cheese and with your hand, press down on the cheese to force out as much liquid as possible, making dry curds.

5. Place the drained cottage cheese in the food processor. Process for 2 minutes, or until absolutely smooth, without a trace of graininess. Add the cream cheese, eggs, brown sugar, and vanilla. Pulse until blended and smooth. Add the flour mixture and pulse 3 or 4 times, just to blend. Do not overmix.

6. Turn the batter into the prepared pan and bake for 1 hour and 20 minutes, or until the sides are risen and the top is set but slightly soft. Turn the oven off and leave the cake inside for 1 hour.

7. Set the cake on a wire rack in a draft-free location. Run the blade of a long, thin knife between the cake and the pan sides to release steam. Leave the cake on the rack until thoroughly cool. Then refrigerate for at least 4 hours, or overnight, to firm.

8. About 30 minutes before serving, remove the cheesecake from the refrigerator to come to room temperature. To unmold the cake, release the spring and lift off the sides, leaving the cake on the pan bottom. Serve the cake plain or with the warmed sauce.

Light Touch: When I started working on this recipe, I used 3 cups 2% cottage cheese and 1 pound light cream cheese; with just a few pecans in the crust, I discovered I still had a fat content of 36 percent. Dropping to 1% cottage cheese cut the calories from fat by only 1 percent. Nonfat cottage cheese, which has somewhat less flavor, and a small reduction in the amount of cream cheese brought the total down to 27 percent calories from fat. To compensate for the slight flavor loss, I increased the quantity of brown sugar and added more vanilla.

Nutritional Analysis per serving (without optional sauce)

187 calories

11 g protein

6 g fat

3 g satfat

25 g carbohydrate

409 mg sodium

33 mg cholesterol

Grand Marnier
Cheesecake

◆ · ◆ · ◆

My students call this "Plan-Ahead Cheesecake" because it is made with plain yogurt drained for twenty-four hours until it has the consistency of cream cheese. The process is effortless, however, and well worth the planning, for this cheesecake has extra richness without extra fat, as well as a strong orange flavor. It makes an elegant presentation topped with a decorative layer of glazed orange slices ringed with chopped pistachio nuts. Note: If you plan to glaze the cake more than 2 hours before serving, use Firm Fruit Glaze (page 433).

◆ · ◆ · ◆

Yield

5 cups batter; one 8-inch cake; 10 servings

Advance Preparation

One or two days in advance, make the yogurt cheese, letting it drain for 24 hours in the refrigerator. After baking, the cake needs about 3 hours to cool thoroughly, then another 3 hours minimum to firm in the refrigerator before serving. Cake can be made one day in advance, so with the cheese draining, you should plan on starting this recipe 2 or even 3 days before you plan to serve the cake. Topping glaze needs about 30 minutes refrigeration to set.

Special Equipment

8-inch springform pan, baking parchment or wax paper (optional), pastry brush

Temperature and Time

325°F for 1 hour and 20 minutes plus 30 minutes in oven with heat off and door closed. Then 1 hour in oven with door propped open

Crust

Butter-flavor no stick cooking spray

Graham–Grape-Nuts Crumb Crust (page 282) for 8-inch springform pan, prepared through Step 2

Filling

2 recipes Yogurt Cheese (page 405), made from 6 cups (48 ounces) nonfat plain yogurt

½ cup (4 ounces) low-fat cream cheese

1 cup nonfat sour cream

Pinch of salt

¾ cup granulated sugar

1 large egg plus 2 large egg whites

2 tablespoons unsifted all-purpose flour

1 tablespoon cornstarch

Grated zest of 1 orange (2 tablespoons)

¼ cup Grand Marnier

3 tablespoons frozen orange juice concentrate

2 teaspoons orange extract

Glaze

⅔ cup best-quality apricot preserves or sweet orange marmalade

2 tablespoons Grand Marnier

Topping

    1 15-ounce can mandarin orange segments, well drained and dried on paper towels, or 2 navel oranges, peeled and cut into segments

    2 teaspoons finely chopped peeled pistachio nuts for garnish (optional)

    Fresh mint leaves (optional)

*Nutritional Analysis
per serving*

282 calories

13 g protein

7 g fat

2.2 g satfat

41 g carbohydrate

277 mg sodium

30 mg cholesterol

1. Position a rack in the center of the oven and preheat it to 325°F. Coat the springform pan with cooking spray. If using an aluminum pan, line the bottom with baking parchment or wax paper and spray.

2. Press the crumb mixture into an even layer over the bottom and about 1 inch up the sides of the prepared pan. Set aside in a cool place.

3. In a large bowl, using an electric mixer, or in a food processor, beat together the yogurt cheese, cream cheese, and sour cream until smooth. Add the salt, sugar, egg and egg whites, flour, cornstarch, orange zest, Grand Marnier, frozen juice concentrate, and extract, and beat until creamy and smooth.

4. Place a sheet of aluminum foil on the oven floor to catch possible drips from the butter in the crust. Spoon the batter into the prepared crust. Bake for about 1 hour and 20 minutes, or until the top looks set and is no longer sticky when touched. Turn off the oven and leave the cake inside with the door closed for 1 hour. Then, place the cake on a wire rack in a draft-free location until completely cool.

5. Refrigerate the cake for at least 3 hours to firm before adding the topping. To unmold the cake, release the spring and remove the pan sides; leave the cake on the pan bottom to serve.

6. Up to 2 hours before serving, prepare the glaze and topping: In a small saucepan, stir the preserves until melted. Remove from the heat, strain, and stir in the liqueur. With a pastry brush, coat the top of the chilled cheesecake with some of the glaze.

7. The oranges must be perfectly dry, or the glaze will melt. Arrange the orange segments in a flower-petal pattern on top of the cake. Rewarm the glaze if necessary, then brush the remaining warm preserves over the oranges. Sprinkle the chopped nuts, if using, in a ring around the rim of the cake. Place a sprig of mint in the center if desired. Refrigerate for about 30 minutes to set the glaze.

(continued)

Light Touch: With only 23 percent of the total calories from fat, this cheesecake with its low-fat crumb crust has about one third the fat of a classic version (68 percent calories from fat) made with 1½ pounds cream cheese, 1 cup sour cream, 4 eggs, more than 1 cup of sugar, and a topping with 2 more cups sweetened sour cream, packed into a buttery hazelnut crust. When pistachio nuts are added as a garnish, they add only 3 calories and trace amounts of fat per serving.

I replaced the full-fat cream cheese with homemade nonfat yogurt cheese, supplemented with low-fat cream cheese and nonfat sour cream. To eliminate most of the cholesterol, I dropped 1 egg and 2 yolks. To prevent a soggy crust (because of the reduction in fat), I added a little flour and cornstarch to the batter. To compensate for the flavor lost with the fat, I enhanced the orange taste with extract, juice, and zest.

Elegant Apple
Cheesecake

· ◆ · ◆ · ◆ ·

I first tasted this cake nearly ten years ago in Munich at the Palm Court Conditorei behind the Nymphenburg Palace. I hold a singular memory of the event, sitting with my husband and daughter in the flower-filled garden on a sun-dappled afternoon. We were having our typical lunch—a selection of cakes—when we discovered this delightful combination of apple torte and almond cheesecake: a sugar cookie base cradling a dense almond cheesecake, topped by a great mound of buttery apple slices glazed with apricot jam.

My taste-memory was jogged when I encountered a similar cake while judging the Third Annual Apple Bake-Off sponsored by the New England Culinary Institute and the Vermont Apple Marketing Board. An outstanding apple torte, submitted by Connie Waller of Starksboro, Vermont, won first prize in the apple dessert category. I recognized the flavor combination at once, even though Connie's version also used raspberry jam (a good idea). I decided to experiment with a reduced-fat variation and the result, easily prepared in the food processor, is elegant in taste and appearance. The top is an appealing jumble of golden sugar-glazed apple and almond slices; at first bite, the taste of sweet apples blends into rich almond cream, playing off a hint of tart apricots and a nutty crumb crust.

As an alternative to almond flavoring in the cake, you can omit extract and add 2 teaspoons lemon zest and 2 teaspoons lemon juice to the batter. Instead of nuts on top, brush 2 tablespoons of warmed apricot preserves over the apples after the cake is baked and cooled.

· ◆ · ◆ · ◆ ·

(continued)

One 8-inch cake;
8 servings

After baking and
cooling, the cake needs
to firm up for several
hours in the refrigerator.
It can be made a day in
advance and refrigerated.
Bring to room temp-
erature before serving.

8-inch springform pan,
baking parchment or
wax paper (optional)

375°F for 45 to 50
minutes

Crust

Butter-flavor no stick cooking spray

Graham–Grape-Nuts Crumb Crust (page 282), quantity for
    8-inch springform pan, prepared through Step 2

½ cup apricot preserves

Filling

¼ cup nonfat plain or vanilla yogurt

1 large egg

¾ cup (6 ounces) low-fat cream cheese

¼ cup granulated sugar

¼ cup unsifted all-purpose flour

½ teaspoon almond extract

Topping

2 large Golden Delicious apples, peeled, cored, and very thinly
    sliced (about 2 cups)

⅓ cup plus 1 teaspoon granulated sugar

½ teaspoon cinnamon

3 tablespoons sliced unblanched almonds

1. Position a rack in the center of the oven and preheat it to 375°F.
Coat the springform pan with cooking spray. If using an aluminum pan,
line the bottom with baking parchment or wax paper and spray.

2. Place a strainer over a bowl and add the yogurt. Allow to drain
for 10 to 15 minutes to remove excess liquid.

3. Prepare the crumb crust: Press the crumb mixture evenly over
the bottom and about 1 inch up the sides of the prepared pan.

4. In a small saucepan, stir the apricot preserves over low heat
until liquefied. Pour about half the preserves over the bottom crumb
crust, spreading them evenly with the back of a spoon. Reserve the
remaining preserves. Set the springform pan aside.

5. Combine all the filling ingredients in a food processor and process until smooth. The batter will be quite runny. Pour the batter over
the preserves in the pan. Spoon on the remaining apricot preserves; the
preserves will sink slightly into the batter.

6. Prepare the topping: In a bowl, toss the sliced apples with ⅓
cup of the sugar and the cinnamon. Spread them over the filling. Scatter
the sliced almond over the apples, then sprinkle on the remaining 1
teaspoon sugar.

7. Bake for 45 to 50 minutes, or until the top is lightly golden, the apples are fork-tender, and the filling is set. Cool the cake on a wire rack. Then refrigerate for at least 3 hours, or overnight, to firm the filling.

8. To unmold the cake, loosen and remove the springform sides, leaving the cake on the pan bottom.

Light Touch: This delectable confection obtains only 28 percent of its calories from fat, in contrast to its ultra-rich German predecessor: 55 percent calories from fat. To achieve this reduction, I cut several eggs and reduced the cream cheese content, substituting the low-fat variety plus some nonfat yogurt. The flour gives the substance and solidity originally provided by the cream cheese and additional eggs. The original butter-rich cookie crust is replaced by a low-fat graham–Grape-Nuts crust that provides a crisp texture and offers a nutty flavor as well.

Nutritional Analysis
per serving
....
283 calories

6 g protein

9 g fat

3 g satfat

47 g carbohydrate

266 mg sodium

36 mg cholesterol

Lemon Ricotta Cheesecake

◆ · ◆ · ◆ ·

*T*orta di ricotta *is a famous Italian specialty made in different versions depending upon the region of the country and the holiday for which it is served. This recipe, from a friend living in Venice, has a counterpoint of tart apricots and sweet, rum-soaked golden raisins played against a mild lemon-cheese background. It can be served year-round, but is especially appropriate at Easter. For Christmas, the apricots, raisins, and lemon usually are replaced with almond flavoring and mixed glacéed fruits combined with a little chopped bittersweet chocolate.*

· ◆ · ◆ · ◆ ·

Yield

5 cups batter; one 8-inch cake; 8 servings

Advance Preparation

Cake needs to cool for at least 3 hours after baking. It can be served at room temperature, when the texture will be at its lightest. Or it can be baked up to a day in advance, cooled, and refrigerated; the texture will be denser, but the flavors will be more mellowed. Do not freeze.

Special Equipment

8-inch springform pan, baking parchment or wax paper (optional), heavy baking sheet

Temperature and Time

325°F for 45 to 50 minutes plus 1 hour in oven with heat off and door closed

Crust

> Butter-flavor no stick cooking spray
>
> 2½ tablespoons Grape-Nuts or Cheerios cereal
>
> 1 tablespoon chopped walnuts
>
> 1 tablespoon granulated sugar
>
> Pinch of cinnamon

Filling

> ⅓ cup golden raisins
>
> ⅓ cup dried apricots, diced
>
> ⅓ cup dark rum or Kirsch *or* fresh orange juice
>
> 1¾ cups skim-milk ricotta cheese
>
> 3 ounces low-fat cream cheese, at room temperature
>
> ¾ cup granulated sugar
>
> ¼ cup nonfat plain yogurt
>
> 1 large egg, separated, plus 2 large egg whites
>
> 1 teaspoon grated lemon zest
>
> 2 teaspoons fresh lemon juice
>
> ¼ cup unsifted all-purpose flour
>
> Pinch of salt
>
> Grated nutmeg or 1 tablespoon lightly toasted pine nuts (optional)

1. Position a rack in the center of the oven and preheat it to 325°F. Coat the springform pan with cooking spray. If using an aluminum pan, line the bottom with baking parchment or wax paper and spray.

2. Combine the crust ingredients in a food processor and blend to fine crumbs. Add the crumbs to the prepared pan, and tilt and rotate the pan to coat with crumbs. Set the pan flat on a table and tap so any loose crumbs are spread more or less evenly over the bottom. Set the pan aside.

3. Combine the raisins, apricots, and rum or juice in a small microwaveable bowl; partially cover with plastic wrap and microwave on high for 15 to 20 seconds to heat through, or simmer in a small pan over low heat about 5 minutes. Set aside for about 20 minutes. Drain off the liquid.

4. Meanwhile, place the ricotta in a strainer set over a bowl, and allow to drain for about 10 minutes. Discard the liquid in the bowl, then force the ricotta through the strainer into the bowl with the back of a large spoon.

5. In the large bowl of an electric mixer, beat the cream cheese until smooth. Beat in ½ cup of the sugar. Scrape down the bowl and beaters, and add the ricotta, yogurt, egg yolk, lemon zest, and lemon juice. Beat well to blend thoroughly, then beat in the flour and salt. Stir in the drained raisins and apricots.

6. In a clean, grease-free bowl, using clean beaters, whip the egg whites until foamy. Gradually add the remaining ¼ cup sugar, and whip until the egg whites are stiff but not dry. Fold the whites into the batter.

7. Turn the batter into the prepared pan, and smooth the top. Sprinkle on a light dusting of nutmeg or the toasted pine nuts, if desired.

Set the pan on a heavy baking sheet and bake for about 45 to 50 minutes, or until the edges of the cake are puffed up and light golden, and the center is firm to the touch. Turn off the oven and leave the cake inside with the door closed for 1 hour. Then set the cake on a rack in a draft-free location and let cool completely. Serve at room temperature or refrigerate.

Light Touch: This cheesecake is a low-fat adaptation of one of my favorite recipes. The original, with 52 percent of its calories from fat, is set in a buttery walnut crust and made with 3 whole eggs, regular cream cheese, whole-milk ricotta, regular yogurt, and pine nuts. I have kept the flavor and texture but cut more than half the calories from fat

(continued)

Nutritional Analysis per serving (without pine nuts)

240 calories

11 g protein

7 g fat

3 g satfat

37 g carbohydrate

200 mg sodium

39 mg cholesterol

(to 24 percent) by replacing the crust with a light dusting of low-fat crumbs, eliminating 2 egg yolks, and using low-fat cream cheese, ricotta, and yogurt. The nutmeg adds a satisfactory touch of color on top, but if you want to be traditional and use pine nuts (toasted until golden in a frying pan), note that 1 tablespoon adds just under 1 gram of fat to each serving.

Pumpkin Cheesecake Pie

◆ · ◆ · ◆

At Thanksgiving, my mother used to make a version of this cake combining, in addition to eggs, sugar, and spices, equal parts cream cheese, sour cream, and pumpkin. It blended the best of two worlds, cheesecake and pumpkin pie, in a buttery walnut crust.

This enlightened version retains all the rich flavor and adds two new features: a crunchy crumb crust and a lovely marbleized presentation. The idea and method for marbleizing the cake comes from my colleague Betty Rosbottom, cookbook author and director of La Belle Pomme Cooking School at Lazarus in Columbus, Ohio.

◆ · ◆ · ◆

Yield

3¾ cups filling; one 9-inch pie; 10 servings

Advance Preparation

Pie can be baked 1 day in advance, covered, and refrigerated. Bring to room temperature before serving.

Special Equipment

9-inch pie plate

Temperature and Time

350°F for 30 minutes

Crust

Graham–Grape-Nuts Crumb Crust (page 282) for 9-inch pie, prepared through Step 2

Filling

1½ cups (12 ounces) nonfat cottage cheese

⅓ cup (2¾ ounces) low-fat cream cheese, at room temperature

3 tablespoons nonfat vanilla yogurt

⅓ cup granulated sugar

1½ tablespoons unsifted all-purpose flour

2 teaspoons vanilla extract

2 large egg whites

1½ cups canned pumpkin purée

⅓ cup dark brown sugar, packed

1 teaspoon cinnamon

½ teaspoon nutmeg

½ teaspoon ground ginger

Scant ⅛ teaspoon ground cloves

Generous pinch of salt

1. Position a rack in the top third of the oven and preheat it to 350°F.

2. Press the crumb mixture into the pie plate. Set aside.

3. Place the cottage cheese in a strainer set over a bowl. Cover the cheese with a piece of plastic wrap and press down firmly on the cheese to force out as much liquid as possible, making relatively dry curds. Transfer the cottage cheese to the food processor and process for 2 full minutes, or until absolutely smooth, without a trace of graininess.

4. Add the cream cheese, yogurt, sugar, flour, and vanilla. Process until smooth. Remove ⅓ cup of this mixture and set it aside for marbleizing the top of the pie.

5. Add the egg whites, pumpkin, brown sugar, spices, and salt to the processor. Pulse until thoroughly blended.

6. Pour the pumpkin mixture into the prepared crust, taking care not to dislodge the crumbs. To make the marbleized design, spoon 5 separate pools of the reserved cream cheese batter on the top of the pie. Draw the tip of a knife through the contrasting batters in a swirling pattern (see diagrams on page 228).

7. Bake for 30 minutes, or until the top of the pie is set and no longer sticky to the touch. Cool the pie on a wire rack. Serve at room temperature. (Refrigerate any leftovers.)

Light Touch: This pie filling contains only 11 percent fat. Adding the crumb crust gives a relatively modest total of 19 percent calories from fat. With Elmira and Mary's Pie Pastry (page 276), the total would rise to 34 percent fat, and per serving, boost calories 17 grams and fat 4 grams.

*Nutritional Analysis
per serving*
....

214 calories

8 g protein

5 g fat

1.6 g satfat

37 g carbohydrate

303 mg sodium

8 mg cholesterol

No-Bake Berry Cheesecake

· ◆ · ◆ · ◆ ·

My tattered family cookbook contains a bespattered 1972 note from my good friend Carla Jaeger with her recipe for Refrigerator Cheesecake. Made in a blender from equal parts cream cheese and sour cream flavored with sugar and lemon, bound with a little gelatine, it is set in a granola crumb crust—a nod to the health foods we were aggressively eating (with our cream) in those days.

We have enjoyed this easy-to-make dessert for years, decorating it with seasonal fruits and berries "of contrasting colors and flavors," as Carla suggests. She is the mother of the present recipe, which, twenty years later, is a lot healthier: The fat content is modified without losing the creamy texture or clean, bright flavor.

I find the procedure is streamlined if the berries are simply set in the shell and the filling poured on top, as they will rise to the surface enough to give color—but you can arrange them decoratively on top if you prefer. Flavorful fresh ripe berries are really the only ones to use. Frozen berries, even whole unsweetened ones, bleed into the filling, adding moisture that may prevent the cheesecake from setting.

· ◆ · ◆ · ◆ ·

Yield

One 10-inch pie; 12 servings

Advance Preparation

The yogurt must be drained for about 30 minutes before using. The pie needs to set in the refrigerator for at least 3 hours before serving. It can be made 1 day in advance, covered, and refrigerated.

Special Equipment

10-inch pie plate

Crust

Honey-Graham Crumb Crust (page 281) for 10-inch pie plate, prepared through Step 2 (or other crumb crust of your choice)

Filling

1 cup nonfat vanilla yogurt

¾ cup (6 ounces) nonfat cottage cheese

¾ cup (6 ounces) low-fat cream cheese

1 teaspoon grated lemon zest

¾ cup plus 2 tablespoons granulated sugar

½ teaspoon vanilla extract

2 tablespoons fresh lemon juice

2 tablespoons fresh orange juice

1 envelope (2 generous teaspoons) Knox unflavored gelatine

1 cup fresh blueberries, picked over, rinsed, and gently dried on paper towels

1 cup fresh raspberries, picked over

1. Press the crumb mixture into the pie plate. Refrigerate.

2. Place the yogurt in a fine-mesh strainer and set aside to drain for about 30 minutes. Transfer the yogurt to a bowl.

3. Place the cottage cheese in a strainer set over a bowl. Cover it with a piece of plastic wrap and press down firmly on the cheese to force out as much liquid as possible, making relatively dry curds.

4. Transfer the drained cottage cheese to a blender or a food processor. Process for at least 2 full minutes, or until absolutely smooth, without a trace of graininess. Add the cream cheese, lemon zest, sugar, and vanilla and process until well blended. Add the drained yogurt and pulse to blend.

5. Combine the lemon juice and orange juice in a small saucepan. Sprinkle on the gelatine, and set aside to soften for about 3 minutes. Then stir the mixture over low heat until the gelatine is dissolved; do not boil.

6. With the blender or processor running, add the gelatine mixture, and pulse to combine.

7. Arrange the berries in the bottom of the crumb crust. Pour on the filling. Refrigerate for at least 3 hours, or overnight, before serving.

Light Touch: Made with low-fat cream cheese and nonfat vanilla yogurt, which has a little more complexity of taste than the plain, plus some nonfat cottage cheese for added creaminess, this divine creation gets just 28 percent of its calories from fat. That's quite a drop from the original, made with regular cream cheese and sour cream, and weighing in at 47 percent calories from fat; each serving contained 16 grams of fat, 8 of them saturated.

Nutritional Analysis per serving

233 calories

6 g protein

7 g fat

3 g satfat

38 g carbohydrate

228 mg sodium

12 mg cholesterol

No-Bake Pineapple Cheesecake

· ◆ · ◆ · ◆ ·

L uxuriously rich and creamy with a bright pineapple flavor, this cheesecake is everyone's favorite. I like to prepare it in a springform pan, but you can also use a 10-inch deep-dish pie plate. The unbaked filling firms in the refrigerator, but the crust is bound with a little egg white and so must be prebaked for a few minutes; you can substitute a chilled unbaked crumb crust if you prefer. Serve this with Pineapple Sauce (page 419) or, for color contrast, Raspberry Sauce (page 412). The recipe calls for pineapple extract, which is available in most supermarkets; alternatively, you can substitute ¼ cup frozen pineapple juice concentrate or lemonade concentrate, undiluted, and increase the gelatine to 3¾ teaspoons.

◆ · ◆ · ◆ ·

Crust

> Graham–Grape-Nuts Crumb Crust (page 282) for 8-inch springform pan or 10-inch deep-dish pie plate, prepared through Step 3, prebaked, cooled, and chilled

Filling

> 1¼ cups nonfat vanilla or plain yogurt
>
> 1 20-ounce can crushed pineapple, unsweetened or in regular light syrup
>
> ¾ cup (6 ounces) nonfat cottage cheese
>
> ¾ cup (6 ounces) low-fat cream cheese, at room temperature
>
> ¾ cup granulated sugar
>
> 1 teaspoon vanilla extract
>
> 1½ teaspoons pineapple extract
>
> 3 tablespoons fresh lemon juice
>
> Scant 3½ teaspoons Knox unflavored gelatine
>
> Sprig of mint (optional)

1. Place the yogurt in a fine-mesh strainer set over a bowl and set aside to drain for at least 20 minutes. Then transfer to a small bowl.

2. Drain the crushed pineapple in a strainer set over a bowl. Press the fruit lightly with the back of a large spoon to release all the juice. Transfer the pineapple to a small bowl, and reserve ½ cup of the juice.

Yield

About 4½ cups filling; one 8-inch or 10-inch cake; 10 servings

Advance Preparation

The yogurt must drain for at least 20 minutes before using. After baking and cooling, the cake must be chilled for at least 3 hours to set.

Special Equipment

8-inch springform pan or 10-inch deep-dish Pyrex pie plate

3. Place the cottage cheese in a strainer set over a bowl. Cover it with a piece of plastic wrap, and press down firmly on the cheese to force excess liquid from the curds.

4. Place the cottage cheese and cream cheese in a blender or a food processor. Process for at least 3 full minutes, or until absolutely smooth, with no trace of graininess, stopping once to scrape down the sides with a rubber spatula.

5. Add the sugar, vanilla, pineapple extract, and drained yogurt. Pulse until well blended. Scrape down the sides with a rubber spatula, and pulse several times. Add 1½ cups of the drained crushed pineapple and pulse just to blend.

6. In a small saucepan, combine the reserved ½ cup pineapple juice and the lemon juice. Sprinkle on the gelatine and allow to sit about 3 minutes to soften. Then stir the mixture over low heat just until the gelatine is dissolved; do not boil. With the blender or food processor running, add the gelatine mixture and pulse to blend.

7. Pour the filling into the chilled crust and refrigerate for at least 3 hours, or overnight, before serving. Once the top is firm, cover it with plastic wrap.

8. If desired, garnish the top of the cake with a small sprig of mint before serving.

Light Touch: I am as pleased with the taste and the creamy "mouthfeel" of this dessert as I am with the fact that it contains only 22 percent calories from fat. It has been a long journey from my first efforts. Initially, I wanted to avoid using gelatine and instead follow the traditional, and creamier, method of setting a no-bake cheesecake with sweetened condensed milk. The notion is fine, but sweetened condensed milk, made from whole milk, is fairly high in calories and fat. When I cut it down to an acceptable level, I found I still needed to add gelatine to make it set, and I had most of the can of condensed milk left over—an impractical solution. I decided to forget the condensed milk and use a minimum amount of gelatine dissolved in pineapple juice. I put the filling into a flaky pastry shell and thought I was home free. The flavor was good though the texture was not quite creamy enough, and...it had nearly 40 percent calories from fat! To gain extra richness and body without adding more fat, I added puréed nonfat cottage cheese. Finally, to remove the greatest contributor of fat, I replaced the pastry with a low-fat crumb crust.

*Nutritional Analysis
per serving*

245 calories

8 g protein

6 g fat

0.7 g satfat

42 g carbohydrate

270 mg sodium

10 mg cholesterol

Pudding Cakes
and
Puddings

In my personal culinary lexicon, puddings are comfort foods, sweets with a soft consistency, deeply satisfying flavor, and accessible, appealing presentation. Never are they haughty, forbidding, or threateningly grand; these are the treats you curl up with late at night, to celebrate a quiet moment, to soften a sad one.

The most "down home" are the easily prepared Old-Fashioned Bread Pudding, Creamy Rice Pudding, and Chocolate Pudding. My "company puddings" are equally delectable, if slightly fancier in presentation: Steamed Apricot-Apple Pudding, intoxicating when served with warm Bourbon Sauce, and no-bake Very Berry Summer Pudding, an old English classic and one of the prettiest and tastiest dishes ever.

Pudding cakes, also in the family of comfort foods, are a delightful marriage of cake and flavorful creamy pudding. My fascination with this confection began when, as a child, I would watch my mother prepare what looked like a normal chocolate cake batter and then, just before baking, pour a cup of boiling water over it. I was always sure she had made a mistake. I never trusted the outcome and counted the minutes until the pan emerged from the alchemist's fire: a crisp crunchy brownie cake rippled throughout with dark chocolate pudding! Like a cartoon character, I always did a surprise take. Don't ask how it works, it does. Even in my newly devised variations.

These cakes have other virtues as well: Many are made without any eggs at all (leaving them cholesterol-free); all are reduced in fat, particularly saturated fat; and all are quick and easy to prepare. In fact, simplicity is their leitmotif. In time tests in my kitchen, once the ingredients were measured and eggs separated, these cakes took five minutes to get into the oven; boxed cake mixes took at least nine.

A cautionary note: Packaged pudding cake mixes have no relation to these homemade pudding cakes. They are simply regular cake mixes with the addition of instant pudding.

I have included two types of pudding cake recipes here. For the first one, the dry ingredients are blended with oil, milk, and flavoring (no eggs are used) and spread into a baking pan. The batter is topped with additional flavoring such as cocoa or sugar, and then a cup of boiling liquid is poured on just before it is popped into the oven. This procedure results in a moist cake rippled with pudding, which is best served right from the baking pan.

The second method, for cakes that include eggs, is equally surprising and equally flavorful. The eggs are separated, and the stiffly whipped whites are folded into the batter. The cake is baked in a water bath to maintain an even temperature, and the custard pudding separates into a creamy bottom layer with a delicate sponge-meringue cake that rises like a soufflé on top. The meringue sinks as the cake cools, so it should be served as soon as it is baked.

Light Touch: Pudding cakes have never been loaded with fat, though the presence of some butter and eggs leaves room for improvement. All the pudding cake recipes in this chapter get between 21 and 27 percent calories from fat. To achieve this, in the recipes with eggs, I have adapted classic recipes, cutting out at least 1 yolk and part of the sugar and replacing whole milk with 1% milk. In the egg-free recipes, I have dropped about ½ cup sugar, used low-fat milk, and eliminated ⅓ cup butter. In the original versions of egg-pudding cakes (roughly 30 percent calories from fat), 3 or 4 whole eggs are used, along with at least 1 cup sugar and ¾ cup whole milk. Compared with many other desserts in this book, the calorie count in pudding cakes appears relatively high. Note that although sugar is reduced, it is still present in significant amounts. Console yourself with the fact that both total fat and saturated fat are greatly reduced and in many cases cholesterol is zero.

Mocha Pudding Cake

◆ · ◆ · ◆

This is a chocolate lover's dream: a glazed brownie/cake rippled with rich, coffee-scented chocolate pudding. Served hot from the oven with a glass of cold low-fat milk, this is the ultimate comfort food. This cake is so easy to prepare, it can be pulled from the oven within 45 minutes of the first twitch of a chocoholic's midnight craving.

◆ · ◆ · ◆

Yield

One 8-inch square cake;
6 servings

Advance Preparation

Do not bake this cake in
advance.

Special Equipment

8 × 8 × 1 ½-inch pan

Temperature and Time

350°F for 25 to 30
minutes

Nutritional Analysis
per serving

342 calories

4 g protein

10 g fat

0.8 g satfat

64 g carbohydrate

215 mg sodium

1 mg cholesterol

Butter-flavor no stick cooking spray

1⅓ cups granulated sugar, divided

1 cup unsifted all-purpose flour

¼ teaspoon salt

½ cup unsweetened cocoa (preferably Dutch-processed),
   divided

2 teaspoons baking powder

Pinch of cinnamon

¼ cup canola oil

½ cup 1% milk

1 teaspoon vanilla

2 heaping teaspoons espresso coffee powder *or* regular or
   decaffeinated coffee powder

1 cup boiling water

1. Position a rack in the center of the oven and preheat it to 350°F. Coat the baking pan with cooking spray.

2. In a large bowl, combine ⅔ cup of the sugar, the flour, salt, ¼ cup of the cocoa, the baking powder, and cinnamon and stir well to blend. Whisk in the oil, milk, and vanilla. The batter will be stiff. Scrape the batter into the prepared pan and smooth the top.

3. In a small bowl, stir together the remaining ⅔ cup sugar and ¼ cup cocoa. Sprinkle evenly over the cake batter. Dissolve the coffee powder in the boiling water, and pour it over the batter; do not stir.

4. Bake for about 25 to 30 minutes, or until the top of the cake looks crisp and crackled, and a cake tester inserted in a "cakey" area comes out clean. Cool on a wire rack for about 5 minutes. Serve warm from the baking pan.

Light Touch: See page 251. 25 percent calories from fat.

Orange Pudding Cake

◆ ◆ ◆

This cake has a strong orange flavor and lovely golden-orange color. The taste of the cake will be affected by the type of marmalade you use, and the amount of sugar needed for the topping varies, depending upon the sweetness of the marmalade. You will need to use slightly more for bitter English-type marmalade.

◆ ◆ ◆

Butter-flavor no stick cooking spray

$2/3$ cup plus $1/2$ cup granulated sugar, divided, or to taste

1 cup unsifted all-purpose flour

2 teaspoons baking powder

$1/4$ teaspoon salt

$1/4$ cup canola oil

$1\frac{1}{2}$ cups fresh orange juice, divided

1 teaspoon vanilla extract

1 teaspoon orange extract or orange oil

Grated zest of 1 orange (about 2 tablespoons)

$1/2$ cup regular style best-quality orange marmalade

1. Position a rack in the center of the oven and preheat it to 350°F. Coat the baking pan with cooking spray.

2. In a large bowl, combine $2/3$ cup of the sugar, the flour, baking powder, and salt. Stir well to blend. Whisk in the oil, $1/2$ cup of the orange juice, the vanilla, and orange extract. Scrape the batter into the prepared pan and smooth the top.

3. Sprinkle the remaining $1/2$ cup sugar (or more to taste, depending on the sweetness of the marmalade) over the top of the batter.

4. In a small saucepan, combine the zest and marmalade and the remaining 1 cup orange juice. Stir over medium heat until almost boiling. Pour over the batter; do not stir.

5. Bake for 30 to 35 minutes, or until the top of the cake is golden and a cake tester inserted in a "cakey" area comes out clean. Cool on a wire rack for about 5 minutes. Serve from the baking pan.

Light Touch: See page 251. Twenty-one percent calories from fat.

Yield

One 8-inch square cake; 6 servings

Advance Preparation

Do not bake this cake in advance.

Special Equipment

$8 \times 8 \times 1\frac{1}{2}$-inch pan

Temperature and Time

350°F for 30 to 35 minutes

Nutritional Analysis per serving

402 calories

3 g protein

9 g fat

0.6 g satfat

79 g carbohydrate

202 mg sodium

0 mg cholesterol

Vanilla-Blackberry
Pudding Cake

◆ · ◆ · ◆ ·

While the rich burgundy color of the blackberries is a lovely contrast to the white cake, you can use any type of berries. I like canned blackberries or boysenberries because they are always available and their sweet syrup can be used to flavor the pudding. If you substitute fresh berries, you must purée and strain some of the berries and sweeten the juice to replace the canned syrup.

◆ · ◆ · ◆ ·

Yield

One 8-inch square cake;
6 servings

Advance Preparation

Do not bake this cake in advance.

Special Equipment

8 × 8 × 1½-inch pan

Temperature and Time

350°F for 30 to 35 minutes

Butter-flavor no stick cooking spray

⅔ cup plus ¼ cup granulated sugar, divided

1 cup unsifted all-purpose flour

2 teaspoons baking powder

¼ teaspoon salt

¼ cup canola oil

½ cup 1% milk

2 teaspoons vanilla extract

3 tablespoons Framboise or Grand Marnier (optional), divided

One 17-ounce can fancy blackberries in heavy syrup, well drained, syrup reserved (you should have 1⅓ cups berries and 1 cup syrup; if syrup is scant, mash and strain ⅓ cup of the berries and add the juice to the syrup)

1. Position a rack in the center of the oven and preheat it to 350°F. Coat the baking pan with cooking spray.

2. In a large bowl, combine ⅔ cup of the sugar, the flour, baking powder, and salt. Stir well to blend. Whisk in the oil, milk, vanilla, and 1 tablespoon of the liqueur, if using. The batter will be quite stiff.

3. Spread the drained berries evenly in the bottom of the prepared pan, and top them with the batter. Smooth the top of the batter and sprinkle on the remaining ¼ cup sugar.

4. In a small saucepan, warm the reserved berry syrup until hot to the touch (about 130°F). Stir in the remaining 2 tablespoons liqueur if using. Pour the warm mixture over the batter; do not stir.

5. Bake for about 35 minutes, or until the top of the cake looks crisp and crackled, and a cake tester inserted into a "cakey" area comes out clean. Cool on a wire rack for about 5 minutes. Serve warm from the baking pan.

Light Touch: See page 251. Twenty-two percent calories from fat.

Nutritional Analysis
per serving

389 calories

4 g protein

10 g fat

0.8 g satfat

72 g carbohydrate

212 mg sodium

1 mg cholesterol

Lemon-Raspberry Pudding Cake

◆ · ◆ · ◆

This cake is prepared with stiffly whipped egg whites folded into a batter that magically separates into a creamy fruit-filled pudding topped with a meringue sponge cake. Serve this hot from the oven, before the meringue has a chance to cool and collapse.

◆ · ◆ · ◆

Yield

One 8-inch square cake; 6 servings

Advance Preparation

Do not bake this cake in advance.

Special Equipment

8 × 8 × 1½-inch pan, roasting pan large enough to hold the cake pan

Temperature and Time

350°F for 25 to 35 minutes

Nutritional Analysis per serving

215 calories

4 g protein

7 g fat

1 g satfat

37 g carbohydrate

92 mg sodium

72 mg cholesterol

Butter-flavor no stick cooking spray

¾ cup plus 2 tablespoons granulated sugar, divided

3 tablespoons unsifted all-purpose flour

⅛ teaspoon salt

⅛ teaspoon cinnamon

2 tablespoons canola oil

Grated zest of 1 lemon (about 1 tablespoon)

¼ cup fresh lemon juice

¾ cup 1% milk or buttermilk

2 large eggs, separated, plus 1 large egg white

1 cup fresh raspberries

Pinch of nutmeg

1. Position a rack in the center of the oven and preheat it to 350°F. Coat the baking pan with cooking spray. In a large bowl, combine the ¾ cup sugar, the flour, salt, and cinnamon. Whisk to blend. Whisk in the oil, lemon zest and juice, milk or buttermilk, and egg yolks. Blend well.

2. In a grease-free bowl, using an electric mixer, whip the egg whites until foamy. Add the remaining 2 tablespoons sugar and whip until stiff but not dry. Fold the whites into the batter. Gently fold in the berries. Turn the batter into the prepared pan, and sprinkle the nutmeg on top.

3. Set the cake pan in the larger roasting pan. Carefully add hot water to the roasting pan to reach about one third of the way up the sides of the cake pan, and set in the oven. Bake for about 25 minutes, or until the top of the cake is golden brown. Remove the cake pan from the water bath and cool it on a wire rack for about 5 minutes. Serve warm from the baking pan.

Light Touch: See page 251. Twenty-seven percent calories from fat.

Almond-Chocolate
Pudding Cake

◆ ◆ ◆

Delicately almond scented, this white cake is glazed on top with specks of chocolate and layered with a deep rich chocolate pudding.

◆ ◆ ◆

Butter-flavor no stick cooking spray

1⅓ cups granulated sugar, divided

1 cup unsifted all-purpose flour

¼ teaspoon salt

2 teaspoons baking powder

¼ cup canola oil

½ cup 1% milk

1 teaspoon vanilla extract

½ teaspoon almond extract

¼ cup unsweetened nonalkalized cocoa

1 cup boiling water

1. Position a rack in the center of the oven and preheat it to 350°F. Coat the baking pan with cooking spray.

2. In a large bowl, combine ⅔ cup of the sugar, the flour, salt, and baking powder. Stir well to blend. Whisk in the oil, milk, and both extracts. The batter will be quite stiff. Scrape the batter into the prepared pan and smooth the top.

3. In a small bowl, stir together the cocoa and the remaining ⅔ cup sugar. Sprinkle this mixture over the batter. Pour the boiling water over the batter; do not stir.

4. Bake for 25 to 35 minutes, until the top of the cake looks crisp and crackled and a cake tester inserted into a "cakey" area comes out clean. Cool on a wire rack for about 5 minutes. Serve warm from the baking pan.

Light Touch: See page 251. Twenty-seven percent calories from fat.

Yield

One 8-inch square cake; 6 servings

Advance Preparation

Do not bake this cake in advance.

Special Equipment

8 × 8 × 1½-inch pan

Temperature and Time

350°F for 25 to 35 minutes

Nutritional Analysis per serving

337 calories

3 g protein

10 g fat

1.2 g satfat

61 g carbohydrate

211 mg sodium

1 mg cholesterol

Maple-Apple Pudding Cake

· ◆ · ◆ · ◆ ·

M ade with a whipped meringue, this maple pudding is topped with a delicate cinnamon-scented sponge cake flecked with bits of chopped apple. This is an unusual and delicious addition to a fall brunch; be sure to serve it warm from the oven, when the cake texture is high and light; the soufflé will fall as it cools.

Select a soft eating apple such as Macintosh or Opalescent rather than a hard apple for this recipe because the baking time is so short.

· ◆ · ◆ · ◆ ·

Yield

One 8-inch square cake; 6 servings

Advance Preparation

Do not bake this cake in advance.

Special Equipment

8 × 8 × 1½-inch pan; roasting pan large enough to hold the cake pan

Temperature and Time

350°F for 30 to 35 minutes

Butter-flavor no stick cooking spray

½ cup plus 2 tablespoons granulated sugar, divided

3 tablespoons unsifted all-purpose flour

⅛ teaspoon salt

Generous pinch of cinnamon

2 large eggs plus 1 large egg white

2 tablespoons canola oil

3 tablespoons pure maple syrup

1 teaspoon maple extract

1 teaspoon vanilla extract

¾ cup 1% milk

1 medium apple, peeled, cored, and finely diced

Pinch of nutmeg

1. Position a rack in the center of the oven and preheat it to 350°F. Coat the baking pan with cooking spray.

2. In a large bowl, combine ½ cup of the sugar, the flour, salt, and cinnamon. Whisk to blend.

3. In another bowl, whisk together the egg yolks, oil, maple syrup, both extracts, and the milk. Whisk the dry ingredients into the liquids, blending well; the batter will be quite thin.

4. In a grease-free bowl, using an electric mixer, whip the egg whites until foamy. Add the 2 tablespoons sugar and whip until stiff but not dry.

5. Whisk the maple batter once, then add half the whipped whites and blend with the whisk. Then fold in the remaining whites and the diced apples. (Because the batter is so thin, blending in the whites may look improbable at first, but gentle whisking will accomplish the task.) Turn the batter into the prepared pan and sprinkle on the nutmeg.

6. Set the cake pan in the larger roasting pan. Carefully add hot water to the roasting pan to reach about one third of the way up the sides of the cake pan, and set in the oven. Bake for about 35 minutes, or until the cake is golden on top and dry and springy to the touch. Remove the cake pan from the water bath and cool on a wire rack for about 5 minutes. Serve warm from the baking pan.

Light Touch: See page 251. Twenty-four percent calories from fat.

Nutritional Analysis per serving

245 calories

4 g protein

7 g fat

1 g satfat

44 g carbohydrate

102 mg sodium

72 mg cholesterol

Indian Pudding

◆ ◆ ◆

Indian Pudding should really be called Settlers' Pudding. Far from being a Native American dish, it was concocted by British colonists who adopted the Indians' corn for their puddings when the grains they had brought with them failed to thrive here. It is a rich dish that blends spices and molasses with the nutty taste and grainy texture of cornmeal.

Indian Pudding was one of my father's favorite dishes, and when I was a child, it was a favorite family dessert—usually bought in a can, steamed, and served hot with a great scoop of vanilla ice cream. My husband and daughter now enjoy it with me, though we have come to prefer the softer, creamier texture of the home-baked pudding. Vanilla yogurt is a good (virtuous) accompaniment. Don't even think about heavy cream.

◆ ◆ ◆

Yield

6 servings

Advance Preparation

Pudding can be made several hours in advance, but is best served warm from the oven.

Special Equipment

1½-quart ovenproof baking dish, roasting pan large enough to hold the baking dish

Temperature and Time

325°F for 1 hour and 30 to 40 minutes

Butter-flavor no stick cooking spray

3½ cups 2% milk, divided

½ cup yellow cornmeal

½ cup unsulfured molasses

2 tablespoons granulated sugar

¾ teaspoon salt

1 teaspoon cinnamon

½ teaspoon nutmeg

½ teaspoon ground ginger

1 tablespoon cornstarch

1 large egg

1 large egg white

Low-fat vanilla yogurt (optional)

1. Position a rack in the center of the oven and preheat it to 325°F. Coat the baking dish with cooking spray.

2. Pour 2¾ cups of the milk into a large heavy-bottomed saucepan, and set it over medium heat until the milk is scalded (small bubbles appear at the edges).

3. Meanwhile, in a small bowl, whisk the cornmeal into ½ cup of the remaining milk.

Have Your Cake and Eat It, Too

4. Whisk the cornmeal mixture into the scalded milk and bring to a gentle boil over medium heat. Reduce heat and simmer, whisking frequently, for 15 minutes, or until the mixture has thickened enough to coat a metal spoon. Stir in the molasses, sugar, salt, and spices, and remove from the heat.

5. In a small bowl, dissolve the cornstarch in the remaining ¼ cup milk. Whisk in the egg and egg white.

6. Add about a cup of the hot cornmeal mixture to the egg-cornstarch mixture, whisking vigorously to prevent the eggs from curdling. Then, while continuing to whisk, turn the egg mixture into the hot pudding and blend thoroughly. Whisk until smooth.

7. Pour the pudding into the prepared baking dish. Set it in the roasting pan. Add hot water to the roasting pan to come about one-third of the way up the sides of the baking dish. Set in the oven and bake for about 1 hour and 30 to 40 minutes, or until the pudding is browned on top and a knife inserted near the edge (not in the center) comes out clean. Remove the baking dish from the water bath, and cool slightly on a rack. Serve warm, or at room temperature, plain or with vanilla yogurt. (The pudding firms as it cools.)

Light Touch: Classic recipes for Indian Pudding vary slightly—some include raisins, some have more or less eggs and butter, but all have the characteristic molasses-spice flavor. It has never been a very high-fat dish, but when made with whole milk, 3 eggs, and a few tablespoons of butter, it manages to get about 37 percent calories from fat before adding the traditional vanilla ice cream topping.

Because this pudding has an egg custard base, reducing the fat creates problems. When I eliminated 2 of the eggs, used skim milk, which tends to curdle if boiled, and cut the butter, the custard "broke" (separated) on my first two tries. I then increased the cornmeal slightly, added cornstarch to stabilize the mixture, and used 2% milk, which worked better than skim. The pudding now gets only 16 percent of its calories from fat. The butter is not essential; however, you can add 1 tablespoon butter (in the hot milk) if you wish to add richness, as well as 17 calories, 2 grams of fat, and 6 milligrams of cholesterol per serving. Because the molasses is so sweet, I dropped the amount of sugar to 2 tablespoons. I do not like this dish when cloying, but use up to ¼ cup sugar, if you prefer.

217 calories

7 g protein

4 g fat

2 g satfat

39 g carbohydrate

362 mg sodium

46 mg cholesterol

Very Berry Summer Pudding

∙—◆—◆—◆—∙

The very essence of summer is in this simple, colorful fruit dessert. There is no baking involved; the berries are barely cooked with some sugar, then set into a bowl lined with bread or cake slices and allowed to stand, weighted, overnight, until the juices soak into the lining and the pudding becomes firm enough to unmold and slice. Serve it plain or with a dab of vanilla yogurt and garnish with a few fresh berries.

The recipe is very low in fat, cholesterol-free, and as flexible as it is easy to prepare. Summer pudding is a British classic, originally made with stale bread, but I prefer to line the mold with fresh but firm sandwich bread. Angel food or chiffon cake slices will do as well; avoid cottony or fluffy white bread. For filling, use any combination of berries at hand; I prefer half blueberries, half raspberries.

∙—◆—◆—◆—∙

Yield

6 servings

Advance Preparation

Pudding must be made at least 12 hours before it is served; it may be kept covered in the refrigerator for 1 more day before becoming too soggy.

Special Equipment

1½-quart bowl; small dish, or paper plate or cardboard disk trimmed as necessary, to fit inside the top of the bowl; 2-pound weight (such as 1 or 2 large cans) to set on top of the mold; flat serving platter with a lip

7 cups fresh berries or frozen whole unsweetened berries (blueberries, raspberries, blackberries, or any combination), divided

2 tablespoons water

½ to ⅔ cup granulated sugar, to taste

2 to 4 tablespoons dark rum or Framboise, to taste (optional)

1 1-pound loaf store-bought or homemade sliced firm white sandwich bread, crusts removed (about 15 slices)

1. Combine 6 cups of the berries, the water, and sugar in a large heavy saucepan and set it over medium-high heat. Cook, mashing and stirring the berries with a potato masher or the back of a wooden spoon, for about 3 or 4 minutes, until the sugar dissolves and the berries release their juice. Remove the pan from the heat. Stir in the rum or Framboise, if using it, and set aside to cool.

2. Line the 1½-quart bowl with a sheet of plastic wrap large enough to overhang the edges. Cut 11 slices of the bread in half on the diagonal. Arrange 9 or 10 triangular pieces of bread in a pinwheel pattern, slightly overlapping, to cover the bottom of the bowl completely. Cut 3 or 4 slices of bread into 1- to 2-inch-wide strips and stand them on end, side by side, to line the sides of the bowl. Add extra bread, cut to fit, as needed to line the bowl right up to the rim.

3. Stir the berry mixture, and spoon about half into the bread-lined bowl. Smooth the top, and arrange 6 or more bread triangles in a pinwheel pattern to cover the berries. Spoon on the remaining berries, and arrange 6 or more bread triangles in another pinwheel covering the berries. Cut small pieces of bread to patch any holes. The pattern does not matter; this will be the bottom when the pudding is unmolded. Fold the flaps of the plastic wrap over the bread.

4. Cover the pudding with another piece of plastic wrap slightly larger than the diameter of the bowl, then top it with a plate or cardboard round that fits just inside the bowl (it should not rest on the rim). Set a 2-pound weight on top, and refrigerate the pudding for at least 12 hours.

5. To unmold, remove the weight and uncover the top of the pudding. Fold back the flaps of the plastic wrap and top the pudding with a flat serving plate with a lip. Invert, and peel off the plastic wrap. Cut into wedges and garnish each serving with a few of the remaining fresh berries.

Light Touch: The only fat and cholesterol (if any) in this dessert come from the bread or cake used for the liner. Made with plain, firm sandwich bread such as Pepperidge Farm, it gets only 9 percent of its calories from fat and has no cholesterol. As a bonus, the fruit provides 6 grams of dietary fiber per serving.

Nutritional Analysis per serving

297 calories

6 g protein

3 g fat

0.5 g satfat

63 g carbohydrate

300 mg sodium

0 mg cholesterol

Steamed Apricot-Apple Pudding

◆ - ◆ - ◆

Filled with tangy apricots, sweet apples, and rum-soaked golden raisins, this moist, rich dessert lacks nothing but fat. Like plum pudding, but with a better flavor, it is best when served warm, with Bourbon Sauce—a perfect midwinter dessert to enjoy with a glass of port beside a roaring fire. Or douse it with warm brandy and flambé it for Christmas or New Year's Eve dinner. The notion of including steamed puddings in this book was suggested by my thoughtful friend Ann Amendolara Nurse, inspired cook, benevolent mother to—and founding member of—the New York Association of Cooking Teachers.

Don't let the idea of steaming put you off. Pack the batter into a 2-quart pudding mold if you have one, or substitute any 2-quart heatproof bowl topped with foil. The steamer itself is simply a large covered pot.

◆ - ◆ - ◆

Yield

8 servings

Advance Preparation

Pudding can be made up to 3 days in advance and kept covered in the refrigerator. Allow at least 30 minutes to rewarm the cold pudding in a 325°F oven or 35 to 45 seconds per portion in the microwave before serving.

Special Equipment

2-quart pudding mold with lid or 2-quart heatproof soufflé or baking dish, with aluminum foil and cotton string or a heavy-duty rubber band to fit the circumference of dish; Dutch oven or other large pot with lid to hold the steaming mold; steamer rack or trivet (I often use several metal Mason jar lids, wired together side by side into a ring.)

Temperature and Time

Stovetop steaming minimum 1 hour and 20 to 40 minutes

½ cup golden raisins

Grated zest of 1 orange (about 2 tablespoons)

¼ cup dark rum, bourbon, or orange juice

1 cup unsifted all-purpose flour

1 teaspoon baking powder

½ teaspoon baking soda

¼ teaspoon salt

1 teaspoon cinnamon

1 teaspoon ground ginger

½ teaspoon cardamom, optional

½ teaspoon nutmeg

1 cup dried apricots, lightly packed

¼ cup plain dried bread crumbs

1 large Granny Smith or other tart apple, peeled, cored, and diced

⅓ cup orange or apple juice

3 tablespoons canola or safflower oil

1 large egg

½ cup dark brown sugar, packed

¼ cup unsulfured molasses

¼ cup honey

2 teaspoons vanilla extract

Butter-flavor no stick cooking spray

1 recipe Bourbon Sauce (page 418)

Nutritional Analysis per serving (without sauce)

337 calories

4 g protein

6 g fat

0.7 g satfat

65 g carbohydrate

200 mg sodium

27 mg cholesterol

1. In a small microwaveable bowl, combine the raisins, orange zest, and rum, bourbon, or juice. Partially cover with plastic wrap and microwave on High for 30 seconds, or simmer in a small saucepan over low heat about 5 minutes. Set aside to soak.

2. Sift together the flour, baking powder, baking soda, salt, and spices into a bowl or onto a sheet of wax paper.

3. Combine the apricots and bread crumbs in a food processor and pulse to coarsely chop. Add the apple and pulse about 5 times. Put the fruit mixture into a large bowl. Return the work bowl to the processor without washing.

4. Combine the orange or apple juice, oil, egg, brown sugar, molasses, honey, and vanilla in the processor bowl. Pulse several times to blend. Add the flour mixture and pulse about 8 times just to moisten the batter. Do not overprocess, or the pudding will be tough. Add the batter to the fruit in the bowl. Then add the soaked raisin mixture and stir with a wooden spoon to blend well.

5. Coat the inside of the mold or baking dish with cooking spray. Turn the batter into the mold or dish. Oil the lid and fasten it in place, or oil a piece of foil large enough to generously cover the bowl and place it oiled side down on the bowl. Pinch the foil edges tightly around the bowl, then fasten a rubber band or string around the rim to secure it.

6. Place the steamer rack or trivet in the bottom of the steamer pot, set the pudding mold in place, and add hot water to reach about two thirds of the way up the sides of the mold. Cover the pot, set it over high heat, and bring the water to a boil. Reduce the heat to medium and boil very slowly for about 1 hour and 20 to 40 minutes. Add more boiling water as needed to keep the water level constant.

7. Lift the mold from the steamer pot and remove the mold lid or foil. The pudding should be well risen and springy to the touch, and a thin wooden skewer or other long pick inserted into the center of the pudding should come out clean. If necessary, cover the pudding and steam for an additional 15 minutes or so. Uncover the mold and cool

(continued)

the pudding on a wire rack for about 10 minutes. Then top the mold or bowl with a serving platter and invert. Lift off the mold. Serve the pudding warm with the sauce. (The pudding can be made up to 3 days in advance. Allow to cool completely, then cover with foil and refrigerate. Before serving, reheat in a 325°F oven for at least 30 minutes or heat individual portions 35 to 45 seconds in a microwave.)

Light Touch: Steaming a cake is an advantage when fat has been reduced because the process itself helps to produce a moist product. This rich-tasting confection contains an abundance of fruit that contributes 2.2 grams of fiber per serving plus vitamins and minerals, but it receives only 16 percent of its calories from fat because it uses a minimum of oil and just 1 egg. By comparison, a traditional steamed pudding, made with 1 cup beef suet and 4 eggs, weighs in at around 50 percent fat, and 1 serving contains 14 grams of saturated fat.

Old-Fashioned Bread Pudding

·◆·◆·◆·

Warm and custardy, redolent of vanilla and nutmeg, this is one of my favorite comfort foods . . . for breakfast, lunch, or midnight snack. Use leftover or stale French or Italian bread, both of which are made without fat. For a smoother texture, you can bake the pudding in a water bath, though it is not essential. When you taste the rich full flavor, you will never guess this is a really low-fat treat. For variation in flavor, add the grated zest of half an orange or lemon.

To have the proper consistency, it's essential to bake this pudding in the correct size pan; if the pan is too large, the pudding dries out and tastes more like French toast.

·◆·◆·◆·

4 cups diced stale or lightly toasted French or Italian bread
(cut into ¾- to 1-inch cubes), lightly packed

3 cups 1% milk, divided

2 tablespoons brown sugar, packed

Pinch of salt

1 large egg

2 large egg whites

½ cup plus 1 teaspoon granulated sugar, divided

½ teaspoon cinnamon

½ teaspoon nutmeg

1 teaspoon vanilla extract

½ cup seedless raisins

1. Position a rack in the center of the oven, and preheat it to 350°F.

2. Place the bread in the baking pan. In a large bowl, whisk together 2 cups of the milk, the brown sugar, and salt until the sugar dissolves. Pour over the bread and set aside to soak for about 15 minutes, turning the cubes of bread once or twice.

3. In the same bowl, whisk together the remaining 1 cup milk, the 1 egg and egg whites, ½ cup of the sugar, the cinnamon, nutmeg, and vanilla.

4. Spread the bread cubes evenly in the pan. Sprinkle the raisins over the soaked bread. Then pour on the egg mixture. Sprinkle the remaining 1 teaspoon sugar over the top.

5. To bake in a water bath, set the baking pan in a roasting pan. Add hot water to come about one third of the way up the sides of the baking pan, and place in the oven. Or simply place the baking pan directly in the center of the oven. Bake for 50 to 55 minutes in the water bath, about 45 minutes without it, or until the pudding is set and a knife inserted in it comes out clean. (With the water bath, the knife should come out clean 1 inch from the edge but the pudding should remain creamy in the center.) Serve warm.

Light Touch: Although this pudding tastes rich and creamy, it gets only 11 percent of its calories from fat and has less than 1 gram of saturated fat per serving. If you wish, you can increase the richness slightly without radically altering the numbers: If you use 2 whole eggs plus 1 white, you add only 8 calories and a trace more saturated fat per serving (but you nearly double the cholesterol, to 57 milligrams).

This is a far cry from my old standby recipe, which got 30 percent of its calories from fat, and was made with 3 cups whole milk, 4 whole eggs, and 2 tablespoons of butter. Each serving contained 296 calories, 10 grams fat (of which 5 were saturated), and 127 milligrams cholesterol.

Yield

8 servings

Advance Preparation

Pudding is best served the day it is made, best of all warm from the oven. However, it keeps well refrigerated and may be baked a day or 2 in advance and warmed in the microwave or oven before serving.

Special Equipment

8 × 8 × 2-inch pan or 6-cup (1½-quart) oven-proof casserole, large roasting pan for water bath (optional)

Temperature and Time

350°F for about 50 to 55 minutes with water bath, 45 minutes without water bath

Nutritional Analysis per serving

227 calories

8 g protein

3 g fat

0.9 g satfat

43 g carbohydrate

261 mg sodium

30 mg cholesterol

Creamy Rice Pudding

◆·◆·◆·

A custardy rice pudding studded with plump juicy raisins, this is comfort food at its best. It is heaven when served warm for breakfast.

For the creamiest results, use medium-grain rice such as River brand, available in supermarkets, or Italian Arborio. Both types have more of the desired starch than long-grain rice; Arborio has the most, so it makes a slightly thicker pudding. Regular "converted" rice will also work. To enhance creaminess, dried milk powder is added to the pudding made with medium-grain rice; it is not needed for an Arborio rice pudding.

·◆·◆·◆·

Yield

4 servings

Advance Preparation

Rice pudding is best warm from the oven, but keeps well for several days covered and refrigerated. To serve, warm it in the microwave, oven, or double boiler.

Special Equipment

1½- or 2-quart heavy-bottomed saucepan with lid

½ cup medium-grain white rice or Arborio or other short-grain rice (or substitute regular converted rice)

¼ cup seedless raisins

1¾ cups plus 2 tablespoons 1% milk, divided

Pinch of salt

3 tablespoons granulated sugar, or to taste

1 tablespoon instant nonfat dry milk (if using medium-grain rice)

1 large egg

¼ teaspoon nutmeg

Pinch of cinnamon

1 teaspoon vanilla extract

1. Do not wash or rinse the rice; the starch makes the pudding creamy. Combine the rice, raisins, 1¾ cups of the milk, the salt, sugar and dry milk (if using) in a medium heavy-bottomed saucepan. Stir well, then bring to a boil, uncovered, over medium-high heat. Stir for several seconds, then lower the heat so the mixture simmers gently. Cover and cook, stirring several times, for 25 to 30 minutes, or until most of the milk has been absorbed; the rice should not be dry. Remove from the heat.

2. In a small bowl, whisk together the egg, the remaining 2 tablespoons milk, the nutmeg, and cinnamon. Add to the cooked rice and stir well.

Have Your Cake and Eat It, Too

3. Return the pot to the lowest heat and stir constantly for 4 to 5 minutes, until most of the liquid is absorbed and the mixture is very creamy. Remove from the heat and stir in the vanilla. Serve warm. (To reheat cold pudding, add about 2 tablespoons 1% milk per serving and heat in a microwave, oven, or double boiler.)

Light Touch: Traditional rice pudding recipes vary from a meager "Poor Man's Pud" containing rice, water, molasses, and a touch of milk to a German variation oozing goose fat. My own old favorite includes lots of eggs, milk, a cup of heavy cream, and 2 tablespoons butter. Weighing in at 41 percent calories from fat, it offered about 397 calories, 18 grams fat (with 10 grams saturated fat), and a serious 186 milligrams cholesterol per serving.

My light version tastes like "Rich Man's Pud," but gets only 11 percent of its calories from fat. I achieved this by using low-fat milk, cutting the eggs and sugar, and eliminating cream and butter.

Nutritional Analysis per serving

228 calories

8 g protein

3 g fat

1.2 g satfat

43 g carbohydrate

150 mg sodium

58 mg cholesterol

Chocolate Pudding

◆ ◆ ◆

Yield

2½ cups (enough to fill one 9-inch tart or pie shell or 8 mini-tartlet shells); 8 servings

Advance Preparation

Pudding needs an hour or two to cool and set. It can be made a day in advance and refrigerated.

Special Equipment

1½-quart heavy-bottomed saucepan

T*his is a rich, silky, dark chocolate pudding that will satisfy the craving of any chocoholic. It is quickly and easily made, and richer than any packaged pudding mix (see below) because it contains a whole egg. The origin of this recipe is buried in my mother's 1943 edition of* The Joy of Cooking. *I can still turn to that chocolate-smudged page I loved as a child and see the Chocolate Cornstarch Pudding (made with 1 ounce chocolate [or ¼ cup cocoa], ¼ cup cornstarch, 2 cups whole milk, ⅛ teaspoon salt, ½ teaspoon vanilla, and served with cream on top) and my penciled-in girlish variations: Add up to 4 ounces of semisweet chocolate and a touch of almond or orange extract. When I am in the mood for really good chocolate pudding, this is still my favorite recipe, even when made with cocoa and low-fat milk.*

Serve this in stemmed glasses topped by a dab of vanilla yogurt and a chocolate-covered coffee bean, or a colorful (and edible) nasturtium blossom; or use the pudding to fill a tart or pie shell.

◆ ◆ ◆

⅓ cup granulated sugar

¼ cup plus 2 tablespoons unsweetened nonalkalized cocoa

¼ cup cornstarch

Pinch of salt

2 cups 1% milk

¼ cup dark corn syrup

1 large egg

2 teaspoons vanilla extract

1. In a heavy-bottomed medium saucepan, whisk together the sugar, cocoa, cornstarch, and salt. Whisk in the milk and corn syrup. Set the pan over medium-high heat and whisk constantly until the mixture comes to a full rolling boil. Then whisk for 1 full minute longer, and remove from the heat.

2. In a small bowl, beat the egg lightly. Whisk in a few tablespoons of the hot pudding to temper (warm without scrambling) the egg. Add the egg mixture to the pudding in the pan and whisk well to blend.

3. Return the pan to medium-low heat and cook, whisking continually, for 45 to 60 seconds. Remove the pan from the heat and stir in the vanilla. Cover with plastic wrap to prevent a skin from forming as it cools. Allow to cool, then refrigerate until thoroughly chilled.

Light Touch: To reduce the fat in my favorite chocolate pudding, I have used cocoa rather than chocolate, and low-fat milk. To add flavor, I have increased the amount of cocoa in the original recipe by 2 tablespoons. To add depth of flavor, I have added dark corn syrup and reduced the sugar slightly. The whole egg adds some of the richness and creamy "mouthfeel" supplied by whole milk or cream, but does not add too much to the calories or fat (although it raises the cholesterol).

This recipe for lowfat "scratch" pudding takes just about the same time as opening and cooking a packaged pudding mix. To be fair, when the mix is made with low-fat milk, it tastes good and has nearly the same amount of calories and fat (one serving from a mix made with 2% milk has roughly 99 calories and 2 grams fat). But it gets 17 percent of its calories from fat while my recipe gets only 12 percent. In addition, the mix contains additives, including artificial flavor and artificial coloring, that I prefer to do without.

Nutritional Analysis per serving

121 calories

4 g protein

2 g fat

0.6 g satfat

25 g carbohydrate

84 mg sodium

29 mg cholesterol

Pies
and
Tarts

American-style pies, as a general rule, have one or two crusts enveloping sweet or savory fillings baked in shallow round pans. Open-face pies have no top crust; deep-dish pies always have an upper crust and almost never a bottom crust. A tart is the European cousin of the open-face pie, with a bottom crust and a filling of sweetened fruit or custard, or a savory mixture. Both tarts and pies can be covered with a lattice crust.

How do you reduce the fat in a pie? The easiest place to start is the crust. Eliminate one crust from a double-crust pie and thereby cut the fat from the pastry in half automatically. Go for a bottomless deep-dish fruit pie and make the top crust a lattice, or use a simple pattern of cut-out pastry leaves to reduce the amount of fat still further. Or choose a topping of low-fat streusel crumbs to add texture while cutting fat. An open-face tart with only a bottom crust has its fat reduction built in. For a pie crust without any fat at all, select a meringue crust.

Cobblers, crisps, and pandowdies are all pie variations, with toppings made of crumbs or low-fat pastry or biscuit-type dough. I have stretched the category slightly to include the delicious French clafoutis, loosely related because it is a mélange of fruit set into a batter, baked, and served cut into wedges.

Most of the pie and tart fillings in this chapter are fruit-based and quite low in fat and cholesterol. In the pie or tart pastry, however, there are relatively few ingredients so the fat contributes a disproportionately high amount of the total calories. Even reduced-fat pastry has relatively high proportions of total fat. Fortunately, when an empty pie shell is filled with a low-fat fruit filling and divided into, say, ten portions, the calories-from-fat count is greatly reduced. For this reason, I have not provided nutritional analyses for individual crust recipes.

In this chapter, I have included a basic repertoire of reduced-fat pastry and crumb crust recipes, plus meringue shell recipes for full and individual pies. There are pies with traditional fruit fillings and no-bake fruit fillings, mousse pies set with gelatine, and an open-face fruit soufflé pie. Two angel pies fill the meringue shells with delectable mousses. If you are concerned about the fat content of a particular no-bake pie filling, put it into a meringue shell for a fat-free crust. The two tarts I include are classic examples of the genre: one a baked fruit tart and the other a beautiful array of fresh fruit set atop a sweetened cream filling.

Low-Fat Pie Pastry

If you are using a conventional recipe for butter pastry, chances are it has far more fat than necessary for a flavorful pie. A single conventional crust made with butter and an egg yolk gets about 60 percent of its calories from fat; the equivalent of one unfilled serving contains about 141 calories, 9 grams of fat, 4 grams of saturated fat, and 43 milligrams of cholesterol. What to do? Omit the yolk and reduce the butter, or replace it with oil. Since oil is 100 percent fat (butter is about 80 percent fat) you won't cut total fat, but you will drastically drop the saturated fat and eliminate the cholesterol.

Oil pastry has the least saturated fat, but I have never liked working with it. Conventional oil pastry is so fragile and difficult to handle it must be rolled between sheets of wax paper; when baked, it has a sandy, rather than flaky, texture. A breakthrough came last summer when two dear friends shared their favorite recipe with me: Elmira and Mary's Pie Pastry (page 276). The recipe combines oil with skim milk; the pastry is mixed and pressed in place right in the pie plate, eliminating the need for rolling; and the crust is tender/flaky, delicious, and a success every time! It quickly became my favorite pie pastry.

As a bonus, the recipe contains virtually no cholesterol and only 0.6 gram of saturated fat per serving, though the calories (138) and total fat (9 grams) remain nearly the same as for the butter crust.

The flakiest crusts are those made with solid fat that stays separate from, and layers with, the flour. One way to achieve this while reducing saturated fat (butter) is to freeze a soft dough "slurry" made of a little melted butter plus oil and flour. When frozen, this can be cut into the remaining flour; then the liquid is sprinkled on and the dough mass is brought together. To enhance the rich nutty flavor of the butter, I like to brown it first. This technique, used in the recipe for Browned Butter Tart Pastry (page 278), was developed in conjunction with the test kitchen of *Eating Well* magazine, though I have since modified it slightly.

Elmira and Mary's
Pie Pastry

❖ · ❖ · ❖

Yield
Pastry for one single-crust 9-inch pie

Advance Preparation
Unbaked crust can be stored, covered, in the refrigerator for up to 2 days. Or it can be wrapped airtight and frozen for up to 1 month. Thaw overnight before rolling out.

Special Equipment
9-inch pie plate

T*his recipe was shared with me by two friends who live near the Connecticut shore. Both beautiful, highly spiritual, strong women, Elmira Ingersoll and Mary Muhlhausen inspire, cook for, and entertain countless friends with great enthusiasm and creativity.*

I have adjusted the proportions slightly from Elmira and Mary's original recipe, but this is the easiest pie crust I have ever made, as well as one of the best. The procedure is the key to its success. Use your fingertips or a fork to mix the ingredients directly in the pie plate, then pat the dough in place. No rolling, no overworking the pastry—hence a light, tender crust. The addition of milk gives the pastry a greater degree of flakiness than traditional oil crusts. (The dough can be rolled out between two sheets of wax paper if you wish.)

I have been unable to trace the origin of this old-fashioned recipe, but there is a similar formula in the King Arthur Flour 200th Anniversary Cookbook *by Brinna Sands. Brinna tells me that she likes to beat the oil and milk together into an emulsion before adding it to the dry ingredients.*

❖ · ❖ · ❖

1 cup unsifted all-purpose flour
½ teaspoon granulated sugar
½ teaspoon salt
⅓ cup canola or safflower oil
1½ tablespoons skim milk, or as needed

1. Combine the flour, sugar, and salt in a 9-inch pie plate, and stir with a fork to blend. Drizzle the oil and milk over the mixture, and lightly toss it with the fork or your fingertips until crumbly. Pinch the mixture together; if it is too dry and crumbly, add a few more drops of milk.

2. With the back of a spoon or your fingers, press or pat the dough evenly over the bottom and up the sides and rim of the pie plate, taking care not to build it up in the corners.

3. To crimp the edge, either press the floured tines of a fork onto the dough on the rim, or pinch the dough into a fluted pattern with your fingers. Refrigerate the crust for at least 30 minutes.

To partially or completely pre-bake (blind-bake) the pie crust: Position a rack in the lower third of the oven, and preheat it to 425°F. Line the dough with a sheet of aluminum foil (shiny side down), and top it with a layer of pie weights (sold in bakeware shops) or dried rice or beans.

To partially prebake the shell: Bake for about 10 minutes. Remove the foil and weights and bake for an additional 3 to 5 minutes, until the dough is no longer raw or translucent but has not begun to color.

To completely prebake the shell: Bake for about 10 minutes. Lower the oven heat to 350°F. Remove the foil and weights from the pie shell, and bake for an additional 10 to 15 minutes, or until the pastry is golden brown.

Browned Butter
Tart Pastry

◆ ◆ ◆ ◆

T his oil crust is enhanced with the addition of a little browned butter to give it a rich, nutty flavor. To achieve a flaky texture, part of the flour is combined with the oil and butter and frozen for 30 minutes, then cut into the remaining flour. This recipe has a larger yield than the Low-Fat Pie Pastry (page 275) and is suitable for an 11-inch tart shell or 10-inch single-crust pie. Do not make this recipe in a food processor.

◆ ◆ ◆ ◆

2 tablespoons unsalted butter

2½ cups unsifted all-purpose flour

½ cup canola or safflower oil

2 tablespoons granulated sugar

1 teaspoon salt

4 to 6 tablespoons cold skim milk

1. Melt the butter in a small saucepan over low heat, and cook until the butter begins to turn golden brown and has a nutty aroma, about 4 minutes. Watch carefully so the butter does not burn.

2. In a medium bowl, combine 1 cup of the flour and the oil. Add the browned butter and toss with a fork, blending until smooth. Set in the freezer for about 30 minutes.

3. Remove the bowl from the freezer and add the remaining 1½ cups flour, the sugar, and salt. With a pastry cutter or 2 knives, cut the frozen butter mixture into the dry ingredients until the dough is in pea-sized lumps. Sprinkle on the milk 1 tablespoon at a time, adding only enough to hold the dough together. Gather the dough into a ball, wrap in plastic or wax paper, and refrigerate for 30 minutes.

4. To roll out the dough, unwrap it and place it between 2 sheets of wax paper. Roll into a circle 1½ inches in diameter larger than the pie or tart pan. Lift and readjust the paper as necessary to eliminate wrinkles. Peel off the top sheet and carefully flip the pastry circle over into the tart or pie pan, according to the specific recipe. Gently ease the

Yield

Pastry for an 11-inch tart or single-crust 10-inch pie, with scraps left for decorations

Advance Preparation

Plan ahead, because a portion of this dough must be frozen for 30 minutes, and then the pastry should be refrigerated for 30 minutes before rolling out. The unbaked crust can be refrigerated, covered, for up to 1 day. Or it can be wrapped airtight and frozen for up to a month.

Special Equipment

Pastry cutter or 2 table knives, 11-inch tart pan with a removable bottom or 10-inch pie plate

Have Your Cake and Eat It, Too

pastry into the pan and peel off the paper. Fit the pastry in place. If necessary, patch any tears or holes by touching the torn edges with water and pressing on a bit of excess pastry.

5. Trim away excess overhanging pastry and crimp the edges, or fold them over and press them against the inside of the pan. If desired, roll out any pastry scraps and cut or shape into decorative leaves. Press "veins" in the leaves using the back of a paring knife. Place the leaves on a piece of wax paper or foil and set them temporarily in the tart shell or pie plate. Cover the crust and decorations with plastic wrap and refrigerate, or freeze. Bake as directed in the filling recipes.

Crumb Crusts

Crumb crusts are easier to make than pastry crusts; they are a good choice for the timid baker. And crumb crusts need much less fat than pastry crusts, making them the best choice for reduced-fat pies.

Conventional full-fat crumb crusts are bound with up to one third cup melted butter, which gives the classic crust about 53 percent of its calories from fat but enables it to firm neatly when chilled, holding the crust in place when the pie is sliced. Without butter or margarine, each bite is likely to leave you with a fork full of filling and a lap full of crumbs.

Trying to solve this problem with low-fat crumb crusts, I have tried many alternatives to butter or margarine: vegetable oil, nut oils, water, fruit juice, skim milk, yogurt, peanut butter, egg whites, honey, and maple syrup. Most of these will moisten the crumbs or clump them together, but not all will hold them together through baking and serving, or even through filling and chilling.

After many failures, my solution for unbaked crumb crusts is to combine oil and water or fruit juice for the moistening agents and to use honey with a small amount of melted butter for flavoring and binding. This technique cuts out about half the traditional calories from fat, and brings the calories-from-fat count down to 27 percent.

For a baked crumb crust, which holds together a little better and is more crisp than an unbaked one, I use oil, a little water, plus half an egg white for moistening and binding; for flavor, I use sugar instead of honey, with a touch of butter.

Graham crackers, a staple for crumb crusts, are relatively low in fat. To save time, it helps to know that four (2½-inch) squares make ¼ cup crumbs. Other low-fat crisp cookies such as amaretti, or low-fat crunchy cereals such as Shredded Wheat, Cheerios, or Special K, can be substituted. I like to combine graham crackers with Grape-Nuts cereal, low in fat and high in crunch.

Either canola or safflower oil is fine to use; however, in crumb crusts made without nuts, a little hazelnut or walnut oil imparts a nutty flavor. You can further enhance the nuttiness by adding ½ teaspoon almond or maple extract to the crumb crust.

Honey-Graham
Crumb Crust

◆ ◆ ◆

Graham cracker crumbs and crunchy Grape-Nuts are bound together with honey, oil, and melted butter in this easy-to-make food processor recipe. The crust firms as it chills, and it holds together when sliced. If you prefer a crisper crust, you can bake the unfilled crumb crust at 350°F for 7 minutes, then cool it completely before filling. Instead of Grape-Nuts, you can use crumbs of any low-fat cereal (such as Shredded Wheat or Cheerios).

The recipe is written for a 9-inch pie crust, with adjustments for a 10-inch pie pan or 8-inch springform pan noted in parentheses after certain ingredients.

◆ ◆ ◆

14 2½-inch graham cracker squares (18 squares for 10-inch plate)

½ cup Grape-Nuts cereal

2 tablespoons unsalted butter, melted

2 tablespoons canola or hazelnut oil

2 tablespoons honey

1 tablespoon water or fruit juice, or as needed (2 to 3 tablespoons liquid for 10-inch plate)

1. Crumble the graham crackers into the bowl of a food processor. Pulse to form crumbs. Add the Grape-Nuts cereal and pulse 5 or 6 times. Add the melted butter, oil, honey, and 1 tablespoon (2 tablespoons for a 10-inch plate) water or juice and pulse until the crumbs are evenly moistened. Check to see that the crumbs hold together well; if necessary, add a few more drops of liquid and pulse once or twice.

2. Turn the crumbs into the pie plate (or springform pan) and use your hand or the back of a metal spoon to press an even layer around the sides of the pan. Spread the remaining crumbs evenly over the pan bottom, top with a piece of wax paper, and press to form an even layer. Refrigerate until chilled and firm before filling.

Yield

Scant 1½ cups total crumbs, for one 9-inch pie crust (or scant 1⅔ cups total crumbs for 10-inch pie crust or 8-inch springform pan crust)

Advance Preparation

Crust can be prepared and stored, covered, in the refrigerator a day before filling.

Special Equipment

9-inch or 10-inch pie plate or 8-inch springform pan

Graham-Grape-Nuts Crumb Crust

◆ · ◆ · ◆

*T*he crunchy Grape-Nuts cereal in this graham cracker crust provides the texture of nuts without the fat. But you can use all graham crackers or add some nuts if you prefer (see Light Touch). Because this crust contains only a very small proportion of fat, it uses egg white to bind the crumbs. Because of the raw egg white, the crust must be baked in the oven for a short time; the baking also firms and crisps the crust so it holds together better than unbaked low-fat crumb crusts. (The trick to measuring half an egg white is to use a paring knife and fork to break it up; then the egg white can be measured with a measuring spoon.)

After baking and cooling, this crust can be filled with any non-baked (refrigerator) filling. If the crust is to be used with a filling that must be baked, it's not necessary to prebake it.

The recipe is written for a 9-inch pie crust, with adjustments for a 10-inch pie plate or 8-inch springform pan noted in parentheses after certain ingredients.

◆ · ◆ · ◆

Yield

About 1⅓ cups total crumbs for 9-inch pie crust (about 1⅔ cups total crumbs for 10-inch pie crust or 8-inch springform crust)

Advance Preparation

The unbaked pie shell can be prepared a day before filling and kept covered in the refrigerator. The baked pie shell can be prepared a day in advance and kept covered at room temperature.

Special Equipment

9-inch or 10-inch pie plate or 8-inch springform pan

Temperature and Time

Bake unfilled pie shell at 350°F for 7 minutes.

12 2½-inch graham cracker squares (16 squares for 10-inch plate)

⅓ cup Grape-Nuts cereal (½ cup for 10-inch plate)

2 tablespoons granulated sugar

1 tablespoon hazelnut, walnut, or canola oil

1 teaspoon unsalted butter, melted (2 teaspoons for 10-inch plate)

½ large egg white (1 tablespoon for 10-inch plate)

1 to 2 teaspoons fruit juice or water, or as needed (1 tablespoon for 10-inch plate)

1. If the crust is to be prebaked, position a rack in the center of the oven and preheat the oven to 350°F.

2. Crumble the graham crackers into the bowl of a food processor and process until crumbs form. Add the Grape-Nuts cereal, sugar, oil, melted butter, egg white, and 1 teaspoon juice or water. Pulse until the crumbs are evenly moistened. Pinch a spoonful of crumbs together, and test to see if they are moist enough to hold the print of your finger. If necessary, add a few more drops of juice or water and pulse once or twice.

3. Turn the crumbs into the pie plate (or springform pan) and use your hand or the back of a metal spoon to press an even layer around the sides of the pan. Spread the remaining crumbs evenly over the pan bottom, top with a piece of wax paper, and press to form an even layer, taking care not to build up the crumbs in the corners.

If you will be using an unbaked pie filling, bake the shell for 7 minutes. Cool completely on a wire rack before filling. The crust firms and crisps as it cools.

If you will be using a filling that must be baked, set the unbaked shell aside in a cool location, or refrigerate until ready to be filled and baked.

Light Touch: I like to use hazelnut oil or fresh walnut oil for its nutty taste because nuts are omitted from this crunchy crust; you can substitute canola or safflower oil. If you would like to add 2 tablespoons chopped walnuts (which contain 81 percent fat) to the recipe, add another 10 calories and 1 gram of fat per serving of a 9-inch pie made with this crust.

Chocolate Crumb Crust

· ◆ · ◆ · ◆ ·

Yield

About 1⅓ cups crumbs, for one 9-inch pie crust

Advance Preparation

Crust can be prepared several hours in advance and refrigerated before filling.

Special Equipment

9-inch pie plate

About 25 chocolate wafer cookies, crumbled

2 tablespoons canola or safflower oil

1 tablespoon unsalted butter, melted

1 tablespoon skim milk, or as needed

½ teaspoon cinnamon

1. Process the crumbled cookies into crumbs (1½ cups) in the food processor. Add the remaining ingredients and pulse just to blend.

2. Turn crumbs into the pie plate and pinch them together. They should cling together well; if they seem too dry and crumbly, add another drop or two of milk. Press the crumb mixture firmly and evenly against the sides and bottom of the pan. Refrigerate to chill, and firm before filling.

Meringue Shells

· ◆ · ◆ · ◆ ·

*T*he ultimate fat-free pie shell is the meringue, or *vacherin. It can be made for a large pie, or in individual nest shapes, called* petits vacherins. *Meringue-shell pies are also known as angel pies, presumably because the filling is surrounded by heavenly white clouds.*

Meringue shells are baked until crisp. Their taste and texture complement any no-bake filling, whether fruit or chiffon. Since meringues contain no fat, they are a good choice for a relatively high-fat filling such as a mousse that, if served in a pastry crust, would be too high in total fat for our purposes.

· ◆ · ◆ · ◆ ·

Butter-flavor no stick cooking spray

3 large egg whites, at room temperature

¼ teaspoon cream of tartar

⅛ teaspoon salt

¾ cup superfine sugar

½ teaspoon vanilla or almond extract

1. Position a rack in the center of the oven and preheat it to 275°F. If making a pie shell, lightly coat a 9-inch pie plate with cooking spray. If making individual nests, line 2 baking sheets with parchment paper, brown paper, or foil.

2. In the large bowl of an electric mixer, combine the egg whites, cream of tartar, and salt. Beat until foamy. Gradually add ¼ cup of the sugar and beat for 30 seconds, then slowly beat in the remaining ½ cup sugar. Add the extract, and beat for about 7 to 10 minutes longer, stopping occasionally to scrape down the bowl and beater, until the sugar is completely dissolved and the meringue is stiff and shiny.

3. To form a pie shell, spread the meringue onto the bottom and sides of the prepared pie plate. Using the back of a large spoon, spread the meringue up to the rim, forming a decorative edge. Alternatively, use a pastry bag fitted with a ½-inch star tip to pipe meringue around the rim. Bake for about 1 hour and 15 minutes, or until firm and crisp. The meringue should remain white or pale beige; do not allow to brown. Lower oven heat if browning starts to occur. Cool the shell on a wire rack.

4. To form individual shells, use the back of the spoon to spread the mixture and form the meringue into eight 3-inch-diameter nests with high sides. Or, alternatively, spoon and spread eight 3-inch-diameter disks of meringue, then use a pastry bag fitted with a ½-inch star tip to pipe sides around each disk. Bake for about 1 hour, or until crisp and firm; do not allow to color. While still warm, remove from the baking sheets and set to cool on a wire rack.

Yield

One 9-inch pie shell or eight 3-inch meringue nests

Advance Preparation

Meringue shell(s) can be prepared ahead and stored, covered, in an airtight container for up to 1 week.

Special Equipment

Electric mixer with balloon whisk; 9-inch pie plate (for large pie shell) or 2 baking sheets and baking parchment, brown paper, or foil (for individual meringue nests)

Temperature and Time

275°F for 1 hour and 15 minutes for pie shell, 1 hour for individual nests

Apple Pie

◆ ◆ ◆

Yield

One 9-inch pie; 10 servings

Advance Preparation

Pastry can be prepared in advance and refrigerated or frozen. Thaw overnight in the refrigerator before rolling out. Pie is best served the day it is made.

Special Equipment

9-inch pie plate, pastry brush

Temperature and Time

425°F for 15 minutes, then 350°F for 30 to 40 minutes

*T*he all-American original: A great mountain of a pie loaded with apples and spice, topped by a golden, sugar-glazed pastry crust. As it bakes, its perfume will fill your kitchen and your family with all the nostalgia and sentiment that apples and cinnamon can conjure. It lacks only one thing . . . the bottom crust.

◆ ◆ ◆

Filling

> 8 large cooking apples (such as Granny Smith or Greening), peeled, cored, and thinly sliced
>
> 3 tablespoons fresh lemon juice
>
> 1/3 to 1/2 cup dark brown sugar, packed, to taste
>
> 3 tablespoons unsifted all-purpose flour
>
> 1 teaspoon cinnamon
>
> 1/2 teaspoon nutmeg
>
> 1 recipe Elmira and Mary's Pie Pastry (page 276), prepared through Step 1, gathered into a ball, and refrigerated for 30 minutes

Glaze

> 1 large egg white
>
> 1 tablespoon skim milk or water
>
> 1 tablespoon granulated sugar

1. Position a rack in the center of the oven and preheat it to 425°F.

2. In a large bowl, toss the sliced apples with the lemon juice, brown sugar, flour, and spices.

3. Arrange about one third of the apples in the bottom of the pie plate and pack them down neatly. Add half the remaining apples and pack down. Then add the rest, mounding them into a tall dome. With your palms, gently compress the dome into a firm shape. Molding the apples this way ensures that the pie will remain high after baking.

4. Roll out the pastry between two 14-inch sheets of lightly floured wax paper, lifting and repositioning the paper as necessary to prevent wrinkles, to an 11½-inch circle. Remove the top sheet of paper and invert the pastry over the apples, centering the dough over the pie plate. Carefully peel off the backing paper. With your palms, gently mold the pastry over the fruit mound. If there are cracks, moisten the edges with water and press on a pastry patch.

5. Leaving a 1-inch overhang, trim away excess pastry. Fold under the 1-inch border and crimp the pastry along the rim of the plate.

6. In a cup, lightly beat together the egg white and milk or water. Brush the glaze over the pastry, and sprinkle on the granulated sugar. With the tip of a paring knife, cut a ½-inch steam hole out of the center of the pastry, then cut 5 or 6 steam vents around it.

7. Bake at 425°F for 15 minutes, then reduce heat to 350°F and bake for about 30 minutes longer, or until the pastry is golden brown and the fruit is tender when pierced with a knife (through a vent hole). Check the pie halfway through the baking time; if it is overbrowning, cover loosely with a piece of foil (shiny side down). Cool the pie for a few minutes on a wire rack. Serve warm.

Bourbon-Apple Pie

Prepare the pie as directed, but sprinkle about 3 tablespoons of bourbon over the apple slices.

Honey-Apple Pie

This recipe, from Ruby Rossi of Basking Ridge, New Jersey, won the Grand Prize for Best Apple Pie at the third Annual Apple Bake-Off sponsored by the New England Culinary Institute and The Vermont Apple Marketing Board. I was one of the judges and the competition was very stiff. The day she won was Ruby's birthday, but it wasn't just luck; it was a special recipe, passed down to her from her grandmother. Ruby prefers Cortland or Northern Spy apples. I have used my own reduced-fat pastry and omitted 3 tablespoons butter in the filling:

Slice 8 large cooking apples and toss with ⅓ cup honey, 3 tablespoons granulated sugar, 2 tablespoons cornstarch, 1 teaspoon cinnamon, and ¼ teaspoon salt. Proceed as directed.

Apple-Pear Pie

Prepare the pie as directed, but replace half the apples with peeled, cored, and sliced pears.

(continued)

Nutritional Analysis per serving

227 calories

2 g protein

8 g fat

0.6 g satfat

39 g carbohydrate

113 mg sodium

0 mg cholesterol

Light Touch: A traditional two-crust apple pie made with rich pastry weighs in at about 34 percent calories from fat; because of the butter in the crust, each slice packs 13 grams of fat, 7 of which are saturated. Compare this to my one-crust low-fat pastry pie, which has 30 percent total calories from fat, but only 8 grams fat and 0.6 grams saturated fat per slice. And there is an additional bonus: You don't have to worry about soggy-bottom underbaked lower crusts.

Peach-Plum
Deep-Dish Pie

❖ ❖ ❖

*B*rimming with the flavors of summer, plums and peaches complement each other in taste and color. As they bake, ruby-hued plums blend their rosy color with the golden peaches, making a beautiful pie seasoned with a hint of spice and topped by a sugar-glazed pastry crust. This is easy to make and always a hit.

❖ ❖ ❖

Yield
....
One 9-inch deep-dish pie; 10 servings

Advance Preparation
....
Pastry can be prepared in advance and refrigerated or frozen. Thaw overnight in the refrigerator before rolling out. Pie is best served the day it is baked.

Special Equipment
....
1½- to 2-quart round or oval baking dish

Temperature and Time
....
425°F for 15 minutes, then 350°F for 20 to 25 minutes

Filling

> 3 cups peach slices (3 or 4 ripe peaches, peeled, stoned, and sliced) or frozen unsweetened peach slices
>
> 3 cups sliced pitted fresh plums (such as Italian Prune, Santa Rosa, or Emperor)
>
> 3 tablespoons fresh lemon juice
>
> ½ cup dark brown sugar, packed, or to taste
>
> ½ teaspoon cinnamon
>
> ½ teaspoon ground ginger
>
> 3 tablespoons quick-cooking tapioca or cornstarch
>
> 1 recipe Elmira and Mary's Pie Pastry (page 276), prepared through Step 1, gathered into a ball, and refrigerated for 30 minutes

Glaze

> 2 tablespoons skim milk
>
> 1 tablespoon granulated sugar

1. Position a rack in the center of the oven and preheat it to 425°F.

2. To peel peaches, drop them into a large pot of boiling water for about 2 minutes, then remove with a slotted spoon to a bowl of cold water. Drain when cool. The skins should slip off easily. Combine all the filling ingredients in the baking dish and toss gently to coat the fruit.

3. Roll out the pastry between two 14-inch sheets of lightly floured wax paper, lifting and repositioning the paper as necessary to prevent wrinkles, to a 10-inch circle (or about 1 inch larger than the diameter of the baking dish). Remove the top sheet of paper and invert the pastry over the fruit. Peel off the paper.

4. Leaving a 1-inch overhang, trim away excess pastry. Fold under the 1-inch border and crimp the pastry along the rim of the dish.

5. To glaze the pastry, brush the skim milk over it, then sprinkle with the sugar. With the tip of a paring knife, cut several steam vents in the pastry.

6. Bake at 425°F for 15 minutes, then reduce the heat to 350°F and bake for 20 to 25 minutes, or until the pastry is golden brown and the fruit is tender when pierced with the tip of a sharp knife (through a vent hole). Check the pie halfway through the baking time; if over-browning, cover loosely with a piece of foil, shiny side down. Cool for a few minutes on a wire rack. Serve warm.

Light Touch: Though this pie is cholesterol-free and very low in saturated fat, the total calories from fat (30 percent) appear at first to be relatively high. This is because the other ingredients are so low in calories that the calories from the small amount of oil in the pastry ranks disproportionately high. This recipe can easily fit into a low-fat plan for healthy eating.

Nutritional Analysis per serving

208 calories

2 g protein

7 g fat

0.5 g satfat

36 g carbohydrate

113 mg sodium

0 mg cholesterol

Nectarine-Raspberry Crumble

◆ ◆ ◆

As easy as pie! This flavorful blend of fruit topped by a mound of crisp crumbs is heavenly served warm for brunch. The crumbs are made with part whole wheat flour, but you can use all white flour if you prefer.

◆ ◆ ◆

Yield

One 9-inch pie; 10 servings

Advance Preparation

Crumb mixture can be prepared up to a day in advance and refrigerated. Serve the crumble the day it is baked.

Special Equipment

9-inch pie plate

Temperature and Time

350°F for 35 to 40 minutes; if using frozen berries, increase baking time.

Nutritional Analysis per serving

185 calories

3 g protein

5 g fat

1.4 g satfat

34 g carbohydrate

30 mg sodium

5 mg cholesterol

Filling

3 cups sliced unpeeled ripe nectarines (sliced ⅛ inch thick)

1 cup fresh raspberries or frozen whole unsweetened raspberries, unthawed

2 tablespoons fresh lemon juice

2 tablespoons granulated sugar

2 tablespoons unsifted all-purpose flour

½ teaspoon nutmeg

1 recipe Plain Crumb Topping (page 427)

1. Position a rack in the center of the oven and preheat it to 350°F.

2. In a large bowl, combine all the filling ingredients. Toss gently to blend. Turn the mixture into the pie plate.

3. Spread the crumbs evenly over the fruit. Bake for 35 to 40 minutes, or until the crumbs are golden brown, the filling is bubbling, and the nectarines are tender when pierced with the tip of a sharp knife. Cool a few minutes on a wire rack. Serve warm.

Light Touch: This dessert is so tasty you may feel like my daughter who, when about two years old, said pleadingly, "Some people like cookies so much they have two." If you want a second helping, it won't be fatal, because the recipe has only 26 percent calories from fat. If you divide the crumble into 8 instead of 10 servings, you add 46 calories and 1.3 grams of fat per serving.

Apple-Pear-Prune Crumble

◆ · ◆ · ◆

delicious winter dessert for a family supper. Serve warm from the oven with Maple-Yogurt Sauce (page 416).

◆ · ◆ · ◆

Filling

2 large apples (such as Golden Delicious, Rome, or Cortland), peeled, cored, and thinly sliced (2 cups slices)

2 to 3 pears (such as Bartlett, Bosc, or Anjou), peeled, cored, and sliced (2 cups slices)

1 cup dried pitted prunes, cut in quarters

2 tablespoons fresh lemon juice

2 tablespoons dark brown sugar, packed, or to taste

2 tablespoons unsifted all-purpose flour

1 teaspoon cinnamon

¼ teaspoon ground ginger

1 recipe Plain Crumb Topping (page 427)

1. Position a rack in the center of the oven and preheat it to 350°F.

2. In a large bowl, combine all the filling ingredients. Toss to blend and coat the fruit. Turn the mixture into the pie plate.

3. Spread the crumbs evenly over the fruit. Bake for 35 to 40 minutes, or until the crumbs are golden brown, the filling is bubbling, and the fruit is tender when pierced with the tip of a sharp knife. Cool a few minutes on a wire rack. Serve warm.

Light Touch: With only 21 percent of its calories from fat, this is a deliciously healthful dessert. The crumb topping adds 3.3 grams of dietary fiber. If you want to live dangerously, sprinkle 2 tablespoons chopped walnuts on top of the crumbs just before baking; the nuts will add texture, flavor, and, per serving, an additional 10 calories and 0.9 gram of fat.

Yield

One 9-inch pie; 10 servings

Advance Preparation

Crumb mixture can be prepared up to a day in advance and refrigerated. Serve the pie the day it is baked.

Special Equipment

9-inch pie plate

Temperature and Time

350°F for 35 to 40 minutes

Nutritional Analysis per serving

212 calories

3 g protein

5 g fat

1.5 g satfat

41 g carbohydrate

31 mg sodium

5 mg cholesterol

Strawberry-Rhubarb
Streusel Pie

⬥ ⬥ ⬥

I have replaced the top crust of this classic pie with a streusel crumb topping, but you can leave it off if you wish (see Light Touch). Use fresh fruit in season, or make this at any time of year with frozen fruit.

⬥ ⬥ ⬥

Yield

One 9-inch pie; 10 servings

Advance Preparation

Crust can be prepared ahead and refrigerated or frozen. Pie is best freshly baked.

Special Equipment

9-inch pie plate, pastry brush

Temperature and Time

425°F for 15 minutes, then 350°F for 40 to 50 minutes

Filling

2 cups (about 12 ounces) fresh strawberries, rinsed, dried, hulled, and halved, or frozen unsweetened whole berries, partially thawed

2 cups (about 12 ounces) fresh rhubarb stalks, cut into 1-inch pieces, or frozen rhubarb pieces, partially thawed

1¼ cups granulated sugar or light brown sugar, packed

¼ cup all-purpose flour, plus 1 tablespoon additional flour if using frozen fruit

½ teaspoon nutmeg

Pinch of salt

½ teaspoon vanilla extract

1 egg white, lightly beaten with 1 teaspoon water for egg glaze

1 recipe Elmira and Mary's Pie Pastry (page 276), prepared through Step 3 and refrigerated

Topping

3 tablespoons unsifted all-purpose flour

3 tablespoons old-fashioned rolled oats

1½ tablespoons dark or light brown sugar, packed

1 tablespoon unsalted butter, cut up

1 tablespoon canola or walnut oil

1. Position one rack in the lower third of the oven and another in the center, and preheat it to 425°F.

2. In a medium bowl, combine all the filling ingredients. Toss well to coat the fruit.

3. Brush the egg glaze over the inside of the chilled pastry shell. Add the filling, spreading it evenly in the shell.

4. To prepare the crumb topping, in a small bowl, toss together the dry ingredients. Pinch in the butter. Add the oil and toss with a fork or your fingers until crumbs form; add a few drops of water if needed. Spread the crumbs evenly over the fruit.

5. Place the pie in the lower third of the oven, and bake for 15 minutes. Raise the pie to the center rack, reduce the heat to 350°F, and bake for 40 to 50 minutes longer, or until the filling is bubbling and the crumbs are golden brown. Cool a few minutes on a wire rack. Serve warm.

Light Touch: This favorite pie has never been very high in fat, but with a full double crust, it gets almost 40 percent of its calories from fat. Take off the top crust entirely and you cut back to a respectable 29 percent. Or remove the bottom pastry, so you have a fruit crisp with just a crumb topping, and you plummet to 15 percent calories from fat.

Personally, I like the works—a crust plus a crumb topping—so I push my luck and settle for a compromise at 33 percent calories from fat; the saturated fat is very low and the per serving figures are still within reason. Some things are just worth it.

*Nutritional Analysis
per serving*

274 calories

3 g protein

10 g fat

1.4 g satfat

44 g carbohydrate

141 mg sodium

3 mg cholesterol

Mango-Peach Cobbler

◆·◆·◆·◆

Mango adds an exotic flavor, blending with ripe peaches in a sweet-tart filling covered with a biscuit-like cake. There is no flour added to the fruit so the cake absorbs the fruit juices. This is a great brunch dish, served warm from the oven. You can substitute any other fruit combination for the mangoes and peaches.

◆·◆·◆·◆

Yield

One 10-inch cobbler; 10 servings

Advance Preparation

Cobbler is best fresh from the oven, but it can be made a day in advance and warmed before serving.

Special Equipment

10-inch deep-dish Pyrex pie plate

Temperature and Time

375°F for 30 to 35 minutes

Filling

> 4 cups peach slices (4 or 5 ripe medium peaches, peeled, stoned, and thinly sliced)
>
> 1 large ripe mango, peeled and fruit sliced off the pit (about 1½ cups slices)
>
> 2 tablespoons fresh lemon juice
>
> ¼ teaspoon cinnamon
>
> 3½ tablespoons granulated sugar

Topping

> 1 large egg
>
> 3 tablespoons canola or safflower oil
>
> ¾ cup low-fat buttermilk
>
> 1½ cups unsifted all-purpose flour
>
> 1½ teaspoons baking powder
>
> ¼ teaspoon salt
>
> ¼ cup granulated sugar

1. Position a rack in the center of the oven and preheat it to 375°F.

2. To peel peaches, drop them in a pot of boiling water for 2 minutes, then remove with a slotted spoon to a bowl of cold water. Drain when cool. The skins should slip off easily. Combine the peaches, mango slices, lemon juice, cinnamon, and 2 tablespoons of the sugar in the pie plate. Stir to blend, and spread evenly in the pan.

3. In a large bowl, whisk together the egg, oil, and buttermilk. Set a strainer over the bowl and add the flour, baking powder, salt, and ¼ cup of the sugar. With a spoon, stir and sift onto the egg mixture. With the spoon or an electric mixer on low speed, blend well.

4. Spoon the batter over the fruit in the pie plate. Sprinkle the remaining 1½ tablespoons sugar over the top. Bake for about 35 minutes, or until golden brown on top and a cake tester inserted into the cake comes out clean. Cool a few minutes on a wire rack. Serve warm.

Light Touch: With no fat in the fruit and just a little oil in the cake topping, this cobbler obtains 23 percent of its calories from fat. My favorite traditional cobbler recipe uses similar ingredients, but includes ¾ cup butter—4 tablespoons combined with the fruit and 8 in the cake, rather than oil. The result is about twice as rich at 48 percent total calories from fat, with 15 grams of fat per serving, 9 of them saturated.

Nutritional Analysis per serving

190 calories

4 g protein

5 g fat

0.5 g satfat

34 g carbohydrate

129 mg sodium

22 mg cholesterol

Strawberry-Blueberry Crisp

◆ ・ ◆ ・ ◆

A perfect, easy-to-make spring dessert with a flavor as bright as its color. Serve this warm with a spoonful of vanilla yogurt alongside. Its cool mellow taste is a perfect complement to the tang of the fruit and crunch of the topping.

The quantities given here are generous, and although they will fit into a 9-inch pie plate, the filling sometimes overflows; I prefer to use a 10-inch pie plate. If you don't have one, use a 9-inch pan plus one Pyrex custard cup.

◆ ・ ◆ ・ ◆ ・

Filling

2 cups fresh strawberries, rinsed, gently dried on paper towels, hulled, and cut in half, or frozen unsweetened whole strawberries

2 cups fresh blueberries, picked over, rinsed, and gently dried on paper towels, or frozen unsweetened whole blueberries

1¼ cups granulated sugar

¼ cup unsifted all-purpose flour

Pinch of salt

½ teaspoon nutmeg

½ teaspoon vanilla extract

1 recipe Oat Streusel Topping II (page 430)

1. Position a rack in the center of the oven, and preheat it to 350°F.

2. In a large bowl, toss all the filling ingredients together. Spread the filling evenly in the pie plate.

3. Sprinkle about half the crumb mixture over the filling, and, using the palms of your hands, pat down very gently to slightly compress the fruit. Scatter on the remaining crumbs.

4. Bake for about 45 to 55 minutes, until the topping is browned and the strawberries can be pierced easily with the tip of a sharp knife. Cool a few minutes on a wire rack. Serve warm.

Yield

One 10-inch crisp; 10 servings

Advance Preparation

Crumbs may be prepared a day ahead and refrigerated. Crisp is best when freshly baked, but can stand a day before the crumbs begin to soften.

Special Equipment

10-inch pie plate

Temperature and Time

350°F for 45 to 55 minutes

Nutritional Analysis per serving

278 calories

4 g protein

5 g fat

0.5 g satfat

58 g carbohydrate

62 mg sodium

0 mg cholesterol

Light Touch: There is practically no fat in the filling; the meager 15 percent calories from fat comes from the topping. The small quantity of nuts in the crumbs add flavor and texture without excessive fat.

Ginger-Peach Pandowdy

❖ · ❖ · ❖

*J*uicy *spiced peaches bubbling over the edges of crisp golden sugar-glazed pastry, served warm for brunch or Sunday supper . . . hard to resist. A pandowdy is a New England specialty related to cobblers, slumps, and grunts. The term refers to a unique baking technique wherein a fruit pie filling is topped by a pastry crust and half-baked. The crust is then "dowdied," or cut up and pressed down into the bubbling fruit juices, which enrich and flavor it. Then, by the time the baking is complete, the crust has risen and regained its crispness. Serve this pandowdy warm from the oven, garnished with low-fat vanilla yogurt.*

❖ · ❖ · ❖

Filling

6 cups ripe peach slices (6 to 8 ripe peaches, peeled, stoned, and sliced)

1 to 3 tablespoons candied crystallized ginger, or to taste

1 teaspoon ground ginger, or to taste

¼ teaspoon nutmeg

2 tablespoons unsifted all-purpose flour

2 tablespoons fresh lemon juice

⅓ cup pure maple syrup or ¼ cup dark brown sugar, packed

Crust

1 recipe Elmira and Mary's Pie Pastry (page 276), prepared through Step 1, gathered into a ball, and refrigerated for 30 minutes

Glaze

2 tablespoons skim milk

1 tablespoon granulated sugar

(continued)

Yield

One 10-inch pandowdy; 10 servings

Advance Preparation

Pastry can be prepared in advance and refrigerated or frozen. Thaw overnight in the refrigerator before rolling out. Pandowdy is best served the day it is baked.

Special Equipment

10-inch pie plate, pastry brush

Temperature and Time

400°F for 1 hour

1. Position a rack in the center of the oven and preheat it to 400°F.

2. To peel peaches, drop them in a pot of boiling water for 2 minutes, then remove with a slotted spoon to a bowl of cold water. Drain when cool. The skins should slip off easily. Combine all the filling ingredients in the pie plate and toss gently to coat the fruit.

3. Roll out the pastry between two 14-inch sheets of lightly floured wax paper, lifting and repositioning the paper as necessary to prevent wrinkles, to an 11-inch circle. Remove the top sheet of paper and invert the pastry over the fruit. Peel off the paper. Don't worry if there are cracks or tears; simply moisten the edges and set patches on top (this is a casual project). With a paring knife, cut around the pastry at the *inside* edge of the pie plate, and remove the excess.

4. To glaze the pastry, brush it with the skim milk, then sprinkle with the sugar. With a sharp paring knife, cut a few steam vents in the pastry.

5. Bake for 30 minutes. Remove from the oven and cut the pastry layer into 9 big squares. With a pancake turner or spatula, gently but firmly press the pastry squares under the bubbling fruit juices. Bake for another 30 minutes, until the topping is crisp and brown. Cool a few minutes on a wire rack. Serve warm.

Light Touch: Though the pandowdy is cholesterol-free and very low in saturated fat, the total calories from fat (34 percent) appears, at first, to be relatively high. This is because the other ingredients are so low in calories that the calories from the small amount of oil in the pastry rank disproportionately high. This recipe can easily fit into a low-fat plan for healthy eating.

No-Bake Berry Pie

◆ · ◆ · ◆

An easy, lazy-summer-day pie, this is simply a crush of berries cooked up with sugar and wine, mixed with a little gelatine, and poured into a crumb crust. If you have had an exhausting day at the beach, forget the crumb crust and serve the fruit filling in wine goblets topped with a sprig of mint.

The recipe calls for berries, but you can substitute any blend of ripe fruit: peeled and chopped peaches, nectarines, or pears, alone or blended *with some berries. Wine gives the most sophisticated flavor, but white grape juice or other fruit juice can be substituted. If you prefer not to turn the oven on to prebake the crumb crust, substitute the unbaked Honey-Graham Crumb Crust (page 281).*

◆·◆·◆·

Filling

> 2 cups fresh blueberries, picked over, rinsed, and dried, or frozen unsweetened whole blueberries
>
> 2 cups fresh raspberries or frozen unsweetened whole raspberries
>
> ⅔ cup granulated sugar
>
> ¼ cup dry white wine
>
> 2½ tablespoons fresh lemon juice
>
> ¼ cup water
>
> 2 teaspoons Knox unflavored gelatine
>
> 2 tablespoons crème de cassis

Graham–Grape-Nuts Crumb Crust (page 282) for 9-inch pie, prepared through Step 3, baked, and cooled

1. In a 1½-quart nonreactive saucepan, combine 1 cup of the blueberries, 1 cup of the raspberries, the sugar, wine, and lemon juice. Set over low heat and cook gently, crushing the fruit with a potato masher or the back of a large spoon, until the sugar dissolves. Remove from the heat.

2. Pour the water into a small saucepan, sprinkle on the gelatine, and allow to sit for about 3 minutes to soften. Then stir the mixture over low heat just until the gelatine is dissolved; do not boil.

3. Stir the dissolved gelatine into the berry mixture, then stir in the remaining berries and the crème de cassis.

4. Transfer the hot berry mixture to a heatproof bowl and set it in a larger pan of ice water. Cool, stirring on and off, for about 5 minutes, until the mixture thickens to the consistency of raw egg whites. Turn the filling into the prepared crumb crust, cover, and refrigerate until set, at least 3 hours, or overnight.

Light Touch: With only 18 percent of its total calories from fat, this recipe is so light that you can have a second piece!

Yield

One 9-inch pie; 10 servings

Advance Preparation

Crumb crust can prepared up to a day ahead; it has to cool completely before it is filled. The filling needs at least 3 hours to set. Pie may be made a day in advance and refrigerated.

Special Equipment

9-inch pie plate, potato masher or large spoon, heatproof bowl

Nutritional Analysis per serving

125 calories

2 g protein

3 g fat

0.5 g satfat

22 g carbohydrate

85 mg sodium

1 mg cholesterol

Apricot-Orange Soufflé Pie

◆ · ◆ · ◆ ·

T his baked soufflé in a pastry shell combines meringue with apricot-orange purée to create a slightly tart, light-textured pie with intense flavor. Serve a dollop of low-fat vanilla yogurt alongside each slice.

◆ · ◆ · ◆ ·

Yield

One 9-inch pie; 10 servings

Advance Preparation

The texture is best if the pie is served within several hours of baking.

Special Equipment

9-inch pie plate

Temperature and Time

425°F for 18 to 20 minutes to blind-bake the pastry shell; 325°F for 20 to 25 minutes to bake filled pie

Crust

> 1 recipe Elmira and Mary's Pie Pastry (page 276), prepared through Step 4

Filling

> 2 cups (8 ounces) dried apricot halves
>
> ½ cup plus 3 tablespoons granulated sugar, divided
>
> ⅔ cup orange juice, plus up to 3 tablespoons more if needed
>
> 1 teaspoon grated orange zest
>
> 3 large egg whites
>
> Pinch of salt

1. Following the procedure on page 277, partially prebake the pie shell for 10 minutes with foil and weights, then for 8 to 10 minutes longer without foil and weights, until just set. Transfer the pan to a wire rack to cool. Reduce the oven heat to 325°F.

2. In a 1½-quart nonreactive saucepan, combine the apricots, ½ cup of the sugar, ⅔ cup orange juice, and the zest. Cover and bring to a boil. Reduce the heat to low and simmer, covered, for 10 minutes. Remove the lid and simmer for another 5 minutes, or until the apricots are tender.

3. Set aside 6 nicely shaped apricot halves for garnish. Transfer the remaining apricots, with their cooking juices, to a food processor or a blender, and purée until smooth. If the purée is too stiff to spread easily, add 2 to 3 tablespoons orange juice and process to blend. Turn the purée into a large mixing bowl.

4. In a large grease-free bowl, combine the egg whites and salt, and whip with an electric mixer on medium speed until foamy. Gradually add the remaining 3 tablespoons sugar, and whip until stiff but not dry.

5. Whisk about one quarter of the whipped whites into the apricot mixture to lighten it, then fold in the remaining whites. Spoon the mixture into the partially baked pie shell.

6. Place the pie in the center of the oven, and bake for 20 to 25 minutes, or until the top is lightly browned. Cool on a wire rack.

7. To garnish the pie, blot the reserved apricot halves on paper towels. Set 1 apricot half, cut side down, in the center of the pie and arrange the remaining halves around it like the petals of a flower.

Light Touch: I used to make this pie in a butter-rich crust with a topping of crushed caramelized walnuts; when I felt really decadent, I sometimes added a cup of whipped cream to the filling. My excesses were delicious but the price was between 49 and 62 percent calories from fat. Did I care? I do now. The responsible me is pleased to have cut total calories from fat down to only 28 percent while keeping the great flavor and a tender pastry shell.

*Nutritional Analysis
per serving*

227 calories

3 g protein

7 g fat

0.5 g satfat

39 g carbohydrate

155 mg sodium

0 mg cholesterol

Raspberry Mousse Angel Pie

· ◆ · ◆ · ◆ ·

M eet a slender (though not quite X-ray) cousin of classically zaftig raspberry Bavarian cream. This glamorous new creature is just as rich and delectable. No one will guess that beneath the berries, yogurt replaces heavy cream. Once you try this, you will throw caution— and the meringue shell—to the wind and serve the mousse alone in wine goblets garnished with a dash of Chambord, a sprig of fresh mint, and an Almond Tile Cookie (page 322).

· ◆ · ◆ · ◆ ·

Yield

One 9-inch pie; 10 servings

Advance Preparation

Meringue crust can be prepared up to 1 week ahead. The filled pie needs 3 hours to set. It can be made 1 day in advance.

Special Equipment

9-inch pie plate, heatproof bowl

Filling

> 3 cups fresh raspberries, or 1 12-ounce package frozen unsweetened whole berries, partially thawed
>
> ½ cup cold water
>
> 3 level teaspoons Knox unflavored gelatine
>
> ¼ cup orange or apple juice
>
> 1 tablespoon fresh lemon juice
>
> ¼ cup granulated sugar
>
> ¼ teaspoon salt
>
> 2 tablespoons Chambord or Framboise
>
> 1½ cups nonfat vanilla yogurt

> 1 9-inch Meringue Shell (page 284), baked and cooled
>
> Mint sprigs (optional)

1. If using fresh berries, set 6 or 7 aside to garnish the pie. Purée the remaining berries in a food processor or blender. If desired, pass the purée through a strainer to remove the seeds (I don't bother). Set aside.

2. Pour the water into a medium saucepan, sprinkle on the gelatine, and allow to sit for about 3 minutes to soften. Stir in the orange or apple juice and lemon juice, set the pan over low heat, and stir just until the gelatine is dissolved; do not boil.

3. Stir in the berry purée, sugar, and salt, increase the heat to medium, and cook, stirring, for 3 to 4 minutes, or until the sugar is dissolved. Remove from the heat and stir in the liqueur.

4. Transfer the raspberry mixture to a heatproof bowl and set it in a larger bowl of ice water. Cool, stirring on and off, for about 15 minutes, or until the mixture thickens to the consistency of raw egg whites.

5. While the mixture chills, set the yogurt in a strainer over a bowl and allow to drain for about 10 minutes.

6. Whisk the yogurt into the raspberry mixture. Pour the mousse into the meringue crust. Cover loosely with plastic wrap and refrigerate for at least 3 hours, or overnight, to set. Before serving, garnish the pie with the reserved fresh raspberries and mint sprigs, if desired.

Light Touch: With only 1 percent calories from fat, this is one of the lightest recipes in the whole book, as well as one of the most delicious. Compare it with a classic raspberry Bavarian cream pie, in a hazelnut-butter crumb crust with a mousse enriched by 1 cup heavy cream: It gets about 54 percent calories from fat, with each serving offering 316 calories and 20 grams of fat). For extra richness, add ½ cup heavy cream, whipped, in Step 6 (22 percent calories from fat, 5 g fat, 3 g satfat, and 17 mg cholesterol per serving).

Nutritional Analysis per serving

138 calories

4 g protein

0 g fat

0 g satfat

31 g carbohydrate

120 mg sodium

1 mg cholesterol

Chocolate-Peppermint Angel Pie

◆ · ◆ · ◆

A whisper of peppermint cuts the sweetness of this silken chocolate mousse embraced by a crisp meringue shell. It really is an angel of a pie, every bit as rich-tasting as the original version, although meringue replaces whipped cream and egg yolks. The deep chocolate flavor results from a blend of cocoa and semisweet chocolate.

The mousse, which is not baked, contains whipped egg whites. To prevent any possible health hazard from uncooked whites (page 22), the whites are whipped into a meringue in a double boiler over heat following the standard procedure for 7-minute icing. If you prefer, you can make this pie with a chocolate crumb crust (see Light Touch).

◆ · ◆ · ◆

(continued)

Advance Preparation

Meringue crust can be
prepared up to 1 week
ahead. The filled pie
must be refrigerated for
at least 3 hours, or
overnight, to set.

Special Equipment

9-inch pie plate, hand-
held electric mixer,
candy thermometer
(optional)

Chocolate Mousse Filling

1 cup skim milk, divided

1 large egg plus 2 large egg whites

¼ cup plus 2 teaspoons light corn syrup, divided

½ cup unsweetened cocoa

½ cup plus 1 tablespoon water, divided

2 teaspoons Knox unflavored gelatine

2 ounces semisweet chocolate, finely chopped

¼ cup (2 ounces) low-fat cream cheese, slightly softened and
    cut up

1 teaspoon vanilla extract

½ teaspoon peppermint extract

¾ cup granulated sugar

1 9-inch Meringue Shell (page 284), baked and cooled

1 1-ounce square bittersweet or semisweet chocolate, at room
    temperature or slightly warmed (optional), for garnish

1. In a medium bowl, whisk together ¼ cup of the milk, the whole egg, ¼ cup of the corn syrup, and the cocoa until smooth.

2. In a heavy-bottomed saucepan, heat the remaining ¾ cup milk until bubbles appear around the edge; remove from the heat.

3. Whisk a little of the hot milk into the cocoa mixture to warm it, then whisk the cocoa mixture into the remaining hot milk in the pan. Cook over medium heat, whisking constantly, for about 5 minutes, until slightly thickened. Remove from the heat.

4. Prepare the gelatine: Pour ¼ cup of the water into a small saucepan, sprinkle over the gelatine, and allow to sit for about 3 minutes to soften. Then stir the mixture over low heat just until the gelatine is dissolved; do not boil. Remove from the heat.

5. Add the chopped chocolate and cream cheese to the hot cocoa mixture, and whisk hard until melted and very smooth. Beat in the vanilla and peppermint extracts and the dissolved gelatine. Set aside to cool.

6. To prepare the meringue, set up a double boiler with just enough water in the bottom that the top part can sit above it without getting wet. In the top of the double boiler, combine the egg whites, sugar, the remaining 5 tablespoons water, and the remaining 2 teaspoons corn syrup. Bring the water in the bottom of the double boiler to a boil, and place a hand-held electric mixer next to the stove (keep the cord away from the heat).

7. Set the top of the double boiler over the boiling water and *immediately* begin beating the mixture with the mixer on medium speed. Beat for about 4 minutes, then increase the speed to high, and beat for 2 minutes. The meringue should be satiny and thick, standing in soft peaks. Immediately remove the meringue from the heat and transfer it to a cool bowl to stop the cooking process.

8. Whisk about 1 cup of the meringue into the chocolate mixture to lighten it. Then fold in the remaining meringue. Turn it into the prepared meringue crust, spreading the filling to the edges, and smooth the top. To prevent absorption of other flavors, you can cover the pie loosely with plastic wrap (held off the surface with several toothpicks). Refrigerate for at least 3 hours, or overnight, to set.

9. If you wish to garnish the pie, use a vegetable peeler to shave curls from a square of chocolate onto a piece of wax paper. Arrange the curls in a pile in the center of the pie.

Light Touch: Patricia Jamieson and the staff of *Eating Well* magazine helped me develop the base for this reduced-fat chocolate mousse. I accept the responsibility for the innovation of using a variation of 7-minute icing to replace the classic Italian meringue.

The idea for this recipe originated with an old favorite, Chocolate Mousse–Crème de Menthe Pie set into a chocolate wafer crust. The traditional filling includes 12 ounces bittersweet chocolate, ½ cup butter, 4 whole eggs, and ½ cup whipped heavy cream; the topping adds another ½ cup whipped heavy cream. You won't be surprised to learn that it gets 49 percent of its calories from fat, and a single serving packs 640 calories, 37 grams of fat (13 of them saturated), and 148 milligrams of cholesterol.

My enlightened pie gets only 14 percent calories from fat, with just a tad of saturated fat and cholesterol, while retaining the flavor and creamy texture of its namesake. To achieve this, I replaced nearly all the chocolate with cocoa plus corn syrup. Cocoa alone lacks the complexity and depth of solid chocolate, so I left in 2 ounces of solid chocolate. I dropped 3 eggs and replaced the whipped cream with a fat-free meringue. The classic version of the pie is set through the solidification of the chocolate and butter; this one is set with a little gelatine. To keep down the calories from fat, since the mousse itself is not exactly fat-free, I decided to present it in a meringue shell rather than a crumb or pastry crust. If you would rather substitute the Chocolate Crumb Crust (page 284), you will raise the total fat to 32 percent, adding 46 calories, 6 grams of fat, and 1 gram of saturated fat to each serving.

Nutritional Analysis per serving (without optional garnish)

229 calories

6 g protein

4 g fat

0.1 g satfat

48 g carbohydrate

121 mg sodium

24 mg cholesterol

Cappuccino Mousse Pie

· ◆ · ◆ · ◆ ·

*C*offee liqueur and a touch of real whipped cream add discernible *richness to this no-bake pie. While this is not the lowest-fat recipe in this book, it is one of the best.*

The mousse, which is not baked, contains whipped egg whites. The uncooked egg whites are cooked with a boiled sugar syrup, which will destroy any potentially harmful bacteria (page 23).

· ◆ · ◆ · ◆ ·

Cappuccino Mousse Filling

1¾ teaspoons Knox unflavored gelatine

½ cup cold water, divided

½ cup 1% milk

½ cup plus 3 tablespoons granulated sugar, divided

3 tablespoons instant espresso powder or regular instant coffee

1 teaspoon unsweetened cocoa

⅛ teaspoon cinnamon

Pinch of salt

2 tablespoons coffee liqueur (such as Kahlúa)

1 teaspoon vanilla extract

⅛ teaspoon cream of tartar

2 large egg whites, at room temperature

¼ cup heavy cream, chilled

1 Chocolate Crumb Crust (page 284), prepared through Step 2 and refrigerated

Chocolate-covered espresso beans (optional)

1. Prepare the coffee base for the mousse: In a small saucepan, sprinkle the gelatine over ¼ cup of the cold water, and set aside to soften about 3 minutes. Then place over low heat and stir until the gelatine is dissolved; do not boil. Remove the pan from the heat and whisk in the milk, 3 tablespoons of the sugar, the espresso or coffee powder, cocoa, cinnamon, and salt.

2. Return the pan to low heat and whisk for about 3 minutes, until the sugar is dissolved. Remove the pan from the heat and stir in the

Yield

One 9-inch pie;
12 servings

Advance Preparation

Crust can be prepared several hours in advance; it must chill for at least 30 minutes before it is filled. The filled pie must be refrigerated for at least 3 hours, or overnight, before serving.

Special Equipment

9-inch pie plate, pastry brush, candy thermometer (optional)

coffee liqueur and vanilla. Pour the mixture into a large heatproof bowl and set aside at room temperature.

3. Prepare the meringue: In a 1½-quart saucepan, stir together the remaining ¼ cup water, remaining ½ cup sugar, and the cream of tartar. Set over medium heat and cook, gently swirling the pan several times, until the sugar is dissolved. To prevent sugar crystallization, wash down the pan sides with a pastry brush dipped in cold water. If you have a candy thermometer, clip it to the pan. Increase the heat to medium high and boil without stirring until the thermometer reads 239° to 242°F, or until a drop of the syrup forms a soft ball when dropped in ice water.

4. While the syrup is cooking, begin to whip the egg whites in a medium bowl: Whip until medium peaks form.

5. When the syrup reaches the specified temperature, remove it from the heat, and gradually pour it over the whites while whipping them at medium-low speed. Pour the syrup in a steady stream between the sides of the bowl and the beaters (do not scrape in the hardened bits from the sides). Continue whipping until the whites feel cool and form stiff peaks, about 5 minutes. Set aside.

6. Prepare an ice water bath, with a tray or two of ice cubes in a large bowl, water, and a few sprinkles of salt. Set the bowl of coffee base in the ice water bath and stir until it chills and thickens to the consistency of raw egg whites. Don't let it set completely; if it chills too much and feels stiff, place it over a pan of hot water and stir or whisk briefly until smooth and creamy (like soft pudding).

7. Whisk about 1 cup of the cooled meringue into the coffee mixture to lighten it, then fold in the rest of the meringue.

8. In a clean medium bowl, using clean beaters, whip the cream until soft peaks form. Fold the whipped cream into the coffee-meringue mixture. Don't worry if a few streaks of white remain.

9. Turn the mousse into the chilled crust, and smooth the top. Refrigerate for at least 3 hours, or overnight. Just before serving, if desired, arrange a ring of chocolate-covered espresso beans around the rim of the pie.

Light Touch: A classic mousse made with 4 yolks and 1½ cups heavy cream (plus ½ cup whipped cream on top) can present you with up to 61 percent calories from fat. One serving lays on about 24 grams of fat, 12 of which are saturated, plus a whopping 135 milligrams of

(continued)

182 calories

3 g protein

8 g fat

2 g satfat

24 g carbohydrate

43 mg sodium

11 mg cholesterol

cholesterol. By eliminating the cream topping and the yolks, and replacing almost all the whipped cream in the mousse with whipped egg whites, I have seriously dropped the saturated fat and cholesterol, bringing the total calories from fat down to 38 percent. I can hear you shouting that this is above the magic figure of 30 percent. You're right. It's an exception, and it's worth it; note the low figures for saturated fat and cholesterol. But if it makes you feel better, replace the crumb crust with a meringue shell to get a mere 12 percent calories from fat.

Peach-Raspberry-Blueberry Clafouti

· ◆ · ◆ · ◆ ·

A clafouti is a casual, easy-to-make French fruit dessert with a batter that resembles Yorkshire pudding. It takes only a few minutes to put it together and yet it is a marvel to behold and to taste. When baked, the puffy top is golden brown and crisp, the inside creamy, custardy, and studded with fruit.

Typically made with cherries, the clafouti is delectable when made with any fruit or berry. I prefer a combination, as in this recipe. The process of macerating the fruit in liqueur may be omitted if you don't want the alcohol.

I generally bake this in a 10-inch pie plate for 8 servings. If you prefer to use a 9-inch plate (for 6 servings), cut the fruit down to 2 cups total, but keep the batter quantities the same.

◆ · ◆ · ◆ ·

Butter-flavor no stick cooking spray

6 tablespoons plus 1 teaspoon granulated sugar, divided

1 cup thinly sliced peeled fresh or frozen unsweetened peaches

1 cup fresh blueberries, picked over, rinsed, and patted dry, or frozen unsweetened whole blueberries

1 cup fresh raspberries or frozen unsweetened whole raspberries

3 tablespoons dark rum or fruit-flavored liqueur (optional)

Yield

One 10-inch tart; 8 servings

Advance Preparation

Clafouti is best served warm from the oven, but it may be prepared several hours in advance and rewarmed before serving.

Special Equipment

10-inch pie plate

Temperature and Time

350°F for 35 to 40 minutes

1 cup 1% milk

2 large eggs plus 1 large egg white

2 teaspoons vanilla extract

⅔ cup unsifted all-purpose flour

Pinch of salt

⅛ teaspoon nutmeg

Confectioners' sugar

150 calories

4 g protein

2 g fat

0.6 g satfat

27 g carbohydrate

74 mg sodium

55 mg cholesterol

1. Position a rack in the center of the oven and preheat it to 350°F. Coat the pie plate with cooking spray, then sprinkle it with 1 teaspoon sugar.

2. To peel peaches, drop them into a large pot of boiling water for about 2 minutes, then transfer them with a slotted spoon to a bowl of cold water. Drain when cool. The skins will slip off easily. In a large bowl, combine the fruit, 3 tablespoons of the sugar, and the rum or liqueur, if using it. Toss to blend. Set aside to macerate while you prepare the batter.

3. In a food processor or blender, combine the milk, eggs and egg white, vanilla, the remaining 3 tablespoons sugar, the flour, salt, and nutmeg. Process until smooth.

4. Spread the fruit mixture in the prepared plate, and pour the batter over the top. Bake for about 35 minutes, or until the top is puffed up and golden brown. Allow to cool for about 5 minutes, then sift on some confectioners' sugar and serve warm. (Or set aside at room temperature. Reheat and sift on some sugar before serving.)

Light Touch: A clafouti is traditionally made with a minimum of 3 whole eggs, ¾ cup whole milk, and ¼ cup heavy cream plus fruit. This formula produces a perfectly respectable 26 percent calories from fat. Why tamper with the recipe at all? Because each serving contains a resounding 93 milligrams cholesterol. By cutting out 1 yolk, omitting the cream, and substituting 1% milk, I have kept the great taste but cut a substantial 38 milligrams cholesterol and 43 calories per serving, while reducing overall calories from fat to 11 percent.

Fresh Fruit Tart

·◆·◆·◆·

T his is the bright face of summer... a brilliant display of glazed
ripe red raspberries, golden peaches, blueberries, kiwi slices,
and green grapes set atop a simple vanilla yogurt cream in a prebaked
pastry shell. You can vary the fruit, vary the cream (try Ricotta Cream,
page 403, or Fromage Blanc, page 407) and, in haste, even use a store-
bought shell. What you cannot do, however, is get through summer
without serving this refreshing dessert at least once. Note: The recipe can
be prepared in a 10-inch pie plate instead of a tart pan.

·◆·◆·◆·

Yield

One 11-inch tart;
16 servings

Advance Preparation

Pastry can be prepared
ahead and frozen. Pastry
shell can be baked a day
in advance. Vanilla
cream can be made a
day in advance and
refrigerated. Fill and
glaze the tart up to 2
hours before it is to be
served (the cream filling
thickens as it chills). If
you must glaze the tart
more than 2 hours in
advance, use Firm Fruit
Glaze (page 433) instead
of the plain fruit
preserves.

Special Equipment

11-inch tart pan with
removable bottom or 10-
inch pie plate, pastry
brush

Temperature and Time

425°F for 12 minutes,
then 350°F for 10 to 15
minutes for prebaked
tart shell

1 recipe Browned Butter Tart Pastry (page 278), prepared
though Step 4

Glaze

⅔ cup apricot preserves

2 tablespoons kirsch or orange-flavored liqueur (such as Grand
Marnier)

Filling

½ recipe (1 cup) Vanilla Cream (page 402), chilled

1 kiwi

½ to 1 ripe peach

2 tablespoons fresh lemon juice

½ to ⅔ cup fresh raspberries

⅓ to ½ cup fresh blueberries, picked over, rinsed, and patted
dry

1 small bunch seedless green grapes, rinsed, stemmed, and
patted dry

1. Roll out the pastry and fit it into the pan following the directions
on page 278. Then completely bake the tart shell according to the directions on page 277. Set aside to cool.

2. Prepare the glaze: Put the preserves in a small saucepan set
over low heat and stir until smooth and of spreadable consistency. Remove from the heat and stir in the kirsch or liqueur.

3. Brush a coating of the glaze over the bottom of the cooled tart
shell. Set aside the remaining glaze.

4. Peel and slice the kiwi and peach, and toss with the lemon juice to prevent discoloration.

5. To assemble the tart, stir the vanilla cream well. Spread it in the bottom of the glazed tart shell. Arrange the fruit slices, berries, and grapes in an attractive pattern of alternating colors over the top; use paper towels to pat dry the peach and kiwi slices before adding them to the tart. Warm the glaze if it is too stiff, then brush the fruit with the glaze, and refrigerate until serving time.

Light Touch: With vanilla cream filling, this recipe gets 39 percent calories from fat. To drop to 33 percent, spread ½ cup warmed apricot preserves beneath the fruit instead of cream. The per serving figures with the cream are, however, not only well within acceptable limits (the saturated fat is especially low), but dramatically lower than for a classic fruit tart. Compare this, for example, to one made with all-butter pastry and, under the fruit, my old favorite, Double Cream Filling (8 ounces cream cheese plus ¾ cup heavy cream, whipped). It gets 58 percent calories from fat, and each slice contains double the fat—and 10 times the saturated fat (11.5 grams).

Nutritional Analysis per serving

227 calories

3 g protein

10 g fat

1.5 g satfat

31 g carbohydrate

183 mg sodium

7 mg cholesterol

Cranberry-Raisin Tart

◆ · ◆ · ◆

Gleaming like a ruby, this glazed cranberry tart makes an elegant presentation, especially when decorated with pastry leaves; for Christmas, shape holly leaves.

The recipe can be prepared in a 10-inch pie plate instead of a tart pan.

◆ · ◆ · ◆

1 recipe Browned Butter Tart Pastry (page 278), prepared through Step 4

Filling

3 cups fresh or frozen whole cranberries, picked over, rinsed, and blotted dry with paper towels (or 2 cups cranberries plus 1 cup fresh or frozen unsweetened whole raspberries)

1 cup seedless raisins

1 tablespoon grated orange zest

½ cup fresh orange juice (1 orange)

¾ cup plus 2 tablespoons granulated sugar

½ cup dark brown sugar, packed

2 tablespoons quick-cooking tapioca

½ teaspoon cinnamon

½ teaspoon nutmeg

1 egg white, beaten with 1 teaspoon water, for egg glaze

½ cup sweet orange marmalade

⅓ cup walnuts, finely chopped

Granulated sugar

Glaze

½ cup red currant jelly

1. Roll out the pastry, and fit it into an oiled tart pan following the directions. Roll out the pastry scraps and use a paring knife to cut out leaf shapes. Mark leaf veins with the back of the knife blade. Place the leaves on a piece of foil, set them on the pastry shell, and refrigerate while you prepare the filling.

Have Your Cake and Eat It, Too

Yield

One 11-inch tart; 16 servings

Advance Preparation

Pastry shell can be prepared ahead and refrigerated or frozen.

Special Equipment

11-inch tart pan with removable bottom or 10-inch pie plate, pastry brush

Temperature and Time

425°F for 15 minutes, then 350°F for 30 to 35 minutes

2. Position a rack in the lower third of the oven and preheat it to 425°F.

3. In a medium bowl, stir together the cranberries, raisins, orange zest and juice, both sugars, the tapioca, cinnamon and nutmeg.

4. In a cup, lightly beat together the water and egg white. With a pastry brush, spread a little of the egg glaze over the bottom of the chilled pastry shell.

5. In a small saucepan, stir the marmalade over low heat until warm and spreadable. Spoon it over the pastry shell, and sprinkle on the walnuts. Add the cranberry-raisin mixture, spreading it evenly in the pan.

6. Brush a little egg glaze over each pastry leaf, then sprinkle on a tiny bit of granulated sugar. Set the leaves on a small baking sheet; they are baked separately so the cranberry juice doesn't discolor them, then set on the glazed tart.

7. Place the tart in the lower third of the oven and bake for 15 minutes. Reduce the heat to 350°F, and raise the tart to the center of the oven. Place the sheet of pastry leaves in the oven. Bake for 30 to 40 minutes longer, or until the tart pastry is golden brown. If the pastry browns too quickly, cover it with a piece of foil. Cool the baked tart and leaves on a wire rack.

8. In a small saucepan, stir the currant jelly until melted. Brush it over the cooled tart. Place the pastry leaves on top and refrigerate for at least 15 minutes to set the glaze. Before serving, remove the edge of the tart pan and slide the tart (on the pan bottom) onto a flat serving plate.

Light Touch: This rich and flavorful tart gets only 29 percent of its calories from fat. If you want to shave that down to 24 percent, omit the walnuts.

Nutritional Analysis per serving

305 calories

3 g protein

10 g fat

1.6 g satfat

53 g carbohydrate

144 mg sodium

4 mg cholesterol

Cookies
and
Biscotti

Cookies depend upon solid fats for their buttery taste and crisp or soft texture, but these fats vary enormously. Different fats have different melting points, and they contain different quantities of water, requiring different amounts of flour to make the dough hold together. The ideal fat for cookies is either butter (good flavor, but packed with cholesterol and saturated fat; and it has a low melting point, which causes thin, flat cookies) or a blend of butter and solid shortening like Crisco (with one third the cholesterol of butter but some saturated fat, it retains moisture and has a higher melting point, enabling the cookie to set its shape before the fat melts). When you reduce the fat in cookies, you alter a delicate balance of fat, starch, and sugar. The results are often dramatically different, sometimes surprisingly good, often disappointing.

It is difficult to make crisp cookies without using a high proportion of solid fat. It's much easier to reduce fat in soft or chewy cookies with a high fruit content, such as fruited drop cookies, bars, and balls. My first experiments were with oatmeal cookies. When I removed most of the shortening and replaced it with a small fraction of oil, the cookies were tough and flavorless. After replacing a high proportion of the fat with applesauce and substituting all-purpose flour for low-gluten cake flour, which needs less to fat to tenderize it and absorbs less liquid, I began to see improvement. When I added a little more oil and increased the spices and vanilla, the taste returned to normal. Finally, chopped apples and raisins added texture and moisture.

Loss of crispness during storage is the biggest problem with reduced-fat cookies such as the Oatmeal Raisin Cookies. When fresh from the oven, they are crisp outside, slightly chewy inside, and thoroughly appealing. Stored at room temperature overnight in an airtight container, they lose their crispness and become slightly sticky on the outside. Leave them loosely covered at room temperature and they go stale. What is the solution? First, I recommend making the batter ahead but baking the cookies in small batches. Freeze any remaining batter for later use. My colleagues at *Eating Well* magazine recommend cooling the cookies thoroughly on wire racks, then storing them in the freezer in an airtight container, separated from each other with layers of plastic wrap. (Thaw before serving.)

My second round of experiments dealt with crisp cookies that could be rolled out and cut into shapes. My tests failed until I began treating the dough like pie crust. First, I replaced some of the butter with low-fat cream cheese plus a little oil. Then I browned a small amount of butter to enhance its flavor, mixed it with a little flour, and froze it until firm so I was able to cut it into the remaining flour as I had always done with solid fat. This gave me a flavorful dough I could roll out, cut into shapes, and bake into crisp thins. Good in taste and texture, and low enough in fat to consider it a victory. These Cut-Out Cookies are fine for decorating with icing, and they remain crisp when stored in an airtight tin or left loosely covered at room temperature.

Brandy Snaps, Almond Tile Cookies, and Tulip Cookies all contain a little butter and bake into thin wafers that remain crisp and can be successfully stored.

Ladyfingers and Meringue Angel Kisses fit naturally into the low-fat category; both can be combined with other recipes to create new desserts (see Mandarin Orange Charlotte, page 186) or simply served with berries and Fromage Blanc (page 407).

Biscotti, crisp dry rusks of ancient origin, are low in fat, high in flavor, elegant, and Italian—is there a more irresistible combination?

The name *biscotti* refers to their cooking method (*bis cotto,* "twice cooked"); *biscotto* is the singular form, *biscotti* the plural. The flavorful dough, usually studded with nuts and/or dried fruits, is shaped into long logs, partially baked, then cut into slices. The slices are baked again to dry them out, removing moisture so they will keep without spoiling. Mandlebrot, from the German for almond bread, is the Jewish version of biscotti.

Because biscotti are crisp and dry, they do not require fat to retain moisture. Many biscotti recipes contain no added fat other than that present in the egg yolks and nuts. For a slightly more tender product, a little butter can be added, as it is in the mandlebrot recipe. When storing mandlebrot or biscotti, be sure to dry them completely before packing them into an airtight container.

Tulip Cookies

◆·◆·◆·

These fragile, buttery wafers are classics in French confectionery. They are made with a very thin batter, which spreads during baking; while still warm, the wafers can be molded into various shapes—rolled up on a wooden spoon handle into "cigarettes," or, as here, set into muffin tins to form "tulipes," tulip-shaped cups. Sometimes they are eaten as plain cookies, but more often they serve as containers for fruit or cream fillings.

The basic procedure is deceptively simple. Follow instructions carefully, because if the batter is too stiff, the wafers will not mold; if too thin or overbaked, they will shatter. A nonstick cookie sheet is helpful.

·◆·◆·◆·

¼ cup plus 2 tablespoons unsifted all-purpose flour

⅛ teaspoon salt

¼ cup plus 2 tablespoons granulated sugar

2 tablespoons unsalted butter, melted and cooled

2 tablespoons hazelnut or walnut oil *or* canola or safflower oil

2 large egg whites

1½ teaspoons vanilla extract

1 teaspoon grated lemon zest

1. Position a rack in the center of the oven and preheat it to 400°F. Coat the cookie sheets with cooking spray.

2. Sift together the flour, salt, and sugar into a bowl.

3. In another bowl, whisk together the melted and cooled butter, oil, egg whites, vanilla, and lemon zest. Add the dry ingredients and whisk until smooth.

4. Make only 2 to 3 wafers per cookie sheet, so they have room to spread: For each one, drop 1 tablespoon of batter onto the sheet, then use the back of the spoon to spread it into a 4-inch disk without any holes or air bubbles. Leave about 3 inches between wafers.

5. Bake for 4 to 5 minutes, until the wafers are golden on top and the edges are golden brown. Do not overbake.

Yield

Ten 4-inch cookies

Advance Preparation

Tulips can be baked ahead and stored for 24 hours in an airtight container, or frozen for up to a week.

Special Equipment

Cookie sheets, preferably nonstick, muffin tin (approximately 2½-inch-diameter cups)

Temperature and Time

400° for 4 to 6 minutes per batch

6. As soon as the wafers are baked, place the baking sheet on a wire rack, and immediately use a broad spatula to lift each warm wafer and place it in a muffin cup, gently crimping the edges to ease it down into the cupped shape. Let set until cool and crisp. Repeat with the remaining batter. If wafers stick to the pan, return it to the oven briefly to warm.

Light Touch: Butter is essential to the flavor and texture of these delicate wafers. When all butter (4 tablespoons) is used, the total calories from fat actually drops slightly, to 47 percent, but 29 percent of this fat is saturated; with oil replacing half the butter, the total calories from fat is 49 percent, because oil is 100 percent fat and butter is only about 80 percent, but only 16 percent of the fat is saturated. For this reason, I prefer to use oil for half the fat. Hazelnut oil or walnut oil give extra flavor, but canola oil is equally good.

Because this recipe contains few ingredients, and few of these contribute calories, it appears to get a high percentage of calories from fat. However the amount of fat and saturated fat in each wafer is low. When the wafers are used as the base for an assembled dessert, the total calories come from all the ingredients involved (see, for example, Tulip Fruit Crisps, page 385, with 29 percent calories from fat).

*Nutritional Analysis
per cookie*

95 calories

1 g protein

5 g fat

1.7 g satfat

11 g carbohydrate

39 mg sodium

7 g cholesterol

Brandy Snaps

◆·◆·◆

Yield

About 16 5½-inch cookies or rolled cylinders or 8 large tulip cups

Advance Preparation

Brandy snaps can be made at least 1 week ahead and stored in an airtight container.

Special Equipment

Cookie sheets, preferably nonstick; for rolled cookies, wooden spoon; for large tulip cups, 4 small custard cups or juice glasses with bottoms approximately 1¾ inches in diameter

Temperature and Time

400°F for 7 to 8 minutes

A British classic, these paper-thin, crisp wafers are flavored with butter, ginger, and brandy. The finest I ever tasted were made by my English friend Thérèse Davies, a dazzlingly beautiful woman who triumphs in baking as well as in singing and acting in the musical theater. Thérèse serves brandy snaps in the traditional manner, rolled up into narrow tubes and filled with piped-in brandy-scented whipped cream. British brandy snaps are made with either treacle, a type of molasses, or Lyle's Golden Syrup, a cane sugar syrup available here in specialty food shops and some supermarkets. I have adapted Thérèse's recipe and partially combined it with one developed by the test kitchen of Eating Well magazine. My version substitutes dark corn syrup plus a touch of molasses for the traditional syrups.

While still warm, the cookies are simply wrapped around the handle of a wooden spoon to shape them. They taste delicious plain, but can be filled with Vanilla Cream (page 402), Ricotta Cream (page 403), or Fromage Blanc (page 407).

Large brandy snaps can be formed into serving cups (tulips) by molding the warm wafers over inverted custard cups. They can be filled with frozen yogurt, Pineapple Buttermilk Sherbet (page 379), Apple Snow (page 382), or Fromage Blanc (without gelatine), topped by slivers of Homemade Candied Citrus Peel (page 449). Since the tulips can be made up to a week ahead, this recipe is as practical as it is chic to serve as a dinner party dessert.

◆·◆·◆

Butter-flavor no stick cooking spray
¼ cup dark brown sugar, packed
¼ cup dark corn syrup
2 teaspoons unsulfured molasses
2 tablespoons unsalted butter
2 tablespoons canola or safflower oil
¼ cup brandy
½ teaspoon ground ginger
¼ teaspoon cinnamon
⅔ cup sifted all-purpose flour

1. Position a rack in the center of the oven and preheat it to 400°F. Coat the cookie sheets with cooking spray.

2. In a large heavy-bottomed saucepan, combine the sugar, corn syrup, molasses, butter, oil, brandy, and spices. Stir to blend, then bring to a boil over medium-high heat. Boil vigorously, stirring, for 1 minute. Remove from the heat and whisk in the flour, beating until absolutely smooth.

3. To form average-size wafers to leave flat or roll into cylinders, drop the batter by the generous teaspoonful onto the cookie sheet, placing 4 to 5 per sheet, spaced 3 to 4 inches apart so they can spread. Smooth the batter with the back of a spoon to about 3½ inches round. To form large tulip cups, use 2 teaspoons of batter per wafer, and place only 2 per baking sheet. Smooth the batter with the back of a spoon to about 5½ inches round.

4. Bake for about 7 to 8 minutes, until a rich golden brown. Watch the cookies, not the clock, and begin checking after 6 minutes; they burn quickly.

5. While the brandy snaps bake, set up the equipment needed to mold the wafers, if you will be doing so: a wooden spoon for rolling cylinders, or 4 custard cups or small juice glasses, bottoms up.

6. Set the baking sheet on a heatproof surface or wire rack, and allow the wafers to cool for about 2 minutes. Then use a pancake turner or metal spatula to lift them up, one at a time, and immediately roll the warm cookies loosely around the handle of the wooden spoon to make cylinders; slip off rolls and cool seam down on wire rack. Or invert the wafers over the custard cups or glasses to form tulip cups. If you try to lift the cookies when they are too hot, they will pull apart. If they become too cool and stiff to lift from the cookie sheet, return the sheet briefly to the hot oven to soften them.

7. The cookies will firm and crisp in a matter of minutes; set them on a wire rack to cool completely, and repeat with the remaining batter. If the batter becomes too stiff to scoop, return the pan to the stove and stir until softened.

Light Touch: Thérèse's traditional brandy snap recipe contains ½ cup butter; the recipe obtains half its calories from fat. When she fills them with 1 cup heavy cream, whipped, plus 2 tablespoons brandy and a little sugar, the ante is raised to 64 percent calories from fat, and each filled cookie contains 12 grams of fat, 7 of which are saturated. My lightened brandy snap has all the flavor and crisp texture of the original,

(continued)

*Nutritional Analysis
per 5½-inch
brandy snap*

85 calories

1 g protein

3 g fat

1 g satfat

11 g carbohydrate

5 mg sodium

4 mg cholesterol

with 32 percent calories from fat. While this is not quite the magic figure of 30 percent, I couldn't remove more fat and retain the texture; the per serving figures are well within acceptable limits.

The dramatic fat reduction from the original is achieved by cutting the total fat in half and substituting oil for half the butter. When the light brandy snaps are filled with Fromage Blanc (containing real whipped cream), total calories from fat rises 2 percent, but each filled brandy snap has only 5 grams of fat (2 grams saturated), about half the original version. Believe me, you will love every gram.

Almond Tile Cookies

◆ ‑ ◆ ‑ ◆ ‑

These thin, deliciously crisp French almond cookies are molded while warm to resemble roofing tiles. Traditionally, the just-baked cookies are draped over a broom handle, but I find it easier to set them into the curve of a French bread pan; they may also be left flat, or rolled around the handle of a wooden spoon to make cigarettes. Serve them for an elegant dessert alongside fresh berries and a fruit compote.

◆ ‑ ◆ ‑ ◆ ‑

Yield

Twenty-four 4-inch cookies

Advance Preparation

Cookies can be baked in advance and stored for several days in an airtight tin, or frozen for up to a week.

Special Equipment

Cookie sheets, preferably nonstick; French bread pan or similar curved surface for molding cookies

Temperature and Time

400°F for 4 to 6 minutes

Butter-flavor no stick cooking spray

2 tablespoons (¾ ounce) slivered blanched almonds

1 cup plus 1 tablespoon sifted confectioners' sugar, divided

¼ cup unsifted all-purpose flour

Pinch of salt

2 large egg whites, at room temperature

1 tablespoon unsalted butter, softened

1 tablespoon canola or safflower oil

1 teaspoon vanilla extract

1 teaspoon almond extract

1. Position a rack in the center of the oven and preheat it to 400°F. Coat the cookie sheets with cooking spray.

2. To toast the almonds (and increase their flavor), place them in a small frying pan set over medium-high heat. Toast, stirring and tossing with a wooden spoon, just until they turn golden in color (2 to 3 minutes) and smell aromatic. Remove from the heat and place them in a food processor. Add 1 tablespoon of the confectioners' sugar and pulse to chop fine (don't reduce them to powder).

3. Turn the almonds into a large mixing bowl. Set a strainer over the bowl and add the remaining 1 cup sugar, the flour, and salt. Stir and sift the dry ingredients over the nuts. Toss to blend well.

4. Add all the remaining ingredients to the bowl. With an electric mixer on low speed, blend together. Increase the speed to medium and beat for about 30 seconds. The batter will be runny.

5. Drop the batter by single teaspoonfuls onto the prepared cookie sheets, and use the back of the spoon to spread the batter to 2½-inch disks. Leave about 2 inches between each cookie so they can spread during baking. You can bake 2 sheets in the oven at a time.

6. Bake for 4 to 6 minutes, or just until the cookies are dark beige with golden-brown edges. Do not overbake.

7. As soon as the cookies are baked, place the baking sheet on a wire rack, and immediately use a broad spatula to lift up each one and set it in the curve of the bread pan. Let cool for 3 to 5 minutes, until completely cool and crisp. Repeat with the remaining batter.

Light Touch: Traditionally, this recipe is made with ⅔ cup chopped almonds, 1 whole egg plus 1 egg white, and 2 tablespoons butter; it gets about 45 percent of its calories from fat. To cut this to 34 percent, the lowest I could go while retaining the desired taste and texture, I shaved the almonds to 2 tablespoons and added almond extract to strengthen the flavor. To cut saturated fat and cholesterol, I replaced half the butter with oil. The amount of total fat and saturated fat in each cookie is minimal. This recipe easily fits into a low-fat plan for healthy eating.

*Nutritional Analysis
per cookie*

37 calories

1 g protein

1 g fat

0.4 g satfat

6 g carbohydrate

16 mg sodium

1 mg cholesterol

Almond-Hazelnut Madeleines

◆ · ◆ · ◆ ·

The technique for making traditional madeleines is similar to preparing a genoise: Whole eggs are warmed and whipped, then sugar is added before sifting on flour and folding in butter. This method does not work well when the fat is reduced, so I have substituted a sponge cake technique, wherein the eggs are separated and stiff whites are folded into the batter. This method, although I have adapted and changed the ingredients somewhat, was suggested by (and is used with the permission of) Nina Simonds, in her "Lemon Madeleines" recipe published in Eating Well *magazine (July/August 1992).*

Madeleine pans are available in specialty cookware shops and from cookware suppliers (see page 460). These madeleines have a tendency to stick to the pan unless the pans are thoroughly oiled and floured.

To vary the flavor (without changing the nutritional analysis), substitute orange extract for almond and use Curaçao or Grand Marnier instead of hazelnut liqueur.

◆ · ◆ · ◆ ·

Butter-flavor no stick cooking spray

2 large eggs, separated, at room temperature

Pinch of salt

¼ cup granulated sugar, divided

1 teaspoon almond extract

1 teaspoon vanilla extract

1 tablespoon Frangelico liqueur or water

1 tablespoon hazelnut or canola oil

2 teaspoons unsalted butter, melted

¼ cup plus 2 tablespoons sifted cake flour

Confectioners' sugar

1. Position a rack in the center of the oven, and preheat it to 325°F. Whether using a nonstick or plain madeleine pan or cookie sheet, coat it with cooking spray, then dust generously with flour, and tap out excess flour.

2. In a medium bowl, using an electric mixer, whip the egg whites with the salt until foamy. Gradually add 2 tablespoons of the sugar, and whip until the whites are nearly stiff but not dry. Shake off the beaters into the bowl, and without washing them, return them to the mixer.

3. In a large bowl, combine the egg yolks with the remaining 2 tablespoons sugar and whip on high speed for about 3 minutes, until light yellow and creamy. Add both extracts, the liqueur or water, oil, and melted butter, and whip for 2 minutes.

4. Fold about one third of the whipped whites into the yolk mixture, then alternately fold in the flour and the remaining whites.

5. Drop about 1 tablespoonful of batter into each madeleine shell, nearly filling it. Or drop the batter by tablespoonfuls onto the prepared mini-cupcake pan or cookie sheet. Bake for about 12 to 14 minutes if using a mold, or about 10 minutes if using other pans, until the tops are golden. Cool in the pan on a wire rack for about 3 minutes. Then, run the tip of a paring knife around each madeleine to release it, pry out gently, and set to cool completely on a wire rack; or use a spatula to lift the cookies off a cookie sheet.

6. When the madeleines are cool, turn them shell pattern up, and sift on a light dusting of confectioners' sugar. Or dust confectioners' sugar over the cooled drop cookies or mini-cupcakes.

Light Touch: I'm willing to bet even Proust wouldn't notice that these madeleines lack two thirds of the sugar and nearly all the butter (¾ cup) found in the original version—60 percent calories from fat)—still baked in Proust country near Commercy, France.

By altering the traditional mixing technique and the proportions of the ingredients, I dropped total calories from fat to 29 percent, making each madeleine nearly sin-free. If you replace the liqueur with water, you drop 3 calories per cookie.

Nutritional Analysis
per madeleine

31 calories

1 g protein

1 g fat

0.3 g satfat

4 g carbohydrate

17 mg sodium

19 mg cholesterol

Ladyfingers

◆·◆·◆·

Homemade ladyfingers are delicate sponge biscuits with a light, eggy flavor and a crisp topping resulting from a dusting of confectioners' sugar just before baking. Serve as you would cookies to accompany a fruit dessert, or use them to line a charlotte mold (see page 187) filled with mousse.

◆·◆·◆·

see page 187

Butter-flavor no stick cooking spray

⅔ cup sifted cake flour

¾ teaspoon baking powder

2 large eggs, separated, plus 1 large egg white, at room temperature

Pinch of salt

½ cup plus 2 tablespoons sifted superfine or granulated sugar, divided

1 teaspoon vanilla extract

2 teaspoons water

About 3 tablespoons confectioners' sugar

1. Position 2 racks to divide the oven equally in thirds. Preheat the oven to 300°F. Line 2 cookie sheets with baking parchment or foil, dabbing the sheets with a few spots of shortening to anchor the paper or foil. Spray covered sheets with cooking spray and dust with flour; tap off the excess flour.

2. Sift the flour and baking powder together. Return them to the sifter and gently set it into a small bowl. Set aside.

3. In a large grease-free bowl, combine the egg whites and salt. Using an electric mixer on medium speed, whip until foamy. Gradually add 2 tablespoons of the superfine or granulated sugar and whip until nearly stiff but not dry. Set the whites aside. Shake the beaters into the bowl and, without washing the beaters, return them to the mixer.

4. In another large bowl, combine the egg yolks, the remaining ½ cup superfine or granulated sugar, the vanilla, and water. Beat with the electric mixer on medium speed until the mixture is thick and light-colored, and forms a flat ribbon falling back upon itself when the beater is lifted. Scrape down the bowl and beaters once or twice.

Yield

Twenty-four 1½ × 4-inch ladyfingers, (enough to line a 2-quart charlotte mold)

Advance Preparation

Ladyfingers can be baked ahead, wrapped airtight, and kept at room temperature about a week, or frozen.

Special Equipment

2 cookie sheets, baking parchment or foil, 16- to 18-inch pastry bag, ½-inch (#6) plain round tip, small (about 3-inch diameter) strainer

Temperature and Time

300°F for 15 to 17 minutes

5. Using a rubber spatula, alternately fold the whipped whites and the flour mixture, sifting it on, into the egg mixture. There should be some streaks of white remaining.

6. Set out a large measuring cup or mug to serve as a stand for the pastry bag: Fasten the ½-inch tip to the pastry bag, fold back a generous 4- to 5-inch cuff, and set the bag tip-down in the cup. Scoop about one third to one half of the batter into the bag, close it, and twist to compress the batter.

7. To shape the ladyfingers, pipe neat fingers about 3 inches long and 1 inch apart on the prepared sheets. Lift the pastry tip and flip the batter back onto itself at the end of each finger to make a neat break. Repeat with the remaining batter. Then, using the small strainer, sift confectioners' sugar onto the top of each ladyfinger.

8. Bake for about 15 to 17 minutes, or until the ladyfingers are a light golden color around the edges and the tops look slightly crackled. Set the sheets on a rack and let the ladyfingers cool 3 to 5 minutes. Lift ladyfingers with a spatula and set them on a wire rack to cool completely.

Light Touch: Ladyfingers have never been a particularly high-fat item, but when made with a classic recipe using 3 whole eggs, they obtain 14 percent of their total calories from fat; each one contains 26 milligrams cholesterol and 1 gram fat. Because I dropped 2 yolks to reduce cholesterol, I also reduced the leavening action of the classic egg/sugar foam. To compensate, I added a little baking powder. This lightened version obtains only 10 percent of its calories from fat, and cuts out 9 milligrams cholesterol and about 0.3 gram of fat per ladyfinger.

Nutritional Analysis
per ladyfinger

40 calories

1 g protein

0.4 g fat

0.1 g satfat

8 g carbohydrate

18 mg sodium

18 mg cholesterol

Meringue Angel Kisses

◆ ◆ ◆

As sweet as a kiss, as light as a whisper ... these easy cookies please everyone. Make them in a variety of flavors—vanilla, chocolate, almond, orange, or lemon—and serve them with fresh fruit or berries. For a creative and elegant dessert, prepare a soft Buttermilk Fromage Blanc (page 408) sweetened with a little sugar or honey and stir in a pint of raspberries. Then sandwich spoonfuls of the berry mixture between meringue kisses.

◆ ◆ ◆

Yield

About 42 cookies

Advance Preparation

Stored airtight, the kisses will keep up to 2 weeks.

Special Equipment

2 cookie sheets, baking parchment or aluminum foil, 2 teaspoons or pastry bag fitted with $1/2$-inch (#6) star tip

Temperature and Time

250°F for 40 to 45 minutes

3 large egg whites, at room temperature

$1/8$ teaspoon cream of tartar

$1/8$ teaspoon salt

$3/4$ cup granulated sugar

1 teaspoon vanilla extract

$1/2$ teaspoon almond extract (optional)

1. Position 2 racks to divide the oven in thirds, and preheat the oven to 250°F. Line 2 cookie sheets with baking parchment or foil.

2. In a large grease-free bowl, combine the egg whites, cream of tartar, and salt. Using an electric mixer on medium speed, whip until foamy. Gradually add the sugar, and whip until the whites hold medium-stiff peaks. Add the extract(s) and whip until whites are satiny and hold stiff peaks.

3. Drop the meringue by the teaspoonful onto the prepared sheets, or scoop the meringue into a pastry bag fitted with a $1/2$-inch star tip and pipe 1-inch round rosettes, leaving about 1 inch between kisses.

4. Bake for 40 to 45 minutes, until the tops of the kisses feel dry to the touch; they should remain white or ivory in color. Reduce the heat if they begin to color. Set the sheets on a rack and allow to cool for 3 to 5 minutes, then peel away the backing paper or foil.

Light Touch: These cookies contain neither fat nor cholesterol, yet they are a satisfying dessert sweet. The variations do not noticeably change the nutritional analysis.

Orange or Lemon Kisses

Prepare the recipe as directed but reduce the vanilla to ½ teaspoon and omit the almond extract, add 1 teaspoon orange *or* lemon extract plus 2 teaspoons grated orange *or* lemon zest.

Chocolate Kisses

Prepare the recipe as directed, using the almond extract. Fold 2 tablespoons sifted unsweetened cocoa, preferably Dutch-processed, into the whipped meringue, leaving it slightly streaked. These kisses will flatten slightly as they bake.

15 calories

0 g protein

0 g fat

0 g satfat

4 g carbohydrate

11 mg sodium

0 mg cholesterol

Cut-Out Cookies

◆ · ◆ · ◆

These are crisp cookies, perfect for rolling and cutting into fancy shapes for holidays. Or the dough can be rolled into logs and frozen (so-called refrigerator cookies) to slice and bake whenever you wish. For decorations, use Vanilla Icing Glaze (page 435), Cookie Frosting (page 445), or Royal Icing (page 443), or brush on a little skim milk and sprinkle with plain or colored sugar crystals before baking. To change the flavor, add a teaspoon of almond, orange, or lemon extract in addition to the vanilla.

While this recipe contains much less butter than traditional rolled cookies, it still has a fine flavor and texture. The same technique is used here as with the pie crust on page 278. A small amount of butter is cooked until it is brown in color and nutty in aroma, then frozen with a little flour. This solid fat is then worked into the flour and blended with the remaining ingredients.

◆ · ◆ · ◆

Yield

Rolled and cut shapes, 2½-inch diameter, 3 dozen cookies; frozen log sliced into ⅛-inch wafers, about 6 dozen cookies

Advance Preparation

Cookies can be baked in advance, frosted, and kept fresh for a week at room temperature in an airtight container, or frozen. Batter can be prepared ahead, wrapped airtight, and frozen.

Special Equipment

Cookie sheets

Temperature and Time

350°F for 12 to 14 minutes for rolled and cut shapes, 8 to 10 minutes for thin-sliced refrigerator cookies

3 tablespoons lightly salted butter

2 cups sifted all-purpose flour, or as needed

¾ teaspoon baking powder

¼ teaspoon salt

2½ tablespoons sifted confectioners' sugar

½ cup granulated sugar

2 ounces light cream cheese or Neufchâtel cheese, at room temperature

1 large egg

3 tablespoons canola or safflower oil

2 teaspoons vanilla extract

1 teaspoon almond extract or 1½ teaspoons orange or lemon extract

Butter-flavor no stick cooking spray (optional)

Vanilla Icing Glaze (page 435) or Cookie Frosting (page 445) or Royal Icing (page 443) (optional)

1. Position 2 racks to divide the oven in thirds, and preheat the oven to 350°F.

2. Melt the butter in a small saucepan set over medium heat, and cook until the butter begins to turn golden brown and have a nutty aroma, about 4 minutes. Watch carefully so the butter does not burn. While the butter melts, measure the flour onto wax paper or into a bowl.

3. Transfer the browned butter to a small bowl and stir in about 2 tablespoons of the sifted flour. Place the mixture in the freezer until solid, about 10 minutes. Add the baking powder, salt, and confectioners' sugar to the sifted flour. Stir the mixture together.

4. In a large bowl, using an electric mixer, cream the granulated sugar and cream cheese. Add the egg, oil, vanilla, and other extract, and beat well.

5. Scrape the frozen butter mixture into the flour mixture. With your fingertips, pinch the butter into the flour, creating coarse flakes. Add the flour mixture to the egg mixture and beat with the mixer on low until incorporated. Scrape down the bowl and beaters once or twice. Add 1 or 2 tablespoons more flour if the dough feels too sticky.

6. Gather the dough into a ball, wrap it in plastic wrap, and chill until ready to roll out.

To make rolled and cut cookies: Roll out a portion of the dough between sheets of wax paper. Remove the top paper and cut shapes with lightly floured cookie cutters. Peel away the excess dough between shapes (use the tip of a paring knife to pry up the scraps of dough) and slide the sheet of wax paper with the cookies on it onto a baking sheet. If you don't plan to frost the cookies, brush them with skim milk and sprinkle on sugar crystals now. Bake until the cookies are golden around the edges, about 12 to 14 minutes.

Slide the wax paper sheet onto a wire rack, and allow the cookies to cool for 3 or 4 minutes. Then peel them off the paper and set them on a wire rack to cool completely. Chill and roll out scraps.

Alternatively, the dough can be rolled out on a lightly floured surface, cut into shapes, and the shapes lifted with a floured spatula onto baking sheets coated with cooking spray. The dough tends to be soft, however, so the wax paper method is much easier.

To make refrigerator cookies: Divide the dough into 2 or 3 portions. Roll each one into a log about 1½ to 2 inches in diameter, double-wrap in plastic wrap or wax paper, then put into a heavy-duty plastic bag and freeze until firm, or up to 2 months.

(continued)

Nutritional Analysis per cookie (for 3 dozen cookies)

58 calories

1 g protein

2 g fat

0.7 g satfat

8 g carbohydrate

33 mg sodium

9 mg cholesterol

To bake the cookies, use a sharp or serrated knife to slice ⅛-inch wafers from the frozen log. Set the wafers (still frozen) on lightly oiled baking sheets, and bake for 8 to 10 minutes, or until golden around the edges. (Because these are baked frozen, they may take a little more time.)

Light Touch: Creating a crisp, tasty, cut-out cookie is one of the most difficult tasks of low-fat baking. I have made over a dozen versions of this recipe: the less fat, the more tasteless and rubbery. With just oil replacing the solid fat entirely, the texture is all wrong. Finally, I settled on a combination of oil plus browned butter and low-fat cream cheese. This gives the best taste and texture but brings the calories from fat to 38 percent. That may seem slightly high, but the per cookie figures are well within acceptable limits—and when there is less fat, the result is simply not worth eating. Consider the fact that each cookie contains 30 percent less fat than the 54 percent calories from fat of a traditional rolled cookie made from a recipe using 1 cup butter and 2 eggs.

Oatmeal Raisin Cookies

·◆·◆·◆·

These are chewy cookies, not too sweet, with a satisfying texture and flavor. They are at their best fresh from the oven, or within a few hours of baking, while they retain their crispness. Serve them with a cup of steaming tea for an infusion of positive energy.

After standing, these cookies lose their crispness and become chewy throughout. Since I prefer the crisp texture, I recommend baking as many as you will eat in one sitting and freezing the remaining batter in heavy-duty plastic bags to bake fresh as desired.

·◆·◆·◆·

Butter-flavor no stick cooking spray

1 cup dark brown sugar, packed

1 large egg

3 tablespoons canola or safflower oil

1 tablespoon vanilla extract

¾ cup unsweetened applesauce

½ cup very finely chopped peeled apple

2 cups old-fashioned rolled oats

1½ cups sifted cake flour

1 teaspoon baking soda

½ teaspoon salt

1 teaspoon cinnamon

½ teaspoon nutmeg

3 tablespoons toasted wheat germ

1 cup seedless raisins

1. Position 2 racks to divide the oven in thirds, and preheat the oven to 350°F. Coat the cookie sheets with cooking spray or line them with baking parchment.

2. In a large bowl, combine the sugar, egg, oil, vanilla, applesauce, and chopped apple. Whisk to blend, or beat well with an electric mixer.

3. In another bowl, combine the oats, flour, baking soda, salt, spices, wheat germ, and raisins. Toss to blend well. Add to the sugar-egg mixture and blend with a wooden spoon or the electric mixer on medium-low speed. Do not overmix.

4. Drop the batter by the tablespoonful onto the prepared sheets, spacing the cookies about 2 inches apart. Bake for 12 to 15 minutes, until golden brown; the longer cooking time results in a crisper cookie. Use a spatula to transfer the cookies to wire racks to cool.

Light Touch: With only 17 percent calories from fat, each cookie offers vitamins, minerals, and 1 gram of dietary fiber, making these a healthy snack. Traditional recipes for oatmeal cookies vary; some include nuts, others additional eggs and egg yolks. My classic version is quite similar to this lightened variation but uses ½ cup shortening plus a little butter, weighing in with 30 percent calories from fat.

Advance Preparation

Batter can be prepared ahead and refrigerated for up to 3 days, or frozen for up to 1 month. The baked cookies are best fresh; if desired, bake small batches, and store any unbaked batter in the refrigerator or freezer.

Special Equipment

Cookie sheets, baking parchment (optional)

Temperature and Time

350°F for 12 to 15 minutes

Nutritional Analysis per cookie

88 calories

2 g protein

1.7 g fat

0.2 g satfat

17 g carbohydrate

57 mg sodium

6 mg cholesterol

Pfeffernüsse

◆ · ◆ · ◆

Yield

About 60 to 65 ¾- to 1-inch cookies

Advance Preparation

Cookies keep for at least a month in an airtight container at room temperature, or longer in the freezer.

Special Equipment

Cookie sheets

Temperature and Time

350°F for 12 to 15 minutes

*I*n Germany, many feel that the scent of baking pfeffernüsse signals the start of the Christmas season. Recipes for pfeffernüsse date back at least to the Middle Ages, and ever since, bakers have toyed with the meaning of the name. My German dictionary translates pfeffernüsse as "gingerbread nut," which is a fairly apt description. Some believe both the pfeffer ("pepper") and the nüsse ("nut") refer to the peppercorns traditionally ground and added to the spices. Others hold that the small brown ball-shaped cookies resemble nuts.

Don't be put off by the long list of ingredients: It includes many spices, but the procedure is actually very simple. Young children love to help roll the balls of dough. These sturdy cookies with their shiny hard glaze can be sent safely through the mail without crumbling.

Pfeffernüsse become very hard when air-dried; for a softer, chewier texture, you can store them with a slice of apple in the container to provide a little moisture.

◆ · ◆ · ◆

Butter-flavor no stick cooking spray

½ cup dark brown sugar, packed

¼ cup honey

¾ cup unsulfured molasses

¼ cup canola or safflower oil

3½ cups unsifted all-purpose flour

1 teaspoon salt

1 teaspoon baking powder

¼ teaspoon baking soda

1 teaspoon cinnamon

1 teaspoon nutmeg

¾ teaspoon ground allspice

¾ teaspoon ground ginger

½ teaspoon freshly ground black or white pepper

¼ teaspoon ground cloves

¼ teaspoon crushed anise seed (optional)

1½ teaspoons grated lemon zest

1 large egg, lightly beaten

Icing

    1 cup sifted confectioners' sugar

    1 teaspoon honey

    2 to 3 teaspoon fresh lemon juice, or as needed

1. Position 2 racks to divide the oven equally into thirds. Preheat oven to 350°F. Coat the cookie sheets with cooking spray.

2. In a large heavy-bottomed saucepan, combine the brown sugar, honey, molasses, and oil. Set over medium heat and stir with a wooden spoon until the sugar melts; do not let the mixture boil. Remove from the heat and let cool to lukewarm.

3. In a large mixing bowl, combine all the remaining ingredients except the egg. Set aside.

4. Beat the egg into the cooled sugar-molasses mixture. A little at a time, stir in the flour-spice mixture, stirring vigorously after each addition. If the dough feels runny or soft, chill it in the refrigerator for 15 to 30 minutes.

5. Prepare the icing: In a small bowl, whisk together the confectioners' sugar, honey, and 2 teaspoons lemon juice. Beat in additional lemon juice as needed until the icing glaze is the consistency of very softly whipped cream. Cover with plastic wrap until ready to use.

6. To form the cookies, dampen your hands. Pinch off small lumps of dough, and roll the dough between your palms into balls about ¾ to 1 inch in diameter. Set the balls on the prepared baking sheets, and bake for 12 to 15 minutes, until golden brown on top.

7. Transfer the cookies to wire racks set over wax paper. While the cookies are still warm, "paint" the top and sides of each one with icing, using your finger or the back of a spoon. The warmth of the cookies will melt the icing. Let the iced cookies air-dry completely on the racks.

Light Touch: Older recipes for pfeffernüsse contained no butter; its addition (up to 1 cup, bringing calories from fat to 36 percent) represents a fairly recent attempt to add tenderness to a very hard cookie once valued for its long keeping qualities. To remove most of the 12 milligrams cholesterol per cookie from the butter version, I have reduced the fat drastically and replaced the butter with some oil. These cookies get 15 percent of their calories from fat.

*Nutritional Analysis
per cookie
(for sixty ¾-inch
cookies)*

64 calories

1 g protein

1 g fat

0.1 g satfat

13 g carbohydrate

47 mg sodium

4 mg cholesterol

Granola Bars

◆ ◆ ◆

One of my daughter's earliest cooking memories is of making Rice Krispies candy at her grandmother's house. Children love to blend the sticky mass of melted marshmallows and cereal, press it into a pan, then munch on the crisp sweet bars. This recipe is a reduced-fat variation of that Kellogg's back-of-the-box standby; the big boost in nutritional value comes from substituting homemade granola for half the cereal. All-granola bars would be too dense and tough to chew. For the other cereal, you can use either Kellogg's Special K or Kellogg's Rice Krispies (see Light Touch).

◆ ◆ ◆

Yield

25 1½-inch-square bars

Advance Preparation

Bars can be prepared a day or two ahead and refrigerated in an airtight container. They need to chill for 20 minutes to firm before cutting.

Special Equipment

8 × 8 × 1½-inch baking pan

Nutritional Analysis per bar

82 calories

2 g protein

2 g fat

0.3 g satfat

15 g carbohydrate

50 mg sodium

0 mg cholesterol

Butter-flavor no stick cooking spray

2 tablespoons margarine or butter

7 ounces marshmallows (28 to 40 depending on brand)

2 cups Crunchy Granola (page 72)

2 cups Kellogg's Special K cereal or Rice Krispies

1. Coat the baking pan with cooking spray or vegetable oil.

2. Melt the margarine or butter in a large heavy-bottomed pot set over medium-low heat. Add the marshmallows and stir with a wooden spoon until they are melted. Remove from the heat and cool for a minute or 2.

3. In a bowl, toss the cereals together. Add them to the melted marshmallows and blend well, using a wooden spoon or, if the mixture is cool enough, your slightly dampened hands. (If a child is doing the mixing, turn the entire mixture into a big bowl; the saucepan retains the heat and may cause burns.)

4. Press the mixture evenly into the prepared pan. Refrigerate for about 20 minutes, or until firm. Cut into squares, and store in an airtight tin.

Light Touch: With only 23 percent calories from fat, this is a low-fat, highly nutritious snack. Other dried chopped fruits or dried berries can be added. In selecting the cereal to blend with granola, note that both brands have, per 1 ounce, nearly the same amount of calories and total fat. However, Rice Krispies has 340 milligrams of sodium while Special K has 265; for this reason, I prefer the latter.

Low-Flying Saucers

◆ ◆ ◆

*C*ommercial soft–ice cream vendors originated the frozen flying saucer: ice cream sandwiched between wafer cookies rolled in crunchy crumbs and/or nuts. Friend and cookbook author Lora Brody suggested this enlightened version made entirely from store-bought elements (no, you will not be struck by lightning). All you have to do is assemble these and freeze: ready at a moment's notice for a pool party or a snack. I dedicate this recipe to my dear friend the Flying Dutchman, Jan Pieter Hoekstra, who pilots planes as well as computers while keeping an eye out for flying saucers.

This recipe is for mocha saucers; if chocolate and coffee are not your favorites, use any other flavor frozen yogurt and omit the coffee granules in the crunchy crumb mixture.

◆ ◆ ◆

1½ pints (3 cups) chocolate low-fat (98% fat-free) frozen yogurt
2½ cups Grape-Nuts cereal
¼ cup granulated or light brown sugar, packed
2 teaspoons instant coffee powder or granules, or to taste
1 9-ounce box Nabisco Famous Chocolate Wafers

1. Remove the frozen yogurt from the freezer about 10 minutes before you will use it to soften slightly. Line a flat, shallow pan with a sheet of aluminum foil.

2. In a shallow bowl, toss together the Grape-Nuts, sugar, and coffee powder.

3. Scoop 2 tablespoons of the frozen yogurt onto a chocolate wafer, cover with another wafer, and compress the "sandwich" slightly. Set it on its edge and roll it in the crumb mixture.

4. Place the flying saucer on the foil-covered pan and repeat, making a total of 22 sandwiches. If you are taking your time and the kitchen is warm, transfer the completed sandwiches to a tray in the freezer as you work. Freeze the sandwiches until frozen hard, then wrap airtight individually in foil or plastic wrap and then in heavy-duty plastic bags.

(continued)

Yield

22 servings

Advance Preparation

Saucers can be prepared up to 1 month ahead and frozen. After about 2 days in the freezer, the chocolate wafers lose their crisp texture, but they still taste fine.

Nutritional Analysis per serving

140 calories
3 g protein
2 g fat
0 g satfat
28 g carbohydrate
188 mg sodium
2 mg cholesterol

Light Touch: These are "low"-flying saucers because they get only 13 percent calories from fat. You can feel smug comparing this to the roughly 40 percent calories from fat present in commercial versions made with full-fat soft ice cream sandwiched between calorie-laden cookies rolled in high-fat chocolate crumbs.

Prune Brownies

◆·◆·◆

*C*ocoa Brownies with Prunes? Cocoa-Prune Purée Brownies? Brownies with Dried-Plum Paste, as the California Prune Board euphemistically prefers? Dreaming up titles for this chocolaty, cake-type brownie could become a life's work. Well, to be honest, these are not your basic old-fashioned brownies because they do have the, er, unmentionable ingredient added, both to replace fat and to add moisture. But it works, and if I hadn't put it into the title, you would not guess it from the taste. The only tip-off is the slightly sticky top. These delicious brownies are rather like a dense devil's food cake, and that's pretty good since they contain less than half the fat of traditional brownies.*

I have studied the considerable literature on the subject of prune purée as a fat substitute, have spent the better part of one autumn immersed in batters thick with the stuff, and have baked more than my share of prune cookies, muffins, and brownies. I have puréed dried prunes in the food processor with hot water (sometimes it works, sometimes it is too dry), I have puréed prunes after simmering and soaking (the best method), I have tried baby-food puréed prunes (usually too liquid), I have used jars of prune butter (lekvar; a good convenience but usually too thick and viscous). Believe me when I tell you that you do not want to eat the majority of baked goods made with prune purée as a replacement for all the fat. All is the operative word. Forget it. They are very sticky, among other problems. I have rejected so many recipes that I am honestly surprised, as well as delighted, to have come up with this one, which works because some fat is added. Considering the few calories and the fraction of fat and cholesterol present in each brownie, this recipe is a welcome addition to the low-fat repertoire.

This recipe uses prunes that are simmered, soaked, then puréed in the processor. This method produces a brownie superior, in my opinion,

Yield

4 cups batter; 24 brownies

Advance Preparation

Brownies stay fresh, covered, at room temperature for at least a week. For longer storage, wrap them airtight and freeze.

Special Equipment

9 × 13-inch baking pan, food processor or blender

Temperature and Time

350°F for 30 to 35 minutes

to one made using the thicker bottled prune butter. *This recipe is my own variation (fat added, eggs adjusted, nuts reduced) of one sent to me by the California Prune Board for Lite 'n Dark Brownies with Dried-Plum Paste.*

Butter-flavor no stick cooking spray

1 cup pitted prunes (about 18)

1½ cups water, divided

1½ cups unsifted cake flour

1⅓ cups granulated sugar

1 cup unsweetened nonalkalized cocoa

2 teaspoons baking powder

½ teaspoon baking soda

½ teaspoon salt

1 large egg

2 large egg whites

3 tablespoons canola or safflower oil

2 teaspoons vanilla extract

3 tablespoons chopped walnuts

1. Position a rack in the center of the oven and preheat it to 350°F. Coat the baking pan with cooking spray.

2. Combine the prunes with 1 cup of the water in a saucepan, and bring to a boil. Lower the heat and simmer, covered, for about 5 minutes until soft. Remove from the heat and stir in the remaining ½ cup water. Transfer to a food processor or blender, and purée. Set aside.

3. Sift together the flour, sugar, cocoa, baking powder, baking soda, and salt into a large bowl. Make a well in the center and add the egg and egg whites, oil, vanilla, and puréed prunes. With a whisk or an electric mixer on low speed, blend well.

4. Spread the batter evenly in the prepared pan and sprinkle on the chopped nuts. Bake for about 30 to 35 minutes, or until a cake tester inserted in the center comes out clean; do not overbake. Cool on a wire rack, then cut into 24 brownies.

Light Touch: With only 21 percent of its calories from fat, this brownie recipe is a best bet. It has half the calories, and about one fifth the fat and one sixth the cholesterol of one of my old favorites that weighed in at 58 percent calories from fat—it was made with ½ pound butter, 4 ounces chocolate, and 4 whole eggs.

Nutritional Analysis per brownie
....
107 calories

1 g protein

3 g fat

0.2 g satfat

20 g carbohydrate

97 mg. sodium

9 mg cholesterol

Fruit Bars

◆ ◆ ◆

M y tasters could not decide whether these were cookies, cakes, or candies. I think of them as light dried-fruit snack cakes. Whatever you call them, they are easy to make and the perfect not-too-sweet, chewy dessert bar or snack to take on a picnic, pack in a lunch box, or add to a Christmas cookie platter. They pack and mail well, making them good candidates for camp or college care packages or holiday gift packs.

◆ ◆ ◆

Butter-flavor no stick cooking spray

½ cup sifted cake flour

¼ cup sifted whole wheat pastry flour (or use a total of ¾ cup sifted cake flour)

½ teaspoon baking powder

⅛ teaspoon salt

1 teaspoon cinnamon

⅔ cup light brown sugar, packed

¼ cup chopped walnuts

½ cup chopped peeled apple

1 cup chopped pitted dates

½ cup chopped dried apricots

½ cup chopped dried peaches or pears

¼ cup golden or seedless raisins

1 large egg plus 1 large egg white

2 tablespoons apple or orange juice

1 tablespoon canola oil

1. Position a rack in the center of the oven and preheat it to 350°F. Line the pan with baking parchment or wax paper and coat the paper with cooking spray.

2. In a bowl, toss together both flours, the baking powder, salt, cinnamon, brown sugar, and nuts to blend well.

3. In another bowl, combine all the fruits and toss to blend. Add the fruits to the dry ingredients and toss well with your hands, separating the pieces of fruit and coating them well with the dry mixture.

Yield

3 cups batter; 25 bars

Advance Preparation

Bars can be made a week in advance and stored in an airtight container or wrapped airtight and frozen.

Special Equipment

9 × 9 × 1½-inch pan, baking parchment or wax paper

Temperature and Time

350°F for 25 minutes

4. In a cup, lightly beat together the egg and egg white, juice, and oil. Stir into the fruit mixture and stir hard with a wooden spoon until thoroughly mixed and moistened.

5. Turn the batter into the prepared pan and press down evenly on the top to spread it out. Bake for about 25 minutes, until golden on top and slightly springy to the touch, and a cake tester inserted in the center comes out clean. Cool for about 10 minutes in the pan on a wire rack. Then use a sharp paring knife to cut into 25 squares. Cool bars completely. Serve from the pan, or remove and store in an airtight container.

Light Touch: These nutritious whole wheat bars contain a mix of dried fruits high in vitamins, minerals, and natural sugar. They get only 17 percent calories from fat and offer 1.3 grams dietary fiber per bar.

Nutritional Analysis per bar

85 calories

1 g protein

2 g fat

0.1 g satfat

18 g carbohydrate

25 mg sodium

9 mg cholesterol

No-Bake Fruit Balls

◆ · ◆ · ◆

E asy to make, especially with children, these no-bake treats are a healthy mixture of chopped dried fruits and grains held together with a slightly spiced, lightly buttered syrup. Roll the fruit balls in powdered sugar and include them on a tray of holiday cookies, or pop them into plastic bags for a nutritious lunch-box snack. Add other chopped dried fruits, such as figs, dried sour cherries, dried cranberries, or dried blueberries, as desired.

◆ · ◆ · ◆

Yield

About 32 1-inch balls

Advance Preparation

Fruit balls can be made up to 2 week in advance and stored in an airtight container in a cool dry location.

2 tablespoons unsalted butter

½ cup dark brown sugar, packed

1 tablespoon honey

2 tablespoons apple or orange juice

½ teaspoon nutmeg

¼ teaspoon cinnamon

½ cup dried pitted prunes, chopped

½ cup dried pitted dates, chopped

½ cup dried apricots, chopped

½ cup golden raisins, chopped

1 cup confectioners' sugar, sifted

½ cup Crunchy Granola (page 72)

½ cup Rice Krispies or Special K cereal

1. In a heavy-bottomed medium saucepan, combine the butter, sugar, honey, juice, and spices. Stir with a wooden spoon over medium heat for 3 to 5 minutes, or until the sugar is dissolved. Remove from the heat.

2. Combine the dried fruits and 2 tablespoons of the confectioners' sugar in a food processor, and pulse to chop. Or chop the fruits on a cutting board, using a sharp knife.

3. Add the chopped fruits, granola, and cereal to the warm syrup. Stir well to coat. Set aside until cool to the touch.

4. Spread the confectioners' sugar in a shallow bowl. With slightly dampened fingers, pinch off small lumps of the fruit mixture and roll between your palms into 1-inch balls. Roll the balls in the confectioners' sugar, and set on wax paper to dry. To store, place in an airtight container and sift on a little more sugar.

Light Touch: With only 15 percent calories from fat, each of these nutritious fruit balls provides lots of vitamins, minerals, and 1 gram dietary fiber. Even the youngest chefs love rolling the mixture into balls, and if they nibble on the batter, so much the better. Noshers can't resist this treat—it's not overly sweet and has an appealing variety of textures. This delicious recipe is significantly lighter than the version I have been making for twenty years, which contains nearly three times as much fat (43 percent calories from fat) and adds such high-fat items as shredded coconut, butter, and chopped nuts.

59 calories

1 g protein

1 g fat

0.5 g satfat

13 g carbohydrate

11 mg sodium

2 mg cholesterol

Hazelnut-Cocoa Biscotti

◆ ◆ ◆

These crisp chocolate cookies are flavored with cocoa, toasted hazelnuts, and hazelnut liqueur. Theoretically, biscotti have a long shelf life; these have never stayed around long enough for me to prove it. If you can find hazelnut extract (see page 460), use it in place of almond extract. Pecans, walnuts, or almonds can be used in place of hazelnuts.

◆ ◆ ◆

(see page 460)

Yield

About 36 to 42 ½-inch-thick biscotti

Advance Preparation

Biscotti can be stored for at least a month in an airtight container, or wrapped airtight and frozen.

Special Equipment

Heavy cookie sheet(s), baking parchment (optional), serrated knife

Temperature and Time

350°F for 20 to 22 minutes, then 300°F for 15 to 20 minutes

Butter-flavor no stick cooking spray

½ cup (4 ounces) hazelnuts, shelled

2½ cups sifted all-purpose flour, or more if needed

1½ teaspoons baking powder

¼ teaspoon salt

¼ cup unsweetened cocoa, preferably Dutch-processed

2 tablespoons lightly salted butter, softened

1 cup granulated sugar

2 large eggs plus 1 large egg white

1 teaspoon vanilla extract

1 teaspoon almond or hazelnut extract

3 tablespoons Frangelico (optional)

1. Position a rack in the center of the oven and preheat it to 350°F. Lightly coat the cookie sheet with cooking spray or line it with baking parchment.

2. Place the hazelnuts in a shallow baking pan or pie plate and toast in the oven for about 8 minutes, tossing occasionally, until golden and aromatic. Wrap the nuts in a kitchen towel, and let them steam for a few minutes, then rub the nuts in the towel to remove the skins. Transfer the nuts to a food processor, add about 2 tablespoons of the flour mixture, and chop coarsely. Set aside.

3. Sift together the flour, baking powder, salt, and cocoa into a bowl.

4. In a large bowl, using an electric mixer, cream the butter and sugar until light and fluffy. Add the eggs and egg white one at a time, beating well after each addition. Beat in the vanilla, almond or hazelnut extract, and liqueur, if using it.

5. Add the flour mixture all at once, and with the mixer on low speed, blend well. Scrape down the bowl and beaters. Add the chopped nuts and beat just to incorporate. Gather the dough into a ball. The dough should feel quite dry; if it sticks to your fingers, work in a little more flour, a tablespoon at a time.

*Nutritional Analysis
per biscotti
(for 36 biscotti)*

76 calories

2 g protein

2 g fat

0.6 g satfat

12 g carbohydrate

38 mg sodium

14 mg cholesterol

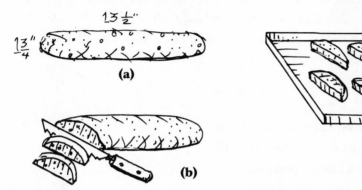

6. On a lightly floured surface, divide the dough evenly in half. Shape each half into a roll about 13 to 14 inches long, 1 inch high, and 1½ inches wide. Place the rolls about 2 inches apart on the prepared baking sheet, and gently flatten the top of each one until it is slightly domed, ¾ inch high, about 1¾ inches wide, and 13½ to 14 inches long (a).

7. Bake for 20 to 22 minutes, or until the rolls are dry on top and firm to the touch, and a wooden toothpick inserted in the roll comes out nearly clean. Just a trace of chocolate batter should remain on the pick; if necessary, return the pan to the oven for 5 more minutes. Remove the pan from the oven and reduce the heat to 300°F. With a long flat spatula, transfer each roll to a cutting board and allow to cool for 4 to 5 minutes.

8. With a serrated knife, cut the still-warm logs on the diagonal into ½-inch-thick slices (b). Place the slices cut side down (c) on the same baking pan (do not regrease). If necessary, use a second pan. Place the pan(s) in the oven and bake for another 15 to 20 minutes, until the slices are dry and crisp. The longer they bake, the harder and more crisp they will be; they crisp further as they cool. Transfer the biscotti to wire racks to cool.

Light Touch: These biscotti contain a small amount of fat and cholesterol because of the butter, but the strong chocolate flavor comes from cocoa instead of higher-fat solid chocolate. The small amount of butter balances the drying effect of the cocoa and provides a little tenderness. They obtain 25 percent of their calories from fat. When cut into 42 slices instead of 36, each cookie drops to 65 calories.

Orange-Walnut Biscotti

◆ ◆ ◆

I n my taste tests, this was the most popular biscotti. It has a strong orange flavor and a crunchy nut-studded texture. There is no fat in this recipe, so it is slightly drier than those that contain a small amount of butter.

◆ ◆ ◆

Butter-flavor no stick cooking spray

2 cups plus 3 tablespoons sifted all-purpose flour

1½ teaspoons baking powder

⅛ teaspoon salt

½ cup walnuts, coarsely chopped

¾ cup granulated sugar

2 large eggs

Grated zest of 1 orange (about 2 tablespoons)

1 teaspoon orange extract

1 tablespoon frozen orange juice concentrate

2 tablespoons orange-flavored liqueur (such as Grand Marnier) (optional)

1. Position a rack in the center of the oven and preheat it to 350°F. Lightly coat the baking pan with cooking spray or line it with baking parchment.

2. Sift together the flour, baking powder, and salt into a bowl.

3. In a small bowl, combine the chopped walnuts with 2 table-spoons of the flour mixture, and toss well.

4. In a large bowl, whisk together the sugar, eggs, orange zest, orange extract, juice concentrate, and liqueur if using it.

5. Add the flour mixture all at once, and using an electric mixer on low speed, blend well. Scrape down the bowl and beaters. Add the nuts and beat just to incorporate. Gather the dough into a ball. The dough should feel quite dry; if it sticks to your fingers, work in a little more flour, ½ teaspoon at a time.

6. On a lightly floured surface, divide the dough evenly in half. Shape each half into a roll about 13 inches long, 1 inch high, and 1½ inches wide. Place the rolls about 2 inches apart on the prepared baking sheet and gently flatten the top of each one until it is slightly domed, ¾ inch high, and about 1¾ inches wide.

7. Bake for about 20 minutes, or until the rolls are dry on top and firm to the touch and a wooden toothpick inserted in the roll comes out clean. Remove the pan from the oven and reduce the heat to 300°F. With a long flat spatula, transfer each roll to a cutting board and allow to cool for 4 to 5 minutes.

8. With a serrated knife, cut the still-warm logs on the diagonal into ½-inch-thick slices. Place the slices cut side down on the same baking pan (do not regrease). If necessary, use a second pan. Place the pan(s) in the oven and bake for another 15 to 20 minutes, until the slices are golden and crisp. Transfer the biscotti to wire racks to cool. Store in an airtight container.

Light Touch: This recipe obtains 21 percent of its calories from fat. The small amount of fat present comes from the egg yolks and the nuts.

Nutritional Analysis per biscotti

44 calories

1 g protein

1 g fat

0.1 g satfat

8 g carbohydrate

19 mg sodium

9 mg cholesterol

Almond-Raisin
Mandlebrot

◆ · ◆ · ◆ ·

Mandlebrot is a Jewish version of biscotti. It is made the same way, with a double baking to create crisp, dry slices. This recipe is a reduced-fat version of one of my family's favorites, Anne Sternberger's Mandlebrot. Anne shared her specialty with me when I was first married. I still love the delicate almond flavor with the nuts and the blend of dark and golden raisins. The original recipe contains butter, and I have kept a very small amount to retain the characteristic tenderness and richness.

◆ · ◆ · ◆ ·

Yield

About 4 dozen ½-inch-thick mandlebrot

Advance Preparation

Mandlebrot can be stored for up to a month in an airtight container, or wrapped airtight and frozen.

Special Equipment

Heavy cookie sheet(s), baking parchment (optional), serrated knife

Temperature and Time

350°F for 20 to 25 minutes, then 300°F for 15 to 20 minutes

Butter-flavor no stick cooking spray

2 cups sifted all-purpose flour

1½ teaspoons baking powder

⅛ teaspoon salt

½ cup blanched almonds, coarsely chopped

¼ cup seedless raisins, packed

¼ cup golden raisins, packed

2 tablespoons lightly salted butter, at room temperature

½ cup plus 2 tablespoons granulated sugar

2 large eggs

1 teaspoon vanilla extract

¾ teaspoon almond extract

1. Position a rack in the center of the oven and preheat it to 350°F. Lightly coat the baking pan with cooking spray or line it with baking parchment.

2. Sift together the flour, baking powder, and salt into a bowl.

3. In a small bowl, combine the nuts and raisins with 2 tablespoons of the flour mixture, and toss well. Set aside.

4. In a large bowl, using an electric mixer, cream the butter and sugar until light and fluffy. Add the eggs one at a time, beating after each addition. Beat in the vanilla and almond extracts.

5. Add the flour mixture all at once, and, with the mixer on low speed, blend well. Scrape down the bowl and beaters. Add the raisin-nut mixture and beat a few seconds on low just to incorporate. Gather the dough into a ball. The dough should feel quite dry; if it sticks to your fingers, work in a little more flour, ½ teaspoon at a time.

6. On a lightly floured surface, divide the dough evenly in half. Shape each half into a roll about 13 inches long, 1 inch high, and 1½ inches wide. Set the rolls about 2 inches apart on the prepared baking sheet, and gently flatten the top of each one until it is slightly domed, ¾ inch high, and about 1¾ inches wide.

7. Bake for 20 to 25 minutes, or until the rolls are pale golden on top and firm to the touch and a wooden toothpick inserted into the roll comes out clean. Remove the pan from the oven and reduce the heat to 300°F. With a long flat spatula, transfer each roll to a cutting board and allow to cool for 4 to 5 minutes.

8. With a serrated knife, cut the still-warm logs on the diagonal into ½-inch-thick slices. Place the slices cut side down on the same baking pan (do not regrease). If necessary, use a second pan. Place the pan(s) in the oven and bake for another 15 to 20 minutes, until the slices are golden and crisp. Transfer the mandlebrot to wire racks to cool. Store in an airtight container.

Light Touch: Anne Sternberger's original recipe is very similar to this but contains ½ cup butter, bringing the total calories from fat to 42 percent. By dropping all but 2 tablespoons of the butter, I cut the calories from fat to 26 percent yet retained the basic character of the recipe.

Nutritional Analysis per cookie

48 calories

1 g protein

1 g fat

0.4 g satfat

8 g carbohydrate

19 mg sodium

10 mg cholesterol

Cream Puffs
(Pâte à Choux)

◆ · ◆ · ◆ ·

The French call them choux ("cabbages"), a fair description of these puffed-up, rounded pastry shells created when the eggy batter literally blows up in the heat of the oven. This pastry is the base for éclairs, cream puffs, profiteroles, and many other elegant desserts. When I was growing up, my mother used to make them as a special treat: oversize crisp golden rounds filled with creamy vanilla pudding and topped with a faint sifting of confectioners' sugar. I still love them.

You can shape the dough into small or large balls, long ribbons, or other designs, fill them with anything from frozen yogurt to Light Lemon Curd, and serve them with warm Spiced Blueberry Sauce, Raspberry Sauce, or any other fruit sauce.

◆ · ◆ · ◆ ·

Pastry

Butter-flavor no stick cooking spray

1 cup unsifted all-purpose flour

$\frac{1}{2}$ teaspoon salt

1 cup water

1 teaspoon unsalted butter

1 tablespoon hazelnut or canola oil

2 large eggs

2 large egg whites

Filling

Fromage Blanc (page 407), Shortcut Vanilla Pastry Cream
(page 401), Vanilla Cream (page 402), Light Lemon Curd
(page 404), Chocolate Pudding (page 270), or $1\frac{1}{2}$ to 2
cups any flavor low-fat frozen yogurt

Confectioners' sugar or Vanilla Icing Glaze (page 435)
(optional)

1. Position the rack in the center of the oven and preheat it to 400°F. Lightly coat the baking sheets with cooking spray.

2. Sift the flour and salt together in a small bowl.

3. In a large heavy-bottomed nonreactive pan, combine the water, butter, and oil and bring to a boil. Remove from the heat, add all the

Yield

24 small puffs (1½-inch diameter), 12 large puffs (3-inch diameter), or 12 4-inch-long éclairs

Advance Preparation

Shells can be made ahead and stored in an airtight container for a day or 2. Or they can be wrapped airtight and frozen for up to a month.

Special Equipment

Baking sheets, pastry bag and tip (optional)

Temperature and Time

400°F for 25 to 35 minutes

flour mixture at once, and beat hard with a wooden spoon until the batter forms a smooth ball that pulls away from the sides of the pan. Return the pan to low heat and beat about 1 minute longer. Then remove from the heat and cool for 3 or 4 minutes.

4. While you can beat the eggs into the dough with a wooden spoon, the easiest method is to transfer the dough to a food processor or the bowl of an electric mixer. Add the eggs and egg whites one at a time, pulsing or beating until smooth after each addition. When each egg or white is first added, the batter will look lumpy and slimy, but after a few seconds of hard beating, it smooths out. Don't skimp on the beating here, because it is what makes the dough light. When the dough is smooth, shiny, and thick, but able to drop, slowly, from a spoon, process for another 10 seconds or beat for another 30 seconds.

5. To form the cream puffs, you can either pipe the dough through a pastry bag fitted with a ½- to ¾-inch star tip, or simply drop lumps from a spoon. To make small puffs or profiteroles, form rounded 1- to 1¼-inch lumps about 1 inch apart on the sheet. To shape éclairs, pipe the dough into strips ½ inch wide and 4 inches long. For large cream puffs (3 inches, baked), pipe balls of dough about 1½ inches in diameter or shape balls with a spoon.

6. Bake for about 25 to 35 minutes, depending on size, until the puffs are golden brown and crisp. Test one by cutting into it: If the inside is still doughy or pasty, bake for 3 to 5 minutes longer. Transfer the puffs to wire racks, and prick each one in the side with a fork to let out the steam and keep them crisp. Cool completely.

7. Slice open the puffs, add the filling of your choice, and put the tops back in place. (There will be some soft dough inside the puffs; you can either ignore it or scrape it out with a fork before adding the filling.) Top the filled puffs with a light sifting of confectioners' sugar or drizzle on Vanilla Icing Glaze if desired.

Light Touch: The classic French recipe for pâte à choux uses ½ cup butter and 4 eggs to 1 cup flour and 1 cup water; this formula gets 66 percent of its calories from fat. In order to retain the special puffing ability of this dough, the basic proportions of fat and eggs can be cut only by half (to 33 percent calories from fat). With less fat or fewer yolks, the dough does not react properly. However, the per serving amount of fat is so low that one does not have to be alarmed that the total calories from fat is slightly above 30 percent.

Nutritional Analysis per small puff (without filling or topping)

33 calories
1 g protein
1 g fat
0.3 g satfat
4 g carbohydrate
55 mg sodium
18 mg cholesterol

Baked Soufflés

The cook is nervous, the dinner guests more so. As the entrée is cleared and thoughts turn toward dessert—an interlude usually filled with pleasant anticipation—blood pressure begins to rise. How high will it (the soufflé, not the blood pressure) rise? Will it fall? Collapse? Do we care? Couldn't we have a plain layer cake? Furtive glances at the clock. Finally, the cook dashes out (on tiptoe lest the floor shake), extricates the soufflé from the oven, tiptoes back, and with lightning speed serves her creation while admonishing the hapless victims, "Eat quickly before it utterly disappears, you know how delicate soufflés are ... but aren't they worth it?" In a word, no. Not *that* kind of soufflé. Too delicate, too much anxiety, a test of stress management skills.

There are two types of classic hot fruit soufflés: One is made with a base of starch-butter-egg yolks (high in saturated fat), the other is a simple fat-free blend of puréed fruit and meringue. If the latter is so clearly the more healthful, you ask, why isn't it the darling of low-fat bakers? It is too unreliable and fragile. The texture can vary from watery sludge to dry cotton foam depending upon the weight, sweetness, and moisture content of the fruit. These soufflés have an unnerving tendency to collapse upon even the most experienced bakers because while they lack fat, they also lack a stabilized starch base to support the fruited meringue.

After countless experiments, I have devised a soufflé that is utterly reliable and does not fall. For overcoming this long-known and greatly feared kitchen terrorist, the falling soufflé, I should win a Nobel peace (or chemistry) prize.

My soufflé is not only divine to behold and sublime to taste, it is quick and simple to make and based on classic techniques with a new twist. The first trick is to cook a flavored fruit purée thickened and stabilized with cornstarch and sugar. This flavor base can be made ahead and refrigerated, but must be at room temperature before blending it (the only last-minute task) with stiffly beaten egg whites just before baking.

The second trick is to bake the soufflé in a water bath, which guarantees gentle even heat, a slow and steady rise, a creamy texture, and a stable product. A traditional baking technique, it never fails.

The third trick is to use an instant-read thermometer to test the internal temperature of the soufflé. Fruit soufflés are perfectly baked when the thermometer inserted 1 inch from the rim reads 160°F and 150°F at the center. (The soufflé is hotter near the rim, so check both.) At this point the texture will be light and still moist, but does hold its shape. The center will be set but smooth and creamy, the edges slightly firmer and drier. Chocolate soufflés bake slightly longer, until the temperature in the *center* is 160°F.

When first taken from the oven, the soufflé is puffed to its greatest height, and it should be presented and served right away (take a bow). However, this soufflé will not collapse seconds after it is taken from the oven, nor will it fall when you spoon out the first serving. It will sink about one inch, then hold its shape for two to six hours—if there are leftovers.

Here are some tips for successfully making soufflés.

• These soufflés do not need paper or foil collars.

• Plan your time so the fruit base, if it has been made in advance, can be brought to lukewarm temperature (about 70°F) before folding it into the meringue. Make the sauce, if any, well in advance.

• Be sure to preheat the oven for at least 15 minutes before baking the soufflé. Place the soufflé in its water bath in the oven about 35 minutes before you plan to serve it.

• Remember that eggs separate most easily when cold but whip to greater volume when at room temperature. If your egg whites are cold, place them in a bowl set into a larger bowl of warm water. Stir until the whites are warm to the touch.

• Treat the egg whites with care—they are the leavening for the soufflé. The bowl and beaters must be completely free of fat; wipe them with a paper towel dampened with white vinegar. Whip the whites until foamy before adding the sugar. Then whip until stiff but not dry; at this point, the whites will be smooth, glossy, and just hold their shape. Do not overbeat, or the soufflé may collapse when baked.

Light Touch: A classic vanilla soufflé made with a cooked béchamel sauce base (flour-butter-yolks), using 4 or 5 whole eggs, receives approximately 45 percent calories from fat. Each serving packs a relatively minor 9 grams of fat but a huge 157 millligrams of cholesterol. A classic meringue/fruit soufflé has the same amount of fat as it has dependability: None. All of my soufflés are dependable, and, with one exception, they contain virtually no fat (they range from 0 to 2 percent calories from fat). The one exception is the chocolate soufflé (14 percent) because it contains a little solid chocolate, high in cocoa butter, which is a saturated fat.

Chocolate Soufflé

Yield

6 to 8 servings

Advance Preparation

Cooked chocolate base can be prepared ahead and stored, covered, in the refrigerator for up to 2 days. Bring to room temperature (70°F) before combining with the meringue.

Special Equipment

2-quart (8-cup) soufflé mold or six 1½-cup individual soufflé dishes, baking pan large enough to contain soufflé mold(s), instant-read thermometer (optional)

Temperature and Time

350°F for 35 to 40 minutes for large soufflé (internal temperature near the center of 160°F, about 25 minutes for individual soufflés

The intense chocolate flavor of this soufflé comes from cocoa and a small amount of grated unsweetened chocolate. Serve this for a dramatic finale at a dinner party, napped with Raspberry Sauce (page 412) or sprinkled with a few drops of coffee liqueur.

This recipe makes a slightly larger soufflé than the other ones in this book, because it is typically served as a party dessert and I wanted it to have an exceptionally high rise. Read Baked Soufflés (page 354) before beginning the recipe.

⅔ cup nonalkalized unsweetened cocoa
¾ cup plus 2 tablespoons granulated sugar, divided
4 teaspoons cornstarch
⅛ teaspoon cinnamon
1 cup skim milk
2 teaspoons vanilla extract
Butter-flavor no stick cooking spray
7 large egg whites, at room temperature
Pinch of salt
¼ teaspoon cream of tartar
½ ounce unsweetened chocolate, grated
Confectioners' sugar

1. Prepare the chocolate base: In a heavy-bottomed nonreactive saucepan, combine the cocoa, ¼ cup of the sugar, the cornstarch, and cinnamon. Whisk to blend well. Whisk in the milk. Set over medium heat and whisk constantly, for 5 to 7 minutes until it reaches a boil. Then boil, stirring, making sure to reach into the corners, for 1 minute, or until the mixture is as thick as pudding and generously coats a spoon. Remove from the heat and stir in the vanilla. Let cool to room temperature. (The base can be prepared ahead, covered with plastic wrap, and refrigerated; bring to room temperature before proceeding.)

2. Arrange a rack in the lower third of the oven and preheat it to 350°F. Coat the soufflé mold(s) with cooking spray. Sprinkle bottom and sides with 2 tablespoons of the sugar, and tap out excess sugar.

3. In a large grease-free bowl, using an electric mixer on medium speed, whip the egg whites with the salt and cream of tartar until foamy. Gradually add the remaining ½ cup sugar and whip until the whites are medium-stiff but not dry.

4. Be sure the chocolate base is at room temperature. Stir it well. Using a whisk, fold about 1 cup of the whipped whites into the chocolate mixture to lighten it. Sprinkle in the grated chocolate and then fold the chocolate mixture into the remaining whites. Turn the mixture into the prepared mold(s) and smooth the top(s) with a spatula.

5. Place the mold(s) in a baking pan, and add hot water to come about one third of the way up the sides of the mold(s). Bake until well risen and firm when lightly jiggled with your hand, 35 to 40 minutes for a large soufflé (an instant-read thermometer inserted near the center should read about 160°F) or about 25 minutes for individual soufflés. Remove from the oven and sift on a little confectioners' sugar. Serve at once.

Light Touch: See page 355. Fourteen percent calories from fat.

Nutritional Analysis per serving (based on 6 servings, without sauce)

172 calories

7 g protein

3 g fat

1 g satfat

34 g carbohydrate

86 mg sodium

1 mg cholesterol

Raspberry Soufflé

◆ ◆ ◆

E thereal in texture, bright pink in color, and delectable in taste, this fat- and cholesterol-free soufflé can be made in any season because frozen raspberries work as well as fresh. Complement the flavor with a spoonful of Raspberry Sauce (page 412) or Chocolate Sauce (page 411). Read Baked Soufflés (page 354) before beginning the recipe.

The raspberry flavor of this soufflé is intensified by using either Chambord (a sweet raspberry liqueur) or Framboise (raspberry eau-de-vie).

◆ ◆ ◆

Yield

6 servings

Advance Preparation

Fruit base can be prepared up to 2 days in advance, covered, and refrigerated. Bring to room temperature (70°F) before combining with the meringue.

Special Equipment

1½-quart (6-cup) soufflé mold or six 1½-cup individual soufflé dishes, baking pan large enough to contain soufflé mold(s), instant-read thermometer (optional)

Temperature and Time

350°F for 30 to 35 minutes for a large soufflé (internal temperature in the center of 150°F), about 25 minutes for individual soufflés

1⅓ cups fresh raspberries or frozen unsweetened whole raspberries

5 tablespoons granulated sugar, divided

1½ teaspoons grated orange zest

1 tablespoon water

2 tablespoons cornstarch

2½ tablespoons fresh lemon juice

2 tablespoons Chambord or Framboise

Butter-flavor no stick cooking spray

5 large egg whites, at room temperature

¼ teaspoon cream of tartar

Pinch of salt

Confectioners' sugar

1. Prepare the raspberry base: In a heavy-bottomed nonreactive saucepan, combine 1 cup of the raspberries, 2 tablespoons of the sugar, the orange zest, and water. Set over medium heat and bring to a boil, stirring and mashing the berries with a wooden spoon. Meanwhile, dissolve the cornstarch in the lemon juice.

2. Stir the cornstarch mixture into the raspberries and bring back to a boil, stirring constantly. Then boil, stirring, for about 45 seconds, or until the mixture is no longer cloudy and is as thick as preserves. Remove from the heat and stir in the Chambord or Framboise and the remaining ⅓ cup whole raspberries. Let cool to room temperature. (The raspberry base can be made ahead, covered, and refrigerated; bring to room temperature before proceeding.)

3. Position a rack in the lower third of the oven and preheat it to 350°F. Coat the mold(s) with cooking spray. Sprinkle bottom and sides with sugar, and tap out excess sugar.

4. In a large grease-free bowl, combine the egg whites, cream of tartar, and salt. Using an electric mixer on medium speed, whip until foamy. Gradually add the remaining 3 tablespoons sugar and whip until the whites are medium-stiff but not dry.

5. Be sure the raspberry base is at room temperature. Stir it well. Using a whisk, fold about 1 cup of the whipped whites into the raspberry base to lighten it, then fold the mixture into the remaining whites. Turn the mixture into the prepared soufflé mold(s) and smooth the top(s) with a spatula.

6. Place the mold(s) in the roasting pan, and add hot water to come about one third of the way up the sides of the mold(s). Bake until well risen, medium-brown in color, and fairly firm when lightly jiggled with your hand, about 35 minutes for a large soufflé (an instant-read thermometer inserted in the center should read about 150°F) or about 25 minutes for individual soufflés. Remove from the oven, and sift on confectioners' sugar. Serve immediately.

Light Touch: See page 355. One percent calories from fat.

Apricot Soufflé

◆ · ◆ · ◆

T his delightfully tart soufflé is light but intense in flavor. The soufflé rises into a dome shape, rather than the familiar "high hat," because the meringue is weighted slightly by the dense apricot purée. Serve this with Apricot-Orange Sauce (page 413) if you like. Read Baked Soufflés (page 354) before beginning the recipe.

◆ · ◆ · ◆

Serve this with Apricot-Orange Sauce (page 413) if you like. Read Baked Soufflés (page 354) before beginning the recipe.

(page 413)

Yield

6 servings

Advance Preparation

Fruit base can be prepared up to 2 days in advance, covered, and refrigerated. Bring to room temperature (70°F) before combining with the meringue.

Special Equipment

1½-quart (6-cup) soufflé mold or six 1½-cup individual soufflé dishes, baking pan large enough to contain soufflé mold(s), instant-read thermometer (optional)

Temperature and Time

350°F for 35 to 40 minutes for a large soufflé (internal temperature in the center of about 150°F) or about 25 minutes for individual soufflés

8 ounces dried apricots (1½ cups)

1 cup water

2 tablespoons cornstarch

⅓ cup fresh orange juice

2 teaspoons fresh lemon juice

6 tablespoons granulated sugar, divided

1 teaspoon vanilla extract

Butter-flavor no stick cooking spray

6 large egg whites, at room temperature

¼ teaspoon cream of tartar

Pinch of salt

Confectioners' sugar

1. Prepare the apricot base: In a heavy-bottomed nonreactive saucepan, combine the apricots and water. Cover and bring to a boil, then reduce the heat and simmer for 15 to 20 minutes or until fruit is soft. Transfer to a food processor and purée until smooth (you should have a scant 1¼ cups). Return the purée to the saucepan.

2. In a small bowl, dissolve the cornstarch in the orange juice. Add to the apricot purée, along with the lemon juice and 3 tablespoons of the sugar.

3. Set the saucepan over medium heat, and bring to a boil, whisking constantly. Then boil, continuing to whisk, for about 45 seconds, until the sauce is no longer cloudy. Remove from the heat and stir in the vanilla. Set aside to cool. (The apricot base can be prepared ahead, covered, and refrigerated; bring to room temperature before proceeding.)

4. Position a rack in the lower third of the oven and preheat it to 350°F. Coat the soufflé mold(s) with cooking spray. Sprinkle the bottom and sides with sugar, and tap out excess sugar.

5. In a large grease-free bowl, combine the egg whites, cream of tartar, and salt. Using an electric mixer on medium speed, whip until foamy. Gradually add the remaining 3 tablespoons sugar, and whip until stiff but not dry.

6. Be sure the apricot base is at room temperature. Stir it well. Using a whisk, fold about 2 cups of the whipped whites into the apricot base to lighten it; this takes some work if the purée has been made in advance, but a smooth blend is critical to the final texture. Fold this mixture into the remaining whites a little at a time, until well blended and smooth. Turn the batter into the prepared mold(s) and smooth the top(s) with a spatula.

7. Place the mold(s) in the baking pan, and add hot water to come about one third of the way up the sides of the mold(s). Bake until well risen, quite brown on top, and fairly firm to the touch, about 35 minutes for a large soufflé (an instant-read thermometer inserted in the center should register about 150°F) or about 25 minutes for individual soufflés. Remove from the oven and sift on a little confectioners' sugar. Serve immediately.

Light Touch: See page 355. One percent calories from fat. As a bonus, the apricots contribute a generous 3 grams of dietary fiber to each fat- and cholesterol-free serving.

Nutritional Analysis per serving

158 calories

5 g protein

0 g fat

0 g satfat

37 g carbohydrate

60 mg sodium

0 mg cholesterol

Plum Soufflé

◆·◆·◆·

This unusual soufflé has a light pink color and a delicate but definite plum flavor, brought out by slivovitz, a plum brandy. Because the skins are left on the plums, they contribute both color and textural contrast. In late summer and fall, I use Italian prune plums, but you can substitute others such as Emperor or Santa Rosa, or use whole canned plums in light syrup (well drained). Serve this plain or with Raspberry Sauce (page 412), or make a quick sauce by warming half a cup of plum preserves and stirring in three or four tablespoons of dry white wine. Read Baked Soufflés (page 354) before beginning the recipe.

·◆·◆·◆·

Raspberry Sauce (page 412)
Read Baked Soufflés (page 354)

1¾ cups sliced pitted fresh plums, unpeeled (10 ounces Italian prune plums)

6 tablespoons granulated sugar, divided

Pinch of cinnamon

¼ cup water

2 tablespoons cornstarch

3 tablespoons fresh lemon juice

¼ cup plum preserves

3 tablespoons slivovitz or kirsch

Butter-flavor no stick cooking spray

5 large egg whites, at room temperature

¼ teaspoon cream of tartar

Pinch of salt

Confectioners' sugar

1. Prepare the plum base: In a heavy-bottomed 1½-quart non-reactive saucepan, combine the plums, 3 tablespoons of the sugar, the cinnamon, and water. Cover and bring to a boil, then reduce the heat and simmer for 10 minutes, or until the plums are tender. Transfer to a food processor and purée until bits of skin are no larger than ¼ inch. Return the purée to the saucepan.

2. Dissolve the cornstarch in the lemon juice, and add it to the plum purée. Set over medium heat and bring to a boil, whisking constantly. Then boil, whisking, for about 45 seconds, or until the sauce thickens to the consistency of preserves and is no longer cloudy. Re-

---

Sidebar

Yield

6 servings

Advance Preparation

Fruit base can be prepared up to 2 days in advance, covered, and refrigerated. Bring to room temperature (70°F) before combining with meringue.

Special Equipment

1½-quart (6-cup) soufflé mold or six 1½-cup individual soufflé dishes, baking pan large enough to contain soufflé mold(s), instant-read thermometer (optional)

Temperature and Time

350°F for 35 to 40 minutes (internal temperature in the center of about 150°F) or about 25 minutes for individual soufflés

move from the heat and stir in the plum preserves and slivovitz or kirsch. Let cool to room temperature. (The plum base can be prepared ahead, covered, and refrigerated; bring to room temperature before proceeding.)

3. Position a rack in the lower third of the oven and preheat it to 350°F. Coat the soufflé mold with cooking spray. Sprinkle the bottom and sides with sugar, and tap out excess sugar.

4. In a large grease-free bowl, combine the egg whites, cream of tartar, and salt. Using an electric mixer on medium speed, whip until foamy. Gradually add the remaining 3 tablespoons sugar and whip until medium-stiff but not dry.

5. Be sure the plum base is at room temperature. Stir it well. Using a whisk, fold about 1 cup of the whipped whites into the plum base to lighten it, then fold it into the remaining whites. Turn the batter into the prepared mold(s) and smooth the top(s) with a spatula.

6. Place the mold(s) in the baking pan, and add hot water to come about one third of the way up the sides of the mold(s). Bake until well risen, golden brown on top, and fairly firm when lightly jiggled with your hand (an instant-read thermometer inserted in the center should read about 150°F), 35 to 40 minutes for a large soufflé or about 25 minutes for individual soufflés. Remove the soufflé(s) from the oven, and sift on confectioners' sugar. Serve immediately.

Light Touch: See page 355. Zero percent calories from fat.

Nutritional Analysis per serving

136 calories

3 g protein

0 g fat

0 g satfat

30 g carbohydrate

94 mg sodium

0 mg cholesterol

Peach Daiquiri Soufflé

◆ ◆ ◆

M *ake this delectable soufflé with ripe peaches. To intensify the flavor, the fruit is blended with frozen peach daiquiri mix and spiked with dark rum or peach schnapps. For the full effect, serve this soufflé with Peach Daiquiri Sauce (page 420). Read Baked Soufflés (page 354) before beginning the recipe.*

◆ ◆ ◆

Yield
....

6 servings

Advance Preparation
....

Peach base can be prepared up to 2 days in advance, covered, and refrigerated. Bring it to room temperature (70°F) before combining with the meringue.

Special Equipment
....

1 ½-quart (6-cup) soufflé mold, roasting pan large enough to contain soufflé mold, instant-read thermometer (optional)

Temperature and Time
....

350°F for 35 to 40 minutes (internal temperature in the center of about 150°F)

1 generous cup peeled sliced peaches (from 1 large ripe peach) or frozen dry-pack unsweetened sliced peaches
¼ cup Bacardi Peach Daiquiri Mix Frozen Concentrate
¼ cup hot water
2 tablespoons cornstarch
1 tablespoon fresh lemon juice
6 tablespoons granulated sugar, divided
3 tablespoons dark rum or peach schnapps
Butter-flavor no stick cooking spray
5 large egg whites, at room temperature
¼ teaspoon cream of tartar
Pinch of salt
Confectioners' sugar
Peach Daiquiri Sauce (page 420)

1. To peel peaches, drop them into boiling water for about 2 minutes, then transfer to a bowl of ice water to cool. The skins should slip off easily.

Prepare the peach daiquiri base: Purée the peach slices in a food processor. Set aside.

2. In a heavy-bottomed saucepan, blend the frozen daiquiri mix and hot water. Measure 3 tablespoons of this liquid into a cup, and stir in the cornstarch until dissolved.

3. Add the cornstarch mixture, puréed peaches, lemon juice, and 3 tablespoons of the sugar to the daiquiri mixture in the saucepan. Bring to a boil over medium heat, stirring constantly. Then boil for about 1 minute, stirring, until the mixture thickens to the consistency of preserves and is no longer cloudy. Remove from the heat and stir in the rum or liqueur. Let cool to room temperature. (The peach base can be prepared ahead, covered, and refrigerated. Bring to room temperature before proceeding.)

4. Position a rack in the lower third of the oven and preheat it to 350°F. Coat the soufflé mold with cooking spray. Sprinkle bottom and sides with sugar, and tap out excess sugar.

5. In a large grease-free bowl, combine the egg whites, cream of tartar, and salt. Using an electric mixer on medium speed, whip until foamy. Gradually add the remaining 3 tablespoons sugar, and whip until the whites are medium-stiff but not dry.

6. Be sure the peach base is at room temperature. Stir it well. Using a whisk, fold about 1 cup of the whipped whites into the peach base to lighten it. Then fold the peach mixture into the remaining whites. Turn the batter into the prepared mold(s) and smooth the top(s) with a spatula.

7. Place the mold(s) in the baking pan, and add hot water to come about one third of the way up the sides of the mold(s). Bake until well risen, golden brown, and quite firm when lightly jiggled with your hand (an instant-read thermometer inserted in the center should read 150°F). Remove from the oven, and sift on some confectioners' sugar. Serve immediately, with the sauce.

Light Touch: See page 355. One percent calories from fat.

*Nutritional Analysis
per serving
(including sauce)*

194 calories

4 g protein

0 g fat

0 g satfat

40 g carbohydrate

94 mg sodium

0 mg cholesterol

Orange Soufflé

◆ ◆ ◆

*A*s bright in flavor as it is in color, this high-rising soufflé is the perfect dessert for an elegant dinner. The orange taste is intensified by the addition of marmalade. Use the best quality available, and avoid bitter or "burned-style" orange marmalade, which would leave an unpleasant aftertaste. Serve this with Apricot-Orange Sauce (page 413) or Chocolate Sauce (page 411). Read Baked Soufflés (page 354) before beginning the recipe.

◆ ◆ ◆

Yield

6 servings

Advance Preparation

Fruit base can be prepared up to 2 days in advance, covered, and refrigerated. Bring to room temperature (70°F) before combining with the meringue.

Special Equipment

1½-quart (6-cup) soufflé mold or six 1½-cup individual soufflé dishes, baking pan large enough to contain soufflé mold(s), instant-read thermometer (optional).

Temperature and Time

350°F for 35 to 40 minutes for a large soufflé (internal temperature in the center of about 150°F, 1 inch from rim, 160°F) or about 25 minutes for individual soufflés

½ cup granulated sugar, divided

2 tablespoons cornstarch

¾ cup hot water

¼ cup frozen orange juice concentrate

2 teaspoons fresh lemon juice

2 teaspoons grated orange zest

3 tablespoons orange marmalade

1 teaspoon orange extract

½ teaspoon vanilla extract

Butter-flavor no stick cooking spray

5 large egg whites, at room temperature

¼ teaspoon cream of tartar

Pinch of salt

Confectioners' sugar

1. Prepare the orange base: In a small nonreactive heavy-bottomed saucepan, whisk together ¼ cup of the sugar and the cornstarch. Gradually whisk in the hot water, orange juice concentrate, lemon juice, and orange zest. Bring to a boil over medium heat, whisking constantly. Then boil, whisking, for 45 to 60 seconds, or until thickened to the consistency of preserves and no longer cloudy.

2. Remove from the heat and stir in the marmalade, orange extract, and vanilla. Let cool to room temperature. (The orange base can be made ahead, covered, and refrigerated; bring to room temperature before proceeding.)

3. Position a rack in the lower third of the oven and preheat it to 350°F. Coat the soufflé mold(s) with cooking spray. Sprinkle bottom and sides with sugar, and tap out excess sugar.

4. In a large grease-free bowl, combine the egg whites, cream of tartar, and salt. Using an electric mixer on medium speed, whip until foamy. Gradually add the remaining ¼ cup sugar, and whip until medium-stiff but not dry.

5. Be sure the orange base is at room temperature. Stir it well. Using a whisk, fold about 1 cup of the whipped whites into the orange base to lighten it, then fold it into the remaining whites. Turn the batter into the prepared mold(s) and smooth the top(s) with a spatula.

6. Place the mold(s) in the baking pan, and add hot water to come about one third of the way up the sides of the mold(s). Bake until well risen, golden brown in color, and fairly firm when lightly jiggled with your hand, about 35 minutes for a large soufflé (an instant-read thermometer inserted in the center should read about 150°F, 1 inch from the rim, 160°F), or about 25 minutes for individual soufflés. Remove from the oven, and sift on confectioners' sugar. Serve immediately.

Light Touch: See page 355. Zero percent calories from fat.

*Nutritional Analysis
per serving
(without sauce)*

131 calories

3 g protein

0 g fat

0 g satfat

30 g carbohydrate

94 mg sodium

0 mg cholesterol

Lemon Soufflé

- ◆ - ◆ - ◆ -

*L*ike a cool breeze on a hot evening, this fat- and cholesterol-free soufflé is welcome and refreshing. Light, zesty, and not too sweet, it has a touch of orange juice and orange liqueur to mellow the sharpness of the lemon. For flavor and color contrast, serve it with Raspberry Sauce (page 412). Read Baked Soufflés (page 354) before beginning the recipe.

- ◆ - ◆ - ◆ -

³⁄₄ cup granulated sugar, divided

2 tablespoons cornstarch

¹⁄₄ cup cold water

¹⁄₃ cup fresh lemon juice

2 tablespoons orange juice

2 teaspoons grated lemon zest

2 tablespoons orange-flavored liqueur (such as Grand Marnier)

Butter-flavor no stick cooking spray

5 large egg whites, at room temperature

¹⁄₄ teaspoon cream of tartar

Pinch of salt

Confectioners' sugar

1. Prepare the lemon base: In a small nonreactive heavy-bottomed saucepan, whisk together ¹⁄₄ cup of the sugar and the cornstarch. Gradually whisk in the water, lemon juice, orange juice, and 1¹⁄₂ teaspoons of the lemon zest. (Reserve the remaining lemon zest for garnish.) Bring to a boil over medium heat, whisking constantly. Then boil, whisking, for about 45 seconds, or until thickened to the consistency of preserves and no longer cloudy.

2. Remove from the heat and stir in the orange liqueur. Let cool to room temperature. (The lemon base can be made ahead, covered, and refrigerated; bring to room temperature before proceeding.)

3. Position a rack in the lower third of the oven and preheat it to 350°F. Coat the soufflé mold(s) with cooking spray. Sprinkle bottom and sides with sugar, and tap out excess sugar.

Yield

6 servings

Advance Preparation

Fruit base can be prepared up to 2 days in advance, covered, and refrigerated. Bring it to room temperature (70°F) before combining with the meringue.

Special Equipment

1¹⁄₂-quart (6-cup) soufflé mold or six 1¹⁄₂-cup individual soufflé dishes, baking pan large enough to contain soufflé mold(s), instant-read thermometer (optional)

Temperature and Time

350°F for 35 to 40 minutes for large soufflé (internal temperature in center of about 150°F, 1 inch from rim, 160°F) or about 25 minutes for individual soufflés

4. In a large grease-free bowl, combine the egg whites, cream of tartar, and salt. Using an electric mixer on medium speed, whip until foamy. Gradually add the remaining ½ cup sugar, and whip until medium-stiff but not dry.

5. Be sure the lemon base is at room temperature. Stir it well. Using a whisk, fold about 1 cup of the whipped whites into the lemon base to lighten it, then fold it into the remaining whites. Turn the batter into the prepared mold(s) and smooth the top(s) with a spatula.

6. Place the mold(s) in the baking pan, and add hot water to come about one third of the way up the sides of the mold(s). Bake until well risen, golden brown, and fairly firm when lightly jiggled with your hand, about 35 minutes for a large soufflé (an instant-read thermometer inserted in the center should read about 150°F, 1 inch from the rim, 160°F), or about 25 minutes for individual soufflés. Remove from the oven, and sift on confectioners' sugar. Sprinkle the reserved lemon zest over the top. Serve immediately.

Light Touch: See page 355. Zero percent calories from fat.

*Nutritional Analysis
per serving
(without sauce)*

133 calories

3 g protein

0 g fat

0 g satfat

30 g carbohydrate

91 mg sodium

0 mg cholesterol

Pineapple Soufflé

◆ ◆ ◆

Serve this not-too-sweet soufflé with warm Pineapple Sauce for an elegant and refreshing dessert.

Both the soufflé and the sauce can be made from the one 20-ounce can of crushed pineapple. Drain the fruit well and reserve all the juice (3 tablespoons are used for the soufflé, ¾ cup reserved for the sauce); you should have sufficient ingredients for both recipes. Read Baked Soufflés (page 354) before beginning the recipe.

◆ ◆ ◆

2 tablespoons cornstarch

1 cup well-drained crushed canned pineapple (plus 3 tablespoons of the juice)

1 tablespoon fresh lemon juice

6 tablespoons granulated sugar, divided

1 teaspoon vanilla extract

Butter-flavor no stick cooking spray

5 large egg whites, at room temperature

¼ teaspoon cream of tartar

Pinch of salt

Pineapple Sauce (page 419), warmed

1. Prepare the pineapple base: In a heavy-bottomed saucepan, dissolve the cornstarch in the reserved 3 tablespoons pineapple juice. Add the crushed pineapple, lemon juice, and 3 tablespoons of the sugar. Bring to a boil over medium heat, whisking constantly. Then boil, whisking, for about 45 seconds, or until the mixture thickens to the consistency of preserves and is no longer cloudy.

2. Remove from the heat and stir in the vanilla. Set aside to cool to room temperature. (The pineapple base can be made ahead, covered, and refrigerated; bring to room temperature before proceeding.)

3. Position a rack in the lower third of the oven and preheat it to 350°F. Coat the soufflé mold with cooking spray. Sprinkle the bottom and sides with sugar, and tap out excess sugar.

4. In a large grease-free bowl, combine the egg whites, cream of tartar, and salt. Using an electric mixer on medium speed, whip until

Yield

6 servings

Advance Preparation

Pineapple base can be prepared up to 2 days in advance, covered, and refrigerated. Bring it to room temperature (70°F) before combining with the meringue. Sauce can be made a day or two in advance.

Special Equipment

1½-quart (6-cup) soufflé mold, baking pan large enough to contain soufflé mold, instant-read thermometer (optional)

Temperature and Time

350°F for 35 to 40 minutes (internal temperature in center of about 150°F)

foamy. Gradually add the remaining 3 tablespoons sugar and whip until the whites are medium-stiff but not dry.

5. Be sure the pineapple base is at room temperature. Stir it well. Using a whisk, fold about 1 cup of the whipped whites into the pineapple mixture to lighten it, then fold it into the whites. Turn the batter into the prepared mold and smooth the top with a spatula.

6. Place the mold in the baking pan, and add hot water to come about one third of the way up the sides of the mold. Bake for about 35 minutes, or until well risen, golden brown, and fairly firm when lightly jiggled with your hand (an instant-read thermometer inserted near the center should read about 150°F). Remove from the oven and serve immediately, with the warm sauce.

Light Touch: See page 355. Two percent calories from fat.

*Nutritional Analysis
per serving
(including sauce)*

126 calories

3 g protein

0 g fat

0 g satfat

29 g carbohydrate

93 mg sodium

0 mg cholesterol

Exotic Fruit Soufflé

◆ · ◆ · ◆

Created by Chef Jean-Pierre Vuillermet of Robert Henry's Restaurant in New Haven, Connecticut, this remarkable confection was the finale to a dazzling banquet held at the restaurant in December 1992, in honor of Jacques Pépin. Produced by owner/restaurateur Jo MacKenzie, the outstanding and flawlessly prepared menu included consommé with foie gras and polenta croutons, yellow pike and lobster fricassée with sautéed cèpes, roasted capon with truffles, cheese and walnut galettes, mâche salad, and a fabulous selection of Champagnes, wines, and chocolate truffles.

A hard act to follow? Not, apparently, for Jean-Pierre, who told me he worked for several months in search of a flavorful soufflé that could be prepared well ahead, frozen, baked at the last moment, and unmolded without collapsing before being served to over eighty gourmets and food professionals. A tough audience, a resounding success. The chef received a well-deserved standing ovation.

You will, too! Just follow my adaptation of Jean-Pierre's recipe to prepare a cornstarch-stabilized purée of fresh tropical fruits folded into a meringue. Spoon the mixture into individual molds, freeze, and bake just before serving. Unmold the soufflés, nap with sauce, and garnish with fresh fruit.

My own contribution is a variation on the presentation: I like to unmold the soufflés onto individual meringue shells and spoon the sauce over both. This presents a contrast in textures as well as tastes. It looks much more difficult than it is, because you can make all the parts well in advance. I served this at the end of our traditional groaning board Christmas dinner and it was perfection: stunning in presentation, light but flavorful and refreshing, and an unusual conversation piece as well.

◆ · ◆ · ◆

Yield

12 servings

Advance Preparation

The soufflés can be prepared in advance and frozen up to two weeks. Don't thaw before baking.

Special Equipment

Twelve ½-cup ovenproof ramekins or custard cups, baking pan(s) large enough to hold the ramekins for a water bath

Temperature and Time

350°F for about 15 minutes

Soufflé

Butter-flavor no stick cooking spray

4 medium ripe mangoes, peeled, pitted, and diced (2 cups)

1½ cups peeled, cored, and diced ripe pineapple

1¼ cups peeled and finely diced passion fruit or ripe cantaloupe

1 teaspoon fresh lemon juice, divided

1½ tablespoons cornstarch

2 tablespoons cold fruit juice or water

4 large egg whites, at room temperature

⅓ cup plus 3 tablespoons granulated sugar, divided

½ teaspoon lemon or orange extract *or* ¼ teaspoon pineapple extract, or to taste (optional)

Twelve 4-inch-diameter baked meringue nests made from double recipe Meringue Shells (page 284), optional

1 kiwi, peeled and diced

½ cup finely diced fresh ripe pineapple and/or cantaloupe

Nutritional Analysis per serving (without optional meringue shell)

127 calories

2 g protein

1 g fat

0 g satfat

31 g carbohydrate

26 mg sodium

0 mg cholesterol

1. Generously coat the ramekins or custard cups with cooking spray. (Do not sugar.)

2. Combine the mangoes, pineapple, and passion fruit or cantaloupe in a food processor or blender, and purée until nearly smooth. (You should have about 4 cups purée.)

3. Place 2½ cups of the purée in a large nonreactive pan. (Cover and reserve the remaining purée for the sauce.) Bring the purée to a simmer over medium heat, and cook, stirring on and off, for about 5 minutes to reduce slightly.

4. Stir ½ teaspoon of the lemon juice into the purée. Dissolve the cornstarch in the cold fruit juice or water, add to the purée, and bring to a boil. Boil for 2 minutes, stirring constantly. Remove from the heat.

5. Transfer 1½ cups of the purée to a bowl, leaving the remaining purée in the pan. Set it aside.

Let the purée in the bowl cool. To speed this process, place the bowl of purée in a larger bowl of ice water and stir until the purée is cool to the touch.

6. In a grease-free bowl, using an electric mixer on medium speed, whip the egg whites until foamy. Gradually add ⅓ cup of the sugar, and whip until the whites are stiff but not dry. In several additions, fold

(continued)

Baked Soufflés

in the cooled 1½ cups fruit purée. Divide the batter among the pre-pared ramekins, filling them about three quarters full. Cover the ramekins with plastic wrap, place them on a sturdy tray or in a box, and freeze for up to 2 weeks. (To bake without freezing, see the variation below.)

7. To complete the sauce, add the reserved 1¾ cups fruit purée to the thickened purée in the saucepan. Stir in the remaining 3 table-spoons sugar and ½ teaspoon lemon juice. Set over medium heat and stir for 3 or 4 minutes until the sugar is dissolved. If you have not used passion fruit (which has a strong, distinctive flavor) stir in the optional extract. Transfer the sauce to a bowl, cover, and refrigerate for up to 1 week or freeze for up to 2 weeks. Thaw overnight in the refrigerator before serving.

8. Preheat the oven to 350°F. About 30 minutes before you plan to serve the soufflés, remove from the freezer, and unwrap them.

9. Place the frozen soufflés in a baking pan, and add warm water to come halfway up the sides of the ramekins. Bake for 15 to 17 minutes, until the soufflés are puffed up slightly above the rim of the ramekins and look dry on top.

10. Remove the baking pan from the oven. One by one, lift each ramekin from the pan and wipe off the bottom with a towel. Run the tip of a paring knife around the edge of each soufflé to loosen it, then top it with a meringue shell, if used, or a plate, and invert. Give a sharp shake to the mold, then lift it off, leaving the soufflé upside down. If a soufflé doesn't come out easily, run the tip of a longer knife between the side of the mold and the soufflé, and invert again.

11. Spoon about 2 tablespoons of the sauce around each soufflé and sprinkle on some diced fruits. Serve at once while the soufflés are still warm.

Baked Fruit Soufflé

This is a classic hot soufflé that must be served as soon as it is baked. You can prepare the purée up to 2 days in advance, cover, and refrigerate, but bring it to room temperature (70°F) before adding it to the meringue. Whip the meringue no more than 30 minutes before you are ready to serve the soufflé.

Prepare the recipe as directed, but preheat the oven to 350°F before you prepare the meringue in Step 6, and sprinkle sugar inside the greased molds.

Set the filled molds in a hot water bath as above, and bake for 15 to 20 minutes, until the soufflés are golden on top and risen about ½ inch above the rim of the ramekins. Sift a tiny bit of confectioners' sugar over the tops, and serve at once, without unmolding. Pass the fruit sauce in a pitcher.

Light Touch: This is the ultimate in light, chic desserts: It has all the class you could wish for but only 3 percent calories from fat. If you add the meringue nests, you drop to 2 percent total calories from fat—but add 60 calories per serving.

Fruit
Desserts

M any of the desserts found throughout this book contain fruit. However, desserts in which the fruit itself is the primary focus, or in which fruit determines the essential nature of the dessert, deserve a category of their own. The range of desserts within this section is extremely broad, from incredibly easy Pineapple Buttermilk Sherbet to Iced Oranges Filled with Orange Sherbet to Apple Snow. There are fruit-filled crêpes and strudels (both large and mini-versions), Baked Peaches in Phyllo Cups, and a unique Plum Soup. The selection is rounded off with two simple compotes, one of fresh fruit, the other a combination of fresh and stewed dried fruit.

Pineapple Buttermilk Sherbet

❖ ❖ ❖

Here is one of those recipes you share only with your closest friends... it is too simple and too delicious to be true. Rich and creamy, punctuated by chunky bits of sweet-tart fruit, a sublime refresher on a hot summer afternoon, this is nothing more than a frozen blend of buttermilk and crushed canned pineapple sweetened with a little sugar. Freeze it in a bowl and mix it with a fork; no special equipment needed. For an elegant summer party dessert, scoop the sherbet into delicate cup-shaped cookies such as Tulip Cookies (page 318) or Brandy Snap tulip cups (page 320) and top it with Pineapple Sauce (page 419).

This is my adaptation of a recipe I found years ago in Elsie Masterton's wonderful Blueberry Hill Menu Cookbook.

❖ ❖ ❖

2 cups nonfat buttermilk
1 20-ounce can crushed unsweetened pineapple
¾ cup superfine or granulated sugar

1. In a bowl, stir together all the ingredients until the sugar is completely dissolved. (Superfine sugar dissolves more quickly than granulated.)

2. Transfer mixture to a freezer container, and set it in the freezer for about 30 to 45 minutes (timing varies with freezers), or until the mixture has begun to harden. Stir it well with a fork until it becomes slushy, recover and return to the freezer for about 2 hours, at which point it should be hardened enough to serve. The sherbet can be left in the freezer for up to 1 week, but it will freeze much harder. If it has frozen very hard, remove it from the freezer about 30 minutes before serving to soften slightly.

Light Touch: This is really something for nothing: high flavor, rich, creamy texture, lots of fruit (which contributes 1 gram of dietary fiber per serving), and a nearly invisible 2 percent calories from fat.

Yield

1 quart; 8 servings

Advance Preparation

Sherbet needs about 2 to 3 hours to freeze, or it can be made up to a week in advance and kept frozen. Remove from the freezer about 30 minutes before serving, so it is not too hard.

Special Equipment

Sturdy 1½-quart bowl or freezer container or 2 large ice cube trays without dividers

Nutritional Analysis per serving

120 calories
2 g protein
0.3 g fat
0 g satfat
28 g carbohydrate
64 mg sodium
0 mg cholesterol

Iced Oranges Filled
with Orange Sherbet

❖ ◆ ❖ ◆ ❖

*T*his is a dessert I remember with pleasure from childhood summers, when we hollowed out lemons as well as oranges, filled them with store-bought sherbet, and then served them frozen hard with jaunty caps of the fruit peel on top.

The presentation is still a refreshing idea on a hot summer evening. A decided improvement on nostalgia, this version is a rich, buttermilk-orange confection quickly and simply made at home, without any special equipment. If you find exotic red-gold blood oranges, use the shells for a dramatic presentation, but blend their pulp with some from regular juice oranges, or add more sugar, as they can be tart.

If you prefer, serve the sherbet by itself in crystal goblets or scoop it into Tulip Cookies (page 318), and top it with Apricot-Orange Sauce (page 413). Let the children help with this one. There is no cooking required.

❖ ◆ ❖ ◆ ❖

Yield

1 quart; 10 servings

Advance Preparation

Sherbet must chill for 2 to 3 hours to reach the proper texture to fill the oranges; the filled fruit needs a minimum of 3 hours to freeze hard. This dessert is best made a day in advance, and it can be made up to a week ahead, wrapped airtight, and kept frozen.

Special Equipment

2-quart metal bowl or 9 × 5 × 3-inch metal loaf pan, grapefruit knife

11 medium juice oranges, washed and dried

2½ cups low-fat buttermilk

¾ cup frozen orange juice concentrate, undiluted

½ cup superfine or granulated sugar, or more to taste

1 tablespoon fresh lemon juice

1. Grate the zest from 1 orange. Place the zest in the metal bowl or loaf pan, then cut the orange in half and squeeze the juice into the bowl or pan. Discard the orange rind.

2. Prepare the remaining orange shells: With a sharp knife, slice off the top quarter of each orange. Set the small pieces ("hats") aside. With a grapefruit knife, remove most of the pulp from 4 of the oranges, leaving walls about ¼ inch thick. Remove the pits, and put the pulp in a food processor. Hollow out the remaining 6 oranges, but reserve the inner pulp for another purpose (or eat it). Place the hollowed-out oranges and their "hats" in a large plastic bag (don't squash them), and refrigerate until needed.

3. Pulse the pulp in the processor until finely chopped. Transfer all the juice and pulp to the metal bowl or loaf pan. Remove and discard any chunks of fruit core or unchopped pulp. Add the buttermilk, orange juice concentrate, sugar, and lemon juice. Stir well until the sugar is completely dissolved. Taste and add more sugar if needed; oranges vary in sweetness.

4. Cover with foil or plastic wrap and place in the freezer for about 2 hours, or until the sherbet has just begun to solidify. Stir it with a fork until slushy, scraping down any frozen bits from the sides. Freeze for 30 minutes longer, or until the sherbet scoops easily but is not frozen solid.

5. Set the hollowed-out oranges on a tray with sides or place them in loaf pans so the pan sides support them upright. Spoon the sherbet into the oranges, filling generously, and placing crumpled foil or wax paper around the oranges to prop them upright if necessary. If the sherbet starts to melt as you work, place the filled oranges in the freezer. Top each orange with a "hat."

6. Cover the oranges with plastic wrap and place in the freezer. Freeze until the sherbet is hard, at least 3 hours. If the sherbet freezes very hard, remove it from the freezer about 30 minutes before serving, so it can soften slightly. (In summer, serve the oranges directly from the freezer.)

Light Touch: With a rich, creamy texture but only 5 percent calories from fat, this dessert is a real crowd pleaser. The minimal amounts of fat and cholesterol come from the low-fat buttermilk; the nonfat type can be substituted, but I like the extra richness of this since there is no other fat in the dessert.

Nutritional Analysis per serving

105 calories

3 g protein

1 g fat

0.3 g satfat

24 g carbohydrate

65 mg sodium

2 mg cholesterol

Apple Snow

· ◆ · ◆ · ◆ ·

Yield

10 servings

Advance Preparation

Made with uncooked meringue, the snow will hold in the refrigerator for about 4 hours; with cooked meringue, it will hold for at least 8 hours.

*A*pple snow comes under the heading of something for nothing: It is an old-fashioned, easy-to-make dessert in which applesauce is whipped into meringue. It is related to spooms and fools, in which fruit purées are blended with whipped cream or stiffly beaten egg whites.

Apple snow is a refreshing, light, versatile sweet that can be served in plain or fancy dress. Spoon it into wine goblets or ice cream sundae dishes and top with a little Caramel Sauce (page 421), serve it over a slice of Spice Cake (page 170) napped with warm Bourbon Sauce (page 418), or mound it in crisp cookie containers such as Tulip Cookies (page 318) garnished with thin apple wedges or curls of Candied Citrus Peel (page 449).

The meringue can be either uncooked (which I find safe in my own home, but see page 22) or cooked, following the procedure for Seven-Minute Icing. The cooked meringue uses more sugar and holds its stiffness longer than the fresh; be sure to use it if you are making the dessert well in advance. The volume of the whipped apple snow will vary somewhat depending upon the exact size and temperature of your egg whites and the type of electric mixer used; heavy-duty machines with balloon whisks whip in more air than hand-held electric beaters, but either kind is fine.

· ◆ · ◆ · ◆ ·

Method I

Uncooked Meringue

> 2 large egg whites, at room temperature
>
> ⅛ teaspoon cream of tartar
>
> Pinch of salt
>
> ½ cup superfine sugar
>
> 2 cups unsweetened applesauce (not chunky)
>
> ¼ teaspoon vanilla extract
>
> ¼ teaspoon cinnamon, or to taste
>
> Pinch of ground ginger (optional)

1. In a large grease-free bowl, combine the egg whites, cream of tartar, and salt. Using an electric mixer on medium speed, whip until foamy. Gradually add the sugar, whipping until soft peaks form and the beater leaves tracks on the surface.

2. Add the applesauce ⅓ cup at a time, whipping for about 15 seconds after each addition. At first the applesauce softens the meringue, but it quickly stiffens again as the whipping continues. Increase the speed to high and whip for several minutes longer, until medium-stiff peaks form. Add the vanilla, cinnamon, and ginger, if using it, and whip just to blend.

3. Transfer the apple snow to a covered container and refrigerate until ready to serve.

Method II

Cooked Meringue

> 2 large egg whites
>
> ¾ cup superfine or granulated sugar
>
> 5 tablespoons cold water
>
> 2 teaspoons light corn syrup
>
> ¼ teaspoon cream of tartar
>
> 2 cups unsweetened applesauce (not chunky)
>
> ¼ teaspoon vanilla extract
>
> ¼ teaspoon cinnamon, or to taste
>
> Pinch of ground ginger (optional)

1. Combine egg whites, sugar, water, corn syrup, and cream of tartar in the top pan of a double boiler set over boiling water. Immediately begin beating with a hand-held electric mixer; reduce heat so water simmers gently. With the beater on medium-low speed, beat for about 3½ minutes, or until the meringue forms soft peaks. Add the applesauce gradually while continuing to beat. Increase beater speed as needed. Continue beating until all the applesauce is added and the meringue forms stiff peaks.

2. Remove the top of the double boiler from the heat. Stir in the vanilla and spices, then beat hard for 1 full minute longer, until the mixture is slightly thicker.

3. Transfer the apple snow to a covered container and refrigerate until ready to serve. This snow will hold about 8 hours before breaking down.

Light Touch: Both methods are as light as they come: zero percent calories from fat. Method II uses ¼ cup more sugar and has 30 more calories per serving.

Nutritional Analysis per serving for Method I

....

60 calories

1 g protein

0 g fat

0 g satfat

15 g carbohydrate

40 mg sodium

0 mg cholesterol

Nutritional Analysis per serving for Method II

....

91 calories

1 g protein

0 g fat

0 g satfat

23 g carbohydrate

15 mg sodium

0 cholesterol

Crêpes with Apple Snow Flambé

◆–◆–◆–

Apple Snow is simply applesauce whipped into meringue. It is an old-fashioned nineteenth-century dessert, brought up to speed for the twenty-first century by my daughter, Cassandra, who dreamed up the notion of folding it into crêpes sauced with apricot preserves and topped with flaming apple brandy. Serve this unusual, light, but satisfying finale after a hearty repast.

◆–◆–◆–

1 recipe Basic Crêpes (page 78)

½ recipe Apple Snow following either Method I or II, pages 382 and 383

Sauce

1 cup apricot preserves

Grated nutmeg

6 to 8 tablespoons Armagnac, applejack, Cognac, or other brandy

1. To assemble the crêpes, place a crêpe pale side up on a work surface. Following the diagrams on page 81, place a tablespoon or 2 of the apple snow on the crêpe. Lift up the bottom edge of the crêpe over the filling, fold over the sides, and roll up from the bottom. Set the filled crêpe seam side down in a baking dish or on a heatproof serving platter. Repeat with the remaining crêpes. Refrigerate for up to 2 hours. Reserve and refrigerate any remaining apple snow.

2. About 30 minutes before serving time, preheat the broiler for about 10 minutes and remove the crêpes from the refrigerator. Spread the apricot preserves around and between the crêpes, but don't cover them with it. Sprinkle on a little nutmeg.

3. Set the dish or platter of crêpes under the broiler for about 1 to 2 minutes, or until the tops of the crêpes are slightly browned and the preserves are nearly melted; watch closely so the crêpes don't burn.

Meanwhile heat the Armagnac or other brandy over low heat in a small pan.

4. To present the crêpes, flambé them at the table: Pour the hot spirits over the crêpes and simultaneously touch a match to the warmed liquid, so it flames as it runs over the crêpes. (If you have a highly developed sense of drama, turn out the lights before striking the match.) As soon as the flames die down, transfer the crêpes to individual dishes, scooping some of the apricot sauce over each crêpe and adding a dollop of the reserved apple snow alongside.

Light Touch: With only 5 percent calories from fat, this recipe has become a successful addition to my enlightened dessert repertoire. Guests are surprised by the combination of ingredients and give it rave reviews.

Tulip Fruit Crisps

·❖·❖·❖·

T his is a perfect quick and easy summer dessert: feather-light tulip cookie shells filled with vanilla yogurt or fromage blanc and sugared fresh fruit topped by crisp homemade granola. If you are pressed for time, or caught by surprise guests, use store-bought cookies such as amaretti or graham crackers as the base.

·❖·❖·❖·

8 Tulip Cookies (page 318)

Filling

    2 ripe peaches, peeled, stoned, and thinly sliced

    2 ripe plums (such as Santa Rosa or Emperor), pitted and thinly sliced

    1 generous cup fresh raspberries or blueberries

    2 tablespoons granulated sugar

    2 tablespoons crème de cassis (black currant liqueur) or orange-flavored liqueur

    1 cup nonfat vanilla yogurt or Fromage Blanc (page 407) or Buttermilk Fromage Blanc (page 408)

½ cup Crunchy Granola (page 72)

Yield

....

8 servings (The Tulip Cookie recipes make 10 shells, use 8.)

Advance Preparation

....

Tulips can be made a day or two in advance and kept in an airtight container; recrisp if necessary at 300°F for about 10 minutes. The granola can be made up to 2 weeks in advance.

(continued)

190 calories

4 g protein

6 g fat

1.8 g satfat

29 g carbohydrate

73 mg sodium

7 mg cholesterol

1. To peel peaches, drop them in a pot of boiling water for 2 minutes, then remove with a slotted spoon to a bowl of cold water. Drain when cool. The skins should slip off easily. Stone and slice the peaches.

In a medium bowl, toss the sliced fruit and berries lightly with the sugar and liqueur.

2. Place a tulip cookie on each of 8 serving plates. Place 2 tablespoons of the vanilla yogurt or Fromage Blanc in each cookie, and top with the fruit mixture. Sprinkle 1 tablespoon of the granola over each dessert, and serve.

Light Touch: Though it is easy to assemble, this dessert has a complex blend of delicious flavors and textures and obtains only 29 percent of its calories from fat. Some brands of low-fat vanilla yogurt are more flavorful than the nonfat version; if you prefer to use the low-fat, it will push up the total fat to 30 percent, not a serious jump.

Apple-Apricot Strudel

◆ · ◆ · ◆ ·

*T*his delicious strudel is made with store-bought phyllo pastry leaves. It is layered with far less butter than traditional strudel, but has just enough to retain the flavor. The recipe makes two strudel rolls, enough for twelve generous portions, but you can bake just one and freeze the other for another occasion; it's a two-for-one special.

The filling is especially flavorful because it combines chopped apples and apricot preserves with two types of raisins, as well as dried apricots and dried peaches or pears. The naturally concentrated sweetness of the dried fruit supplements the small amount of sugar in the recipe.

Phyllo is available in the freezer case of most supermarkets and specialty food stores. When working with phyllo pastry, be sure to keep the unused pastry leaves completely covered at all times with a sheet of plastic wrap or aluminum foil topped by a tea towel; the phyllo dries out very quickly in the air.

For this recipe, butter flavor is essential, and, real butter is supplemented by butter-flavor cooking spray; regular vegetable spray has a less rich flavor.

◆ · ◆ · ◆ ·

Butter-flavor no stick cooking spray

Filling

1 cup apricot preserves

2 tablespoons applejack or fruit juice

2 tablespoons unsalted butter

2 tablespoons canola or safflower oil

½ cup golden raisins

¾ cup seedless raisins

½ cup dried apricots, packed, cut into ¼-inch slivers

1 cup dried peaches or pears, packed, cut into ¼-inch slivers

2 Golden Delicious or other eating apples, peeled, cored, and cut into ¼-inch dice (about 2 cups)

Grated zest and juice of 1 lemon (about 2 teaspoons zest and 2½ tablespoons juice)

½ cup light brown sugar, packed

½ teaspoon cinnamon

3 tablespoons unflavored dried bread crumbs

3 tablespoons granulated sugar

8 sheets frozen phyllo dough (each about 13 × 17 inches), thawed overnight in the refrigerator

Confectioners' sugar

1. Position a rack in the center of the oven and preheat it to 425°F. Coat the baking sheet with cooking spray.

2. In a small saucepan, combine the apricot preserves with the applejack or juice, and stir over low heat until melted and spreadable. Remove from the heat and set aside.

3. In another small saucepan, melt the butter over low heat. Remove from the heat and add the oil. Set aside.

4. In a large bowl, toss together all the fruit, the lemon zest and juice, brown sugar, and cinnamon. In a cup, stir together the bread crumbs and the granulated sugar.

5. Lay the sheets of phyllo pastry flat on a tray and cover immediately with a sheet of plastic wrap or foil large enough to cover the edges of the pastry. Top with a large, slightly damp tea towel.

6. Remove 1 sheet of phyllo, recovering the rest, and place it on a work surface with a short edge toward you. Brush lightly with some

(continued)

Yield

Two 13-inch-long strudel rolls; 12 servings

Advance Preparation

Strudel is best when freshly baked, but it can be assembled early in the day and baked before serving. Fruit filling can be prepared several hours in advance and kept covered in the refrigerator. The frozen phyllo must be thawed overnight in the refrigerator. If you want to freeze one of the filled strudel rolls, leave it unbaked, place it on a stiff cardboard base, double-wrap it, and freeze. To serve, bake unthawed for about 10 to 15 minutes longer than the time specified.

Special Equipment

Baking sheet with edges (such as a jelly-roll pan), tray at least 14 × 18 inches, tea towel at least 14 × 18 inches, pastry brush

Temperature and Time

425°F for 15 minutes, then 350°F for 15 minutes

*Nutritional Analysis
per serving*
....

332 calories

3 g protein

5 g fat

1.6 g satfat

72 g carbohydrate

87 mg sodium

6 mg cholesterol

of the butter mixture, spray with the cooking spray, and sprinkle with some of the bread crumb mixture. Place a second sheet of phyllo directly over the first, brush with butter, spray with cooking spray, and sprinkle with crumbs. Add a third sheet and repeat. Top with a fourth sheet of phyllo, dab with the butter, and lightly spray. Using the back of a spoon, spread half the warmed preserves over the phyllo sheet.

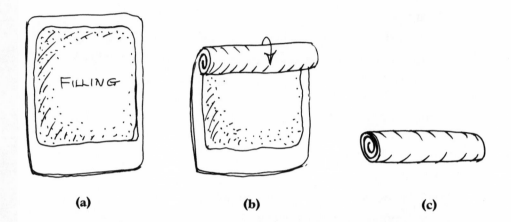

(a)　　　　　　　(b)　　　　　　　(c)

7. Spread half of the fruit mixture evenly over the preserves (see diagram (a), starting about 1 inch down from the top edge. Leave a 1-inch border along each side, and a 2-inch border across the bottom. Brush the bottom edge lightly with melted butter. Fold the top edge of the pastry over the filling and roll over twice (b), then fold in the sides and roll as compactly as possible to the bottom (c). Set the strudel roll seam side down on the prepared baking sheet. Brush with butter, and sprinkle some of the crumb-sugar mixture along the top. Repeat to make a second strudel roll, and place it on the baking sheet.

8. Bake for 15 minutes, then reduce the heat to 350°F and continue to bake for 15 minutes longer, or until golden brown and crisp. Use a long, wide spatula to slide the strudels onto a wire rack or board to cool. Just before serving, sift a little confectioners' sugar on top. Use a serrated knife to slice each strudel, straight across or on the diagonal, into 6 pieces.

Light Touch: "Delicate, divine, buttery" are the comments written in the margin of my recipe after a taste test with friends. With so much flavor, it is surprising to find it gets only 14 percent calories from fat. Compare this to a strudel using the same filling but layered with the more conventional ¾ cup melted butter: This weighs in at 32 percent calories from fat, but each serving has 90 more calories, about three times the fat (16 grams), and four times the saturated fat (8 grams).

Apple-Pear-Plum
Mini-Strudels

◆ • ◆ • ◆ •

T he beauty of these delicate individual strudels is that, while
they are best prepared fresh, they also can be made ahead for a
party and frozen. Serve the mini-strudels warm with a dollop of low-fat
vanilla yogurt alongside.

Classic strudel is prepared with butter slathered between the layers;
in this recipe, butter-flavor cooking spray is used instead either alone for
the lowest of fat content, or in combination with a small amount of
melted butter for richer flavor (see Light Touch). Before working with
phyllo, read the recipe introduction to Apple-Apricot Strudel (page 386).

◆ • ◆ • ◆ •

Butter-flavor no stick cooking spray

Filling

    1 Golden Delicious or other eating apple, peeled, cored, and
        cut into ¼-inch dice

    1 medium Bosc, Anjou, or Bartlett pear, peeled, cored, and cut
        into ¼-inch dice

    3 purple plums or 4 Italian prune plums, pitted and finely
        chopped

    3 tablespoons dried currants or seedless raisins

    2 tablespoons all-purpose flour

    3 tablespoons dark brown sugar, packed

    ½ teaspoon cinnamon

    ½ teaspoon nutmeg

    1 tablespoon fresh lemon juice

    ½ cup granulated sugar

    1 teaspoon cinnamon

    4 tablespoons unsalted butter (optional; see Light Touch)

    8 sheets frozen phyllo dough (each about 13 × 17 inches),
        thawed overnight in the refrigerator

1. Position a rack in the center of the oven and preheat it to 350°F.
Coat the baking pan with cooking spray or line it with baking parchment.

(continued)

Yield

16 mini-strudels (about
2 × 3 ¼ inches);
8 servings

Advance Preparation

Fruit filling can be
prepared a day in
advance and kept,
covered, in the
refrigerator. Filled
unbaked strudels can be
set on a stiff board,
wrapped airtight, and
frozen for up to 1
month; bake without
thawing for about 10
minutes longer than the
time specified.

Special Equipment

Baking sheet with edges
(such as a jelly-roll pan),
baking parchment
(optional), tray at least
14 × 18 inches, tea
towel at least 14 × 18
inches, pastry brush (if
using butter)

Temperature and Time

350°F for 15 to 20
minutes (about 30
minutes if frozen)

2. To prepare the filling, combine all the ingredients in a large bowl. Toss gently to coat the fruit, and set aside.

3. Stir the sugar and cinnamon together in a small bowl. Set aside. If using the butter, melt it in a small saucepan set over low heat. Remove from the heat and set aside.

4. Lay the sheets of phyllo flat on a work surface, and slice in half crosswise, making 16 sheets about 8½ × 13 inches. Cover with a sheet of plastic wrap topped by a tea towel, to prevent the phyllo from drying out.

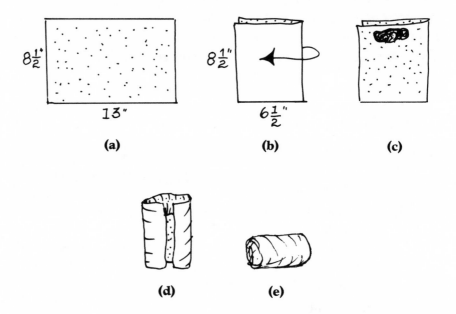

5. Remove 1 sheet of the phyllo, recovering the remaining pieces. Following the diagrams, place the phyllo on a work surface with the long edges at the top and bottom (a). Using a pastry brush, dab on a little butter. Lightly coat the phyllo with cooking spray and sprinkle with about 1 teaspoon of the cinnamon sugar. Bring the *short* edges together, folding in half to 6½ × 8½ inches (b). Fold should be at the right side. Lightly spray and sugar the surface. Place about 1½ tablespoons of the fruit filling about 1 inch below the center of the top of the phyllo (c). Fold the top over the fruit, then fold over the sides so they meet in the center (d). Dab the phyllo with butter, then spray with cooking spray and sprinkle on about ½ teaspoon cinnamon sugar. Finally, roll up the packet from top to bottom, like an egg roll (e), and place seam side down on the prepared baking sheet. Repeat to make a total of 16 strudels.

6. Brush a little butter over the top of each mini-strudel, or spray with a little cooking spray, and sprinkle with cinnamon sugar. Bake for 15 to 20 minutes, or until golden brown and crisp. Set the pan on a wire rack to cool for several minutes, then transfer the strudels to a wire rack to cool slightly. Serve warm.

Light Touch: Without butter, these pastries still have plenty of flavor and contain no cholesterol; they get only 7 percent of their total calories from fat. When 4 tablespoons melted butter is used in addition to the butter-flavor spray, the flavor is enriched and the total calories from fat rises to 26 percent, still not too high. For each mini-strudel, there is an increase of about 30 calories, 3 grams of fat, 2 grams of saturated fat, and 8 milligrams of cholesterol. These figures are modest when compared with a traditional strudel made with about ½ cup butter—weighing in at about 47 percent calories from fat.

Baked Peaches
in Phyllo Cups

◆ ·◆· ◆· ◆·

Yield

8 servings

Advance Preparation

Prepare the fruit and baked phyllo nests on the morning of the day they are to be served. The vanilla sauce should be cooled before serving; you can prepare it 1 day in advance and store it, covered, in the refrigerator.

Special Equipment

3-inch muffin cups, preferably nonstick (note that 2½-inch cups are too small), 9 × 12-inch Pyrex baking dish

Temperature and Time

350°F for about 30 minutes for peaches; 350°F for 7 to 10 minutes for phyllo cups

A baked peach sprinkled with toasted pecans and napped with vanilla custard nestles in a crisp golden nest of phyllo leaves . . . the elegant finish to a gala feast.

To give the peaches a lovely rosy glow, leave the skins on while they bake. The fruit and the phyllo nests are prepared separately in advance and combined just before serving to preserve the crispness of the pastry. For an alternative sauce, use Apricot-Orange Sauce (page 413).

In season, freestone peaches are easy to locate. They bake well and their baked skins peel off with ease. Out of season, different varieties appear, some clingstone, and often their skins are difficult to remove even after baking. I recommend baking an extra peach or two in case you have problems and prefer not to use the less lovely specimens that don't peel neatly. The alternative, out of season, is simply to use canned Elberta peach halves in light syrup, well drained.

For this recipe, butter flavor is essential. Real butter is replaced here by butter-flavor spray; regular nonstick spray has a less rich flavor. Before working with phyllo, read the recipe introduction to Apple-Apricot Strudel (page 386).

◆ ·◆· ◆· ◆·

Butter-flavor no stick cooking spray

Filling

4 ripe freestone peaches, skins left on, halved and stoned

½ cup apple or orange juice *or* dry white wine, or more if needed

¼ teaspoon cinnamon

4 sheets frozen phyllo dough (each about 13 × 17 inches), thawed overnight in the refrigerator

About 3 tablespoons granulated sugar

3 tablespoons chopped pecans, walnuts, or almonds

1 recipe Vanilla Custard Sauce (page 410)

1. Position a rack in the lower third of the oven and preheat it to 350°F. Lightly coat the muffin cups with cooking spray.

2. To prepare the peaches, set them cut side down in the baking dish. Add the juice or wine and cinnamon. Bake for about 30 minutes, until the fruit is tender when pierced with the tip of a knife. Add a little more liquid if it evaporates during baking.

3. Let the peaches cool for 5 to 10 minutes. Then slip the skins off; if they cling, use a paring knife. Let the peaches cool in the baking pan, then cover and refrigerate.

4. To make the phyllo cups, lay the sheets of phyllo flat on a work surface and cut lengthwise in half. Then cut crosswise in thirds (making 6 pieces about $5\frac{1}{2} \times 6\frac{1}{2}$ inches from each full sheet). Cover the phyllo with plastic wrap and then a tea towel to prevent drying out.

5. Place 1 of the phyllo squares in a coated muffin cup and press gently down, easing it into the cup. Spray it lightly with cooking spray and sprinkle with a pinch of sugar. Add a second phyllo square, setting it on top of the first but slightly turned so the corners do not match up. Ease this second layer down into the cup and spray and sugar it; be sure the spray reaches the edges of the phyllo. Add a third piece of phyllo, and spray and sugar it. Repeat the process to make a total of 8 cups each with 3 layers. Be sure the central cavity is large enough for a peach half; if you wish, crumple a ball of foil into the bottom to hold space as it bakes.

6. Bake for 7 to 10 minutes, or until light golden brown and crisp. Remove from the oven and cool on a wire rack. Leave the fragile phyllo cups in the muffin pans until ready to serve.

7. To toast the nuts, place them in a small frying pan set over medium heat, and shake and toss for 3 to 5 minutes, until they begin to darken in color and become aromatic. Transfer to a small bowl until ready to assemble the dessert.

8. Shortly before serving, carefully transfer each phyllo nest to an individual serving bowl or plate. Spoon a little of the custard sauce inside, and top with a peach half, cut side down. Sprinkle on the toasted nuts. Pass any remaining sauce in a pitcher at the table.

Light Touch: This dessert gets 28 percent of its calories from fat. The 2 yolks in the custard sauce are responsible for the cholesterol. I like this combination and find its richness appealing. However, you can eliminate cholesterol entirely and cut more than half the calories from fat (to 12 percent) if you serve this with Apricot Orange Sauce instead of the custard sauce.

Nutritional Analysis per serving (with Vanilla Custard Sauce and pecans)

139 calories

4 g protein

4 g fat

0.7 g satfat

22 g carbohydrate

76 mg sodium

54 mg cholesterol

Individual Meringue Shells
with Berries and Cassis

◆·◆·◆·

*C*risp meringue shells filled with ripe juicy berries and topped *with cassis sauce make a refreshing light dessert. Be creative and set the berries on scoops of nonfat frozen yogurt or on Light Lemon Curd (page 404) or Shortcut Vanilla Pastry Cream Filling (page 401); use any combination of berries and/or sliced ripe fruit in season.*

◆·◆·◆·

Sauce

   1 cup red currant jelly

   ¼ cup crème de cassis

   1½ cups nonfat vanilla frozen yogurt (optional)

Eight 3-inch Meringue Shells (page 284), baked and cooled

4 cups fresh strawberries, rinsed, dried, and hulled, or any
     combination of fresh raspberries, blueberries, and/or
     blackberries

1. To prepare the sauce, combine the jelly and the cassis in a small saucepan. Stir over low heat until the jelly melts.

2. Shortly before serving, scoop a spoonful of frozen yogurt, lemon curd, or cream filling if using, into the bottom of each meringue shell. Top with the berries and nap generously with the sauce. Serve immediately.

Light Touch: Even with the frozen yogurt, you get only 2 percent total calories from fat. Drop the yogurt, and the dessert is virtually fat-free (1 percent). This is one indulgence that practically makes you thin!

Yield

8 servings

Advance Preparation

Meringue shells can be made ahead and stored in an airtight container for up to a week.

Nutritional Analysis per serving (with optional frozen yogurt)

252 calories

3 g protein

1 g fat

0 g satfat

58 g carbohydrate

49 mg sodium

0 mg cholesterol

Plum Soup

◆ ◆ ◆

This lovely burgundy-hued soup is flavored with sherry and yogurt. I prefer to serve it warm as an unusual start to a special dinner. However, it is equally good chilled, as a dessert or appetizer. For best flavor and color, use fully ripe red plums in season; my favorite variety is Santa Rosa, but I also use Italian prune plums.

◆ ◆ ◆

22 to 24 ripe Santa Rosa plums or other plums of similar size or about 35 Italian prune plums, halved and pitted (do not peel)

¼ cup water or apple juice

2 tablespoons cornstarch

¾ cup dry sherry or dry white wine, divided

½ cup granulated sugar

½ cup low-fat plain or vanilla yogurt, plus additional yogurt for serving (optional)

Freshly grated nutmeg

1. Put the plums in a large nonreactive saucepan, add the water or juice, and bring almost to a boil. Immediately reduce the heat, and simmer for about 15 minutes, or until plums are fork-tender.

2. Transfer the plums and their liquid to a food processor or blender and purée (you may need to do this in batches in the blender); set the saucepan aside.

Purée the plums until the pieces of skin are no more than ⅛ inch across. You should have about 4 cups of purée; the amount varies depending upon the plum variety and size. Purée extra plums if necessary, to make 4 cups.

3. Return the purée to the saucepan. Stir the cornstarch into ½ cup of the dry sherry or wine until dissolved, then stir into the plum purée. Stir in the sugar and yogurt. Place over medium heat and cook, whisking on and off for 5 to 7 minutes, or until thickened and smooth. Remove from the heat and stir in the remaining ¼ cup sherry or wine. Taste and adjust flavoring; add sugar or wine if needed. Serve warm, or refrigerate and serve chilled. Top each serving with a scant teaspoon of yogurt and a pinch of grated nutmeg.

(continued)

Yield

About 5 cups; 6 to 8 servings

Advance Preparation

Soup can be prepared up to 2 days before serving and stored, covered, in the refrigerator. It can also be frozen; but it may darken in color slightly. Thaw overnight in refrigerator, then taste and correct flavor.

Nutritional Analysis per serving (based on 6 servings)

255 calories

4 g protein

2 g fat

0.5 g satfat

55 g carbohydrate

22 mg sodium

2 mg cholesterol

Light Touch: This rich-tasting and flavorful soup gets only 7 percent of its calories from fat. The high concentration of fruit adds vitamins, minerals, and a generous 6 grams of fiber per serving.

Fresh Orange-Raspberry Compote

◆·◆·◆·

*T*his blend of lightly sweetened uncooked fruit and liqueur is a refreshing, fat-free accompaniment to a slice of Orange Chiffon Cake (page 214). It can also be served on its own.

◆·◆·◆·

Yield
....
About 3 cups; 12 servings

Advance Preparation
....
Compote can be prepared ahead and refrigerated, covered, for 2 days.

Nutritional Analysis per serving
....
39 calories

0 g protein

0 g fat

0 g satfat

8 g carbohydrate

0 mg sodium

0 mg cholesterol

2 cups well-drained canned mandarin orange segments

1 cup fresh raspberries or frozen unsweetened whole raspberries, (thawed)

¼ cup orange-flavored liqueur or light rum or orange juice (fresh or from canned segments)

2 tablespoons granulated sugar

Fresh mint leaves

In a serving bowl, stir together the oranges, raspberries, liqueur or rum, and sugar. Serve immediately, or cover and refrigerate. Garnish with mint leaves before serving.

Light Touch: There is virtually no fat in this quick and easy compote.

Dried Fruit Compote

. ◆ . ◆ . ◆ .

U se any combination of fresh and dried fruits in this easy fruit compote. The flavors meld and mellow as they macerate, so put it together well in advance. Serve the compote warm or chilled—with pancakes or waffles for brunch, with a roast meat entrée, or with plain cake or cookies for a homey, comforting dessert.

. ◆ . ◆ . ◆ .

1 cup dried apricots, packed

½ cup golden or seedless raisins

½ cup dried pitted prunes (packed), cut in half

3 Bosc or Anjou pears, unpeeled, cored, and cut lengthwise into eighths

3 medium, firm apples, such as Rome or Jonathan, peeled, cored, and cut into thick chunks

2 or 3 thick lemon slices

2 tablespoons fresh lemon juice, or more to taste

1 large cinnamon stick or ¼ teaspoon ground cinnamon

⅓ cup honey or pure maple syrup *or* brown sugar, packed, or more to taste

1 cup water or apple juice

1. Combine all the ingredients in a large heavy-bottomed non-reactive pan. Add the lemon slices and juice, cinnamon stick, honey, and water. Cover the pan, set it over medium heat, and bring to a boil. Immediately lower the heat to a simmer and cook for about 15 to 20 minutes, or until the chunks of pear and apple are very tender when pierced with a sharp knife. Remove from the heat, taste, and add more sweetening or lemon juice if needed.

2. Transfer the fruit and juices to a bowl. If preparing ahead, cover and refrigerate. Serve warm or at room temperature.

Light Touch: There's scarcely any fat in this dish (2 percent calories from fat), but there are plenty of vitamins and minerals, and 6 grams of dietary fiber per serving.

Yield

About 6 cups; 6 to 8 servings

Advance Preparation

Prepare the compote a day or 2 in advance to allow the flavors to blend; store covered in the refrigerator.

Nutritional Analysis per serving (based on 6 servings)

262 calories

2 g protein

1 g fat

0.1 g satfat

68 g carbohydrate

7 mg sodium

0 mg cholesterol

Fillings, Sauces,
and
Syrups

The fillings in this chapter are to be used inside cakes and pastries. The sauces and syrups are embellishments, added on top of or alongside a variety of desserts. To get the most out of this chapter, mix and match the recipes using your own creativity.

To fill a jelly roll or roulade or line a fresh fruit tart, try Shortcut Vanilla Pastry Cream Filling, Light Lemon Curd, or Cream Cheese Filling. Fromage Blanc, made with drained, smoothly puréed cottage cheese enriched with a little whipped heavy cream, can be set with unflavored gelatine and used as a cake or tart filling; without the gelatine, it is a softer sauce, perfect for serving with ripe fruit. Buttermilk Fromage Blanc, depending on the method of preparation, can be served as a sauce or used as a substitute for cottage cheese in any recipe in this book. Ricotta Cream is a sauce with the consistency of sour cream; serve it with cake or fruit. Homemade Yogurt Cheese, a remarkable product made simply by draining plain yogurt through cheesecloth for up to twenty-four hours, has the consistency of a soft cream cheese and can be used in many recipes, from cheesecake to creamy dessert sauces.

I offer a wide variety of fruit sauces, including Raspberry, Any-Berry, Spiced Blueberry, Apricot-Orange, and Peach Daiquiri; all are excellent served over a slice of plain cake or a serving of fruit soufflé. Maple Yogurt Sauce and Yogurt Rum Sauce make creamy toppings for fruit pies or crisps, gingerbread, or spice cake. Chocolate Sauce and Vanilla Custard Sauce go with almost any dessert, while Blueberry and Orange syrups are perfect on pancakes and waffles.

Shortcut Vanilla
Pastry Cream Filling

❖ ▪ ❖ ▪ ❖

I have tried many versions of homemade reduced-fat pastry cream, and I'm not ashamed to admit that I like best the packaged mix for vanilla cooked-style "pudding and pie filling." It is sweeter than I would wish, but otherwise as good as homemade, just as low in fat, and easier to prepare—and you can add your own flavoring to disguise its origins. I'll never tell. Unlike the Vanilla Custard Sauce (page 410), this cream is thick enough to fill cream puffs or roulades. For an even thicker filling, use only 1¾ cups milk.

To make a coffee-flavored cream, dissolve one to two tablespoons instant coffee granules in the milk before adding it to the powdered mix. To make a chocolate version, whisk two tablespoons unsweetened cocoa into the dry powdered mix before adding the milk (or use packaged chocolate pudding and pie filling with 1 tablespoon cocoa).

❖ ▪ ❖ ▪ ❖

1 3¼-ounce package vanilla pudding and pie filling (cooked style)

2 cups 2% milk

2 teaspoons vanilla extract *or* 1 teaspoon almond or maple extract

1. Prepare the filling according to the directions on the package, whisking the powdered mix into the milk over medium heat and stirring continually until it comes to a full bubbling boil. Remove from the heat, stir in the extract, cover with plastic wrap placed directly on the cream (to prevent a skin from forming), and let cool. Refrigerate. The filling thickens as it cools.

Light Touch: When made with 2% milk, this pastry cream has only 15 percent calories from fat; made with whole milk, it has 24 percent calories from fat. The powdered mix contains just a trace of fat and no cholesterol.

Yield

2 cups; 16 2-tablespoon servings or 8 ¼-cup servings

Advance Preparation

The cream can prepared up to 2 days in advance, covered, and refrigerated.

Nutritional Analysis per 2-tablespoon serving

35 calories

1 g protein

1 g fat

0.3 g satfat

7 g carbohydrate

56 mg sodium

2 mg cholesterol

Nutritional Analysis per ¼-cup serving

70 calories

2 g protein

1 g fat

0.7 g satfat

13 g carbohydrate

112 mg sodium

5 mg cholesterol

Vanilla Cream

◆ · ◆ · ◆ ·

*T*his rich, thick sauce can be served over fresh fruit or used as a filling in a fruit tart or between cake layers. The consistency of the cream cheese gives it enough body to hold without running; it will thicken even more after chilling. Unlike Fromage Blanc (page 407), this cream is thick enough to be used as a cake filling without adding gelatine. To fill a sponge roll, halve the recipe, but use 1 full teaspoon vanilla (or almond or orange) extract.

◆ · ◆ · ◆ ·

Yield

2 cups; 16 servings

Advance Preparation

The cream can be prepared up to 2 days in advance, covered, and refrigerated.

Nutritional Analysis per serving

49 calories

2 g protein

3 g fat

0 g satfat

5 g carbohydrate

90 mg sodium

5 mg cholesterol

1 cup low-fat vanilla yogurt (without added gums)

1 cup (8 ounces) low-fat cream cheese, at room temperature

1 teaspoon vanilla extract

2 tablespoons granulated sugar, or to taste

1. Measure the yogurt into a strainer set over a bowl and allow to drain for about 15 minutes to remove excess liquid. Discard the liquid in the bowl.

2. Combine the drained yogurt and the remaining ingredients in a medium bowl. Using an electric mixer, whip until smooth. Refrigerate until needed.

Light Touch: "Light" Philadelphia cream cheese, with half the fat of regular cream cheese, blends beautifully with drained yogurt to make a thick, delightfully rich, slightly tangy spread. With 46 percent of its calories from fat, it appears to be wildly high in fat. However, note that the per serving figures are low and you will be combining this cream with fruit and other low-fat elements to further reduce the total fat. In any event, compare this recipe to my classic model made with 8 ounces regular cream cheese and ¼ cup heavy cream: It has 68 percent calories from fat and 13 grams fat per serving. This recipe can easily fit into a low-fat plan for healthy eating.

Ricotta Cream

◆ ◆ ◆

his is a light, creamy blend of ricotta cheese and yogurt, with the consistency of sour cream. Serve it with fresh fruit, mound it in an individual tart shell and top with fresh fruit, or serve it as a sauce with a stewed fruit compote or a plain cake along with raspberry sauce.

A blender gives a much smoother product here than a food processor.

◆ ◆ ◆

16 ounces part-skim ricotta cheese (or one 15-ounce container)

⅓ cup nonfat plain yogurt

Scant ¼ teaspoon salt

1½ teaspoons vanilla extract, or to taste

3 tablespoons granulated sugar, or to taste

Fresh lemon juice (optional)

1. In a blender, combine all the ingredients except lemon juice. Purée for 2 to 3 minutes, until absolutely smooth, without a trace of graininess. Stop once to scrape down the sides of the blender container.

2. Transfer to a bowl and refrigerate, covered, for about 12 hours, for the flavors to blend. Taste and adjust flavoring if necessary. Add a drop or two of lemon juice if the cream tastes flat.

Orange Ricotta Cream

Prepare the recipe as directed, but add 1 teaspoon grated orange zest, ½ teaspoon orange extract, and 2 tablespoons orange-flavored liqueur.

Light Touch: This recipe gets 39 percent calories from fat, but that is significantly less than for an equal quantity of whipped heavy cream (96 percent calories from fat). Note that the per serving figures are low, and, in fact, the cream will be served with other low-fat ingredients to further reduce the total fat.

Yield

About 2 cups; 8 servings

Advance Preparation

Cream can be made up to 2 days in advance; it benefits from at least 12 hours refrigeration to blend the flavors.

Nutritional Analysis per serving

98 calories

7 g protein

4 g fat

2.6 g satfat

8 g carbohydrate

140 mg sodium

17 mg cholesterol

Light Lemon Curd

◆ - ◆ - ◆

Yield

1 cup; enough to cover 1 cake layer or 1 jelly roll

Advance Preparation

Curd can be prepared in advance and refrigerated, covered, for 1 or 2 days. If it is too thick to spread after chilling, warm it for a few seconds in the microwave.

Nutritional Analysis per 1⅓ tablespoons

46 calories

0 (trace) g protein

1 g fat

0.5 g satfat

10 g carbohydrate

25 mg sodium

3 mg cholesterol

*T*his easy-to-prepare pastry filling is thickened with cornstarch and enriched with a little heavy cream—instead of the traditional complement of five yolks and half a cup of butter. It has a fine tart flavor but, without the yolks, lacks the deep yellow color of the classic. The trick is to color it with a tablespoon of frozen orange juice concentrate; if you don't have any, you can use orange juice or water and the curd will be cream color instead of yellow.

◆ - ◆ - ◆

½ cup granulated sugar

1½ tablespoons cornstarch

1 teaspoon all-purpose flour

Pinch of salt

½ cup hot water

1 tablespoon frozen orange juice concentrate *or* 1 tablespoon orange juice or water

1 teaspoon grated lemon zest

4 tablespoons fresh lemon juice

2 tablespoons heavy cream

1. In a medium heavy-bottomed nonreactive saucepan, whisk together the sugar, cornstarch, flour, and salt.

2. In a small bowl, whisk together the hot water and frozen orange juice concentrate, or juice or water, the lemon zest, and lemon juice. Whisk the liquid into the dry ingredients. Place the pan over medium heat and whisk until the mixture comes to a boil. Boil, whisking constantly, for 1 minute, or until thickened and clear. Remove from the heat.

3. Whisk in the cream. Set the curd aside until cool, then refrigerate. The curd thickens as it cools.

Light Touch: My old-fashioned yolk- and butter-rich lemon curd recipe gets an apparently acceptable 30 percent of its calories from fat, but each serving has 23 grams of fat, 13 of them saturated. To remove about half the fat, and nearly all the saturated fat, I dropped the yolks and butter. Even though I added 2 tablespoons of heavy cream for richness, the count is now only 17 percent calories from fat. To shave this to 10 percent calories from fat, drop 1 tablespoon of the cream.

Yogurt Cheese

❖ ❖ ❖

When plain yogurt is drained of all excess liquid (whey), it becomes a low-fat, low-calorie, low-cholesterol cheese, known in the Middle East as labna and in India as dehin. In texture and taste, it resembles the soft French cheese Boursin; it is delicious on its own, or blended with herbs or pepper or spices for a cracker spread. In cheesecakes as well as many other baked goods, yogurt cheese can be used as a substitute for cream cheese or even sour cream.

Different brands of yogurt contain different additives. To make yogurt cheese, select a yogurt that does not contain modified food starch, vegetable food gums, or gelatine, all of which inhibit the draining of the whey, which contains lots of calcium plus other valuable vitamins and minerals and may be saved for use in muffins and breads or soups and gravies.

Yogurts also differ in the amount of liquid they contain. Therefore, it is impossible to be absolutely specific about the proportion of yogurt that will remain after draining. As a general rule, plan on ending up with slightly over one third of the original volume. (In other words, start with 3 cups of yogurt to make a little more than 1 cup yogurt cheese; 6 cups yogurt to yield 2¼ cups cheese.)

The yogurt needs to drain for about twenty-four hours, or at least overnight, to turn into cheese. Plan ahead.

❖ ❖ ❖

3 cups nonfat plain yogurt

Here are two different easy methods to drain the yogurt:

1. Set a colander or strainer over a deep bowl, and line it with a triple thickness of cheesecloth. Add the yogurt, cover with plastic wrap, then refrigerate and let drain for 24 hours.

2. Cut or fold a triple thickness of cheesecloth into a 14-inch square. Spoon the yogurt into the center of the cheesecloth, gather up the edges, and tie them together with a rubber band. Insert a chopstick through the knot and balance the chopstick over the edges of a deep bowl, so the cheesecloth bag hangs suspended inside. Refrigerate for 24 hours to drain.

(continued)

Yield

1 ¼ cups yogurt cheese; 10 servings

Advance Preparation

Yogurt cheese takes about 24 hours to drain. It keeps, refrigerated, for up to 1 week.

Special Equipment

Cheesecloth, colander, deep bowl

Nutritional Analysis per serving

38 calories

4 g protein

0 g (trace) fat

0 g satfat

5 g carbohydrate

52 mg sodium

1 mg cholesterol

3. Whatever the method, drain the yogurt until it stops dripping completely. Squeeze the cheesecloth gently to extract any remaining drops of whey. Turn the cheese into a clean container, cover, and refrigerate.

Light Touch: This versatile cheese gets just under 3 percent of its calories from fat.

Cream Cheese Filling

◆ ◆ ◆

T his orange- or lemon-flavored cream cheese mixture can be spread in a pie shell and topped with fresh fruit, or mounded in baked peach or pear halves. The quantity is just enough to cover a 9-inch-diameter surface. To extend the recipe, beat in some apricot preserves or marmalade.

◆ ◆ ◆

Yield
....
Generous ½ cup

Advance Preparation
....
Filling can be made a day in advance, covered, and refrigerated.

Nutritional Analysis per scant 1 tablespoon
....
36 calories
2 g protein
2 g fat
0 g satfat
3 g carbohydrate
80 mg sodium
5 mg cholesterol

5 ounces low-fat cream cheese

½ teaspoon orange or lemon extract

1 teaspoon frozen orange juice concentrate or lemonade concentrate

1 tablespoon grated orange zest or 2 teaspoons grated lemon zest

1 tablespoon granulated sugar

In a bowl or blender, beat or blend all the ingredients together until smooth. Refrigerate until ready to use.

Light Touch: Although this recipe gets 57 percent total calories from fat, the per serving figures are low. The cream will be combined with other low-fat ingredients to further reduce total fat. The fat content is significantly less than a traditional recipe made with 5 ounces full-fat cream cheese—88 percent calories from fat. This recipe can easily fit into a low-fat plan for healthy eating.

Fromage Blanc

❖ ❖ ❖

T his thick, creamy sauce is delightful over tangy fresh
raspberries, just-picked strawberries, or sliced ripe peaches. Add
the gelatin only when you want to use this as a filling for a roulade or
between layers of a cake, in which case double the recipe; it will set just
enough to slice neatly without being rubbery.

For a description of true "fromage blanc" in France, see page 408.

❖ ❖ ❖

1 cup (8 ounces) 1% cottage cheese

⅓ cup sifted confectioners' sugar

2 teaspoons vanilla extract

¼ cup heavy cream, chilled

Cake filling

¾ teaspoon Knox unflavored gelatine

1 tablespoon cold water

1. To remove excess liquid from the cottage cheese, place it in a
strainer set over a bowl. Cover the cheese with a layer of plastic wrap,
and press down on it for a minute or 2, forcing out as much whey as
possible.

2. Transfer the drained curds to a food processor or blender and
add the sugar and vanilla. Purée until absolutely smooth; it may take
3 minutes or more for any trace of graininess to disappear.

3. In a small chilled bowl, whip the cream until medium-soft
peaks form. Fold the cheese mixture into the whipped cream.

4. If the fromage blanc is to be used as a sauce, cover and refrigerate until needed.

5. If the fromage blanc is to be used as a cake filling, add the
gelatine: Sprinkle the gelatine over 2 tablespoons cold water in a small
pan. Allow to sit for 3 minutes to soften, then stir over low heat just
until the gelatine is completely dissolved; do not boil. Cool the gelatine
to lukewarm, then gently but very thoroughly, without losing volume,
whisk the gelatine into the cheese mixture. Chill until thickened enough
to spread. Then refrigerate the filled cake for at least 2 to 3 hours to
completely set the fromage blanc.

(continued)

Light Touch: A classic version of this recipe blends 1 cup regular cream cheese with the whipped heavy cream; it obtains 68 percent of its calories from fat, and 1 serving has 13 grams of fat, 8 of them saturated. Replacing the cream cheese with low-fat cottage cheese but retaining the heavy cream for its good flavor, we cut 40 percent of the total calories from fat and three quarters of the fat and saturated fat per serving.

Although the per serving figures are low, this recipe still obtains 41 percent calories from fat because of the heavy cream. However, this sauce is meant to be eaten with fruit and other low-fat ingredients, to further diminish the total percentage of calories from fat.

Buttermilk
Fromage Blanc

◆ · ◆ · ◆ ·

A few years ago, I had the pleasure of traveling with my husband and daughter to Lyon, France, to cook with Jeannette Pépin, mother of chef Jacques Pépin. One extraordinary day, we joined Jeannette and her niece, Christiane, at work in the kitchen of Le Relais Bressans, a restaurant the family ran at that time in the village of Port, high in the Jura Mountains. In the middle of a frantically busy afternoon prepping and cooking for an evening banquet, we took an hour off and climbed the hill to the village laiterie to pick up a bucket of fromage blanc freshly made from the milk of the local herd. That night, the sweet yet subtly tangy soft curds were served with a mélange of cut-up fruit for dessert: perfection in its simplicity.

This delightfully mild, faintly acidic, soft cheese resembles a soft small-curd cottage cheese. The process at home is quick, easy, and foolproof. Simply warm buttermilk until the curds and whey begin to separate, then strain the mixture through cheesecloth. You can stop the process at whatever stage you prefer—leave a little whey in for a creamy texture, or drain completely for a drier cheese. Use the fromage blanc as a spread (French homemakers often add chopped fresh chives and tarragon and serve the mixture on crusty bread) or as a dessert sauce over berries or sliced fruit. Serve the curds plain, or stir in some honey or *a little sugar, plus a drop or two of vanilla or orange extract. To make a delicious fruit pie or tart, spread slightly sweetened fromage blanc in a baked pastry shell and top with glazed fruit.*

You can use either regular cultured buttermilk (1% butterfat) or nonfat buttermilk to make this fromage blanc. Both recipes are low in fat, but the latter more so. An instant-read thermometer facilitates the process but is not essential.

· ◆ · ◆ · ◆ ·

1 quart 1% or nonfat cultured buttermilk

1. Line a strainer with a triple thickness of cheesecloth, and place over a deep bowl.

2. Pour the buttermilk into a heavy-bottomed nonreactive saucepan and heat over medium-low heat for about 5 minutes, until you begin to see a clear liquid separating out at the edges of the milk, and an instant-read thermometer registers 95°F. Reduce the heat slightly and heat for about 2 minutes longer, until the milk separates a little more and the thermometer reaches about 100°F (no more than 110°F).

3. Remove from the heat and let stand, without stirring, for about 3 minutes. If you gently shake the pan, you should see softly lumpy curds beginning to form in the center with whey (the clear liquid) around the edges.

4. Pour the contents of the pan into the cheesecloth-lined strainer. Cover with plastic wrap and set aside at cool room temperature, or refrigerate. Allow to drain until the fromage blanc reaches the desired consistency, about 2 to 3 hours.

Light Touch: Made with 1% cultured buttermilk, fromage blanc obtains 20 percent of its calories from fat. It boasts a minimal amount of saturated fat and a healthy 285 milligrams calcium. Substituting nonfat buttermilk cuts the calories from fat to 11 percent and drops 9 calories and 1 gram of fat per serving.

Yield

About 1 cup; 4 servings

Advance Preparation

The draining of the whey takes some time: 2 cups of buttermilk drains completely in about 1 hour; 1 quart takes 2 hours to reach a creamy stage, 3 hours to drain completely. Fromage blanc will stay fresh for a few days, covered in the refrigerator.

Special Equipment

instant-read thermometer (optional), cheesecloth

Nutritional Analysis per serving (1% cultured buttermilk)

99 calories

8 g protein

2 g fat

1.3 g satfat

12 g carbohydrate

257 mg sodium

9 mg cholesterol

Vanilla Custard Sauce

◆·◆·◆·

I developed this recipe in conjunction with Eating Well *magazine*, *when we decided an intensely chocolate soufflé needed a creamy vanilla sauce as a background. Although it includes a small amount of cornstarch, it is a light custard sauce, not to be confused with* crème pâtissière, *a thicker filling. Serve this sauce alongside any chocolate dessert or pour it over fresh fruit or berries.*

◆·◆·◆·

Yield

About 1¼ cups; 8 servings

Advance Preparation

Sauce can be made a day in advance, covered, and refrigerated.

Nutritional Analysis per serving

44 calories

2 g protein

1 g fat

0.4 g satfat

5 g carbohydrate

26 mg sodium

54 mg cholesterol

1 cup plus 1 tablespoon skim milk, divided

1 large egg plus 1 large egg yolk

2 tablespoons granulated sugar

1½ teaspoons cornstarch

1½ teaspoons vanilla extract

1. In a medium saucepan, whisk together 1 cup of the milk, the egg and egg yolk, and the sugar. Dissolve the cornstarch in the remaining 1 tablespoon milk, then whisk it in.

2. Set the saucepan over medium heat and cook, stirring on and off with a wooden spoon, for 4 to 5 minutes. Then cook, whisking constantly, for 2 minutes, or until the custard is thick enough to coat the spoon. (Turn the spoon over and draw a line down the back; if the line does not close up, the custard is done.) Do not allow the custard to come to a boil, or it may curdle. Remove from the heat and stir in the vanilla, then strain into a bowl. Let cool. Refrigerate until needed.

Light Touch: This recipe gets 27 percent of its calories from fat while most traditional custard sauces, made with several yolks, heavy cream, and butter, are at least half fat. There is some fat and cholesterol in this recipe because of the 2 egg yolks, but the servings are small, and the dessert the sauce is served with should also be low in fat. The addition of a little cornstarch stabilizes the custard and ensures reliability; nevertheless, do not let the custard boil, or it may curdle.

Chocolate Sauce

◆ · ◆ · ◆ ·

This rich, gooey chocolate sauce is best when made with Dutch-processed cocoa. You can vary the flavor by adding 2 tablespoons of coffee liqueur, orange liqueur, or raspberry brandy. I adapted this recipe from one I prepared for Eating Well magazine to accompany Raspberry Soufflé (page 358).

◆ · ◆ · ◆ ·

⅓ cup unsweetened Dutch-processed cocoa

1 tablespoon cornstarch

¼ cup plus 2 tablespoons dark brown sugar, packed

⅓ cup skim milk

¼ cup dark or light corn syrup

1 teaspoon vanilla extract or 2 tablespoons coffee- or orange-flavored liqueur

1. In a small saucepan, whisk together the cocoa, cornstarch, and brown sugar. Add the milk and whisk well, then add the corn syrup.

2. Set the pan over medium heat and stir while bringing to a full boil. Lower the heat slightly and cook, whisking constantly, about 1 minute longer, until the sauce has thickened and will generously coat a spoon. Remove from the heat and stir in the vanilla or other flavoring if using it. Cool, then refrigerate in a covered jar.

Light Touch: This rich chocolaty sauce gets only 7 percent of its calories from fat. It lacks butter or oil, and the corn syrup keeps it viscous, so it does not harden when chilled.

Yield

¾ cup; 6 servings

Advance Preparation

Sauce can be made in advance and refrigerated in a covered jar. It keeps well for about 1 week.

Nutritional Analysis per serving

115 calories

1 g protein

1 g fat

0.5 g satfat

28 g carbohydrate

55 mg sodium

0 mg cholesterol

Raspberry Sauce

·◆·◆·◆·

Make this sauce with fresh or frozen berries and serve it with Raspberry Soufflé (page 358) or any sponge roulade or chiffon cake.

Although the recipe uses three cups of berries, nearly half a cup in volume is lost when all the seeds are strained out; this procedure is optional. I usually strain out about half the seeds.

·◆·◆·◆·

Yield
....
1⅛ cups if completely strained, 1½ cups with some seeds; 8 servings

Advance Preparation
....
Sauce can be prepared in advance and kept covered in the refrigerator for 2 or 3 days.

Nutritional Analysis
per serving
....
59 calories
0.4 (trace) g protein
0.3 (trace) g fat
0 g satfat
13 g carbohydrate
0 mg sodium
0 mg cholesterol

3 cups fresh raspberries or 1 12-ounce bag frozen unsweetened whole raspberries

3 tablespoons granulated sugar, or to taste

3 tablespoons water

1 scant tablespoon cornstarch

3 tablespoons Chambord, Framboise, or crème de cassis (optional)

1. In a small heavy-bottomed nonreactive saucepan, combine the raspberries, sugar, and 2 tablespoons of the water. Set over medium-high heat and cook, stirring and mashing the berries with the back of a large spoon, for 2 or 3 minutes to release berry juice and dissolve the sugar.

2. To remove the seeds, transfer the mixture to a strainer set over a small bowl. Stir and press on the berries with a spoon, then scrape any purée on the underside of the strainer into the bowl. Return the purée to the saucepan.

3. In a cup, dissolve the cornstarch in the remaining 1 tablespoon water. Add it to the raspberry purée. Set the pan over high heat, bring to a boil, and cook, stirring constantly, for 45 to 60 seconds, until the mixture thickens, and is no longer cloudy. Remove from the heat.

4. Stir in the liqueur if using it. Taste and add sugar if necessary. Let cool. Serve at room temperature or chilled.

Light Touch: Although luxurious in taste, this sauce gets only 4 percent of its calories from fat.

Apricot-Orange Sauce

· ◆ · ◆ · ◆ ·

U se the best-quality preserves you can find for this fat-free sauce. Serve it warm for maximum flavor, over Orange Soufflé (page 366) or a plain sponge or chiffon cake.

◆ · ◆ · ◆ ·

½ cup apricot preserves

¼ cup fresh orange juice

3 to 4 tablespoons orange-flavored liqueur (such as Grand Marnier) (optional)

1. In a small saucepan, combine the apricot preserves and orange juice. Stir over medium heat until smooth.

2. Remove from the heat and stir in the liqueur if using. Serve warm, or let cool and refrigerate.

Light Touch: Fat- and cholesterol-free, this sauce has zero percent calories from fat.

Yield

1 cup; 6 to 8 servings

Advance Preparation

Sauce can be made in advance and kept covered in the refrigerator for 2 or 3 days. Warm before serving.

Nutritional Analysis per 6 servings

97 calories

0 g protein

0 g fat

0 g satfat

22 g carbohydrate

3 mg sodium

0 mg cholesterol

Any-Berry Sauce

· ◆ · ◆ · ◆ ·

Make this sauce with any type of berries and serve it warm over pancakes and waffles, or sponge or chiffon cake.

· ◆ · ◆ · ◆ ·

Yield

1⅓ cups; 10 servings

Advance Preparation

Sauce can be prepared a day or two in advance and kept covered in the refrigerator.

Nutritional Analysis per serving (includes optional liqueur)

51 calories

0.2 (trace) g protein

0.1 g fat

0.1 (trace) g satfat

12 g carbohydrate

2 mg sodium

0 mg cholesterol

2 cups fresh berries, rinsed, hulled, and sliced (if strawberries), or frozen whole unsweetened berries

⅓ to ½ cup granulated sugar, to taste (depending upon sweetness of the berries)

1½ to 2 tablespoons fresh lemon juice, to taste

Grated zest of ½ lemon or orange (about ½ to 2 teaspoons)

½ cup plus 2 tablespoons water, divided

1 teaspoon cornstarch

3 tablespoons fruit-flavored liqueur, such as Chambord, Grand Marnier, or crème de cassis (optional)

1. In a medium heavy-bottomed nonreactive saucepan, combine the berries, ⅓ cup sugar, 1½ tablespoons lemon juice, lemon or orange zest, and ½ cup water. Set over medium-high heat and cook, stirring and mashing the berries with the back of a large spoon for 2 to 3 minutes to release the berry juice and dissolve the sugar.

2. In a cup, dissolve the cornstarch in the remaining 2 tablespoons water. Stir it into the berry purée. Set the pan over high heat, bring to a boil, and cook, stirring constantly, for 45 to 60 seconds, until the mixture thickens and is no longer cloudy. Remove from the heat.

3. Stir in the liqueur if using it. Taste and add more sugar and/or lemon juice if necessary. Let cool. Serve at room temperature or chilled.

Light Touch: This sauce contains no cholesterol and gets only 2 percent calories from fat.

Spiced
Blueberry Sauce

◆ ◆ ◆

*T*his lightly spiced berry sauce is best served warm. The rich taste is at home almost anywhere: over pancakes, alongside Orange or Lemon Soufflé (pages 366 and 368), or atop a Lemon Roulade and Fresh Berries with Lemon Curd (page 189).

◆ ◆ ◆

2 cups fresh blueberries, picked over, rinsed, and dried, or frozen unsweetened whole blueberries

¼ cup dark brown sugar, packed, or to taste

½ teaspoon cinnamon

½ teaspoon nutmeg

Pinch of ground ginger

Pinch of ground cloves

2 tablespoons fresh lemon juice

¼ cup water or orange juice, divided

1 tablespoon cornstarch

1. In a heavy-bottomed saucepan, combine the berries, brown sugar, spices, lemon juice, and 2 tablespoons of the water or juice. Set over medium-high heat and cook, stirring and mashing the berries with the back of a large spoon, for 2 to 3 minutes, until the berries release their juice and the sugar is dissolved.

2. In a cup, dissolve the cornstarch in the remaining 2 tablespoons juice or water, and stir it into the blueberry mixture. Raise the heat slightly and bring to a boil. Boil, stirring constantly, for 45 to 60 seconds, or until the sauce is thickened and no longer cloudy. Taste, and add sugar if needed. Serve warm.

Light Touch: This sauce tastes luxurious, yet gets only 4 percent calories from fat and has no cholesterol.

Yield

1⅓ cups; 10 servings

Advance Preparation

Sauce can be prepared in advance and kept covered in the refrigerator for 2 or 3 days. Warm before serving.

Nutritional Analysis per serving

39 calories

0.2 (trace) g protein

0.15 g fat

0 g satfat

10 g carbohydrate

4 mg sodium

0 mg cholesterol

Maple Yogurt Sauce

◆ · ◆ · ◆

Blend maple syrup with vanilla yogurt to make a quick, delicious sauce for a fruit pie or fruit crisp. I prefer to use low-fat yogurt in this recipe because it has a more mellow flavor than the nonfat version.

◆ · ◆ · ◆

Yield
....
1 cup; 8 servings

Advance Preparation
....
Sauce can be made a day or two in advance and refrigerated, covered.

Nutritional Analysis
per serving
....
53 calories
2 g protein
0.3 (trace) g fat
0 g satfat
12 g carbohydrate
31 mg sodium
0 mg cholesterol

1 cup low-fat vanilla yogurt
¼ cup pure maple syrup
¼ teaspoon maple extract

In a medium bowl, beat all the ingredients together well. Serve, or cover and refrigerate. Bring to room temperature before serving.

Light Touch: Even made with low-fat yogurt instead of nonfat, this recipe gets just 4 percent calories from fat and has no cholesterol.

Yogurt Rum Sauce

◆·◆·◆

This simple blend of vanilla yogurt, rum, and sugar makes a perfect sauce to accompany gingerbread, spice cake, fruit pie, or cobbler.

◆·◆·◆

1 cup low-fat vanilla yogurt
1 to 2 tablespoons dark rum, to taste
2 teaspoons granulated sugar or light brown sugar, packed

In a medium bowl beat all the ingredients together well. Serve, or cover and refrigerate. Bring to room temperature before serving.

Light Touch: This sauce gets 6 percent of its calories from fat because it is made with low-fat yogurt. I prefer to use it, because it has a more mellow flavor than nonfat vanilla yogurt. The latter can, however, be substituted if you want to drop virtually all the fat.

Yield

1 cup; 8 servings

Advance Preparation

Sauce can be made a day or two in advance and refrigerated, covered.

Nutritional Analysis per serving

37 calories

2 g protein

0.2 (trace) g fat

0 g satfat

5 g carbohydrate

21 mg sodium

0 mg cholesterol

Bourbon Sauce

◆ ・ ◆ ・ ◆ ・

Yield

1⅓ cups; 10 servings

Advance Preparation

Sauce can be made in advance and kept covered in the refrigerator for up to 2 days. Serve slightly warm.

Nutritional Analysis per serving

55 calories

0 g protein

1 g fat

0.5 g satfat

9 g carbohydrate

3 mg sodium

2 mg cholesterol

This spirited sauce is perfect to serve warm with Old-Fashioned Bread Pudding (page 266) or Steamed Apricot-Apple Pudding (page 264), and it is guaranteed to put some life into a slice of plain sponge cake as well.

◆ ・ ◆ ・ ◆ ・

1 cup apple cider or apple juice, divided

¼ cup dark brown sugar, packed

1 teaspoon lightly salted butter or margarine

⅛ teaspoon freshly grated nutmeg

1 tablespoon cornstarch

¼ cup bourbon, applejack, or Calvados

1. In a small saucepan, combine ¾ cup of the cider or juice, the brown sugar, butter or margarine, and nutmeg. Stir over medium heat until the sugar dissolves.

2. In a small cup, dissolve the cornstarch in the remaining ¼ cup cider or juice, and add it to the hot cider mixture. Increase the heat to medium high, bring to a boil, and boil, stirring, for about 45 to 60 seconds, until thickened and no longer cloudy. Remove from the heat and stir in the bourbon. Serve warm.

Light Touch: The touch of butter added to this sauce pushes the calories from fat to 14 percent. It also adds just a touch of cholesterol; the fat content is nearly the same with margarine, but butter adds 0.4 gram more saturated fat per serving. Nevertheless, the butter adds significant smoothness and flavor, and I prefer it.

Pineapple Sauce

❖ · ❖ · ❖ ·

W arm this delightful fruity sauce and pour it over a serving of
Pineapple Soufflé (page 370), Pineapple Buttermilk Sherbet
(page 379), or Pineapple Chiffon Cake (page 212).

· ❖ · ❖ · ❖ ·

½ cup well-drained canned sweetened crushed pineapple
(reserve ¾ cup juice)
1 tablespoon cornstarch
1 tablespoon fresh lemon juice
2 tablespoons granulated sugar, or to taste

1. Measure 3 tablespoons of the pineapple juice into a small
saucepan. Stir in the cornstarch, mixing until it is dissolved. Add the
remaining juice and all the other ingredients.

2. Cook, stirring, over medium heat until the mixture comes to a
boil. Then boil, stirring, for about 45 to 60 seconds, or until the sauce
is thickened and no longer cloudy. Taste, and add sugar if necessary.
Serve warm.

Light Touch: Virtually fat- and cholesterol-free, this sauce gets a
scant 2 percent if its calories from fat.

Yield

1 cup; 6 servings

Advance Preparation

Sauce can be made in
advance and kept
covered in the
refrigerator for 2 or 3
days. Heat before
serving.

Nutritional Analysis
per serving

43 calories

0.2 (trace) g protein

0 g fat

0 g satfat

11 g carbohydrate

1 mg sodium

0 mg cholesterol

Peach Daiquiri Sauce

◆ ‧ ◆ ‧ ◆ ‧

Yield

1 cup; 6 servings

Advance Preparation

Sauce can be made in advance and kept covered in the refrigerator for 2 or 3 days.

Nutritional Analysis per serving

77 calories

1 g protein

0 g fat

0 g satfat

16 g carbohydrate

1 mg sodium

0 mg cholesterol

*T*his flavorful fruit sauce is the perfect complement for Peach Daiquiri Soufflé (page 364), but it will add an exotic touch to a slice of angel food or chiffon cake.

◆ ‧ ◆ ‧ ◆ ‧

Generous ½ cup peeled ripe peach slices (1 small peach) or frozen unsweetened peach slices

¾ cup orange juice, warmed, or hot water, divided

1 tablespoon cornstarch

3 tablespoons Bacardi Peach Daiquiri Mix Frozen Concentrate

1 tablespoon fresh lemon juice

2 tablespoons granulated sugar, or to taste

3 to 4 tablespoons dark rum or peach liqueur, to taste

1. To peel the peach, drop it in a pot of boiling water for 2 minutes, then remove with a slotted spoon to a bowl of cold water. Drain when cool. The skin should slip off easily. Purée the peach in a food processor.

2. Measure 3 tablespoons of the orange juice or water into a medium saucepan, add the cornstarch, and stir until dissolved. Whisk in the remaining juice or water and the frozen daiquiri mix. Stir in the puréed peaches, lemon juice, and sugar. Cook, stirring, over medium heat until the mixture comes to a boil. Boil, stirring, for 45 to 60 seconds, or until thickened and no longer cloudy.

3. Remove from the heat and stir in the rum or liqueur. Add sugar if needed. Serve warm or cold.

Light Touch: Virtually fat- and cholesterol-free, this sauce gets only 1 percent of its calories from fat.

Caramel Sauce

◆ • ◆ • ◆

*T*his is a sweet caramel-flavored sauce to use over Apple Snow *(page 382) or frozen vanilla yogurt scooped into a Brandy Snap tulip (page 320). Evaporated skim milk is used because it is concentrated and so provides greater richness than regular low-fat milk.*

◆ • ◆ • ◆ •

1 cup granulated sugar

⅓ cup water

1 tablespoon unsalted butter

¾ cup evaporated skim milk

1 teaspoon dark corn syrup

1 teaspoon vanilla extract

1. In a heavy-bottomed saucepan, combine the sugar and water. Stir once or twice, then use a pastry brush dipped into cold water to wash down the sides of the pan to prevent sugar crystallization. Clip the candy thermometer to the pan if using. Bring to a boil over medium-high heat, swirling the pan gently once or twice at first but not stirring. Boil for about 15 minutes, or until the syrup turns a medium amber color (300°F on the candy thermometer). Remove the pan at once from the heat, as it can burn quickly at this point.

2. Let cool for about 1 minute, then stir in the butter. Slowly add the milk, stirring constantly. (The cool milk will cause the caramel to solidify somewhat.) Return the pan to low heat and stir constantly for about 2 or 3 minutes, until the caramel dissolves and the sauce is smooth.

3. Remove from the heat and stir in the corn syrup and vanilla. Cool completely before serving. The sauce thickens as it cools.

Light Touch: With a deeply satisfying caramel flavor, this recipe gets only 11 percent of its calories from fat. When made the traditional way, using 1 cup heavy cream instead of evaporated milk and adding 3 tablespoons of butter, the figure leaps to 57 percent calories from fat.

Yield

1 cup; 12 to 16 servings

Advance Preparation

Sauce can be prepared ahead, covered, and refrigerated for up to a week.

Special Equipment

Pastry brush, candy thermometer (optional)

Nutritional Analysis per serving (based on 12 servings)

84 calories

1 g protein

1 g fat

0.6 g satfat

18 g carbohydrate

19 mg sodium

3 mg cholesterol

Orange Syrup

◆ · ◆ · ◆

*T*ry this on pancakes or waffles instead of maple syrup. To make *Spiced Orange Syrup, add ¼ teaspoon each of cinnamon and nutmeg plus ground ginger and cloves to taste.*

◆ · ◆ · ◆

Grated zest of 1 large orange
½ cup plus 2 tablespoons frozen orange juice concentrate
1 tablespoon plus 1 teaspoon fresh lemon juice
1 cup light corn syrup

In a small saucepan, stir together all the ingredients. Warm over low heat and serve.

Light Touch: This fat-free recipe is as light as they come, though the sugar provides plenty of calories.

Yield

1½ cups; 12 servings

Advance Preparation

Syrup can be prepared ahead, covered, and refrigerated up to 2 weeks. Warm before serving.

Nutritional Analysis per serving

99 calories

0.3 (trace) g protein

0 g fat

0 g satfat

25 g carbohydrate

20 mg sodium

0 mg cholesterol

Blueberry Syrup

◆ ◆ ◆

For breakfast or brunch, serve this warm over waffles or pancakes instead of maple syrup. For dessert, spoon it over a slice of Classic Angel Food Cake (page 161) or Old-Fashioned Silver Cake (page 164).

◆ ◆ ◆

1 pint fresh blueberries, picked over, rinsed, and dried on paper towels, or 2 cups frozen unsweetened whole berries, thawed

2 teaspoons fresh lemon juice

¼ teaspoon freshly grated nutmeg

1 cup light corn syrup

Purée the berries in a food processor or blender. Add the lemon juice, nutmeg, and corn syrup, and blend well. Transfer the syrup to a saucepan, and warm over low heat. Serve.

Light Touch: While scarcely calorie-free, this recipe is virtually fat-free, with barely 1 percent of its calories from fat.

Yield

About 1 cup; 10 to 12 servings

Advance Preparation

Syrup can be prepared ahead, covered, and refrigerated up to 2 weeks. Warm before serving.

Nutritional Analysis per serving

94 calories

0.2 (trace) g protein

0 g fat

0 g satfat

24 g carbohydrate

21 mg sodium

0 mg cholesterol

Toppings, Glazes, Icings, and Frostings

All the recipes in this section are meant to go on top of a dessert, either as an integral ingredient or as a finishing touch.

The toppings include two reduced-fat crumb recipes and three streusel blends. Plain Crumb Topping is made with some whole wheat flour; Butter Crumb Topping, with its cookie-like crumb, is perfect on apple crisp.

Dessert glazes are used for a variety of purposes. Fruit glazes atop pies or tarts seal the juices in the fruit, brighten its appearance, and enhance its color as well. Icing glazes are decorative drizzled over cream puffs, profiteroles, or cakes.

Icings and frostings, thicker than glazes, are sugar-based mixtures used to top cakes and cookies with a decorative and tasty finish. In low-fat baking, rich icings and frostings are eliminated or drastically downscaled to cut fat as well as calories. The reduced-fat recipes included here are meant to be used when a frosting is essential to the well-being of the cake or consumer. Often, however, icings can be replaced with a decorative sifting of unsweetened cocoa, cinnamon, or confectioners' sugar. Or plain or cinnamon sugar can be sprinkled on a cake or muffin batter before baking to make a crisp topping.

Plain Crumb Topping

◆ · ◆ · ◆

*A*ll-purpose and whole wheat pastry flours are blended together for a slightly more refined and less crunchy topping than the Oat Streusel on page 429.

◆ · ◆ · ◆

¾ cup unsifted all-purpose flour

¼ cup unsifted whole wheat pastry flour (or use 1 cup all-purpose flour instead of the blend)

2 tablespoons toasted wheat germ (optional)

½ cup plus 2 tablespoons granulated sugar

⅛ teaspoon salt

½ teaspoon cinamon

½ teaspoon nutmeg

1½ tablespoons unsalted butter, at room temperature

2 tablespoons skim milk, or more if needed

2 tablespoons canola oil

1 teaspoon fresh lemon juice

½ teaspoon almond or vanilla extract

1. In a large bowl, toss together all the dry ingredients. Pinch in the butter with your fingertips.

2. In a cup, using a fork, beat together the milk and oil, then add to the crumbs, along with the lemon juice and extract. Stir with a fork until the mixture forms crumbs. Add a few more drops of milk if needed. The topping can be used immediately or refrigerated until needed.

Light Touch: This recipe alone obtains 32 percent of its calories from fat, but when used atop a fruit filling that has no fat added, the amount of fat per serving is very low. The whole wheat flour and wheat germ add 1.2 grams of dietary fiber per serving. To tenderize the crumbs slightly, I added a touch of lemon juice, because the acid inhibits the development of the gluten, which can toughen wheat flour. Almond extract replaces the nuts omitted from the original recipe because of their high fat level.

(continued)

Yield

1⅔ cups crumbs; enough for a 9-inch pie; 10 servings

Advance Preparation

Topping can be prepared 1 day in advance and refrigerated in a covered bowl.

Nutritional Analysis per serving (includes optional wheat germ)

139 calories

2 g protein

5 g fat

1.4 g satfat

23 g carbohydrate

30 mg sodium

5 mg cholesterol

This recipe is a significant reduction in fat from a standard crumb formula, which weighs in at about 55 percent calories from fat.

Streusel Topping for Coffee Cake

◆ · ◆ · ◆ ·

*T*his is a small recipe for a topping to sprinkle over a coffee cake; it adds texture rather than a full thick coating. If you double the recipe, don't double the Grape-Nuts cereal.

◆ · ◆ · ◆ ·

Yield

½ cup; enough to sprinkle lightly over an 8- or 9-inch cake; 10 servings

Advance Preparation

Crumbs can be prepared a day in advance, covered, and refrigerated. Crumble before spreading.

Nutritional Analysis per serving

34 calories

0.4 (trace) g protein

1 g fat

0.5 g satfat

6 g carbohydrate

15 mg sodium

2 mg cholesterol

2 tablespoons unsifted all-purpose flour

2 tablespoons granulated sugar

3 tablespoons Grape-Nuts cereal

½ teaspoon cinnamon

2 teaspoons unsalted butter

1 teaspoon apple juice, or more as needed

1 teaspoon canola oil *or* fresh walnut or hazelnut oil

1. In a bowl, combine all the dry ingredients. Pinch in the butter.

2. Add the juice and oil and toss with a fork until the mixture forms crumbs. Add a drop or so more juice if needed.

Light Touch: While this recipe gets 34 percent of its total calories from fat, the per serving figures are low and the streusel will be spread on a low-fat cake to further reduce total fat per serving.

Oat Streusel Topping

◆ ◆ ◆

These crunchy crumbs can be used in or on top of a coffee cake, a fruit crisp, or a pie.

◆ ◆ ◆

½ cup all-purpose flour or whole-wheat pastry flour

⅛ teaspoon salt

½ teaspoon cinnamon

½ teaspoon nutmeg

⅓ cup dark or light brown sugar, packed

2 tablespoons granulated sugar

¼ cup old-fashioned rolled oats

2 tablespoons toasted wheat germ (optional)

2 tablespoons Grape-Nuts cereal

½ teaspoon vanilla or almond extract

2 tablespoons canola or walnut oil

1 tablespoon plus 1 teaspoon skim milk *or* apple or orange juice, or more if needed

1. In a bowl, combine and toss together all the dry ingredients.

2. Add the extract, oil, and the milk or juice and blend with a fork. If necessary, add more liquid a few drops at a time until the mixture forms crumbs. Use as directed in your specific recipe.

Light Touch: The only fat in this recipe is oil; it gets 26 percent calories from fat. You could add 1 tablespoon unsalted butter, to increase the total fat slightly and add more flavor (along with 11 calories per serving, 1 additional gram total fat, of which 0.7 gram is saturated, and 3 milligrams cholesterol). Without butter, as written, the flavor is strengthened with a little vanilla or almond extract plus some nut oil.

Yield
....
1½ cups; enough for an 8- or 9-inch cake, crisp, or pie; 10 servings

Advance Preparation
....
Crumbs can be prepared a day in advance, covered, and refrigerated. Crumble before spreading.

Nutritional Analysis per serving (includes wheat germ)
....
108 calories

2 g protein

3 g fat

0.3 g satfat

18 g carbohydrate

40 mg sodium

0 mg cholesterol

Oat Streusel Topping II

◆ ◆ ◆

A slightly larger recipe than Oat Streusel Topping, this version includes nuts. If you prefer not to use the nuts in this topping, use one of the nut oils and the almond extract to strengthen the flavor.

◆ ◆ ◆

Yield

2 cups plus 2 tablespoons crumbs; enough for a 10-inch cake, crisp, or pie; 12 servings

Nutritional Analysis per serving

122 calories

3 g protein

4 g fat

0.4 g satfat

20 g carbohydrate

26 mg sodium

0 mg cholesterol

½ cup plus 2 tablespoons unsifted all-purpose or whole wheat pastry flour

⅛ teaspoon salt

⅓ cup granulated sugar

⅓ cup light or dark brown sugar, packed

½ cup old-fashioned rolled oats

⅓ cup toasted wheat germ

2 tablespoons chopped walnuts (see Light Touch)

½ teaspoon cinnamon

½ teaspoon vanilla or almond extract

2 tablespoons canola oil *or* walnut or hazelnut oil

2 tablespoons skim milk or apple juice, or as needed

1. In a bowl, combine and toss all the dry ingredients.

2. Add the extract, oil, and milk or juice, and blend together with a fork to form crumbs. Add more liquid if necessary. Use as directed in your specific recipe.

Light Touch: This recipe gets 26 percent calories from fat. If you replace the walnuts with 3 tablespoons of equally crunchy Grape-Nuts cereal, the total fat drops to 22 percent, and you cut 1 gram of fat per serving.

Cookie Crumb Topping

· ◆ · ◆ · ◆ ·

T his crumble topping has a cookie-like texture and a buttery
flavor because a little bit of the real thing has been included.
Use this to top a pie with apple filling or any other fruit mixture. Add ½
teaspoon vanilla or almond extract to the crumbs for extra flavor.

· ◆ · ◆ · ◆ ·

½ cup plus 2 tablespoons unsifted all-purpose flour or whole
    wheat pastry flour

¼ teaspoon salt

½ teaspoon baking powder

⅓ cup granulated sugar

2 tablespoons toasted wheat germ

2 teaspoons unsalted butter, at room temperature

1 large egg white, at room temperature

1 tablespoon canola or safflower oil

1. In a large bowl, toss together the dry ingredients. Pinch in the
butter with your fingertips.

2. In a cup, using a fork, mix together the egg white and oil. Add
to the crumbs, and stir with the fork until the mixture forms crumbs.
Add a drop or two of water if necessary. The crumbs can be used immediately or refrigerated until needed.

Light Touch: With 24 percent calories from fat, this crumble mixture can be used on any fruit filling without raising fat levels noticeably.
If the pie has no bottom crust, and, as is generally the case, there is no
fat added to the fruit, the total fat per serving will be very small.

Yield

1⅓ cups; enough for an
8- or 9-inch pie or tart;
10 servings

Advance Preparation

Topping can be
prepared 1 day in
advance and refrigerated
in a covered bowl.

Nutritional Analysis
per serving

76 calories

2 g protein

2 g fat

0.6 g satfat

13 g carbohydrate

76 mg sodium

2 mg cholesterol

Fruit Glaze

• ◆ • ◆ • ◆ •

An all-purpose fruit glaze to use on top of fruit tarts, to keep pie crusts from becoming soggy, or to coat cakes before icing them. Use apricot preserves or red currant jelly, whichever flavor and color best complement your tart or cake.

• ◆ • ◆ • ◆ •

Yield

1 cup; enough to coat two 9- to 11-inch tarts or one 8- or 9-inch 2-layer cake

Nutritional Analysis
per generous 1½ tablespoons (with liqueur)

96 calories

0 g protein

0 g fat

0 g satfat

23 g carbohydrate

3 mg sodium

0 mg cholesterol

1 cup apricot preserves or red currant jelly
2 tablespoons kirsch or other fruit-flavored liqueur (optional)

1. In a small saucepan, stir the preserves or jelly over medium heat until melted.

2. Strain the preserves through a fine-mesh sieve (return fruit pieces to the preserves jar). Return the strained preserves to the saucepan, add the liqueur if using it, and bring to a boil over medium heat. Cook for 1 to 2 minutes, or until the glaze begins to thicken. Cool slightly before using to glaze a fruit tart, to moisture-proof a pie crust, or to coat a cake, and chill to set the glaze.

Light Touch: You can't get lighter than this...it's free of everything except a few calories—and some fruit.

Firm Fruit Glaze

• ◆ • ◆ • ◆ •

Firm but not rubbery, this gelatine-set glaze is perfect for topping a fruit tart or cake that must be held several hours before serving. The gelatine keeps the glaze from melting.

• ◆ • ◆ • ◆ •

½ cup apricot preserves or red currant jelly

1½ teaspoons Knox unflavored gelatine

2 tablespoons kirsch or other fruit-flavored liqueur *or* fruit juice

1. In a small saucepan over medium heat, stir the preserves until melted.

2. Strain the preserves through a fine-mesh sieve (return fruit pieces to the preserves jar). Return the strained preserves to the saucepan, add the gelatine and liqueur, and stir over medium-low heat until the gelatine is completely dissolved. (To test, pinch a drop between your fingers; if dissolved there will be no graininess.) Bring the mixture to a gentle boil and cook for 20 to 30 seconds. Let cool slightly before using to glaze a tart or coat a cake, then chill to set the glaze.

Light Touch: Totally fat- and cholesterol-free, this has minimal calories and is as light as they come.

Yield

....

½ cup; enough for a 9- to 11-inch tart or an 8- or 9-inch cake

Nutritional Analysis per ½ tablespoon

....

33 calories

0 g protein

0 g fat

0 g satfat

8 g carbohydrate

1 mg sodium

0 mg cholesterol

Strawberry
Topping and Glaze

◆ ◆ ◆

*T*his virtually fat-free ruby-colored topping is perfect for Vanilla Cheesecake (page 22), but also adds sparkle to a plain chiffon or sponge cake. Use only fresh ripe berries for garnishing the cake; if they aren't available, forget the garnish.

◆ ◆ ◆

Yield

....

About 1⅔ cups; enough for one 8- to 10-inch cake

Nutritional Analysis per generous 2 tablespoons

....

48 calories

0.3 (trace) g protein

0.2 (trace) g fat

0 g satfat

12 g carbohydrate

1 mg sodium

0 mg cholesterol

1 quart fresh ripe strawberries, washed, dried, and hulled, or 2 cups frozen unsweetened whole berries, thawed

⅓ cup granulated sugar, or to taste

2 teaspoons fresh lemon juice

1½ tablespoons cornstarch

¼ cup cold water

1. Pick over the fresh berries and reserve about 1½ cups of the best to garnish the cake. Leave whole, or slice in half if extra-large. Set them aside. Cut up remaining berries.

2. Combine the remaining fresh berries, or the frozen berries, the sugar, and lemon juice in a medium heavy-bottomed nonreactive saucepan. Set the pan over medium heat and cook, stirring and mashing the berries, for 2 or 3 minutes, or until the sugar dissolves.

3. In a cup, stir the cornstarch into the water, then stir into the berries. Raise the heat slightly, and bring to a boil, stirring constantly. Boil, stirring, for 1 minute, or until the glaze is thickened and no longer cloudy. Remove from the heat and let cool completely.

3. Arrange the reserved fresh berries, if using, on top of your cake, then spoon on about ⅔ cup of the glaze. Chill the cake for about 1 hour to set the glaze, and pass the remaining glaze as a sauce at the table.

Light Touch: This sauce has just trace amounts of fat, which contribute to the total 3 percent calories from fat. All the fruit gives over 1 gram dietary fiber per serving.

Vanilla Icing Glaze

• ◆ • ◆ • ◆ •

Drizzle this fat-free icing glaze over cream puffs, Bundt cakes, fruit cakes, the tops of pies, or bar cookies. The glaze hardens as it dries. Change the flavor of the glaze to complement the pastry by substituting almond, maple, or lemon extract.

• ◆ • ◆ • ◆ •

1 cup sifted confectioners' sugar

1½ to 2 tablespoons skim milk *or* orange or lemon juice *or* strong coffee or bourbon

¼ teaspoon vanilla extract

1. Whisk together the sugar, 1½ tablespoons milk or other liquid, and the extract. Add a few more drops of liquid if needed to make the glaze soft enough to drip from a spoon.

2. Drizzle lacy-looking lines of the icing over pastry, or spread it in a thin layer with the back of a spoon, letting it drip down the sides of the pastry or cake.

Light Touch: This glaze is fat free.

Yield

⅓ cup; enough for one 9-inch pie or cake or 12 large cream puffs

Advance Preparation

Glaze can be made several hours in advance but must be kept sealed with plastic wrap or it will develop a crust on top and dry out.

Nutritional Analysis per scant 1 tablespoon

67 calories

0 g protein

0 g fat

0 g satfat

17 g carbohydrate

4 mg sodium

0.1 (trace) mg cholesterol

Cocoa Icing Glaze

◆ · ◆ · ◆

T his chocolate glaze adds a perfect finishing touch to vanilla or chocolate Bundt or tube cakes or to cream puffs.

◆ · ◆ · ◆

1 cup unsifted confectioners' sugar
3 tablespoons nonalkalized unsweetened cocoa
½ teaspoon vanilla extract
3 tablespoons water or skim milk, or as needed

1. Sift together the sugar and cocoa into a medium bowl. Whisk in the remaining ingredients. Then whisk in a few more drops of liquid if needed to make the glaze soft enough to drip from a spoon.

2. Drizzle the icing glaze over a cake or pastry or spread it in a thin layer using the back of a spoon, letting it drip down the sides of the cake or pastry. It hardens as it air-dries.

Light Touch: Both this glaze and the mocha variation are cholesterol-free but the trace amounts of fat in the cocoa give them a scant 6 percent calories from fat.

Mocha Icing Glaze

Prepare the recipe as directed, but substitute espresso or strong coffee for the water.

Orange Icing Glaze

‧ ◆ ‧ ◆ ‧ ◆ ‧

se this to glaze an angel food cake, or any sponge or chiffon cake.

‧ ◆ ‧ ◆ ‧ ◆ ‧

1½ cups sifted confectioners' sugar

1 teaspoon grated orange zest

3 tablespoons fresh orange juice

2 teaspoons fresh lemon juice

Combine all the ingredients and blend until smooth. Adjust for consistency and flavor, adding more sifted sugar or juice if necessary. Glaze should be runny, like heavy cream.

Light Touch: There is practically nothing to this: a few calories, a whisper of carbohydrate, zero fat and cholesterol.

Lemon Icing Glaze

Prepare the recipe as directed but substitute grated lemon zest for the orange and use all lemon juice. Or use the lemon zest, but keep the same blend of orange and lemon juice.

Yield

1 scant cup; enough for an 8- or 9-inch tube cake (double the recipe for a 10-inch tube or angel food cake)

Advance Preparation

Prepare glaze a few hours in advance and cover with plastic wrap to prevent drying.

Nutritional Analysis per 1½ tablespoons

50 calories

0 g protein

0 g fat

0 g satfat

13 g carbohydrate

0.1 (trace) mg sodium

0 mg cholesterol

Brown Sugar Caramel Icing

◆·◆·◆

A caramel-flavored icing perfect for any white, yellow, or chocolate layer cake. For a spice cake, try the spice variation.

◆·◆·◆

Yield

1⅓ cups; enough for an 8 × 12-inch sheet cake or one 8-inch 2-layer cake (double the recipe for larger cakes)

Advance Preparation

Icing can be prepared a couple of hours in advance, covered with plastic wrap pressed on surface to prevent drying, and refrigerated. Warm slightly before using if too stiff to spread.

Nutritional Analysis per 3 tablespoons

317 calories

0.4 (trace) g protein

3 g fat

2 g satfat

75 g carbohydrate

15 mg sodium

9 mg cholesterol

1 cup dark brown sugar, packed

¼ cup plus 2 tablespoons 2% milk

2 tablespoons unsalted butter

2 cups sifted confectioners' sugar

1 teaspoon vanilla extract

1. In a medium heavy-bottomed saucepan, combine the brown sugar, milk, and butter. Set over medium heat and bring to a boil, then reduce heat slightly and cook, stirring constantly with a wooden spoon, until all sugar is dissolved. Remove from the heat, and let cool for 3 to 5 minutes.

2. Stir in the confectioners' sugar and vanilla, and beat hard until very smooth. Use on cake or cover and refrigerate.

Light Touch: Because it contains a little fat from the milk and butter, this icing obtains 9 percent of its calories from fat. The variation has virtually the same fat content.

Caramel Spice Icing

Prepare the recipe as directed, but substitute light brown sugar for the dark, and add ¾ teaspoon lemon juice, 1 teaspoon cinnamon, and ½ teaspoon *each* nutmeg, ground ginger, and allspice. (If doubling the recipe, do not double the spices; adjust them to taste.)

Seven-Minute Icing

· ◆ · ◆ · ◆ ·

Seven-Minute Icing is a quick, easy version of Boiled Icing (page 441). All the ingredients are whipped together in a double boiler, making it unnecessary to cook a sugar syrup to pour over whipped whites. The results are virtually the same: a white satin whipped meringue that makes a luxurious, fluffy cake icing. Even though I call this a Seven-Minute Icing, it usually takes between five and seven minutes to reach the ideal consistency depending on heat, type of beater, and size of eggs.

In my tests with this technique, the whites were heated to a sufficiently high temperature for a long enough time to destroy any possible bacteria; in fact, this method is slightly safer than the boiled icing method because the heat is more direct. Don't try to freeze cakes coated with this icing; it breaks down and becomes runny when it thaws.

· ◆ · ◆ · ◆ ·

2 large egg whites

1½ cups granulated sugar

5 tablespoons cold water

2 teaspoons light corn syrup

1 teaspoon vanilla extract (optional)

1. Set up the bottom of a double boiler, or a saucepan, with just enough water in it that the top part or the bowl can sit above it without getting wet.

2. Combine all ingredients except the vanilla in the top of the double boiler or the bowl. Bring the water in the pan to a simmer.

3. Place the top of the double boiler or the bowl over the simmering water and *immediately* begin whipping with a hand-held electric mixer on medium speed. (You can whip with a rotary beater or wire whisk, but it may take up to 14 minutes to achieve the same results.) Whip on medium speed for about 3 minutes, then increase the speed to high and whip for about 3 minutes more. Remove the top container or bowl from the heat, add the vanilla if using it, and beat for 1 minute longer, or until the whites are satiny and hold stiff peaks. (When using this for cake icing, beat the full 7 minutes; if you will be

(continued)

Yield

About 3 cups icing; enough to fill and frost an 8- or 9-inch 2-layer cake

Special Equipment

Double boiler or saucepan with round-bottomed metal bowl that fits over it

Nutritional Analysis per 5 tablespoons

12 calories

0 g fat

0 g satfat

3 g carbohydrate

1 mg sodium

0 mg cholesterol

adding the meringue to a mousse, whip for only about 6 minutes). Use immediately.

Light Touch: This is what "Pure Light" means: zero fat, zero cholesterol, and just a few calories.

Seafoam Icing

Prepare the recipe as directed, but replace the granulated sugar with 1½ cups dark brown sugar, firmly packed, and add ½ teaspoon almond extract along with the vanilla.

Maple Seven-Minute Icing

Prepare the recipe as directed, but replace the sugar with ¾ cup pure maple syrup. This whips to stiff peaks in about 6 minutes.

Orange Seven-Minute Icing

Prepare the recipe as directed, but substitute ½ teaspoon orange extract for the vanilla and add 2 teaspoons grated orange zest to the finished icing.

Lemon Seven-Minute Icing

Prepare the recipe as directed, but use only 3 tablespoons water, plus 2 tablespoons fresh lemon juice. Add 1 teaspoon grated lemon zest to the finished icing.

Boiled Icing

◆ ◆ ◆

Also called divinity or white mountain icing, this is the thick, shiny, white satin icing of childhood birthday cakes. In fact, it is really a classic cooked-syrup Italian meringue with a slight adjustment in the cooking temperature of the syrup poured over the whipped whites. Be sure the egg whites are at room temperature before starting, to achieve desired volume when whipped. Endless variations on this theme are possible—Lemon, Orange, Cocoa, or Beige Mountain—follow the master recipe.

◆ ◆ ◆

Yield

About 3½ cups; enough to fill and frost an 8- or 9-inch 2-layer cake

Advance Preparation

Boiled Icing is best made just before using.

Special Equipment

Pastry brush, candy thermometer

Nutritional Analysis per serving (based on 10 servings)

74 calories

1 g protein

0 g fat

0 g satfat

18 g carbohydrate

18 mg sodium

0 mg cholesterol

⅓ cup water

¾ cup plus 2 tablespoons granulated sugar

1 tablespoon light corn syrup or ⅛ teaspoon cream of tartar

3 large egg whites, at room temperature

1 teaspoon vanilla extract

1. In a medium heavy-bottomed saucepan, stir together the water, ¾ cup of sugar, and the corn syrup or cream of tartar. Then set over moderate heat and cook until the sugar is dissolved; don't stir again, but swirl the pan several times.

2. To prevent crystallization, wash down sides of the pan with a pastry brush dipped in cold water. Clip a candy thermometer to the pan, and increase the heat to medium-high. Bring the syrup to a boil and cook, without stirring, for 7 to 8 minutes, or until the thermometer reads 239° to 242°F (a little of the syrup will form a soft ball when dropped into ice water).

3. Meanwhile, when the syrup is almost cooked, begin to whip the egg whites: In a grease-free bowl, using an electric mixer on medium speed, whip until the whites are foamy. Add the remaining 2 tablespoons sugar, and whip until the whites are *nearly* stiff but not dry.

4. As soon as the sugar syrup reaches the specified temperature, remove it from the heat. Gradually pour it over the whites while whipping them on medium-low speed. Pour the syrup in a steady stream between the sides of the bowl and the beaters; do not scrape in any hardened bits of syrup. Continue whipping until the whites are stiff, satiny, and cool, about 5 minutes. Whip in the vanilla and use immediately.

(continued)

Light Touch: Besides a few calories, there's nothing in this: zero calories from fat. The variations that follow have slight changes in ingredients, but the fat content varies very little.

Beige Mountain Icing

Prepare the recipe as directed, but substitute 1½ cups dark or light brown sugar, packed, for the ¾ cup granulated sugar.

Lemon Boiled Icing

Prepare the recipe as directed, but substitute 1 tablespoon fresh lemon juice for the vanilla extract and add ½ teaspoon grated lemon zest along with it. If you like a stronger flavor, add ½ teaspoon lemon extract as well.

Orange Boiled Icing

Prepare the recipe as directed, but substitute 1 tablespoon frozen orange juice concentrate for the vanilla extract, and add 2 teaspoons grated orange zest along with it.

Cocoa Boiled Icing

Prepare the recipe as directed, but sift ¼ cup unsweetened cocoa into 1 cup of the cooled icing, then stir this back into the icing and whip for a few seconds just to blend.

Royal Icing

◆ • ◆ • ◆

Thighs icing becomes very hard when it dries. Use it for trimming cookies, especially those that will hang on a Christmas tree. Or use it to write names on square cookies to make place cards for a holiday table or greeting cards (well wrapped) to send friends. The icing can be tinted with a drop or two of food coloring.

Classic Royal Icing contains uncooked egg whites. If you're uncomfortable using this recipe, try Royal Icing with Meringue Powder. Meringue powder is sold in specialty food shops, some supermarkets, and by cake decorating suppliers (see page 460).

◆ • ◆ • ◆

Classic Royal Icing

2 large egg whites, at room temperature

1/8 teaspoon cream of tartar

1/8 teaspoon salt

About 3 1/2 to 4 cups confectioners' sugar, sifted

2 tablespoons fresh lemon juice, strained, or more if needed

In a medium grease-free bowl, beat the whites with an electric mixer om medium speed until foamy. Add the cream of tartar, salt, about 1 cup of the sugar, and the lemon juice, and beat to blend. Then continue to add sugar, about 1/2 cup at a time, beating after each addition, until the icing reaches the consistency of softly whipped cream. If necessary, add more sifted sugar or more lemon juice to reach the desired consistency. If not using immediately, cover well with plastic wrap to prevent drying.

Royal Icing with Meringue Powder

3 tablespoons meringue powder

4 cups sifted confectioners' sugar

5 to 6 tablespoons warm water

Combine the meringue powder, sugar, and 5 tablespoons water in a large bowl. Using an electric mixer on medium speed, beat until the icing forms stiff peaks. Adjust the consistency by adding more water or sugar if necessary. If not using immediately, cover with plastic wrap to prevent drying.

Light Touch: Both the Classic Royal Icing and the version made with meringue powder are fat- and cholesterol-free.

Yield
....
About 2 cups; enough to decorate about 4 dozen medium-size cookies

Advance Preparation
....
Icing is best made just before using so it does not dry out.

Nutritional Analysis per 2 teaspoons
....
33 calories

0 g protein

0 g fat

0 g satfat

8 g carbohydrate

8 mg sodium

0 mg cholesterol

Yield
....
About 3 cups

Light Cream Cheese Frosting

• ◆ • ◆ • ◆ •

A frosting for those who must have some with Carrot Cake (page 172) or Spice Cake (page 170).

◆ • ◆ • ◆ •

12 ounces low-fat cream cheese, at room temperature
½ cup sifted confectioners' sugar
2 teaspoons vanilla extract

In a food processor or blender, combine all the ingredients and process until smooth. Or combine the ingredients in a bowl and beat with an electric mixer.

Light Touch: Although made with light cream cheese, which has half the calories of regular, this is hardly light—with 57 percent of its calories coming from fat. I include the recipe for diehards who want to have their low-fat carrot cake, but won't eat it too,... without frosting. At least this recipe is an improvement on the original. Although formulas vary, one of my old favorites blends ½ cup butter and 8 ounces cream cheese with 4 cups sugar. Calories from fat drops to 48 percent, but each serving contains more than three times the fat and four times the cholesterol.

Cookie Frosting

◆ ◆ ◆

A simple frosting to color and spread on butter cookies. If you wish to avoid food coloring, use seedless raspberry jam for pink and frozen orange juice concentrate for yellow-orange, substituting it for the liquid in the recipe.

To make an easy decorating bag, cut a tiny hole in one corner of a heavy-duty pint-size plastic bag; add the frosting and close the bag. Or drop a metal decorating tip into the hole in the plastic bag and force the frosting through the tip.

◆ ◆ ◆

2 cups sifted confectioners' sugar
1 teaspoon vanilla extract or strained fresh lemon juice
3 to 5 tablespoons skim milk, water, or fruit juice, or as needed

1. Measure the sugar into a bowl. Using an electric mixer on low speed, beat in the extract or juice plus 3 tablespoons milk or other liquid. Slowly beat in additional liquid until the frosting is the desired consistency and perfectly smooth. If you will be spreading it with a knife or piping it through a decorating bag fitted with a small round tip, it should be about the consistency of soft cream cheese. To make a glaze that you can paint on with a new paintbrush, add additional liquid so that the frosting flows freely.

2. To color the frosting, divide it among several small cups and add a drop or two of different vegetable colors.

Light Touch: This is a fat-free icing that can be used on all types of cookies.

Yield

About ¾ cup; enough for 4 dozen cookies

Nutritional Analysis per scant 1 teaspoon

16 calories

0 g protein

0 g fat

0 g satfat

4 g carbohydrate

1 mg sodium

0 mg cholesterol

Quick
and
Easy Garnishes
and
Finishing Touches for Special Desserts

The reduced-fat cakes and pastries in this book do not need rich frostings or icings, but they can still get dressed up to go out! Here are a few ideas for simple but effective presentations of large or small cakes or pastries. Candied orange or grapefruit peel is particularly effective to garnish tarts or individual desserts, such as Apple Snow in a Tulip Cookie or Fromage Blanc in a Brandy Snap tulip cup.

Candied Citrus Peel

◆ ◆ ◆

T his is fun and easy to make at home if you know three tricks. First, blanch the peel to remove its bitterness; second, pay careful attention to removing the white pith after blanching; third, and most important, pay attention to the time and temperature when boiling the peel in the sugar syrup. Don't be tempted to remove the peel with a vegetable peeler; zest alone is too thin.

Homemade candied citrus peel—orange, grapefruit, lemon, or lime— is a great Christmas gift and delectable filler for holiday fruit cakes. The rest of the year it makes a lovely topping for cakes and fruit tarts.

◆ ◆ ◆

4 oranges, or 6 lemons or limes, or 2 grapefruits

2 cups granulated sugar, divided, plus extra for layering stored peel

½ cup water

2 tablespoons light corn syrup or ¼ teaspoon cream of tartar

1. Wash the fruit well to remove any possible chemical residue. With a sharp paring knife, quarter the oranges or grapefruit, then remove the quarter-segments of peel. For lemons and limes, slice off wide strips of peel, with the pith, cutting right down to the fruit. Ideally, the peel should be about ⅛ inch thick, though thicker is all right. You should have about 2 cups of loosely packed peel.

2. Put the peel into a medium heavy-bottomed nonreactive saucepan, add cold water to cover, and bring to a boil. Lower the heat and boil gently for 15 minutes. Remove from the heat and let the peel stand in the hot water for 15 minutes. Drain in a colander and rinse well under very cold water; the peel will feel soft. (Grapefruit peel is more bitter than the other types and is best blanched in 3 changes of cold water, and each time it is brought to a boil, simmered 10 minutes.)

3. With a teaspoon, carefully scrape off and discard the soft white pith inside each segment of peel. Slice the peel into strips about ¼ inch wide.

4. Prepare the syrup: In the same saucepan, combine 1 cup of the sugar, the ½ cup water, and the corn syrup or cream of tartar. Stir, then bring to a boil, swirling the pan several times to help dissolve the sugar.

(continued)

Yield

About 2 cups candied peel

Advance Preparation

Candied peel will last at least a year if packed in layers of granulated sugar in an airtight container and kept in a cool dry place or refrigerated.

Special Equipment

Pastry brush, candy thermometer or instant-read thermometer, slotted spoon.

Nutritional Analysis per 2 tablespoons (nearly identical for all citrus peel)

90 calories

0.1 (trace) g protein

0.1 (trace) g fat

0 g satfat

23 g carbohydrate

sodium—no data

0 mg cholesterol

Wash down the sides of the pan with a pastry brush dipped in cold water. Boil the syrup until it looks clear, then add the prepared peel, immersing it in the syrup. Clip the candy thermometer, if using, to the pan. Boil the peel gently over moderate heat for about 30 minutes, or until the syrup reaches 230°F (a little of the syrup dropped into ice water should form a thread; just before the soft-ball stage) and most of the syrup has been absorbed. Remove from the heat.

5. Put the remaining 1 cup sugar in a bowl or spread it in a pan. With a slotted spoon, transfer the peel to the bowl or pan, and toss well to coat. Transfer the peel to a wax paper-covered baking sheet, or a wire rack set over a sheet of wax paper, to air-dry.

6. After several hours, or overnight, the peel should be crisp outside but flexible and chewy inside. If too flabby and soft, it was not cooked long enough in the syrup to a high enough temperature; if it is crisp enough to crack when bent, it was cooked at too high a temperature but will still taste good. Store the peel between layers of sugar in an airtight container.

Light Touch: Candied peel contains virtually no fat (1 percent); it is flavorful, exotic, versatile. What more could you ask? No, I won't make it for you.

Creative Stencils

◆ ◆ ◆

For an unusual stencil, place 2 or 3 rose or lemon leaves (or leaves of another edible plant) in a pattern on a cake top and sift confectioners' sugar or cocoa over them. Carefully lift the leaves off, leaving their shape below. Lemon leaves, available in many florist's shops, are strong and flexible; you can cut them with scissors to resemble any leaf shape you wish, such as maple or oak.

Be original. Linnea Milliun, a fabulous bread baker now working in Bridgewater, Connecticut, uses a table fork as a stencil, sifting fine bread flour over the fork to leave its pattern atop her rustic crusty loaves. Why not try this, or a knife, fork, and spoon, on top of a cake?

◆ ◆ ◆

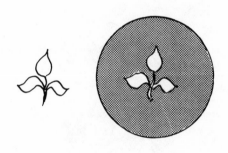

Doilies

◆ ◆ ◆

This old standby is still a good idea. Simply set a store-bought paper doily (or two together, for a stronger stencil) on top of a cake and sift on a small amount of confectioners' sugar (for a spice or chocolate cake) or unsweetened cocoa (for a white cake).

◆ ◆ ◆

Paper Stencils

◆·◆·◆·

C ut your own paper designs from sheets of stiff paper. The
simpler the design, the more effective.

By folding a sheet of paper, as when making folded valentines or
paper dolls, you can create original designs for cake tops. In fact, a chain
of hand-holding paper dolls stretched across a cake top is great for a
child's birthday sheet cake.

To make a snowflake pattern, cut a paper circle the size of the cake
top. Fold it in half, then in quarters, and eighths. Cut out designs from
the two folded edges, then open the paper and press it flat. Set it on the
cake and use as you would a paper doily.

◆·◆·◆·

PAPER DOLLS

SNOWFLAKE

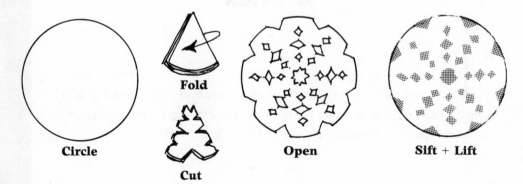

Circle   Fold   Cut   Open   Sift + Lift

Paper Strip Designs

◆ · ◆ · ◆ ·

Another variation on the stencil: Simply cut strips of paper, position them at intervals across a cake top, and sift on confectioners' sugar, cocoa, or cinnamon; for an interesting color and flavor contrast, use all three, alternating them. After sifting, lift off the strips with care. To make a straight plaid or diagonal plaid design, place a second layer of strips over the first at right angles or on an angle. Sift on a little more topping.

◆ · ◆ · ◆ ·

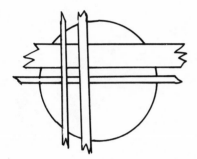 

Appendices

◆ ◆ ◆

The Chemistry of Fats

In terms of its chemical structure, a fat is composed of a chain of carbon atoms linked in different patterns with atoms of hydrogen and oxygen. In its simplest form, this fat chain is composed of a 3-carbon atom molecule called a *glycerol,* which has three links reaching out to clasp free fatty acid chains. These can be of different lengths and structural complexity; they may be short, medium, or long, containing from four to twenty-four carbon atoms to which hydrogen atoms are attached. The pattern, or structure, made when these atoms link up determines whether the fatty acid is mono-unsaturated, polyunsaturated, or saturated. All dietary fats are made up of a variety of chain lengths and varying proportions of mono-unsaturated, polyunsaturated, and saturated fatty acid chains. No food contains only one type of fat. Each type has a different effect on our levels of blood cholesterol.

Triglycerides, Diglycerides, and Monoglycerides

To understand these compounds, visualize the 3-carbon glycerol molecule described above as three figures bound to each other, each with a hand outstretched. When there is a fatty acid chain fastened to each hand (three in all, of varying lengths), the molecule is a *triglyceride.* Triglycerides, the fats most commonly found in food, are both a major source of fatty acids and the most concentrated form in which potential energy can be stored in the body. They provide 95 percent of the energy that comes from dietary fat.

In addition to the glycerol molecule and fatty acids, phosphorus is present in some triglycerides, and these triglycerides are called *phospholipids.* If a sugar containing nitrogen is present, the compounds are called *glycolipids.* All of these can bind to other compounds such as proteins and become part of lipoproteins. In addition, they may serve as the raw material from which cholesterol and other important compounds are derived.

When there are only two fatty acid chains hanging on to the glycerol molecule, the fat is called a *diglyceride.* When there is only one fatty acid chain attached, the fat is a *monoglyceride.* A monoglyceride is an emulsifier because one end of its chain will dissolve in fat and the other in water. Mono- and diglycerides are additives found in many processed foods. They regulate texture and consistency or emulsification.

When mono- and diglycerides are formed from triglycerides, the chains that break off are called *free fatty acids.*

Glycerol Molecule   Triglyceride   Diglyceride   Monoglyceride   Free fatty acids

What Does Saturation Mean?

As seen above, the type of fat (mono-, di-, or tri-glyceride) is determined by the number of chains attached to a basic core: the 3-carbon glycerol molecule.

The fatty acid chains themselves are classified, or distinguished from each other, both by their length and by the pattern in which their atoms are linked. This pattern determines the quality, or degree, of saturation of the fatty acid. Why is this important? Because the degree of saturation (and the predominating length of the chains) determines whether a fat will be liquid or solid at room temperature and how it will affect blood cholesterol levels. Saturated fats (like butter) generally are solid at room temperature, and unsaturated fats are liquid (oils). When extra hydrogen is added to the chain during a process called hydrogenation (see page 30), the unsaturated fatty acid (oil) is changed into a partially hardened fat (shortening or margarine).

The pattern, or structure, of each fatty acid chain is very specific. Every chain begins with a special "head" (in the accompanying diagram, the fat pig head) called a *carboxyl group,* in which a carbon atom is linked with oxygen and a hydroxyl group, and ends with a "tail" called a *methyl group,* in which a carbon atom is joined to three hydrogen atoms. In between the head and tail is a row of carbon atoms that ranges from short (four to twelve), medium (eight to twelve, in fats that are uniquely easy to digest and often used medicinally), or long (fourteen or more, the most prevalent type in dietary fat).

Every carbon atom has four bonds, or hooks, that enable it to attach to four other atoms. To understand a carbon, or fatty acid, chain, visualize each carbon atom with four outstretched hands; one hand on each side grabs an adjacent carbon atom; the remaining two hands reach out top and bottom to grab hydrogen atoms. When all hands are full, the fatty acid chain is said to be *saturated*.

Saturated fatty acids (satfats), which are generally solid at room temperature, are found in animal fats, including meats, butter, and cheese. Almost all vegetable/plant fats are low in satfats; exceptions are tropical oils and cocoa butter. Most satfats are believed to raise the level of LDLs (the "bad guys," see page 4) in blood cholesterol as well as elevate total blood cholesterol levels. However, research has shown that not all saturated fats raise blood cholesterol levels. Some, such as stearic acid, a fat found abundantly in beef, butter, and chocolate, has actually been shown to lower the levels of blood cholesterol!

A saturated short-chain fatty acid looks like this:

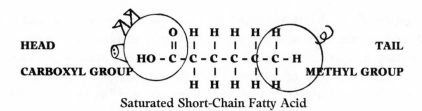

Saturated Short-Chain Fatty Acid

What are Unsaturated (Mono-unsaturated and Polyunsaturated) Fatty Acids?

Sometimes carbon atoms do not "grab on to" four other atoms. Instead, the "hands" of two adjacent carbon atoms will each let go of one hydrogen atom and grab on to each other, forming a double bond between them. Looking at a diagram of such a chain, you see a hole where the two hydrogen atoms were and a double link between the carbon atoms.

Mono-unsaturated Fatty Acid

Polyunsaturated Fatty Acid

If a fatty acid chain contains one or more double bonds, it is said to be *unsaturated*.

If the chain contains just one double bond (missing 2 hydrogen atoms), it is *mono-unsaturated*. Mono-unsaturated fatty acids, which predominate in olive oil, are believed to lower the level of LDLs in blood cholesterol without lowering the levels of HDL's (the "good guys").

If the chain contains two or more double bonds (missing four or more hydrogen atoms), it is *polyunsaturated*. Polyunsaturated fatty acids predominate in most vegetable oils, such as corn and peanut. They are believed to lower the level of LDLs in blood cholesterol while also slightly lowering the level of HDLs.

What Does Saturation Have to Do with the Type of Fats We Eat?

Remember that all fats are composed of a 3-carbon glycerol molecule fastened to one, two, or three different fatty acid chains. The majority of dietary fats are triglycerides (with three chains attached). A fat is identified by the type of fatty acid that predominates within it. For example, olive oil is described as mono-unsaturated because it contains 77 percent mono-unsaturated fatty acids, along with about 14 percent saturated and 8 percent polyunsaturated fatty acids.

What Is a P/S Ratio?

To indicate the value of a fat to health, some cookbooks and product labels express the proportion of polyunsaturated to saturated fat as a ratio, the P/S ratio. For example, one tablespoon of sunflower oil contains 5 grams polyunsaturated fat and 2 grams saturated fat, for a P/S ratio of 5:2. In this example, the first number, representing polyunsaturates is—as it should be—significantly higher than the second (saturated).

The more unsaturated fatty acids present in a fat, the more likely it is to be liquid at room temperature; the more saturated, the more likely it is to be solid. The exceptions are tropical oils such as coconut and palm oil, which are predominantly saturated but stay liquid at room temperature because they contain so many short-chain fatty acids.

What Are Trans Fatty Acids?

When liquid oils are turned into solids, the process is called hydrogenation (see page 30). A problem arises during hydrogenation when some of an oil's fatty acid chains, particularly those that are mono-unsaturated, are transformed. In the new form, trans double bonds are formed, changing the molecular structure of the carbon chain. The new structure is called a *trans fatty acid* (tfa). Trans fatty acids contribute to the stability of hydrogenated fats, helping them avoid rancidity. Trans fatty acids make up a very small proportion (estimates range from 2 to 6 percent) of the total dietary fat intake in the United States.

While research on the subject has been going on for many years, some recent studies have recommended that individual tfa consumption be reduced because tfa's apparently can act like other saturated fats in the body, raising the level of LDLs in blood cholesterol while simultaneously lowering the levels of the good HDLs. While trans fatty acids occur naturally in small amounts in animal products (beef, butter, milk), researchers are now studying whether the levels are excessive in hydrogenated fats such as hard margarines, partially hydrogenated vegetable shortening, and commercial shortenings and frying oils. At present, it is impossible to determine the amounts of tfa's in packaged foods from product labels because the tfa's are grouped with the mono-unsaturated fats.

Further confusion arises for the consumer because we are told that mono-unsaturates are desirable—yet some mono-unsaturates are trans fatty acids, which may not be beneficial at all. Similarly, we are advised that saturated fats are unhealthy, yet stearic acid, a saturated fat, does not appear to raise serum cholesterol levels. Nevertheless, we know for sure that it important to lower overall amounts of saturated fat in the diet. The last word on the subject is likely to be a long time coming. "The fat lady has not yet sung," to quote noted food chemist and writer Shirley Corriher.

Mail Order Sources and Suppliers

General Baking Needs

Bridge Kitchenware Corp.
214 East 52nd St.
New York, NY 10022
212-688-4220
baking pans, cooking
    equipment, utensils

The Broadway Panhandler
520 Broadway
New York, NY 10012
212-966-3434
baking and cake decorating
    utensils

Dean & DeLuca
560 Broadway
New York, NY, 10012
212-431-1691 or 800-221-
    7714
baking supplies, utensils,
    chocolate

Gray's Grist Mill
P.O. Box 422
Adamsville, RI 02801
508-636-6075
brown bread flour, pancake and
    muffin mix, specialty grains

Kenyon Corn Meal Company
P.O. Box 221
West Kingston, RI 02892
401-783-4054
brown bread flour, specialty
    grains

**King Arthur Flour Baker's
    Catalogue**
P.O. Box 876
Norwich, VT 05055
802-649-5635
baking equipment and utensils;
    baking ingredients including
    specialty flours, nuts and
    seeds, pure extracts,
    chocolate and cocoa

Maid of Scandinavia
3244 Raleigh Ave.
Minneapolis, MN 55416
800-328-6722
baking supplies, utensils,
    chocolate

Paprikas Weiss Importer
1572 Second Ave.
New York, NY 10028
212-288-6117
poppy seeds, extracts, flavorings,
    chocolate, baking utensils
    and nut mills

Williams-Sonoma
Mail Order Department
P.O. Box 7456
San Francisco, CA 94120-7456
800-541-2233
baking equipment and utensils,
    baking ingredients, fine
    chocolate and cocoa

Wilton Enterprises, Inc.
2240 West 75th St.
Woodridge, IL 60517
708-963-7100
meringue powder

Gluten-Free Ingredients

Dietary Specialties, Inc.
P.O. Box 227
Rochester, NY 14601
800-544-0099
xanthan gum, gluten-free flours

Ener-G Foods, Inc.
P.O. Box 84487
Seattle, WA 98124-5787
800-331-5222
xanthan gum, gluten-free flours

Selected Technical Bibliography

Bowes, Anna de Planter, and Church, Charles F. *Food Values of Portions Commonly Used.* Revised by Jean A. T. Pennington. 15th ed. New York: Harper & Row, 1989.

Guthrie, Helen A., and Bagby, Robin. *Introductory Nutrition.* 7th ed. Boston: Times Mirror/Mosby College Publishing, 1989.

McGee, Harold. *On Food and Cooking.* New York: Charles Scribner's Sons, 1984.

————. *The Curious Cook.* San Francisco: North Point Press, 1990.

Hole, John W., Jr. *Essentials of Human Anatomy and Physiology.* 3rd ed. Dubuque, Iowa: William C. Brown Publishers, 1989.

Martin, D. W.; Mayes, P. A.; and Rodwell, V. W. *Harper's Review of Biochemistry.* 18th ed. Los Altos, California: Lange Medical Publications, 1981.

Ornish, Dean. *Stress, Diet & Your Heart.* New York: Holt, Rinehart & Winston, 1982.

Styer, Lubert. *Biochemistry.* 3rd ed. New York: W. H. Freeman & Company, 1988.

Sultan, William J. *Practical Baking.* 3rd ed. Westport, CT: AVI Publishing Co., Inc., 1982.

Pamphlets, Newsletters, and References

Corriher, Shirley O. "Fat Expertise for the Cook." *CAREF Research Report,* vol. 7, no. 1. Sponsored by The International Association of Culinary Professionals. Louisville, Kentucky: 1992.

Gershoff Stanley, N. ed. *Tufts University Diet & Nutrition Letter.* New York: 1991–1992.

USDA Agricultural Handbook Series Number 8: *Composition of Foods. Dairy and Egg Products 8-1* (1976); *Fats and Oils 8-4* (1979); *Breakfast Cereals 8-8* (1982); *Fruit and Fruit Juices 8-9* (rev. 1982); *Vegetables and Vegetable Products 8-11* (rev. 1984); *Nuts and Seed Products 8-12* (rev. 1984); *Beverages 8-14* (rev. 1986); *Snacks and Sweets 8-19* (rev. 1991); *Cereals, Grains, and Pasta 8-20* (rev. 1989); *Supplement* (1990).

Webb Denise, ed. *Environmental Nutrition Newsletter.* New York: 1991–1992.

Index

◆ ◆ ◆

wheat germ (*cont.*)
  Cape Cod cranberry upside-down muffins, 105
  fabulous five-week fiber muffins, 118–119
  pineapple upside-down muffins, 105
whipped cream, 15
whisks, wire, 56
whole wheat, 12
  applesauce waffles, 74–75
  blueberry gingerbread, 152–153
  blueberry kuchen, 127–128
  Boston brown bread, 102–103
  bran-raisin-apricot muffins, 110–111

buttermilk wheat-germ muffins, 104–105
cranberry gingerbread, 153
fabulous five-week fiber muffins, 118–119
wire whisks, 56

Y

yogurt, 13, 14, 16–18, 35, 40, 63
  maple sauce, 416
  orange crumb cake, 125
  orange ricotta cream, 403
  plum soup, 395–396
  ricotta cream, 403

rum sauce, 417
scones, 94–95
strawberry shortcake, 174–175
tulip fruit crisps, 385–386
vanilla cream, 402
see also cheesecakes
yogurt, frozen, 17, 18
  low-flying saucers, 337–338
yogurt cheese, 405–406
  Grand Marnier cheesecake, 234–236

Z

zest, 35, 41, 44, 45–46, 62